ROAMIN' THE RANGE

TOGETHER

ROAMIN' THE RANGE

TOGETHER

PART ONE

LIVING IN THE SHADOW OF GIANTS
(1950–1980)

PETE ALLEN

A CIP catalogue record for this book is available from the British Library.

ISBN 978-0-9569733-0-6

Book and cover design by Clare Brayshaw

Prepared and printed by:

York Publishing Services Ltd
64 Hallfield Road
Layerthorpe
York YO31 7ZQ
Tel: 01904 431213

Website: www.yps-publishing.co.uk

For Linda my Wife and Vicky my Step-Daughter
&
In Loving Memory of Walter and Abigail Allen

Contents

About the author

Pete Allen lives in Beverley, East Yorkshire with his wife Linda and step-daughter Vicky, *'Roamin' the Range Together'* is his first book.

Acknowledgements

The author would like to thank the following people without whom this book would not have been possible:-

Linda Allen and Vicky White and Ian, Sarah and Adam Des Forges for their support, and unending encouragement.

Special thanks to Duncan Beal and Clare Brayshaw of YPS for making the book possible, Vicky White for help with the marketing and to the Hull Daily Mail and particularly Hull FC reporter James Smailes for the photographs. Linda Allen, Pete Wood, Derek Clarke and Paul 'Jacko' Jackson for partial proof reading, Lee Jenkinson for his retail advice and Brian Ridley, Kathy Kirk, Barry Edwards, Brian Watson, Steve Roberts, 'Vince', Dick Tingle and Steve Wray for their stories.

Also to Vera Campbell, Phil Arundell, Mike Jacklin, Andrew 'Wolfie' Pahlen and Jim White for their kindness and photographs.

Wilf Rosenberg, Johnny Whiteley, Clive Sullivan, Arthur Keegan, Paul Woods, Terry Kirchin and David Doyle-Davidson for being my heroes, my friends; Locko's Luck, 60532, Standee, FC Eaststander, Touchliner, Staffs FC, Airliebird58, Mick Cranes Sidestep and Hull BG, all readers of the Dentist's Diary and Joe at blackandwhites. com. Everyone at Hull FC, Allen Bagshawe, Chris and Paul Johnson, Ian Pindar and most importantly to all of you for buying this book!

And of course Abbie and Walter my Mum and Dad for giving me my passion and obsession for Hull FC, the greatest Rugby League club in the world. This is also their story and I thank them for making my life so much richer and exciting (and at times frustrating) and giving me something that has taught me so much about life, including the fact that although you can't win all the time..... no one can stop you dreaming about it!

"Winning isn't everything, it's the only thing, each Sunday after the battle one team savours victory and the other wallows in the bitterness of defeat. The many hurts seem a small price to pay for having won, and there is simply no reason at all that is adequate for having lost"

Vince Lombardi (1913-1970)
Head Coach; The Green Bay Packers (1959-1968)

'I know I will never ever get another chance, I have never ever felt so low in my life. It is so unfair, I know someone had to lose ......but why oh why couldn't it be them?"

David Brookes Hull FC forward,
on the occasion of Hull's 4-3 defeat by Halifax in the
Challenge Cup semi final replay of 1988.

Prologue

No doubt it's a ritual that many 'fanatical' sports fans go through with monotonous regularity. You've lost a game, not just 'any' game but one against the 'enemy'. You're walking away from the Stadium in the depth of despair trying not to think about your team, or rugby, or that team from across the City or even about your Club's out of contract players and growing catalogue of injuries.

You're really not bothered are you? It's 'only a game', the sun is shining and you're concentrating all your efforts on holidays, or barbecues, or cold beer, or cars, fast women or even faster horses. That's what life's about, they're the things that really matter. Why should you be getting all wound up about a stupid Rugby League team anyway? You're just into your sixties, you've finished with working for a living and your hearts set on enjoying your retirement. If not exactly 'Last of the Summer Wine', each day should at least be a new adventure, each experience something which you have anticipated and carefully prepared for over those long years of drudgery behind a desk.

That, as you grow older, is the idealist view of things anyway but as most people and all dedicated and obsessive sports fans know, few things are ever ideal and sure enough it's not long before your ageing brain is racing back to focus on the old obsession.

Each morning, like everyone else, you wake up to the experience of those wonderful few seconds of blank, mindless bliss. Then suddenly, as unexpected as it is predictable, reality bites and you're back in turmoil. That's when your mind cranks up for another day and you realise...... it's back! It's match day tomorrow, or the day after, or what's even worse, you lost yesterday and must not at any cost, listen to the radio and risk hearing your hero's sad demise regurgitated by those 'morons' that masquerade under the pretext of local sports journalists. Bollocks to them lot, what do they know about YOUR team!

Even if you have won, there is little time to bask in the reflected glory of a famous victory as those 'great guys' on the radio tell us all how it was. Your favourite players are always about to be out of contract when you need them the most, and the 'vultures' from other clubs are always circling. Perhaps things are bad in the boardroom, you're strapped for cash or there is another injury crisis on the horizon, or worst of all when it comes round to the next match day....you're rubbish again! There's always a crisis, and always another worry. That's just it really, that's life, totally encapsulated for this rugby league fanatic by that stomach churning feeling that only we obsessive sports fans feel before every game of every season. Early in the week you can live with it but as the day of the match gets closer it becomes pretty unbearable and yet every week you still strive to find ways to exist alongside it.

Hull FC, the best (well in my eyes anyway) Rugby League Club in the world, are my team, they always have been and they always will be! Occasionally I wish they weren't, but they are and I can do precious little about it.

As long as my loved ones and friends are healthy and happy, it's probably the only other thing that dominates my life. I guess I have from time to time paid at least lip service to hobbies, 'other interests' and even in my younger days 'girls', however being a life-long fan of my Club is much, much more than any of that.

Of course I was not a "supporter" as such when I was born but from as early as I can remember, and no doubt even before that, the 'Airlie Birds' have always been around me and always there. I often think that it must be great to have come across 'Your team', in later life and to be able to look back on all the years of other interests, like stamp collectors, train spotters and chess players do: boy do I envy those folks sometimes?

It's often said that, 'everyone has a book in them' and after you have endured a few pages of this tome you may think in my case it's the best place for it to remain! But what follows in these pages is nothing more than a simple effort by an ordinary Rugby League fan to encapsulate and explain just what supporting YOUR club throughout YOUR life is about! It's all here, the highs, the lows, the occasional heady moments of real success and the all too regular depths of despair. Here you will experience again the losses and defeats, the getting soaked to the skin, the taunting imbeciles in the away end, and the turncoat player who leaves for the rival club. But then, oh then, just occasionally there are those wonderful fleeting moments when you win, not any game, but THE game, the big one, the one you will remember forever and the one that makes you suddenly realise that it's all, in the end, blissfully worthwhile.

This book spans the first half of my own simple life, from being born into a 'Black and White' family who lived just a 'stone's throw' from the Boulevard Stadium, to living over a pub on Hessle Road in the heart of a wasted and depleted fishing community some 30 years later. It's a cautionary, and probably woeful tale of what can happen to you 'if you aren't careful' and tracks the formative years of someone who has, with age, become an obsessive fanatic and perhaps some would say a fool.

In the rugby bits I do not labour too long on statistics, scorers and league tables, because other people, much better qualified than me do that so much better than I ever could. If that's what you want, then I would suggest you close this book now, put it in the pile for the charity shop, and get yourself a copy of the Gillette Rugby League Year book. This is not just a Rugby League book either, it's the story of a simple lad growing up in that famous community and no doubt some of my recollections about that life and the games and the players involved with Hull FC will be a bit inaccurate, because that's how over time they become, particularly when you're totally biased. There has been no cross referencing, or studious studying of historical documents, so I guess for many of you other fanatics out there, it will just be a case of spot the mistakes. Some of the names of the folks that I met along the way have been changed to, 'protect the innocent', but by and large it's just a simple story about how an ordinary West Hull lad has lived and loved the ultimate and largely unobtainable dream. It's also about a loathing for the rest of the rugby teams we have played over the years and particularly for the old enemy across the river. Once you're born into a family that supports a sports club there is little you can do about it and indeed when someone you know does 'change sides', despite them maybe being a really good friend, it's totally and irretrievably unforgiveable. This is best described I think with the analogy of my best friend leaving his wife and running off with a foxy young female. I would of course be publically 'disgusted', but privately I would probably harbour a modicum of admiration for his actions. However were he to declare that he had abandoned Hull FC to watch Hull Kingston Rovers, I would be totally outraged and would certainly never speak to him again.

I am sure if you've ever really cared about any team in any sport you'll know what I mean when I say that, in the end, it's often really about being an average supporter of an average sports club, who foolishly believes somehow, one day, his team are going to be the best in the world! It's about that unrequited belief, and that's why I honestly pity Manchester United supporters. With all that winning things all the time, it must get terribly boring.

The early years of this book are more like a lesson in social history and are based in part on my recollections, but in the main, as far the Club's fortunes are concerned, on the stories that two great parents who were both fanatical Hull FC supporters told me of their travels, their highs and lows, and their experience of supporting the "Family" team. Most people 'compartmentalise' their lives, some with birthdays others with marriages, new jobs etc, I make no excuses for 'milestoning' mine with rugby matches because quite frankly that's how I remember it. I have forgotten hundreds and hundreds of games but I measure out my life on the ones I remember.

I hope in reading this you will understand what growing up in the fishing community of Hull was like and how a sports club could be woven into the very 'DNA' of that same community. I also hope it gives at least a brief insight into what all this 'Loyal supporter' and 'cross city rivalry' stuff is about, and even perhaps along the way you'll relate to some of my feelings, memories and experiences yourself.

Chapter One

The first game I ever missed

Saturday 9th August 1950   Hull FC 18 - Bradford Northern 10

For this Rugby League fan the first Hull FC game I missed was against Bradford Northern at the Boulevard on 19th August 1950. Of course even though I only lived across the road, at just two months old it would have been a big 'ask' for me to get there. Unlike the explanations of many of those absent fans who call those 'Phone in' sports shows on local radio after games, I believe I had a reasonable excuse. You know the type, the ones that when asked, "Did you go to the game today" always have a readymade excuse to trot out like, "No, I HAD to work..." or "The dog's just died...." or "Just before I was going to set off, my conservatory collapsed...". I suppose, had there been local radio back in 1950 and had I been able to speak, I would have taken great delight in telling the presenter that "I am just two months old, in my cot, and I can't walk or talk, otherwise I would have been there!" That was of course all true, I really couldn't walk, but I somehow know that had I been able to, then I would have got there, although on this occasion, for once, I think I had a pretty good excuse for not attending.

I'd like to think that even at that tender age there was no chance of me being like that lot of committed 'Fair Weather' supporters. We all know them, don't we? The 'sing when your winning' 'only here for the beer' crowd who always have an opinion and invariably an excuse!! Perhaps, if you believe in fate, it explains why I was born just across the road from that most famous of Rugby League Stadiums, The Boulevard! Perhaps what follows in here was just my destiny!!!

Actually, talking of rugby, 1950 was not that good a season for the Club anyway, three wins and a draw from our first 11 games was hardly awe inspiring! A Yorkshire Cup exit in the first round at Dewsbury was another blow, and then Warrington put us out of the Challenge Cup also in the first round and in the end a strong and experienced Workington Town side went on to win the Championship! So I suppose I wasn't really missing much, although one interesting point of note that passed me by completely back then, was that at the end of the campaign we finished the season off with a win against Celtic de Paris in a friendly game staged as part of the Festival of Britain! A friendly game? Now there's a contradiction in terms if ever there was one because I challenge anyone to come forward who has actually witnessed a game of Rugby League that was ever "Friendly". It was then and still is the hardest game in the World.

I say one point of note but of course the most significant thing to happen at my Club that year, took place at York on 23rd December.

Johnny Whiteley takes a bow

Saturday 23rd December 1950   *Hull 19 – York 11*

This was without doubt a massive milestone in the long history of our Club and one that probably a good number of those fans with bereaved dogs and collapsed conservatories missed all together but it was then that the greatest and most popular of all Hull born players Johnny Whiteley made his debut for the Club. His first run out came after playing just two 'A' team games as a trialist and he received the princely sum of £100 as a signing on fee. Several seasoned supporters, relate a great story about how a couple of weeks later, just as he scored his first try for the Club at the Gordon Street end of the Boulevard, a shaft of sunlight pierced the leaden January skies. One supporter that witnessed the event described it to me years later as, 'A spot light from Heaven', it struck the figure of our young loose forward just as he placed the ball over the line to score the first of many touchdowns. Johnny was destined, (as his future career at the Club would subsequently prove) to be the chosen one!

That of course is just a legend and emanates entirely from what I have gleaned from the ageing sages of the 'FC Army' of supporters who remember these types of things. They are those guys who occasionally you bump into and who can, at the drop of the hat, relate tales of post war Rugby League, Duncan Jackson, Bruce Ryan and all. But exactly how far back can I actually remember? And how far back do I have to look to see exactly where this wonderful obsession, nay, love affair with a Rugby League team started!

So that's where it all started then?

Well, I know that I can't remember anything from the early womb days, I doubt anyone can! Some wise men will tell you that their adventures in a bag of amniotic fluid manifest themselves in later life in that secure feeling you get when you wake up in bed with your knees tucked up into your stomach. However if I'm honest I remember very little of what went on up to the age of two, but from then on I can remember quite a lot. That's the funny thing about this sort of reminiscing really, you can remember the finest detail about your life back then and yet as you get older you have difficulty telling anyone what colour socks you wore yesterday!

The stuttering, hazy 'video tape' in my head can flash up tries, bus trips to away games, hotdogs served at half time, being sick in roadside ditches and even injuries from 50 years ago, and yet I constantly struggle to remember when my wedding anniversary is! (28th August I think?)

I will though, here at the very beginning, try my best to fill in the blanks with the stuff my parents told me and what I have gleaned from what I laughingly call my research! I start at the very beginning if for no other reason than to explode the myth that I was found wrapped in a Hull shirt on the terracing at the Airlie Street end of the Boulevard after some muddy 'A' team game, on a foggy Saturday afternoon, back in 1950!

Firstly I have to say that I think it's reasonably safe to presume that things on Anlaby Road back then were a bit quieter than they are now. The road was then the major western artery of Kingston upon Hull leading directly to Boothferry Road and the rest of the country, but it certainly saw a lot fewer motor vehicles (but many more bicycles) than it does today. The old grey haired man sat in the little hut at the railway crossing at 'Boulevard End', would, having heard the electric bell ring, walk out into the traffic, waive his red flag and close the gates for a train. Something he would do, almost mechanically, around one hundred times a day! He just took hold of the gate waived the flag and stepped boldly out into the road. The crossing was replaced by a 'Fly Over' many years later and that's probably a good thing, as had that practise of opening and closing the gates continued today, it is likely the gateman would be doing well to get anywhere near being old and grey haired. There is little doubt that he would have been mowed down long ago by some boy racer or marauding juggernaut!

No doubt too, as the twentieth century marked its half way point, those maroon liveried, battery operated Co-op vans would be speeding backwards and forwards with their daily deliveries, darting between the stately blue and cream East Yorkshire buses which plodded from stop to stop, up and down the highway. There would also be the silent running and slightly phantom, Corporation Transport trolley buses, displaying in their illuminated front panels 69 Meadow Bank Road or 69 Paragon Street depending, on which direction they were travelling. Then there was the hundreds and hundreds of cyclists too who, rain or shine, would make their way to and from work, weaving in and out of the traffic. Their regular sojourn only occasionally interrupted by the changing of the odd set of traffic lights or the closing of that busy railway crossing. It was at those wooden gates that these intrepid riders would line up like international cyclists at the start of the Tour de France waiting to race through the smallest of gap as the gates opened to traffic again.

Day after day, week after week Anlaby Road would be the same, with life continuing at this bustling yet measured pace. I don't suppose any of these comings and goings bothered me much on the 26th June though. For at around ten o'clock that night, as life went on as normal outside the Newington Nursing Home, I was inside, probably more preoccupied with gulping down my first breath, and crying to order after a slap across the backside!

Mum and Dad, Abbie and Wally

In hindsight, I suppose I was a privileged child because back then there were only a few of the more 'modern thinking' families using Nursing Homes for these introductions to the world of West Hull. In most cases the overweight and fresh faced resident midwife Mrs Hayes, was kept busy on her bike, racing up and down the Boulevard to the more traditional births, which the 'more traditional' mothers preferred, "In 'me' own bed!"

Abigail, my Mum, benefiting as she did from the post war euphoria that was everywhere in those days, definitely thought of herself as a modern woman. So, despite her own introduction to the world having been with plenty of 'towels and hot water' in the front room of 22 Carrington Street, she was certainly up for the nursing home bit when it came to giving birth herself. Her husband and my Dad, Charles Walter (or Wally, as he was known by everyone in the Boulevard), was a butcher by trade or as he preferred to be designated whenever he was asked, a 'Master Butcher'. My Dad was very proud of what he had achieved! His long apprenticeship at a Pork Butchers on Beverley Road and his subsequent and mandatory wartime spell in the catering section of the 'Desert Rats', had stood him in good stead to rise through the ranks of his chosen profession. He was, by the time 'Yours Truly' popped out, the Manager of Dewhurst the Butchers at 259 Holderness Road.

The funny thing about the nick name "Wally" is that these days it is a term of ridicule and indicates someone a little stupid, however back then there were a lot of Walters about and the shortened version of their

5

name was seen as a term of endearment! Abbie and Wally, according to everyone who knew them then, had one thing in common, (well hopefully they had more than one but you'll no doubt get the idea), because they were best known around the Boulevard for their keen interest in the game of Rugby League. They were though, more importantly, almost notorious for their long and unswerving love of Hull Rugby League Football Club.

Right up to marrying Wally in 1947, Mum had always lived just off Airlie Street, at number 22 Carrington Street. This was an end terraced house, separated from next door by a short passage, where the back boundary of a tiny back garden was actually the solid concrete wall of the Main, or 'Best Stand' of the Boulevard Stadium. The arena was undoubtedly the centre of the community for everyone in the neighbourhood. There was a lot of local pride in the old place too with it being in the global scheme of things, a world renowned venue for the game of Rugby League!

Amy Johnson knew my Mother!

Abbie had been a bright girl and attended Kingston High School on the Boulevard, a fact that sometimes assisted her in 'breaking the ice at parties' when she would casually announce that she was in the same class as Amy Johnson, the acclaimed long distant aviator. Amy was born not too far away in St George's Road, at number 154 which was a bit more up market than Carrington Street, but still very much in 'Black and White' territory.

Wally alas, was born away from that hot bed of Rugby League in a terraced house in Lilac Avenue in Hardy Street just off Cottingham Road, in an area best described as North/Central Hull. He met Mum, just before the war, at a dance at the then centre of the city's nightlife, the Beverley Road Baths. Shortly after this meeting, the recently qualified butcher, was called up into the R.A.F. to sort out Mr Hitler where he went into the catering corps. and did not return home until 1945. Throughout the war, as millions of other sweethearts did in those days, the pair communicated by hundreds of letters, many of which were lost well before they arrived at their destination. Mum was enlisted to the war effort, making as she put it, "Bits of Spitfires and tanks" at Rosedown and Thompson the Engineers in Cannon Street. By night she did her bit too, acted as an air raid warden and fire watcher around the Hessle Road area.

Wally at first served at local airfields such as Catfoss and Bransburton and was able to get home to see Mum on leave. He was then posted to the Middle East where he catered for the Desert Rats before finally in 1945 he arrived home from Egypt. He brought with him a hand stitched leather camel ornament, a new wallet, a couple of leather lampshades and a bad dose of a Malaria type disease called 'Sand Fly Fever'. Just in case he needed reminding of those years of carving beef and making sausages to feed the lads chasing Nazi's up and down the Sahara, this inflamed rash reoccurred every summer almost up to the day he died in 1980.

23 Aylesford Street – Be it ever so humble …

After being married at St Matthew's the areas (and the rugby club's) Parish Church Mum and Dad decided to settle nearby. In fact, in the traditions of the much vaunted extended family, they ended up not too far away from Mum's original home in Carrington Street, renting a two up two down 'Sham Four' terraced house at 23 Aylesford Street. This fronted that street but had its 'back passage' in Airlie Street just across the road from the front entrance of the Boulevard Stadium. The house itself looks tiny now but back then it seemed like a mansion! There was a front room into which was squashed a gate leg table, a three piece suite, a china cabinet, sideboard and in pride of place in the corner, a 12" Pye television set.

In those days the possession of a TV was still something of a status symbol, and Mum and Dad were the first in the area to have one. Apparently our H Arial was the first to be seen across the rooftops for miles around and I vaguely remember the day when I was three and all the neighbours crammed into our little front room to watch the Coronation!

However, back to 23 where the backroom downstairs was the kitchen which boasted an Ascot gas geyser, a stone sink, a washing machine with wringer and a kitchen table. There was a small pantry in one corner and a flight of stairs that led to the bedrooms in the other. Out through the back door was a yard with a coal house, a shed and next to the back gate an outdoor loo, with a paraffin night light for the cold weather and a rag rug under which the spare house key was always left! We actually had toilet paper, a luxury in those days around our way, with most of our neighbours using small sheets of newspaper. So that these could be hung up tidily the older members of the family often used to sit at night threading the small sheets of newsprint onto a loop of string with a darning needle, whilst listening to Dick Barton and 'Take it from Here' on the radio. Others, who were not so fussed, just jammed yesterday's newspaper behind the plumbing. Some would say, even today, that it's probably not a bad use for the local newspaper!!

Upstairs there were two bedrooms; at the front was my parent's room whilst I was in the back. There were only two things that were special about my room really, the smell and the view from the window. My Dad had made a wooden ottoman for Mum to keep all her bedding and linen in and for some unknown reason he had creosoted it! I can still smell it now! If I knelt on that same piece of aromatic furniture however I could see through the sash window right across the car park of the Boulevard Stadium. In fact if I looked a little further in the gap between the 'Best' stand and the open terrace, or 'Bunker's Hill' as it was known back then, (no doubt after the famous American Battle of 1775) I could just see half the score board which in those days was at the Gordon Street end of the ground. Then, of course, this meant little to me, but in later years that view became very significant indeed!

So that was home, fresh meat every day, brought home by Dad, 'Muffin the Mule' and 'Mexican Pete' on the TV, 'bombed buildings' to play on and Mum's homemade bacon and egg pie, who could wish for more!

Aylesford Street was terraced, in fact at the time of writing, it still is. Each house had a minuscule front garden, often fenced off by smart painted wooden palings. Dad had planted a Privet hedge in there which, I suppose, survived rather than flourished in the shallow soil. The kerbs in front of the houses had knobbly metal stumps along the top that indicated where the cast iron railings had been sawn off as scrap metal for the war effort and never replaced.

On just about every street corner there were butchers, general stores, hairdressers or bakers and all the daily needs of local families were met by these small corner shops. As well as food they provided a social meeting point for the local ladies. In those days it was difficult to keep food fresh and often the pantries were damp and small, so regular visits to these establishments were part of everyday life particularly for the women of the area. Money was tight and often the proprietors of the shops would measure out tiny quantities of tea, sugar, butter or lard to 'tide' the families over till pay day!

One baker called Hudson had a shop on the corner of Airlie Street and the Boulevard. Old Mr Hudson used to bake his own bread daily and the smell was outstanding. One of my first recollections was being pushed down to the shop in my pram and smelling that bread. Even today when I arrive in Argyle Street for Home games at the KC Stadium and smell the aroma from Jackson's Bakery, my mind automatically goes back to Hudson's on the Boulevard with its tiled floor, polished chrome bacon slicer, Rhubarb tarts, fresh custard pies and fat jolly serving ladies in big green aprons!

Another store that stuck in my mind back in those really early days was Crimliss's Fish and Chip shop in Airlie Street. Fish was popular, cheap and very plentiful. When I was little, I can remember Mum taking fish to the shop to be fried for about 2d a piece, but you had to buy chips with it, if you didn't want chips then Mr Crimliss would refuse to fry your fish! Often neighbours who worked on the Fish Docks would bring home a 'fry' of fish, which they would share with us! I guess I didn't know back then, just how lucky I was as far as my nutritional needs go, having a butcher for a Dad and living so near to the docks!

My first encounter with the 'Faithful'.

Saturday 2nd February 1952   Hull 12 - Bradford Northern 8

On Saturdays when there was a rugby game across the road Mum used to proudly sit me in my pram outside the front of the house. There, wrapped in my home knitted Black and White blanket, I would watch with great interest, and not a small amount of delight, the cars, buses and cycles arriving from all angles for the big games!

Although I would have been completely oblivious of what was going on, 1951/52 was a slightly better year for the 'Cream' and ended with a heart breaking defeat by Wigan by 13-9 in the play-off semi final. For the second year running we went out of the Yorkshire Cup in the first round to Wakefield Trinity, whilst the New Zealand tourists thumped us at the Boulevard and Oldham knocked us out of the Challenge Cup in the second round, so in general I suppose I wasn't missing much!

The next season though saw a staggering gate of 20,000 packed into the Boulevard for a game against Bradford Northern; this was the largest crowd to attend any Rugby League ground since the war. We won 12-8 to shatter Bradford's 27 game winning streak and although I cannot remember it now, I bet the houses around us rocked to the roars of the crowd and the chorus' of 'Old Faithful' that day!

Weekend millionaires

I vaguely remember from about the age of two, Mum and I started to venture further afield to the local 'shopping centres' that were either Anlaby or Hessle Road. There, this inquisitive infant would find treasure houses in such establishments as Home and Colonial, Woolworths, Maypole, Boyes and Mallory's. The thing was in those days that people were a lot less worried about child molesters and kidnappers than they are today. So it was, that all along these roads outside the shops we would be deposited in our prams, parked tidily in rows, whilst our Mothers went off to get the weekly provisions.

Hessle Road was of course, in the heart of the fishing industry and in the early 50's around 120 trawlers would set off to ply their trade in the treacherous waters of the North Sea and the Arctic. As you grew up in the area every winter some mate or school pal would lose a father or a brother and, tragic though it was, it was just accepted as part and parcel of living in that fishing community. It was dangerous work on the trawlers and the brave lads who did it used to return home for a few days when a few 'Bevvies' and a bit of fun were always on the agenda. One famous story has a group of seamen being regularly thrown out of the Criterion Pub on Hessle Road at 3-00pm, which was then the afternoon closing time. They would walk to Boyes, the local department store and swap around all the babies in the prams and then hide round the corner and watch the fun when the mothers returned! Those lads certainly worked and played hard.

Waistells the shop at the corner of West Dock Avenue stocked the 'uniform' that these trawlermen used to wear when at home. The younger seamen wore outrageous, flashy outfits that were known in the area as 'Decky Learner' suits, in fact in the later 'Teddy Boy' era of the mid fifties these lads in their powder blue, light grey or cream outfits developed a unique style. The more outrageous the suit worn by these young lads was usually determined by how drunk they were when they visited Waistells to order them!

These fishermen who experienced tremendous hardship everyday of their working lives also really loved their Rugby. It would not be unusual for a trawlerman to come ashore early on a Saturday morning, call at home to see his wife and kids, and then hop into a taxi to go to Huddersfield or Wigan for the game that afternoon! Taxis, although out of my family's price range, were in fact often left with their meters running outside fishermen's houses for hours; there is no wonder these brave lads got the nickname of 'Weekend Millionaires'.

Out and about in the pram

Life in the Boulevard before school was great. I guess looking back money was in pretty short supply but we certainly had a great time.

Dad would get Thursday afternoons off when his shop was closed, and whilst I was still being ferried around in a pram we would all go out exploring on Sundays. This usually took us to West Park to watch the bigger lads fishing for tadpoles, or to go and sit on the seats at the top of the Boulevard and watch the trains go by! Those were great afternoons and I used to be completely mesmerised by the opening and closing of the gates and the goods and passenger trains that would steam by! The seats which were next to Miles, the then famous motor cycle shop, were always occupied by other mothers with their children and several of the older male members of the community. They would sit all day smoking their pipes, discussing the rugby and putting the world to right! Mum would soon join in with the rugby talk, discussing no doubt the current form of say Colin Hutton, Roy Francis or Mick Scott. What better company could you wish for when you were 2 years old!!

Another one of our trips used to take place on Saturdays when Hull City was at home. Mum used to push me all the way up Anlaby Road to Hull City's Boothferry Park Ground. Once there, we would take up position across the road from the ground, me in my pram and Mum sat on a convenient garden wall. There we would watch the trains pulling into the little railway halt bringing supporters from Paragon Station to the match. These keen supporters of the Tigers would open the doors even before the train had stopped, jump out onto the embankment and slide and skid down the muddy bank to the turnstiles at the bottom. It was an amazing sight and probably one of the best and most vivid recollections of my 'pram days'!

Holy wars and Sunday School

As soon as I was out of the pram and falling about the place I was taken every Sunday afternoon to the big 'Parish Hall' of St Matthew's Church which stood imposingly on the front of the Boulevard. Here, at Sunday School, I was introduced to a chap called God. This was a strange ritual where for the most part you sang songs with words you couldn't understand and were taught about Jesus, peace and love! All this after having been thumped on the way in and then again on the way out, by the big lads who were all at least 7 years old.

This atmosphere of 'Holy bullying' came to a head on Palm Sunday 1955 on the day of the Parish Parade. You see if there was one thing that they excelled at down at St Matthew's it was parades. Everyone loved a procession around the district, and once a year on Palm Sunday, the vicar, choir, congregation and the whole Sunday School would process around the parish. We all processed behind the Church banners and all the kids carried the nearest you got to palms in West Hull; Pussy willow branches.

Up front was usually one of the local scrap metal dealer's sons who bedecked in a blanket would re-enact the entry to Jerusalem on the back of one of his Dad's donkeys! We would stop in every street and sing a Lenten song and of course rattle a collection box. That year I was given a beautiful branch that I thought I would take home to Mum so that she could put it in water and watch it burst into leaf! I had seen her do that sort of thing before and I guess in my own little way, I thought this act of unbridled generosity would maybe score some valuable points at home! The other kids, 'Gods battling Urchins', followed the parade, skirmishing amongst themselves and using their branches in mock sword fights, which soon left their Pussy Willow 'Palms' in tatters.

Of course once we got back to the Parish Hall, the inevitable happened and I was set upon by the bad lads, beaten up, and left with a twig about a foot long! I went home in tears to Mum and Dad! If this proved anything to an impressionable four year old it was that all those nice looking missionaries sat in cooking pots surrounded by jolly looking black men, that we saw in our Sunday School books, had it easy. Religious Education was a steep learning curve down the Boulevard!

A rugby orphan ...Play days with Mrs (bloody) Clarkson

Mother, as was the case in those days, did not work, and I would spend almost all my time in her company. I can remember on numerous occasions sitting her on the settee in the front room and aided by a big brass dish for a steering wheel, taking her on imaginary bus trips all over the place! Saturday afternoons however were different!! Although Dad was working, Mum had a season pass for the 'Best Stand' at the Boulevard and every other week during the winter, at about twenty minutes to three I was taken to old Mrs Clarkson's next door. She was charged with looking after me whilst Mum went to 'Cheer on the Cream' across the Road. This of course was in the period which led up to the magnificent late 50's and is talked of by many of those 'sages' I mentioned earlier, as the pinnacle of our Club's post war supremacy. As soon as I could speak and understand what my parents were on about, everywhere we went I would hear folks talking to them about the Drakes, Albert Tripp, Johnny Whiteley, Colin Hutton and Arthur Bedford, Oh and "Bloody Referees!!"

Generally speaking in those days the elderly were valued and appreciated and often taken under the wing of the younger members of the community. As soon as I could walk I would 'go errands' for my Mum taking a plate of food, or some candles, to Mrs Clarkson next door, or taking the evening paper, after my Dad had read it, to old Mrs. Thorpe across the street. The local schools too, I remember, used to make a big thing of bringing the old and infirm produce from their Harvest Festivals and they would often get a few oranges, a jar of jam or a tin of corned beef from this source.

Mrs Clarkson was, I guess, a nice old lady, although when I think back, I suppose that she had probably been around a bit when she was younger. Dad was a bit surprised I think when on a few occasions, after a visit next door I would come out with the odd, 'bloody', or call a Policeman 'a Rosser'! I got some of my first educational pointers from Mrs Clarkson! She was also in charge on Mum and Dad's big night out every year as she 'baby sat' whilst they both put on their 'glad rags' and went to the Annual Supporters' Club Dinner at the Broadway Hotel on Anlaby Road, an event that was always eagerly anticipated in our house.

I don't remember much about Mrs Clarkson's house except for the cast iron doorstop that she used to hold the back door open on warm days. It was a cast iron black man squatting like a Buddha, with one hinged arm stuck out at the front. When you put a penny in his hand the arm went up to his mouth and he would eat the coin whole! It was of course a moneybox but I used to get no end of amusement by tricking him with washers from Dad's shed. Mrs Clarkson affectionately called it Sambo, proving without doubt that back then 'Political Correctness' was still an age away.

Match days in Airlie Street

Every other Saturday throughout the winter, our usually quiet street came alive. Match days in Airlie Street were mayhem. Everybody down our back passage, except ourselves and Mrs Clarkson (and Sambo), took in bikes. This was to offer security during the game for the fans prime mode of transport whilst their owners enjoyed the match across the street. There was a set charge of 1d a bike and all householders who took part in this practise operated a primitive sort of cartel I guess, with most backyards having their own regular customers. So good was trade that Mr Potter who lived four houses down, started an overflow business on the bombed building site at the end of our block of houses. I had never seen so many bicycles, cars and people and even at that tender age the whole match day thing fascinated me! Cars would park down the streets at 45 degrees to the pavement so as to pack more in and it was so quiet and eerie once everyone had got into the ground and the game had started. It was a strange experience seeing all those deserted streets, abandoned vehicles and cycles and hearing the 'oooh's', 'aaaahhhhs' and cheers coming from behind the big brick wall across the road.

What's going on behind that big concrete wall... Granny's rugby commentaries!

Saturday 1st October 1953   *Hull 2 - Bradford 7*

The 1953/54 season was a better one for the Club and the feeling that even a four year old got that something special was happening across the street was probably founded in the fact that we were having a really good run of victories at home. Sadly though we were beaten in the Final of the Yorkshire Cup by Bradford 7-2 although Hull FC managed a very creditable 33 wins out of the 47 games we played. More significantly however the Club was starting to bring together the group of players that would serve us so well in the latter part of the decade. Mum would talk to Dad, the neighbours and anyone who she could get to listen about Johnny Whiteley and the team, whenever she got the chance.

As Mrs Clarkson became more and more infirm her language became even more colourful, and I was shipped off on Saturday afternoons to Granny Evers's house in Carrington Street, where, when Hull scored, the whole house shook with the cheering! It was a strange experience for a four year old, but you got used to it and Granny and I played all sorts of games together. My favourite was "Builders" we would be "Bill" and "Mike" and build pretend walls with dusters and old magazines! Whilst doing this, Granny would keep me up to date with commentary on the game based on the noises coming from the stand at the end of the back yard. She'd say "He's kicked the Goal", "Now the refs copped it!" and "That's a try, Up the Cream". She usually had the score guessed well before Mum arrived back from the game to confirm it and take me home. The "Up the cream" expression, based on the team's faded shirts and shorts, was, my Mum told me many years later, one of the first phrases I ever came out with. Screaming it loud and long in the barber's chair as a three year old, much to Mum's embarrassment! Good old Granny!

I'll always remember Granny Evers as being kind and particularly gentle whilst my Dad's Mum was a formidable woman. She still lived in the family home in Lilac Avenue, where my Dad was born and around 1954 for some unknown reason she suddenly started to visit us every Thursday afternoon to coincide with Dad's half day off. I bet Mum blessed her!!

At about six foot tall she always dressed in a long black coat with a matching brimmed hat that she bought years earlier from the department store Thornton Varleys in Ferensway. She would fill our little front room in Aylesford Street as soon as she walked in. I remember that as she stood there in the doorway pulling her gloves off finger by finger, she would say the greeting "Well, Ow are ya". You can imagine by the age of four I had this off to a tee and used to imitate her whenever I got the opportunity and often, to my mother's acute embarrassment, I'd even perform this party piece in unison, as my Grandma stood there saying it!

Jessie, my Dad's Mum had experienced a sad life really; losing her husband at Passiondale in the Great War just before my Dad was born. In fact Grandma brought my Dad and his sister up herself, never having got round it seemed to getting married again. Although she was quite softly spoken, Jessica was certainly no gentle giant! For someone who won prizes for her embroidery, she was really heavy handed, something that I remember well from the odd occasions when, in an effort to help my Mum, she used to wash me before I went to bed. I can still feel it today. It was as if someone was clamping my head and rubbing my face with sandpaper. The way she screwed the corner of the towel and rammed it in my ear to dry me, made me think that any time soon it would be coming out the other side!

Though they all looked after me really well, I was never cosseted. Kids just weren't in those days and although we were warned not to go too far from home, it was a pretty safe community to live in, with the urban paranoia of the "Don't take sweets from strangers" stuff being still a few years away.

Some women will do anything for a Sherbet Fizz!!

So it was that at about four years old, I started 'Playing Out' with Jacko, David, Ginger, Biffo and my other pals down the street! We usually played on the bombed site across the road that was used on match days as a car park in front of the Boulevard ground. It was mostly Cowboys and Indians, Block or Realleyoo but I remember, being the youngest, it was often hard to understand what the older kids were actually doing. Mostly I think I just used to run around screaming at the top of my voice! However occasionally at the instigation of some of the older girls down the street we played Doctors and Nurses. It was then, I guess, that I first discovered an important truth that has stayed with me for the rest of my life, that being, that some women will do just about anything for a Sherbet Fizz!

The thing is that we were all probably very poor but we did not realise it! The whole community was insular to the point of living in each other's pockets; we were all in the same boat financially and lived to that level of expectation. I never remember wanting anything that I could not have, the fact being that you never really wanted that much! Across the road at the Boulevard major ground improvements were taking place and the constant stream of lorries and cranes arriving in Airlie Street heralded the complete re concreting of the terracing at both the Airlie and Gordon Street ends of the ground and the installation of new perimeter fences that were needed to contain the ever increasing attendances the Club were attracting.

It's the most wonderful time of the year

The days were long, and there were always plenty of adventures to undertake and we got our treats from time to time which we really appreciated. Take Christmas for instance. Wherever you lived at that age it was a magical time. Father Christmas came to Aylesford Street just as he did to every other street in the country. The fact that he brought plastic cars, three-penny bits and oranges to me on Christmas morning, in a pillowcase that amazingly resembled one of my Mum's, made no difference at all. That would be what David next door, or Ginger down the street was getting too, in a pillowcase that looked just like the ones that their parents used! Of course we had the biggest Turkey and lots of joints of meat and everyone crammed into our little front room and drank Hull Brewery Amber and played 'Housey, Housey' (Bingo).

Despite working Saturdays and missing most games at the Boulevard because of work Dad was very active across the road working with Ernie Mason and Jack Hayes on the committee that oversaw the building of the new supporters' Club House on the front of the ground. Throughout the festive period that year we all watched with interest as the brickwork was completed and the asbestos roofing sections were put in place.

There were always parties though particularly at Christmas with jelly and custard, little buns with hundreds and thousands on them, games of musical chairs and at the end, the mandatory and eagerly anticipated visit from Santa. Everyone took their own spoons because it was just impossible to eat jelly or blancmange without one and each utensil had a piece of coloured cotton attached to the handle to ensure that after washing up was completed, it was safely returned to the right child after the party. Well, I say Santa, but usually it was a rather short character, who was anything but jolly. He invariably had a holey, cotton wool beard and wore 'National Health' glasses and sometimes he would even exude the sweet odour of beer or rum but we were pleased to see him just the same, because we knew no different!

I remember one particular party a couple of years later at the newly completed Hull Supporters' Club when Father Christmas was unusual to say the least. We all looked up from our trifle and looked again, because as Santa arrived in the usual garb he appeared to have a real dark 'suntan'. Mum told me later that he had probably been delivering presents in Africa and as he had given me a great game called the Magic Marvello that was good enough for me! In fact on comparing notes next day, Ginger's dad had said he had probably been delivering in Brazil, whilst next door David's mum told him that there had been a heat wave at the North Pole. It was many years before I discovered quite by chance that the Club's great South African coach Roy Francis used to love being Father Christmas at the kid's parties. So that finally explained the bronzed faced Santa!

The Biggest bath I had ever seen!

On another occasion I was taken by my Mum and a Mr Massey around the dressing rooms under the best stand at the Boulevard ground. He was apparently the Club's masseur at the time and he lived in a big house called Foxholes on the Boulevard. I cannot remember too much about that first visit to the hallowed changing rooms except that they let me stand in the massive communal bath that all the players from both sides got into after the game! It seemed gigantic especially as it seemed a long way from down there on the tiles up to where my Mum and Mr Massey were stood looking down at me. I suppose it made me feel even smaller than I was. All I could do was be thankful that there was no water in it at the time! All grounds had these communal 'tubs' back then and all the players from both sides got in together after the game. It was tradition although it's hard to imagine that it would go down too well at the KC Stadium these days. For me the camaraderie and friendship that existed between players from all clubs back then was a real plus for the sport and something that seems to have disappeared somewhat from the modern game.

Some Sundays Dad would take his turn at looking after me and he would take me to the town on the bus before walking me down the dockside to the Pier. On the way along the side of Humber Dock he would point out to me the Associated Humber Lines ships like 'Fountains Abbey' or 'Rieveaux Abbey' that were discharging various cargoes. I can still, to this day, smell the wonderful aroma that came from the banana drying and ripening sheds down there too! This ritual was usually followed by a Steven's Ice cream from the kiosk on the Pier and an afternoon watching the ships go by down the Humber.

As for music, well you will find as you read on that it has played a very important part in my life although back at this time my play list was very limited. It probably included 'The Runaway Train', 'The Big Rock Candy Mountain', 'I Know an Old Lady Who Swallowed a Fly' and 'Old Faithful' all with the exception of the latter which was the family anthem, I had learned 'Parrot Fashion' from listening to Uncle Mac on 'Children's Favourites' on the Radio at nine o'clock every Saturday Morning. 'Old Faithful' is included in this collection of merry melodies simply because it could often be heard drifting up our stairs on Saturday nights after Dad returned from the Supporters' Club, usually smelling a bit like Father Christmas!

Still singing on the terraces long after Halifax had packed up and gone home with the Cup....

Saturday 3ʳᵈ October 1954   *Hull 14 - Halifax 22*

Although unbeknown to me at the time, this period in the history of my Rugby League team was one of the greatest they had experienced since their inception in 1865. With that same Roy Francis as coach and that famous mobile 'Panzer Pack', 'the Cream' terrorised defences through-out the decade. It was in 1954 that the great team really started to tick and the crowds came rolling back to the Boulevard in their thousands. The Club got to the Yorkshire Cup Final and this time after packing me off to Granny's for some more 'Magazine Building', Mum went on a Danby's Motor Coach, with the Hull Supporters' Club to the game against Halifax at Headingley. She told me in later years of her vivid recollections of the match, which she obviously felt was one of the most exciting she had ever seen. Even though for the second year running we lost the final!

What she remembered most and related to everyone who cared to listen, was the number of injuries we incurred in the game. In the second half apparently, the crowd of over 25,000 watched as first Keith Bowman then Johnny Whiteley and finally Tommy Harris were badly injured all in a three minute spell. Harris in fact was knocked out cold but the game still went on for around two minutes, as in those days the rules dictated that the referee had to play on until a try or infringement occurred. There were of course no substitutes then either, so Hull played on with, at one point, just 10 players on the field.

It was a real heroic performance and Harry Markham the massive FC forward even had to play on the wing to bolster the backs. Ailing and patched up players came back onto the field and trailing 22-9 late into the second half Hull, just refused to give up! Driven on by the strains of 'Old Faithful' they moved the ball to the wing and who else but Harry crashed over in the corner, for a try which Hutton goaled. Hull pressed but the loss of critical players at critical times eventually cost them the game 22-14. However the Hull supporters have always been magnanimous when faced with endeavour and courage and my Mum always recalled with much relish the strains of our great anthem ringing around Headingley long after, she said, Halifax had collected the Cup and gone home!

But sadly, at such a tender age, it all passed me by. Although through this early period of my existence I had the occasional brush with the hallowed Boulevard Stadium whilst in the process of 'playing out'.

Back then on game days, to accommodate early leavers, the big wooden gates would rumble open at around three quarter time and I would perhaps daringly run into the entrance, shout abuse at the stewards and then hare out again. However thankfully as yet I had not been hooked, I was still immune, the world was still my oyster, the sky was always blue and everywhere was a playground. Although Hull Rugby League Football Club was always there, it was still tucked away at the back of my mind behind the bogey man, Robin Hood, the Lone Ranger, God and the fear of having to wear corrective shoes or clinic glasses! All us kids just took for granted the lines of Hull FC shirts flapping in the wind on a Monday morning down Graham Avenue after Ernie and Ivy Mason had washed them, (before, that was, they persuaded the Club to buy a washing machine) because it was just all part of everyday life back then. The Club that was to become a way of life was still just the wallpaper that surrounded my existence. I didn't know it then, but it was to become an addiction and a wonderful obsession that would stay with me for the rest of my life!

Chapter Two

All hell breaks loose at Headingley

Saturday 22ⁿᵈ October 1955   *Hull 10 – Halifax 10*

With the exception of my Saturday trips to Granny's and Mum's increasing excitement as Saturdays arrived, I still knew very little of things that were happening across the road at the Boulevard.

I was only just five years old in 1955 and the all consuming world of Hull FC still hadn't infiltrated my life. However had I been of an age to understand, I would probably have deduced that with the increase in people and traffic about on match days things, rugby wise, were really starting to move up a gear. In a season where we had been patchy at times and magnificent at others, we scraped into 4th place and the play-offs. But before that, one of the most notorious games in the Club's history took place at Leeds when we took on Halifax in the final of the Yorkshire Cup. The game itself was a dour affair full of niggling play and bad feeling from both sides, with Hull fighting back from being 10-0 down to draw level through tries from Ivor Watts and Keith Bowman.

But it was what else happened that day that had the national media representatives up in the press box licking their pencils and scrambling for their notebooks, for Saturday 22ⁿᵈ October 1955 was the day all hell broke loose at Headingley. In the first half, the going was really tough for both sides, with some over exuberant tackling leaving several players needing attention to cuts on the face and head. Then in the second half John Henderson was sent off after producing a 'sweet' left hook to flatten our skipper Johnny Whiteley and from then on things turned really nasty with skirmishes and fights breaking out every four or five tackles.

The Hull fans, including my Mum, who had travelled in numbers on two special trains were totally incensed by the refereeing and the conduct of the opposition and as was the norm in those less disciplined times, pelted objects at the Halifax forwards as they left the field at half time. In the second period the inevitable happened as the game finally descended into mayhem when Bob Coverdale, the Hull prop, came out of a scrum with blood pouring down his face. The next scrum saw the Halifax prop, Wilkinson, falling out of the front row with a long cut over his eye that needed four stitches and so it went on. The final whistle went with the scores locked at 10-10 but it was the general opinion of everyone there that the referee George Phillips had totally lost control well before the end.

So bad was the reaction next day in the national media that the Rugby League immediately held an inquiry and both clubs were publicly warned about their behaviour. The statement issued to the media indicated that "These practises must cease" and both clubs were warned about their future actions. However, for a couple of days the traditional northern game of Rugby League got plenty of national publicity, but sadly for all the wrong reasons.

It had been one of the most brutal encounters ever seen on a Rugby League field in this country. The whole thing was re-enacted a week later with the 'Fax' winning the replay at Odsal 7-0. The Hull 'Faithful' were certainly despondent but little did the disappointed fans know that later in the season revenge would be a dish best served in Manchester.

School daze ... The first great betrayal

One thing's for sure in everyone's life and that's when you reach the age of five, with the disclosure of the great Father Christmas swindle still a couple of years off, you invariably experience the first big let down of your life. One minute it seems that the world is one big adventure, you're playing out and 'sleeping tight', digging worms and eating them, falling off back yard walls and making privet soup in your mother's dolly tub, in fact, all in all, life is just full of fun. The next minute however you are taken to this strange place, with no carpets and really high windows. Everything stinks of disinfectant as you're dumped on the floor by your parents, abandoned with some strange adults and all this in the company of some even stranger looking kids. This, it was quickly apparent was what they meant when they talked about school.

I wouldn't have minded really but I could clearly see that Mum was crying when she left me, so why, I thought, should she do it in the first place? It was all really baffling when you were just five. Then, just as I was starting to get used to my new surroundings, playing games and finding a few new friends, back she comes, takes my hand and walks me all the way home for lunch. She told me in later life that it was then, after my first half day at school, and through a mouthful of 'Bullet' Sago, that I announced across the kitchen table, "I don't think I'll go back to school this afternoon".

The admission class at Chiltern Street Infants contained as weird a collection of juveniles as any area in any City could throw together. As children do, my first observation centred on the fact that there were a couple of my classmates with one leg shorter than the other. Three others were really, really over weight with one who wore wiry glasses resembling that porky Billy Bunter character I had seen on the TV back at no. 23. There were also a couple of lads with strange shoes with holes in the side and one whose hair looked as if it had been pulled out of selected areas of his head. I can't quite remember my reaction to this entire menagerie of human kind but I expect it was something along the lines of "what am I doing here with this lot?"

Strange bed fellows!

Once the ice was broken and we started to talk a bit I found that although many of them looked a little weird, we were all just the same really. The main difference seemed to be the level of excitement there was to be found in the jobs that the other kids Dad's did and the amount of kids who didn't have handkerchiefs or even seemed to know what they were used for. Let's face it who needs a handkerchief when your shirt has a sleeve? In Mrs Rutherford's class there were plenty of sons and daughters of fishermen, a couple of the offspring of street sweepers, a sewage worker's daughter and the son and heir to a scrap metal merchant's empire.

From day one, I noticed that a lad called Billy always had a strange odour about him which I suppose, looking back, could have had something to do with his Dad's work; he drove a sort of primitive version of a fork lift truck at the fish manure factory on St Andrews' Dock!

There appeared to be only one rule of uniform dress at Chiltern Infants and that was that there were no rules! That was with the exception that everyone had to wear shoes. It's a bit difficult to imagine these days I know but on the first day I was there, I watched with little interest as two lads were told that they could not sit in their Wellington boots all day and were sent home to get some shoes. As I said earlier, a couple of kids had strange shoes that we all called clodhoppers, these were really old looking and as big and chunky as the description dictates, but they also had holes punched in the sides. These, I found out quite by chance much later in life, had been provided years earlier, for the poor, by the 'Parish Relief' and were punched so that the children's parents could not hawk or 'pop' them at the Porn Brokers to purchase essentials like 'beer and cigs.'

So there we all were, shiny faced and pretty bemused as we all prepared to take the first steps to university, college, the world of work, or Her Majesty's Prison. We were all crammed into a small classroom, where we pulled faces at each other and no doubt picked our noses, all different in our own ways with only our thirst for knowledge and running noses as commonalities. Every day we played in a tabletop sandpit and seemed to do all sorts of wonderful things with plastercine. That was all fine by me and looking back, I really enjoyed it but I could not get on with all that numbers and letters stuff and I was absolutely hopeless at sums and at using that 'dog eared' cardboard money. The latter failing with any sort of currency is something that appears to have stayed with me to this day. 'Green sleeves' Bailey one of the none handkerchief brigade, even tried to buy some milk drops from Mrs. Butter's sweet shop with some of the cardboard coins he had smuggled out of school.

Playtimes however were great, if not a little too short. There were all manners of things to do, fights to support, races to run and games to play. We played Jacks, hopscotch and 'scrapping' and I often used to join some of the older boys as they linked arms and went about the playground singing "Anybody in the road gets a good KICK!" That game, predictably, did not go down too well with the teachers, although generally they turned a blind eye, probably seeing it back then as a character building exercise. Miss Rutherford, the Head Mistress, was a tall elegant grey haired lady who always wore a Tweed two-piece and balanced a pair of silver pince nez on the end of her nose. These unusual spectacles were a far cry from the 'Clinic' glasses that most visually challenged kids wore and were certainly a cause of fascination to us all. She was strict but quite liberal and actually let most of the rough tough stuff in the playground go unchallenged. In school however it was different and when she said "Shut up" you did, immediately.

There was also a lot of what is classed these days as bullying going on too, although then it was just an accepted bi-product of growing up. I suppose I was pretty normal and so I avoided most of that, however if you were particularly rich or poor, fat or thin, smelt or wore anything out of the ordinary, you'd had it at Chiltern Street. 'Green sleeves Bailey' and 'Smelly' Billy, 'the Fishmeal kid' certainly had a rough time.

Everyone got nits and head lice, some got fleas and some caught ringworm. I got nits twice but as a matter of pride, Mum always made sure that she got rid of them before the next visit of the school nurse; 'Nitty Norah the Head Explorer'.

Just another day at school and 'Another brick in the wall'

Looking back you could see exactly what Pink Floyd were on about but 'Infants' was I guess a first chance to learn a little about life although when she met some of my chums for the first time, I think my Mother was convinced that I was already on the rocky road to delinquency. That was a theory, and a fear, which most certainly increased for her one afternoon when I poured glue into Mrs Rutherford's handbag and Mum was summoned to school for me to be unceremoniously marched home and straight to bed.

The typical school day at Chiltern Street began with Assembly, which usually featured discordant renditions of either 'Morning Has Broken', or 'All things Bright and Beautiful' bashed out by Mrs Court on the piano in the corner of the assembly hall. She was a really fat lady who used to play with such gusto that on occasions her glasses would slip down her nose and fall off onto the keyboard. Billy Johnson used to always do his 'Elvis Presley' to this before his impressions were stopped with a swift whack across the head by a teacher who was positioned at the end of his row for that very purpose.

But after the initial shock of experiencing the education system first hand, life just settled into a routine and seemed to be all lessons and playtimes! Monday was Bank Day and Mum used to send me to school with Half a Crown, (which was a lot of money back then) and my Hull Savings Bank book. This was placed in a bag that she had made for me out of scraps of material and which had a draw top and an elastic strap that went over my shoulder. I must have looked what Granny always referred to as a 'real devil' walking to school on Mondays! ! This procedure was, Mum said, so that I could save up for a 'Rainy Day'. It rained a lot back then, but I never recollect ever seeing much of the money.

We are the champions! Or so they told me.

Saturday 12th May 1956   *Hull 10 – Halifax 9*

Despite the commencement of my education, my future as a hooligan and my growing fortune in the bank, Hull FC battled on through the season and finished in fourth position in the final league table. That gave us entry into the play-offs again and this time the Club travelled all the way to Barrow on 12th April and won 30-12. My Mother always told me she did not go to that one simply because it would have meant leaving me too long at Granny's. That was a good decision too although about two hundred Hull FC fans did make the journey, which in those days took around ten hours by coach. I remember being woken by them, in my little bedroom overlooking the car park, as they noisily tumbled off the bus at around 3-00am on Sunday Morning, they were tired, hung over, but happy. We were through to the semi-final.

The success at Barrow meant that we had to go to the Wildespool to play the most feared team in the Rugby League that year, Warrington, or the 'Wire Pullers' as they were nicknamed then. (I often wonder with its modern connotations why they dropped that nickname.) The Hull Directors, sensing a possible final appearance and the revenue that it would bring to the Club, slapped a £25 a man winning bonus on our players, something that was, down our street at least, considered a fortune. They probably thought that their money was reasonably safe anyway because to win at Wildespool would be a really tall order, which was understandable when you consider that Warrington, boasting such famous players as Harry Bath and Brian Bevan, had not been beaten at home by a Yorkshire club for seventeen years (how's that for a statistic?). In contrast this was our first championship play-off semi-final for twenty years. The odds were certainly stacked against Hull FC.

Roy Francis our Coach (and closet Father Christmas) had devised a game plan that was based around creating a fast mobile set of forwards. He had in fact ordered that no one besides the players should be admitted to the two training sessions that week and in this atmosphere of secrecy, he trained with the backs acting as forwards and the forwards playing the game of the backs! It was not unusual in the days when Francis reigned as coach, to see the 'backs' hobbling out of the players gate at the Boulevard on a Tuesday and Thursday night after training.

Years later one of them Brian Darlington told me a story from those days about Francis and how he constantly went on and on about the importance of strong legs at just about every training session. He maintained that they were the most significant and fragile part of a rugby player's metabolism, particularly, he said, if you were a 'back'. To build the players' leg strength up he used to make all the three quarters, full backs and half backs we had on our books, stand in a line at the bottom of the terracing with a rugby ball between their knees. He then made them hop up and down the terrace ten times without dropping the ball, if you did drop it you started again! Most of them, Brian said, collapsed at the end of the session grasping their legs. On the occasion of the big game at Warrington though this intensive training seemed to pay off as Hull scored an early try by Cooper and Hutton kicked a couple of goals and from then on our forwards led by Bill Drake, Bob Coverdale and Johnny Whiteley ground the Wire into the Lancashire mud.

The Hull forwards ran the Warrington pack off their feet that day and once the big Warrington forwards started to capitulate, scrum half Tommy Finn began to run the game and that brought two late tries for Bill Drake and hooker Tommy Harris. It was a magnificent performance with Hull finishing up 17-0 winners. That result shook the world of Rugby League to the core and did not please the Warrington supporters much either. There were reports of one or two fights breaking out in the streets around the ground as the home supporters argued amongst themselves. It was one of the best wins in Hull's long and celebrated history, and back in Airlie Street no one could believe it.

As kids it was hard to understand just what all the fuss in the street that teatime was all about! Most supporters had seen the score quickly flashed up on the TV but everyone thought it must be wrong. With no mobile phones or local radio, everyone had to wait about an hour for confirmation and queued at the newsagents for the Green Sports Mail to be delivered. A big cheer went up across the whole of West Hull as the little red Austin Daily Mail vans delivered the papers and the result was confirmed. The success starved Hull supporters began to make plans to attend the final, which would be against Halifax, the team they all loved to hate, particularly after that early season 'Blood Bath' at Headingley.

So, on 12th May 1956 Hull FC met Halifax in the final of the Championship at Maine Road, Manchester, the home of Manchester City Football Club. Dad got a very rare day off work and accompanied Mum by train to Manchester, whilst no doubt I stayed at Granny Evers, continuing our architectural endeavours with those old magazines and dusters.

Maine Road was packed to the rafters that day. The first half-hour of the game was tight and neither team seemed to be able to make a break or get on top. Slowly but surely though the Hull pack were starting to wrestle the advantage away from the Halifax six and at half time, thanks to a Tommy Harris try, engineered by Whiteley, and a goal by Colin Hutton we were in front. The second half was a real battle, which many that attended thought might any minute erupt as the Yorkshire Cup final had a few months earlier. Then, halfway through the second period of play, Halifax lost the ball at a scrum 10 yards from their line and Tommy Finn nipped in to touch down near the corner flag before the 'Fax' six had even managed to get their heads out of the scrum. Hutton missed the conversion but 'Old Faithful' rang out across Manchester.

Back came Halifax with three unconverted tries in just twenty minutes and they were in the lead. Then it was 'nip and tuck' for the rest of the game. We had Brian Darlington our flying winger playing as an injured passenger on the right and as our forwards started to tire, Halifax moved in for the kill. It looked all over but in the final minute Darlington somehow found the strength to run through the pain barrier on a swerving 30-yard charge that left us just 10 yards from the Halifax line. The Hull crowd cheered the move so loudly that most of them missed the referee blowing for the West Yorkshire outfit being off side at the play the ball and with us trailing 9-8, Hutton had the chance to kick the goal and grab the two points that would herald an unlikely victory for Hull.

In those days before the recent and I think somewhat stupid trend of opposition supporters booing kickers had arrived, the whole place went deathly silent, and you could have heard a pin drop. From about ten yards in from the touch line, to the right of the posts Colin Hutton struck the wet and heavy leather ball with a thud that echoed around the silent terraces, it rose majestically, sailed through the uprights and the place went ballistic! The referee, Charlie 'Apple cart' Appleton, blew the final whistle, and we had won the Championship 10-9 in a game that saw the players pick up pay packets of £33 and my Mum and Dad arrived back home drunk for probably the only time I can ever remember.

'Meadowlark' Lemon might have come to the Boulevard

The Board at Hull FC always had an eye for something a bit different and the following week a big crowd attended the Boulevard to see the famous American basketball team the Harlem Globetrotters take on the Texas Cowboys as part of a national tour. A mat was laid across the centre spot of the ground the size of a basketball court, and the hoops were erected at both ends. On tour with them was probably the most famous basketball player in the world 'Meadowlark' Lemon, although there are conflicting stories as to whether he actually played that afternoon at the Boulevard or not.

Despite these occasional departures from the norm and the heroics from the rugby team across the road at the Boulevard, life in Aylesford Street continued to move along as usual, in fact most things back then were contained within a conventional routine which everyone in the neighbourhood seemed to embrace without question.

We always got up at 7-00, saw Dad off to work on his bike, had porridge in winter and cornflakes in summer, and then it was off to school. This ordered pattern of life was duplicated in all the homes around us and included wash day on Monday, ironing on Tuesday, bath night on Thursdays and house cleaning on Friday. As a kid, if you were not at school, Mondays were a day for keeping out of the way, because the major operation of performing the family wash rendered the whole house a no go area. The washer itself would be ticking over in the middle of the kitchen, clothes were festooned everywhere gently steaming on clotheshorses and there would be condensation on ever window in the house. Dad would drag the hand wringer out of the shed and set it up on the kitchen table before he went to work. There were dolly tubs and poshers and all manner of paraphernalia that any little lad of 7 was best clear of.

Bath nights on Thursdays were another performance too! No one in Aylesford Street had a bathroom so everyone was in the same boat! In our house straight after tea, Dad would unhook the tin bath from the nail in the back yard and set it up in front of the fire in the front room. Then Mum would run backwards and forwards with the kettle, slowly but surely filling it up. I was always despatched upstairs as first Mum and then Dad would have a bath. The water, although never changed, was topped up and re warmed as needed and after about an hour I was called and it was my turn to step into the tepid and by now rather murky waters. I was presented with a big lump of Sunlight soap and told "And don't leave it in the water too long!"

Everywhere in our street it was bath night on Thursdays, and it was a sort of unwritten rule that everyone gave their neighbours the necessary privacy needed in those little houses for this most essential of operations. Sometimes though, people from outside the area would call, and Mum would ask them in, whilst Dad hid me behind a massive bath towel he held up between the bath and the visitor. That towel was never used to get dry on, but specifically kept just for that purpose. There I would be behind the 'modesty' towel, sat hunched in the bath with my knees under my chin, whilst at the other side of the room Mr Hayes was collecting the Littlewoods pools money and chuckling at his own jokes about me "Keeping my hand on my Ha'pney". Bath nights in Aylesford Street was certainly a memorable experience.

'Yours truly' makes his debut at the Boulevard

Saturday 25th March 1957   *Hull 41 – York 3*

At about the same time that I was hiding every Thursday behind that towelling curtain, my Mum and Dad where taking the life changing decision (well as far as I was concerned it was life changing) to introduce their son and heir to his first proper game of Rugby League.

In those days of course there were no floodlights and with Dad being a butcher and working Saturdays the games that he could attend were few and far between so he really looked forward to Bank Holiday games and those over Christmas. It was therefore decided that a Bank Holiday match would be as good as any to be the first that the whole family attended. So it was that at about 2-15pm on Easter Monday 25th March 1957 with around 10,000 other Black and White fanatics in attendance, I made my bow at the Boulevard. We set off from home, crossed the road from our house onto the players' and officials' car park at the front of the ground and before I knew much about it, I was being lifted over the turnstiles and into the Stadium. This was the first time that I had set foot in the place at the beginning of a game, and it marked the moment when this young impressionable and slightly bemused boy was introduced to an obsession that would stay with him for the rest of his life.

Now before I go any further, I have to say that although my memory is reasonably good as far as all things Hull FC are concerned, it is not that good! So what I have to say about this game is a mixture of the facts I have gleaned from various sources and some vague and misty memories. The reports in the local press I researched years later indicated that my parents had made a good choice and stated that the game showed, "a near perfect display of backs and forwards feeding off each other in devastating style", no wonder I was hooked by the time we left.

Mum and Dad certainly picked a great game for my introduction to the obsession, and no doubt because of my young and diminutive frame they chose for us to sit in the 'Best' seats in the 'Best Stand'. The seats actually equated to planks of wood, painted green divided by white lines and with a number to depict your allotted space. I sat on Mum's knee and probably mused on the fact that if those were the 'best', heaven knows what the blocks of seats further down were like.

According to the reports, York was a good side back then and had finished tenth in a league of 30 clubs the previous year. There were some great players in the Hull line up that day, and it was our diminutive scrum half Tommy Finn who took the headlines scoring a hat trick of tries including one of the first two 'nerve settling' scores. Tommy was famous, along with half back partner Rowley Moat, for doggedly following the Hull pack around the ground and feeding off the scraps of ball he could get from the big forwards.

Rowley had a great game that day but failed to get on the score sheet. Turner another long serving Hull back had a good match as well, running all of 80 yards in his centre position to score a great try under the posts. Strangely enough, for a team in good form, Hull started poorly and struggled, showing some signs of nerves by constantly forcing the pass when there was no need. It was therefore no surprise that at first, points were at a premium and after half an hour the visitors led 3-2. All of Hull's 9 tries were scored in the next 50 minutes as our aptly named, 'Panzer' pack, which included that day, Mick Scott, Tommy Harris, Bill and Jim Drake, a very youthful Cyril Sykes and the great Johnny Whiteley at loose forward, dominated the exchanges. By half time the score was 17-3 to Hull and in reality we never looked back.

As the second half started Turner sent Jim Drake crashing over, and the team then finally treated the 10,000 admiring fans to what they had come to expect at home games, as Hull produced another 35 minutes of exhibition rugby. Hooker Tommy 'Bomber' Harris constantly blasted his way through the York ranks whilst there were great performances from Brian Darlington and Ivor Watts, on the wings. The only try I can vaguely remember was one that my Mum constantly reminded me about years later. Johnny Whiteley was her big hero and right there in front of us, it was he who took the ball, swerved round three York players before sending Brian Saville in at the corner. That score was something that I can still see in my mind's eyes, which is hardly surprising because until the day she died, Mum never let me forget the highlight of my first game. I think if I am honest, at the time I really enjoyed the whole experience but found it hard to understand what all the jumping up and down and shouting at the referee was about! I guess I know all about that now.

The fact that Hull won the game and with such ease and style overshadowed somewhat the fact that a little bit of history was made that day when three 'Drakes' played in the same game. The 'Minster Men' of York had a really good winger called Brian Smith who unfortunately missed out when the car he was travelling in from York got a puncture at Hayton. Smith had no spare tyre and the visitors had no spare players, so in desperation they called upon Jim and Bill Drake's younger brother Joe, (who was on York's books anyway, and who had travelled over that morning to watch his brothers play), to fill the breach. Amazingly all three scored too, with Joe getting York's only try at the start of the game and Bill and Jim running in one each for the victorious Airliebirds. The final score was 41-3, and I loved every minute of it.

I remember how all my pals at Chiltern Street gathered round in the playground when we got back to school after the holidays to hear about my trip to the Boulevard, they had all been in at 'three quarter time' when the gates opened, but never sat in the 'Best Seats'! It was a great day out for me and still one of my best memories.

The European Club Championship ... bicycles, onions and stick on moustaches

Monday 15ᵗʰ April 1957   *Hull 19 – Albi 19*

I didn't 'officially' go again that season although I did sneak in a couple of times, (over the wall and through a hole in the fence, at the end of an avenue in Carrington Street). However I was, even at 7 years old, starting to understand just what all the fuss was about as behind that big wall just across the road, things were hotting up for the Airlie Birds. It was season 1956/57 and Hull FC were about to be crowned, for the first and last time in British Rugby League history, European Club Champions!

That was the season when both the British and French leagues agreed to jointly stage a tournament to find Europe's best team featuring as it did the previous years top two clubs from both the French and British Leagues. We had a fantastic tournament, beating Carcassonne home and away and Albi away, although we could only manage a draw against the latter at home.

As for the 'all British' games, the other club involved was of course Halifax the team we defeated in the Championship final the previous year at Maine Road but rather than play extra matches our league games against the West Yorkshire outfit (which we won) were counted as tournament games too. Hull fans have always liked a bit of dressing up and many turned out for the drawn Albi game with either beret's on their heads or strings of onions round their necks, some in fact even sported stick on black curly moustaches made from sticky back paper. It was an amazing sight to see them parading past number 23, looking like those jolly Frenchmen I'd seen in those dog eared geography books at Chiltern Street!

The game turned out to be an exciting affair. Fixture pile-ups were the thing in those days, as with no floodlights and hard winters, it was impossible to play previously postponed games until the end of the season. The Albi game was played with a 6-30 kick off, on Monday 15th April, and 10,000 fans turned up to see the Hull side play their fifth game in ten days, as we chased another top four league finish. Albi looked certain to win as they led 19-17, with a minute to go, when, of all people, our international prop Mick Scott dropped a goal to ensure the points were shared.

The final game that saw us lift the trophy was played a week later on 22nd April at the Boulevard in front of 22,000 fans. We won that match, which was also our 'official' home League game against Halifax, 35-12. Mum of course went along as usual and no doubt came home full of it. The competition lasted for just one year though and as it has not taken place since I expect Hull FC are still officially European Club Champions of the Rugby League World.

Defeat at Odsal in front of 66,190 fans

Saturday 18th May 1957   *Hull 14 – Oldham 15*

However the excitement for that season was not over yet because that win against Halifax also secured our top four spot in the League table, and two weeks later we played Barrow in the Championship play-off semi final at Boothferry Park, in front of another big gate of almost 20,000. We won again 49-14, scoring eleven tries, three of which were memorable 80 yard efforts by our rampaging forwards and so we progressed again to the Final at Odsal on 18th May 1957.

That was a famous occasion for the Black and White army who, along with my Mum, travelled to West Yorkshire for the final decider against Oldham. The crowd that day was an amazing 66,199 and they watched as Hull just missed out 15-14. Many years later Mum used to relate the story about just how well we had played. She said that a minute from the end Stan Cowan snapped up a loose ball to race 40 yards to the line, only for the great Colin Hutton, who had already kicked a then Club record of 166 goals that season, to miss in the dying seconds from just 10 yards out! The hero, who had twelve months earlier kicked us to glory at Maine Road, missed from an easy position, and we fell at the final hurdle, but that's Hull FC for you, it happened then and has continued to happen down the years ever since. Oldham actually won with a disputed penalty when Cyril Sykes was so badly injured that he could not get up and play the ball. Back then, if you could not get to your feet it was deemed an offence, but after this incident in such a high profile game, the rules were subsequently changed so that in future, recovery time would be given to any injured player, however that action by the Rugby League came a bit too late for Cyril, and our hopes against Oldham.

Granny's building site closes for good

For my part I was getting more involved with the Club too and used to line up with my pals on game days at the big gates on the car park ready to run in as soon as they were opened at three quarter time. We would then run up and down the hills that made up the back of the terracing playing cowboys and Indians and other games that involved chasing about. We would occasionally stop momentarily to see what all the fuss was about when the crowd cheered but in general what was happening on the pitch still, by and large, passed me by! During that summer after the season finished, we would sneak into the ground and play in the trenches that had been dug backwards and forwards across the pitch. I found out later that over one and a quarter miles of new drainage was laid under the playing surface that June and July. This work was needed to improve the condition of the pitch but for us it made for a cross between an adventure playground and a First World War re-enactment site. Club records later showed that the work over ran by three weeks probably because the contractors spent as much time chasing us kids out of the ground, as they did laying the drains.

Granny Evers, my main baby sitter and fellow 'duster and magazine' builder, sadly died when I was seven although I don't remember much about it happening, except that Mum cried a lot. However, right up until she passed away suddenly, sat at the kitchen table, I spent more and more of my time after school at her house. There were some great lads living around there and we played 'Out' in the street, at cricket and football for hours, stopping only occasionally to let the odd car or delivery van through the 'outfield'. Cricket usually came somewhere between the marbles and 'conker' seasons, and lamp posts doubled as wickets, with the bat often being a piece of wood roughly honed by some father from an old ironing board or fish box.

On one occasion I remember how Kenny White who lived two doors down Carrington Street from Granny, hit a cricket ball so hard the bat flew out of his hand and straight through Mrs Metcalfe's living room window! We all immediately scampered away and hid down passages and behind dustbins. By the time Mr Metcalfe, who had been asleep in that same sitting room at the time of the incident, came screaming out of the front door, shouting about how he could have been killed, there was not a soul in sight! In fact all it would have needed for the scene to be complete was for some tumbleweed to blow across the pavement. Of course, one by one we emerged from our hiding places and all had to pay towards replacing the window; there was a traditional agreed procedure for these things, because broken windows were a pretty common occurrence around the Boulevard back then.

"Chilly bon bon sells fish tuppence ha'penny a dish ..."

There was much rivalry amongst the schools in the area too and we at Chiltern Street were always at war with the kids from Constable Street, (Or 'Scummy Cunny' as it was generally known). They used to taunt us as we passed them on our way to school. They would be going one way, whilst we were going the other. The bigger urchins from 'Cunny' often used to shout a rhyme across the road, to the tune of Happy Birthday to you. It went something like, "Chilly Bom Bom sells fish, tuppence ha'penny a dish, don't buy it don't buy it, it stinks when you fry it!" We weren't too impressed with this and used to just wave two fingers back at them and run like hell. We didn't really know of the significance of what we were doing, or what it meant, but we had seen the big lads do it and it all seemed pretty 'Hard' to us.

Who is that other Whiteley?

Saturday 17th May 1958   *Hull 20 – Workington 3*

Despite Mum's hero Johnny Whiteley being elected Club Captain, the next season (1957/58) at the Boulevard sadly saw an early sequence of results when much of the promise of the previous two years looked to be ebbing away. We were dumped out of both the Yorkshire Cup and the Challenge Cup following, what my Dad called, "Pretty pathetic performances" against Hunslet and Rochdale respectively. However that was soon forgotten when a total of twenty-nine league wins and two draws saw us get to the Championship final again, this time we were to face the 'Cumbrian giants' of Workington Town.

Firstly though, in the semi final, the Black and Whites had to face Oldham at their Watersheddings ground a week after our league game there had ended in us getting a 43-9 drubbing. Oldham had kicked on from their success the previous season and won the last 11 league games that year and most pundits felt that as far as them retaining the title was concerned it was, for the 'Roughyeds' as they were known, just a formality. Roy Francis, who was gaining a reputation as British Rugby League's master tactician, declined the temptation to make some changes and stuck almost completely to the team that lost the previous week making just one change on the wing.

Watts, Cooper, Drake and Sykes all scored tries and well into the second half Hull were surprisingly leading their Lancashire rivals by 20-3. Then, as often happened in those days, Tommy Harris our international hooker appeared to get a bit bored of playing rugby, and proceeded to lay out the Oldham star Frank Pitchford, with a great right hook. 'Bomber' started his walk to the dressing room even before referee Matt Coates had got his note book out! Reduced to 12 men we really had to scrap to keep the Oldham side at bay but with Brian Hambling taking over Harris's hooking duties, we held out to win the game 20-8. We were in the final again, and this time we were to win!

Over 57,000 people crammed into Odsal Stadium in Bradford for the Championship final against Workington on 17th May 1958, and it was estimated that over 20,000 of those had made the journey from West Hull.

That's a magnificent turnout when you consider the lack of car ownership and motorways back then. British Railways put on six special trains from Hull Paragon Station that morning, but Mum went, as usual, on a Danby's motor coach with Hull Supporters' Club! After those two physical encounters against Oldham, Hull was beset by injuries and both the Drake twins and Tommy Harris cried off with knocks before the game. In came Johnny Whiteley's kid brother Peter and young 'A' team hooker Alan Holdstock. I actually remember seeing Peter Whiteley play several times and although he had a neat crew cut I thought he was a shadow of his brother in pretty much every aspect of his play but every dog has his day and this was to be Peter Whiteley's eighty minutes of fame. This was the day that he was to make his mark for Hull FC.

Mum said that a groan went round the ground when he was named as a late team change but he soon had the crowd cheering with some great breaks and backing up. Workington themselves were dealt a blow too when after only 25 minutes their sensational second rower Cec Thompson was carried off on a stretcher, clearly in a lot of pain with what turned out to be a leg that was broken in three places.

In the early exchanges the Cumbrian pack led by Edgar caused Hull lots of problems as they ground the yards out down the middle of the pitch. Following Thompson's injury, Town went ahead through their flying winger, Ike Southward, who took a pass from Edgar and dived in at the corner. Hull came back with a Colin Cooper try which Bateson goaled from the touch line and we then went ahead when Johnny Whiteley side stepping his way to score from acting half. With 12 man Workington starting to flag, there were further tries for Mick Scott and Tommy Finn which finished the opposition off. Hull FC had won the game 20-3 and with it the Rugby League Championship. I bet 'Old Faithful' rang round the refurbished 'Rubbish Tip' that was the Odsal Stadium that day. That famous victory was followed by a civic reception at the Guildhall with an appearance in front of the fans on the balcony with the trophy, which I witnessed in person perched triumphantly on my Dad's shoulders. It was the culmination of what had turned out in the end, to be a great season.

'Letting it all hang out' on a Hull Corporation bus

As a boy attending Chiltern Street school, (There were girls there, but I never really noticed many of them) the moment you were seven and went up into the 'Juniors' you started to play rugby. Once a week we would all be loaded onto a bus which took us out into 'the country', well actually just about three miles down Boothferry High Road to Anlaby Park Road South, but it was the country to us lot.

'Rain snow or blow' we were all deposited at a marked out playing field surrounded by a high Hawthorne hedge, by an ageing Hull Corporation double decker bus, but there was precious little to see once we arrived.

There were two pitches marked out in creosote and a couple of sets of rugby posts which usually slanted badly in opposing directions. There were no changing rooms either, so we used to change into our various bits of miscellaneous kit at school before we left.

We wore every strip imaginable and it was obvious that Boyes, the economy clothing store on Hessle Road, which sold just about everything and still does to this day, had been doing a roaring trade with seconds of sports kit! Some lads wore hob nailed boots, some played in shoes, whilst others like me, actually wore real rugby boots. Mine were an ancient 'well dubbined' pair that Mum came by at a Jumble Sale at the local Church Hall. The studs underneath were each secured by 3 steel nails, a fact that I remember vividly, because every time I wore them, they used to stick through the sole of the boot and into my foot. I still have the scars to this day.

By the end of these sessions in the rudiments of Rugby League that were carried out under the watchful eye of Mr Chambers, we were covered from head to foot in mud and because the driver of our bus was adverse to getting his upholstery messed up, we used to strip to our underwear under the hedge and then travel back to school semi naked. There were certainly some shocked expressions on the faces of the ladies shopping on Anlaby Road, as the Chiltern Street rugby bus went by. There on show for all to see, were half naked young lads hanging out of the windows, wearing just their tatty underpants, with no doubt, occasionally, other things hanging out on show as well. When we got off the bus back at school in Division Road, we would, there on the pavement, put our muddy gear back on again, ready for the walk home! It was a great show for the mothers and fathers waiting to take the other kids home from school, and they would often laugh, point and direct wolf whistles at us.

Rugby was taken very seriously at Chiltern Street even at an early age; it was much more than just a game, league tables meant little compared with the great honour in beating our local rivals from Constable Street and West Dock Avenue! As I said earlier our 'head coach' was teacher, Mr Chambers, who as well as having a regular third year class was in charge of all boys sport. He was a real disciplinarian when it came to training and took everything very seriously indeed, infact he often ran in and tackled us when our backs were turned, for no apparent reason. Even more remarkable was the fact that he wore a wig, the first I and the other lads, had ever seen. On one occasion it blew off whilst we were up at Anlaby Park Road and I can still see him after that happened, standing on the touch line, barking orders out across the pitch, with one hand permanently clamped to his head! He however was a great guy, and I still see him to this day at Hull FC games.

Old Chambers really believed in toughening us up and made us stay behind at least two nights a week to practise in the playground. This was aimed at improving our ball skills and handling but also included tackling practise on the stone paving, something that really left your legs in tatters! Back then, knees weren't knees if they didn't have scabs on them.

The other excursion of the week was during the summer on Wednesday mornings when, with our 'Cossies' wrapped in a towel, a procession of kids, walking in pairs, would snake through the streets between the School and Madeley Street Public Swimming Baths. There we were taught to swim and to compete for Certificates that displayed the progress we were making. I started well and got a Third Class and 'Diving off the side' diploma and then my pals and I got bored. After that we would spend the sessions splashing each other and causing distress amongst the younger 'learners' by jumping off the side and 'Bombing them'.

I liked the swimming baths and for a couple of years I would go to the same baths with Martin Tomlinson a pal of mine from Airlie Street, whose dad worked on the Railway. On Thursday evenings there was a British Railway's Swimming Club at Madeley Street between 7 and 9pm. Those sessions were great fun and we would call at the Constable Street Chip shop for a bag of scraps and a few chips drenched in vinegar, on our way home.

Johnny Whiteley ... Working class hero

It's funny really how certain things connected to my beloved rugby club constantly circled my development and were woven into the fabric of my very existence even before I was a real 'fan' of Hull FC, that beautiful yet frustrating obsession that was to take over my life. I remember one day whilst Mum and I were on one of our weekly shopping expeditions down Hessle Road I saw a crowd of people gathered round a hole in the ground outside the Criterion pub! All of a sudden as we approached, the crowd burst into applause as a big man in an apron emerged up the ladder from the cellar with an empty beer keg on his shoulder. That was the first time that I ever saw, close up, the great International rugby player, Captain of Hull FC and 'chosen one', Johnny Whiteley. He was at work in his day job as a Drayman for Moore's and Robson's Brewery Company Ltd. Back then Johnny was a real local hero, on the pitch and off it; in fact he still is today.

Johnny was a great ambassador for the Club and became part of local folklore and everyday conversation. He even gave his name to some gent's underwear down our street!! You see, Mrs Mudd across the road, always called her husband George's underpants his "Johnny Whiteley's". I could never understand this strange nomenclature until years later when my Mum explained that apparently George used to roll up his old underpants at the top because they were devoid of any elastic. This was also the trademark of our loose forward, who used to do the same thing with his shorts when he was playing for the Club. So Georgie Mudd's underpants were re christened his 'Johnny Whiteley's'. Whatever happened in the Boulevard area it was hard to escape the influence of Hull FC; it was all around you at the heart of the community. Incidentally the Mudds also had a mongrel dog called 'Bomber' that was named after the Club's great Hooker Tommy Harris.

The haunted house in Camden Street

Once Granny Evers had gone 'to heaven', her sister Auntie Ethel came more into the picture. That's how it happens when you look back on your youth, your development and aging moves from one person to another, as one influence on your life disappears off the scene they are replaced by someone else. Your extended family and friends are the 'Wallpaper' that surrounds your life and seem to form milestones in the process of 'growing up'. Ethel lived in Camden Street the next street along Airlie Street from where Granny had lived. Her home was a similar end terraced house which I remember had both a Grandfather and Grandmother Clock in the front room. The noise of their ticking and chiming dominated the whole house, and there was a musty smell everywhere! It seemed to an 8-year-old that each clock wanted to get to the hour before the other and both were straining to chime first. It was a really bizarre environment for a child.

Ethel had been unmarried for the whole of her life, and I remember thinking "So that's what they mean at church by a 'Spinster of this Parish' is it?" She was, apparently, for many years the private secretary to James Reckitt the managing Director at Reckitt and Colman, the famous 'Brasso' makers of Dansom Lane. She travelled extensively across Europe with her boss and was reported, years later, to have had a brief romantic encounter with an Austrian nobleman along the way. Apparently whilst on a visit to Austria with Mr Reckitt she had fallen for an Austrian Prince and although he was married, a brief and rather scandalous affair had occurred. It finished almost as soon as it started but for years afterwards he would send her gifts and postcards.

Whether that's true or not I'm not sure but it would probably explain a lot, because what I remember most about her house was the amount of German and Austrian stuff there was everywhere, Cuckoo clocks, fancy pipes, paper weights and Beer Steins festooned every shelf, cupboard and wall! Ethel slept at the back of the house and the front bedroom was empty except for a big camp bed positioned from corner to corner across the middle of the floor. This visibly bulged and sagged with postcards, books and memorabilia from Germany and the Tyrol, and provided a wealth of fun for my mates and I, although the sparse furnishings and dust sheet at the window did cause us to believe that the room was probably haunted. Ethel was a frail old lady, who was always well dressed, wore a lot of lace, and silk stockings and what I guess we would now call 'granny shoes', however she always seemed to be surrounded by intrigue and rumour, much of which went right over this young man's head.

The community and the Club

When I was eight, Dad, who had been a member of the Hull Supporters' Club for many years, stood in as their secretary when the previous incumbent died, and this gave me a new opportunity to get into the Stadium across the road! On Sunday mornings after the previous day's game, he would take me with him as we were joined by the grounds man, Ernie Mason the Chairman and a few of the other committee members on the hallowed turf. There they would pull a massive concrete roller up and down the pitch to flatten out the divots created by the game the day before! We would either ride on the roller or run alongside it which was great fun.

On other occasions when the weather forecast predicted frost we would go into the ground and spend most of Sunday afternoon spreading straw over the pitch. This was delivered by a series of tractors and trailers that arrived in Airlie Street throughout the morning. I even remember Mum telling me that on one occasion, last thing at night before her and Dad went to bed, they took hot drinks over the road for the fans who were manning braziers spread across the pitch. They were attempting to stop it from freezing and causing the abandonment of the game next day! The winters seemed a lot harder then with us having at least four or five periods of snow each year. Not that snow lasted long round our way, as it was usually reduced to slush really quickly once the cars and bikes got going! But whilst it was there we loved it.

There was motorised traffic around our neighbourhood of course but there were still a lot of horses and carts used for local deliveries and Rafferty and Watson used to deliver our coal using this mode of transport. As kids one of our favourite pranks was to lead the horse and cart around a corner, whilst the coalman was down a back alley delivering to the coal houses of local homes. If we succeeded, it was great fun hiding round the same corner with the horse and cart and watching the coalman's expression when he returned to find that his transport and all his sacks of coal had completely disappeared.

Remember, remember the 5th of November? The holder of the bell!

Bonfire nights were always a big occasion down Airlie Street and there was invariably one large and several small bonfires on the stadium's car park every year! There was always a great rivalry with the 'gangs' from the adjacent streets, who also had big fires, built on any available land that had been left after the bombing during the war. Often 'raiding parties' would set off to try and pinch wood from these rival operations and we used to take it in turns to guard our pile of wood in the centre of the Boulevard car park in the days leading up to the big night! Local firms would see this as a great time to get rid of their rubbish too and you could often see 'tipper' lorries arriving next to our fire heap from companies like Boggs Fish Merchants to deposit loads of old crates, slimy and stinking of rotting fish, before their drivers beat a hasty retreat.

The Council used to clear any potentially dangerous bonfires away back then, but ours, being well away from the nearest houses, was usually left untouched. That could not be said of the ones that were built about a quarter of a mile away down South Boulevard, in the area just adjacent to the fish docks. The lads who lived down there were a bit braver than us lot and appeared to be fearless as far as authority was concerned. They had little spare land to build on and so usually resorted to constructing their fires on the grass verge often around a telegraph pole! Looking back, the guarding and building of those great bonfires was probably more fun than Bonfire Night itself. This guarding, in Airlie Street, used to involve a long held tradition called the 'Holder of the Bell', a ritual which was part of folklore in Airlie Street back in the fifties.

What happened was this: each morning at about 5-30 it would be someone's turn to get up early and go and guard the fire. Early mornings were a favourite time for raids particularly from the Chiltern or Heron Street gangs. Billy Chapman's Dad was a school teacher and he had an old school hand bell that we would borrow and whoever was guarding the fire that morning would 'hold the bell'. If a raid was threatened it was his job to climb to the top of the fire heap and ring the bell for all he was worth. Then the rest of us would come running out of our houses, often in our pyjamas to defend our fire! All the kids took this very seriously indeed.

Looking back to the night itself it is amazing that more people were not injured on 5th November because there was no such thing as organised displays of fireworks and everyone had to 'make their own amusement' often with dangerous consequences. When the big night arrived people used to purchase their fireworks from Benny Allgood's newsagents in Airlie Street, and then they would proceed to let them off everywhere. Mums and Dads would do their best to try and supervise things but penny bangers would be flying all over the place and rockets were launched from bottles laid on the ground to chase anyone who happened to be riding a bike up the street, it was mayhem, but great fun! One particular lad called Paul, who was nicknamed 'Crazy Horse' had a real speciality of putting two rockets down the ends of his bicycle handle bars. After lighting them both, he would pedal as hard as he could till the rockets flew out on either side. Everyone ducked or ran for cover when you saw 'Crazy Horse's' bike coming down Airlie Street.

Any young people reading this should note that none of these things involving fireworks are clever or should ever be attempted, however we knew little better back then so it just happened and was part of Bonfire Night on the Boulevard. The Casualty Department of the Hull Royal Infirmary was always busy that night. I guess that Bonfire night and holidays were probably the only two things us kids needed money for in those days. However if we did need it, for say a new yo-yo or a catapult we had seen in Boyes, we could soon raise it. You could get a paper round at nine, or even help the milkman with his deliveries, although the best way of raising some cash was usually by holding a jumble sale on an old carpet, on the pavement in front of your house. These seemed to benefit everyone as parents got old toys cleared out of their homes, we kids got extra cash and the buyers usually got a bargain! You just laid out your wares, a crowd gathered and the haggling began.

Another of our money making schemes involved the practise of taking bottles back to the shops to claim the deposit. There was a 'penny back' on most beer and lemonade bottles and they were then subsequently returned by the shop owner to the manufacturers for refilling. To boost my finances I had devised an even more lucrative scheme to re claim these deposits which involved me climbing into the back yard of Harry's 'Off License' shop on the Boulevard. Once inside I would pass a number of bottles back over the wall to my pals and we would then take them around the front of the shop and claim our penny deposits. This practise went on for months and strangely enough we were never detected, however it stopped abruptly one night when I climbed over the wall to find that Harry had made some alterations. All the Murden's and Hull Brewery crates full of empty bottles had been placed in a new padlocked metal cage. Still it was a good scam whilst it lasted.

Six weeks in Mappleton; Billy Butlin, eat your heart out!

Not many kids had proper holidays then and the local parks were really busy throughout the school holidays but I was one of the lucky few and every summer, once school broke up, we went to the village of Mappleton near Hornsea for most of the six weeks. I would always hold a jumble sale before I went to raise some money to spend on some 'Goodies' from the village shop, which was and probably still is, the only shop in the sleepy sea side village.

Dad's Mum, Jessie ("Well ow are ya Then!!") had somehow come by an old wooden Great Central Railway carriage that was converted into a caravan, which made a perfect holiday home. This had been originally sited at Cowden on the East Coast just north of Aldborough, however coastal erosion at the site meant that in 1954 the structure had to be moved, otherwise it would have simply just fallen off the cliff and into the sea. So, in an effort to keep the family holiday 'escape', it was transported to a field behind 'Speight's Farm' at Mappleton, about two miles north of Cowden, on the road towards Hornsea.

At this location there were about 40 caravans and portable homes positioned around a field, most of which had been relocated from Cowden for the same reasons as 'Granny's Carriage' and access to our holiday destination was by a long lane from the main road. This led right through the farmyard and onto the field that doubled as a caravan site. Next to the farm buildings there was an old mill, devoid of any sails, which looked out over the campsite and this was where between the ages of 8 and 11, I spent my summer holidays.

We had a great time, Mum would be there most of the time and Dad would ride all the way from work on Holderness Road most nights to join us! There was one little village shop that supplied all manner of sweets and chews and you could get right down to the beach by using some steps that the fathers hacked out of the clay cliffs at the start of every holiday season. Facilities at the caravan site were a bit basic though to say the least! There was just one tap in the middle of the field for water and every week Mr Speight the farmer would come down the field to empty the contents of our portable toilets. They stank and it was a really messy job! Dad called the tractor and trailer 'The Gravy Boat' and told me the farmer took the contents to put on his turnips. For years after that they were a vegetable I would not entertain at any cost.

I learned quite a few new skills on holiday at Mappleton too! I became a hot shot with a catapult and a dab hand at sea fishing and those six weeks summer holidays seemed to last forever. A mobile fish and chip van used to come onto the site once a week and on occasions we would walk into Hornsea for the day. It was an idyllic way for a young lad from the city to spend his holidays.

Watching trains and training

Back home in Airlie Street, once the summer break was over, I was starting to get increasingly interested in what was happening across the road behind the newly constructed brick wall. This new structure had broken pieces of bottles stuck in cement across the top and had replaced the old tarred wooden fencing. I began to sneak into training on Tuesday and Thursday nights which was great fun because as the players kicked the ball into the stands we would retrieve it for them and kick it back! We got to know many of the players really well and in fact by the age of 9 I could usually tell you who was arriving for training just by seeing a car turning into the far end of Airlie Street. I could name the player long before they parked on the car park and so the adventure began!

Around this time we were visited by the son of one of my Dad's wartime soldier pals, (Tommy, would you believe), who lived in Orpington in Kent. His son Jonathan was about 14 then, and a Queen's Scout and he had been up to Balmoral in Scotland for a national Jamboree and so broke his journey to stay overnight at our house on his way back down south. I was, I remember, a bit put out when I had to sleep on the settee whilst our guest used my bed but number 23 only had two bedrooms. I told him about the famous Hull FC, being across the road, but he had never even heard about Rugby League having played something called 'Union', or 'Rugger' at school.

However I remember he showed some sign of understanding what I was going on about when I mentioned the Cup Final at Wembley! During the day he was with us, all he wanted to do was go to the end of Boulevard and watch the trains go by, for Jonathan was a train spotter!! Within an hour of sitting there with him and listening to his tales of the Mallard, expresses, goods trains and sheds, I was absolutely hooked! For the next ten or so years I was to be a dedicated train spotter which engendered in me a general interest in railways that probably stayed with me for the rest of my life.

Holy orders? Some Tizer and a banana sandwich please!

At Sunday School, when I was nine, I was singled out as having a handy singing voice, and was soon invited to go along to augment the Church choir at St Matthew's when the Bishop of Hull paid his annual visit for a confirmation service. The vicar at the time was a Reverend Dietz, a wonderful man who was rather tubby; with a round face and who always wore a rather unconventional black beret. That day they rigged me out in an ill fitting cassock and surplice and I took my place with the other lads in the choir stalls for the service. I quite enjoyed the whole experience really and was afterwards invited to join the choir full time and as the rest of the members were made up mostly of Hull fans and some of my new train spotting chums, I quickly agreed!

The choirmaster at that time Mr Johns, was also the organist, he too was a really nice chap if not a bit sedentary, he had sparse grey hair, a bit of a twitch and always wore an old suit that smelt of mothballs. It was pretty obvious that his health was failing fast. We did our best as a choir, and although we screeched a bit, we still made half a crown every time we were employed to sing at a wedding on Saturday afternoons, so, financially it proved quite lucrative too! About three months after I joined the choir, 'Johnno' retired through ill health, and the ensemble was amalgamated with another choristers outfit from, I think, Saint Silas, a church in the centre of the City that had just been demolished! This lot was a really professional set up with Tenors, Bass's, Alto, and even girls singing mezzo-soprano! The organist a Mr Watkinson even wrote his own anthems.

St Matthew's was a proud building back then stood as it was at the corner of the Boulevard and Anlaby Road with its almost famous 'Wayside Pulpit' advertisement board outside which displayed 'Jesus Loves You' and 'Heaven Can't wait' type motifs for the passengers on the 69 Trolley Buses to digest as they rode by. Around the same time one had actually made The Hull Daily Mail when in the early part of the year a vigilant cameraman spotted some graffiti that had been added by some of the local kids. The board read, "JESUS SAVES!" To which had been added... "but Dave King nods in the rebounds!" (Dave King was a Hull City player at the time). Another funny one that amused the Mums and Dads of us lot singing in the choir, was when a slogan that read "JESUS IS DEAD GOOD" had an exclamation mark added between the last two words.

They were great days and we had lots of good fun. Often, on Saturdays when there were no weddings, the choir's train spotting fraternity would go off to York or Doncaster together to sit on the station all day collecting numbers! It was the twilight of the steam age and ironically I can still hear us shouting "Scrap the Crate" to engines we had seen before, little knowing that soon they would all indeed be scrapped, steam would have disappeared and we would be left with those horribly impersonal diesel locomotives.

At first, good old Mum would take us all on these trips and looking back now, she was pretty long suffering really. There she would sit at the end of platform 8N at York with 10 or 11 choirboys getting progressively dirtier as each steam engine went by. We of course could simply not imagine anything better as we were happy to spot our trains, drink our Tizer and eat our banana or tomato sandwiches. These meals were always neatly wrapped in that 'waxy' paper that bread loaves used to be sold in and stowed away at the bottom of our ex army rucksacks that we had bought from Boyes.

One of my pals in the Choir and in fact head boy of the whole outfit at St Matthew's back then, was Michael Watts son of the great Hull winger Ivor. In later years some of the other players like Keith Barnwell and Brian and Clive Sullivan would sometimes also attend church as part of the congregation, so once again the influence of the Club was all around me and soon it was to over-take all other interests in my life as I grew from a lad who happened to live opposite a sports stadium, to an incurable rugby fanatic.

In January 1959 the 'Airlie Street and District Tenants Association' for whom Mum was Minute's Secretary, ran their annual trip to the pantomime. This was a great organisation, which featured pretty much the same band of good hearted volunteers that ran Hull Supporters' Club. They regularly promoted shows and parties for us children in St Matthew's Church Hall and in the hall adjacent to St Wilfred's Church on the Boulevard. On this occasion all us kids piled onto a motor coach and were taken to the Regal Cinema in Ferensway to see Lonnie Donegan and his Skiffle Group starring in Mother Goose. It's a little known fact that after one evening performance in late January the theatre was converted into a recording studio as Lonnie and the rest of the group recorded a 'B' side for their single, 'Does your chewing gum lose its flavour on the bed post overnight!' We all loved the 'Panto' and in our street the annual ASDTA trip to see it, which saw us face to face with stars of the day such as Lonnie and in later years, Helen Shapiro and Cliff Richard and the Shadows, was the highlight of the year.

Chapter Three

A Featherstone miner saves Mum's life!!

Saturday 11th April 1959   *Hull 15 – Featherstone 5*

Whilst, as a nine year old, I was happily singing in the choir and train spotting for all I was worth, across the road 1958/59 was another landmark season for Hull FC, because they were to battle their way to the Challenge Cup final at Wembley for the first time ever, where they would meet Wigan on 9th May 1959. The league season had been a disappointing one, particularly following the heights we had scaled the previous year and after some pretty indifferent league performances and being knocked out of the Yorkshire Cup in the second round by Wakefield, the loyal Black and White fans were all pinning their hopes on a good Cup run. Much of this of course was still passing me by a bit, but the Challenge Cup fever that swept West Hull, was none the less the backdrop to my life because it seemed that everyone was talking about it, everywhere I went.

We played Blackpool at home in the first round and were then drawn against Wakefield in the second. This was our chance of revenge for some big league defeats by the men from the West Riding but we blew our opportunities and could only draw 4-4, in a tryless game at the Boulevard. However somehow we managed to win the replay at Belle Vue and then we played Rovers and won 25-9 in front of a massive crowd at the Boulevard. So it was back to Odsal for the semi-final against Featherstone and another 52,000 gate. That day a new star was to emerge from the shadows of Harris, Johnny Whiteley and Co. and that star was George Matthews.

Back at home in Aylesford Street rugby was the predominant topic of conversation, as usual it was there all the time, happening in the background as I chomped on my cornflakes, climbed back yard walls and watched Clint Eastwood in Rawhide on the TV. Those were the things that were important to a young lad back then and in fairness a lot of the rugby stuff still went over my head. Mum usually told Dad about games she had been to and although I am sure there was lots of exciting revelations, there were only a couple of bits that stick in my memory. She always went on about a league game against Rovers that took place on Good Friday 1958, which saw 27,000 people packed into the Boulevard. I found out much later that we won that one 15-8 but the one thing I remembered about my Mother's description of the game was the fact that she always said "Leaving the ground was just like going down Walton Street to Hull Fair. From the back of the best stand to getting out onto the car park my feet never touched the ground!" I tended to think, because of the number of times she related the story, that this experience frightened her somewhat, but it was the other one of her favourite stories that in the end I believe put her off attending the majority of games in future years.

This revelation which she still relived right up to her death in 1979, involved a trip she made to Odsal that year for that Challenge Cup Semi Final game between Hull and Featherstone which took place on 11th April in front of that massive gate. Mum travelled to the game, as usual, with the Hull Supporters' Club bus, along with some of the chaps she sat with at the Boulevard and her pals from the Club. That day there were eleven coaches lined up outside the ABC Regal Cinema with thousands of other fans going on other private coach trips and specially chartered trains.

On arrival Mum positioned herself on the end of the ground which is now the north end terracing. In those days the viewing area was made of wooden sleepers with the occasional crude cast iron crush barrier but this arrangement stopped half way up the bank and the rest of the hillside was covered in black ash. With over 57,000 people in the ground for the game, the only place Mum could get to stand was on this ash slope. Apparently when Hull scored their first try the crowd behind her that ringed the top of the bowl surged forward and she found herself flying down the hill towards a crush barrier in a scrummage of about 4000 people.

Mum continued the story by saying "As I saw the cast iron crush barrier fly towards my head, an arm suddenly wrapped round my waist and somehow just as I lost my footing and fell forward a giant of a man pulled me clear of the barrier and landed me safely on my bottom on the terracing. Another second and I would have been trampled by the avalanche of fans!" There were dozens of injured people that day but my Mum came out pretty unscathed. Later, she related, that she had found the man who had saved her and said "He was about 6ft 4ins tall and weighed at least 18 stone in weight. He explained that he was a miner from Featherstone who was actually a prop forward for the local amateur team, Featherstone Travellers. He had been on shift until early that morning and come straight over for the game" It was one of her favourite stories in later years but she never added how mad I remember my Dad was when she got home, he was shouting at her about her "Nearly getting killed", and I recall a right 'Barney' going on downstairs that night.

I think the reality of that experience and my Father's concern, (because still working as a butcher he was not able to accompany her to games which were still usually played on Saturdays), really unnerved her. In the following days she decided not to attend the final and the next season she missed quite a lot of games too. That game at Odsal saw Hull victorious over a much-fancied Featherstone Rovers team. Again, it was a match we were never expected to win but with the words of Coach Roy Francis ringing in their ears, the two Hull half backs Matthews and Broadhurst, took Featherstone apart.

Francis, it was reported afterwards, had told our two play makers, "From leaving the changing rooms to getting back in there just follow our forwards wherever they go, even if they leave the field" and that's just what they did. As the players took the long walk across the top of the terracing and down that long stairway to the Odsal pitch, it was the forwards that led and the backs that followed. Matthews in particular was a real hero, he scored a hat trick of tries and was the 'toast' of West Hull for a couple of weeks. He had signed to much acclaim, only a year earlier from amateur team Barrow Saint Mary's and his obvious potential had led to an amazing 5000 people attending the under 19's England International's debut in Hull's 'A' team. His performance that day in the semi final at Odsal won us the game and led to our first Wembley appearance against Wigan less than a month later. A game my still 'shaken' Mother and I were to watch at home on our little TV!

Wembley calling!!!

Saturday 9ᵗʰ May 1959   *Hull 13 – Wigan 30*

The week leading up to the Cup Final was filled with excitement, even for a nine-year-old. Shops around the City had their windows decked out in black and white and there was a real buzz of excitement everywhere you went. Several houses in our street decorated their bay windows and there was a special 'Farewell to the Players' evening on the Wednesday night in the Supporters' Club. As kids it was all we talked about at school, although not particularly about the game itself, or even the prestige of winning the cup, all that stuff was still a bit beyond us. However the kids whose parents were making the trip to London talked incessantly about nothing else but what presents they would be bringing back with them from the capital. A few folks in those days went to Wembley for the weekend on organised trips, but that was not the norm and most people went down to the game on the Saturday morning and returned that same night.

Mum and Dad's decision not to go to the final had been made a couple of weeks earlier when the tickets went on sale. That day we were joined by many of the neighbours as we watched in wonder from the top of our back passageway, as 20,000 people queued across the car park to get tickets for the game.

The local newspaper was full of the build up to the match and carried stacks of editorial related to Hull's Final appearance. One such story concerned the National Dock Labour Board who was concerned that the departure of 2000 Dockers (half its work force) to the game would bring the docks to a standstill. Saturdays were a normal working day down on the docks and the management banned the stevedores from taking the day off. Most obeyed the instruction, although several risked their jobs to follow their Club to London.

The day of the final was really exciting, Mum and I got up at half past six as Dad prepared for work and after he had set off on his bike, the two of us went to the railway crossings at the end of the Boulevard and watched the 11 special trains leaving at ten minute intervals all heading for London and the final. It was a train spotter's dream. As the trains rattled across the level crossings wreathed in steam, scarves and rattles could be seen draped out of every window and the saloon tables all seemed to include the mandatory crate of ale.

It was strangely quiet in Airlie Street that day and I remember that by 2-00pm the place was deserted. Mum and I settled down to watch the game in front of our old Pye TV set. I was interested, as you are, in this big event that seemed to be causing such a fuss everywhere but as for the game, I still found it hard to understand my Mum springing from her chair and shouting at the television as I had never seen her before. I did not realise I suppose, that all that manic behaviour was already in my genes, latently laid there, just waiting to emerge very soon indeed.

So we both sat there on the settee following every move on the flickering screen and every glib and often un-necessary comment from Eddie Waring, the commentator, as the action unfolded. The game itself was a bitter disappointment for everyone who went, everyone who watched on TV and indeed everyone in West Hull. We simply did not perform on the day, we had promised so much but once we got on the field, toe to toe with the mighty Wigan, we just froze. How often have I had to say those words since then?

Wigan with Billy Boston, Eric Ashton, David Bolton and Mick Sullivan had clearly the edge in the backs, but Hull seemed, on paper at least, to hold sway in the forwards. The first big disappointment for the fans was that Hull was unable to wear their traditional irregular strip and had to play in white shirts with a black 'V'. It was only a few minutes after the teams had been presented to the Princess Royal and the 80,000 spectators, when the mistakes started with a dropped ball in our own half, from which Ashton and Holden scythed through our defence to go down the field and score. That try was converted but we got a penalty of our own from which a very young Arthur Keegan (In for our regular full back Bateson who was injured) kicked a good goal.

Then with Wigan under pressure inside their 25 yard area Tommy Finn dropped the ball and Bolton scooped it up in a flash to send their mercurial winger Sullivan off on an easy ninety yard run to the try line. Bolton then got on the score sheet himself and Boston got another before the break, by which time we were already 16 points behind. If however anyone ever doubted just how fast Johnny Whiteley was in his prime, they would enjoy my lasting memory from that half, which was the way he left the back of the scrum ran at an angle across the field to catch a 'flying' Mick Sullivan and dump him into touch.

Hull certainly started the second half well with both Saville and Cooper being held short, before Wigan replied in deadly fashion through tries from McTigue and Boston, which really rubbed salt into our wounds. With just 8 minutes remaining we got our only try as Finn steamed in off a Jim Drake pass to run round behind the posts to touch down.

If you're serious about being a sport's fan you have to be able to grieve

When the final whistle went we had lost 30-13 and you could almost taste the disappointment everywhere. Leaving my Mum to her grief I walked out into Aylesford Street where, almost surreally in the blinding sunlight, I discovered several other people just gazing into nothingness.

"It will take a while for our Street to get over this one", I thought. I was glad though that Mum had only had to watch it on the TV with me and Eddie Waring and not made the long journey to London to be there in person. It was to be another year before I was to be able to experience for the first time that feeling of utter despondency that you get when you walk away from the 'twin towers' having lost.

That is, I believe, one of the worst feelings you can experience as a fan (and I know because I have been there, several times) but after 50 odd years of supporting my Club I have come to realise that the team you love can be so inventive in the ways that it can cause you sorrow. Over the years we have, on dozens of occasions, beaten the big boys and been thrashed by a small club the following week, taken the lead in a game and thrown it away and as was the case all those years ago, got to a final and been humiliated. Once you realise that this unrequited love of a sports team is permanent, it soon becomes apparent that it never ends. In fact to this day I sincerely believe that just when you think you have seen it all and there is little else that your Club can do to upset you, they invariably come up with something new.

Eddie Waring ... 'Our Eddie' to the impersonators and just 'A bloody embarrassment' to the fans!

I just mentioned Eddie Waring who was by then the accepted 'Face' of Rugby League on the BBC. He was on everyone's lips back then because whilst the uninitiated potential converts to the game all seemed to love him he was hated by the 'dyed in the wool' supporters. However, looking back now, there is little doubt that wherever you sat on that debate, the portly little man from Dewsbury was certainly doing a lot to 'nationalise' our northern game. Perhaps by way of a digression here it would be a good time for me to pay my homage to that same Eddie Waring because back then in the late fifties he was fast becoming an institution in British Broadcasting. They may not have liked him in the Threepenny Stand but as far as most of the citizens of the country were concerned Rugby League and Eddie Wearing went hand in hand like bacon and eggs. He was a media personality in the eyes of a growing TV audience, hated by many 'real' supporters, tolerated by the majority of fans, but loved by millions who actually had no idea what Rugby League was in the first place and who only watched it because of the antics of one, Eddie Waring.

For some thirty years he commentated on the ups and downs of the game and so distinctive was his voice that no impersonator in the country was worth his salt if he couldn't 'do an Eddie Waring'. He was in fact the mimics dream, introducing as he did phrases such as "It's an up and under", "He's going for an early bath" and "He's a big lad but his mother loves him". He popularised the game across the country particularly in the South, and an amazing 6 million viewers regularly tuned into his Saturday commentaries, most of whom, after the game, switched over to ITV for that other highly cultural pursuit back then, 'Wrestling with Kent Walton'. Next door at number 25 Mrs Potter and her husband Stan had moved into Mrs Clarkeson's house after she died and although they didn't care much for rugby they were big fans of Wrestling. They had their telly turned up really loud when it was on and could both clearly be heard through the walls in our front room shouting at the top of their voices about, Mick McManus, Ricki Starr, Jack Dempsey and Jackie Pallo.

As I said earlier many of the purists said that Eddie Waring gave the game of Rugby League a comedy image but what the hell, the current Rugby League administrators would, I am sure, do anything for an audience of 6 million for a televised game on a Saturday afternoon these days!

Waring had a reputation for being a bit of a strange character though, living for years; it was said, in a hotel and only venturing out once a week to commentate on games. The truth behind this myth is somewhat different however. It appears that Eddie was so put out by the reaction of the traditional supporters to his knockabout style of commentating, that he adopted the Queen's Hotel in Leeds as his accommodation address, whilst actually living in secret in Sowerby Bridge. This paranoia was further born out for me when, in later life, I saw Eddie sneaking into the ground before a Wigan game. I guess if further evidence was needed that his caution was well justified, then you should look no further than the way he was received by the fans on the 'Threepennies' every time he walked round to his commentating position.

In his early life, during the war years, Eddie was a very successful manager at Dewsbury. He was well known back then as a canny operator, signing up all the players that were stationed at army depots and airfields nearby and winning several wartime trophies. After the war he travelled to America where the rumour goes he bumped into Bob Hope who spent some time informing Eddie about the power of television in the United States. Following this chance meeting it was not long before Eddie was one of the first in Great Britain to recognise the potential of televised sport. He courted the BBC in an attempt to persuade them to consider Rugby League for televising and was appointed commentator for their first ever televised match, simply because there was no one else, and he became a fixture thereafter.

On the terraces his glib comments and off the cuff remarks, that were so loved by the uninitiated, were hated by the regulars. How dare he make a mockery of our great game? The unrest amongst traditional supporters grew when the world of show business beckoned and when Katie Boyle (sensible girl) walking out of 'It's a Knockout', (a sort of shambolic holiday camp game show contested between different towns and cities) Eddie was appointed as one of the co-presenters. His style became more and more outlandish as he continued in both jobs; in fact things became so surreal it was often hard to define between his rugby and his 'It's a Knockout' commentaries. My parents and all the diehard FC supporters hated it but he soon gained cult status particularly with students and one university even had an 'Eddie Waring Appreciation Society'. Incidentally, it's interesting to note that both Eddie and Sky TV presenter, Mike Stephenson hails from Dewsbury, it's probably just something in the water.

The BBC even received a 10,000-name petition from outraged diehard fans about his work, but at the height of his popularity the canny Eddie had negotiated himself a contract which tied him to the BBC until he wished to retire. His celebrity status continued unabated and he even appeared on the Morecambe and Wise Christmas Show, although by this time it was hard to tell whether people were laughing with poor old Eddy, or at him.

'Mr Rugby League' finally decided to retire in 1981 aged 71 to be replaced by Ray French, and I guess in hindsight the game owes him a lot for the popularity he brought to it in what were difficult times. For me though he will always be remembered as a commentator who said whatever came into his head, which, in hindsight, was really quiet refreshing. One of his most celebrated and typical comments came at the end of the 1968 cup final when Don Fox missed that conversion under the post that would have won the game for Wakefield, he paused for a second whilst the crowd went mad and then said "Eeee... poor lad!"

But for all his failings he was a character and part of the everyday life of being a supporter back then, every kid on every street corner would do you an Eddie Waring impression. However he played an important part in popularising the game across the country, on the TV at least. I have often thought there should have been some sort of memorial to him and the work he did. Perhaps in hindsight the best way he could be remembered would be for the Queen's Hotel in Leeds to have a plaque by the door which simply says "Eddie Waring Never Lived Here".

At last! ITV comes to No. 23 ... all thanks to Rediffusion!!!

But back to the last year of the decade and whilst I am on the subject of televisions, it was shortly after that Wembley Final that we as a family caught up with all the rest of my pal's households, and exchanged that ageing Pye set for a Rediffusion 17-inch TV. This was a modern marvel and I suppose a piece of state of the art technology that actually gave us for the first time ITV! The TV was connected to a brown Bakelite box on the wall that had a dial that you could use to tune to a couple of radio stations, BBC TV and ITV. Immediately I was able to share and experience all the programmes my pals were always talking about at school, like Robin Hood, Ivanhoe and Wagon Train! Mum and Dad too seemed to enjoy Emergency Ward Ten and were always talking about it and particularly local boy John Alderton from Hessle High Road, who was starring in it at the time. But it was the advertisements that impressed me the most and I was soon singing "Lyons Quick to brew tea means none for the pot" and "Unzip a Banana" at the top of my voice, for this lad, commercial television brought a whole new dimension to the 'in house' entertainment at number 23.

Nine years three months and four days ... The age of enlightenment

Saturday 19th September 1959   *Hull 53 – Doncaster 8*

At the age of nine when I guess I should have had my head down studying for my 11+ Exams (which because of my birthday I had to take at ten) all of a sudden something wonderful and mind blowing happened as the new rugby season started. I suddenly stopped running around the hills at the back of the terracing at the Boulevard after three quarter time and as an uneasy truce fell between the adolescent Cowboys and Indians, I started to take a lot more notice of what was actually going on out there on the pitch! Within the space of three weeks of the campaign beginning I was cadging the admission money from my Mum and going to watch the game from the start! The experience at Odsal had, I think, unnerved my Mum more than she cared to admit and she didn't renew her season ticket for the 'Best Stand' that year. She stopped going to a lot of the games, although she did accompany me to one or two of the bigger fixtures! But I was well into it and so it was that at the tender age of ten, I started the addiction that was to engross my life. It was a game against Doncaster that September when we won 53-8 that, for me, swung the deal completely.

That day I stood on the terracing at the Airlie Street end next to a chap, who, to this day, I have never seen since. He was, I found out later, call Alf, and there with his son, who was about the same age as me. Alf wore a big Duffel coat, a black and white scarf, sported a Woodbine in his mouth all the time and wheezed as he spoke. Seeing me there on my own, he took me with his son, who I think was called Tim, down to the front and sat us on the hooped top metal fencing that separated the viewing areas from the pitch.

Throughout the game he stood behind us and told us both what was happening and who the players were. He was impressed with my knowledge of the Club's stars and what motor cars they drove, and warmed to me as the game went on! I remember he said, on several occasions, when the crowd shouted for a forward pass, "Well off side actually but I suppose they are the same thing". Funny thing to say that, and even funnier how I have remembered it after all these years.

I looked out for Alf and Tim on several occasions after that but did not see them again. From time to time my friends would run up in mid game and ask me to join in with whatever chasing game they were playing that week but by then, I was just too much a fan of the FC to do those sorts of childish things. I was hooked!

A regular fan!

About that time my pal Billy Jenkinson started watching the game with me as well! This was a good thing because it was always good to 'compare notes' on what we thought was going on and to have someone to stand with, in fact Billy and I formed quite a close friendship. Billy lived in a terraced house just across the road from the ground in Division Road not far from Chiltern Street School, at the back of the Threepenny Stand. 'Jenks' was the skinniest kid I had ever seen, who, whatever the weather always seemed to wear short pants that were much too small for him. We were both keen on the players and we waited after games and training to get all the stars' names in our Autograph Books! Once we became established friends, we would play for hours after school against the front wall of the Stadium with chalked wickets, in summer, and goal posts in winter. But mostly we would have 'Kicking Duels', just like the full backs did in games back then. We did this across the Boulevard car park, forcing each other backward with booming punts using the rugby ball I got from Mum and Dad for my ninth birthday.

On match days we would both put on the black and white scarves that our Mothers had knitted for us and I complimented mine with an old Air Raid Wardens rattle I got from Boyes on Hessle Road that Dad had painted black and white for me. This made a hell of a racket and certainly cleared a space around us on the concrete terraces of the Airlie Street end! We were often greeted on arriving before a game with "Oh no not you two again, Bugger off with that bloody rattle".

As for the playing staff back then, well I can remember the likes of the Drakes, Tommy Harris, Cyril Sykes, Tommy Finn and Ivor Watts! Although, most of the others seem to have disappeared into the mists of time. I can however remember well Nan Halifihi a Tongan who played for us; he had a brother Johnny who was a handy Boxer and used to keep fit by attending training at the Club. His was the only signature Jenksy and I had on the 'boxing' page of our autograph albums.

I had better get used to this; queuing for tickets, the 'Threepennies' and Cup glory in the ringside seats

Saturday 19ᵗʰ March 1960   *Hull 12 – Wigan 8*

That year was however a big one for the Club. As I said earlier, Mum and I had watched the previous year's Cup Final defeat by Wigan on the TV but this year, as we started out on another great cup run to a Wembley return, I was a proper fan and so I needed, if not demanded, to be fully involved.

We beat both York and Keithley in the early rounds of the competition before things really warmed up and we were drawn against Wigan at the Boulevard in the quarter finals and what a day that was. Actually, to be honest things started the previous weekend when the quiet of a Sunday morning in Airlie Street was disturbed at about 3-00am as outside my bedroom window I could hear voices in the dark.

Rubbing my eyes and wiping the condensation from the window with my pajama sleeve, I could just make out that across the road, illuminated by the pale street lights at the front of the ground a queue was beginning to form. As a grey dawn broke, the human snake stretched 4 times round the car park, past the front of our house in Aylesford Street to disappear round the far corner and out of sight. By the time the ticket window at the Supporters' Club opened at 10-00am the queue was down the Boulevard and into Selby Street stretching right down to Chiltern Street! In fact the local Daily Mail, next night, stated that at one time around 16,000 people were estimated to be standing in a queue three quarters of a mile long. Mrs. Butters, Benny Allgoods and all the local corner shops opened that Sunday and had sold out of just about everything by 11 o'clock.

It was a freezing cold day too and years later a pal of mine, Vince related how he was in that queue having been bribed by his Dad who said that he would take him to the game if he queued for their tickets!! We got ours I believe from the Supporters' Club so we all just sat in the front room all day and watched the fun as hundreds filed past our bay window.

Mum I guess, realising that there was going to be a big crush and a gate in excess of 20,000 at the game, felt that 'Ring Side' seats were safest for both me and her!! One thing's for sure those ring side seats would never be allowed in modern day sports stadiums, but back then they were just a means of getting a few more folks into the ground for the big games.

Saturday arrived at last and with it being a sell out Cup game the "ALL MUST PAY" signs that usually adorned the turnstiles for these matches were replaced by "TICKETS ONLY" placards pasted over each gateway into the ground. Having got through a turnstile identified by a piece of cardboard with "RINGSIDE SEATS ONLY" scribbled on it in Biro, we then showed our tickets at the big gate in the perimeter fence near the dressing rooms, where the ill and infirm on stretchers and in wheelchairs were brought to the touch line to watch the games. Then we walked, through the discarded heaps of straw around the dead ball line, and took up our seats on park benches positioned in front of the Threepenny Stand at the Gordon Street end of the ground and about 6 foot from the touch line! Seats were also lined up behind the posts at each end too and that's where Vince and his Dad sat that day. The Safety at Sports Ground people would have had a field day!

So there we sat surrounded by piles of discarded straw that had been used to cover the pitch to keep the frost out. It was a real mess! Wherever you looked, the terracing at the ends of the ground seemed to be bulging as thousands packed into the old stadium. It was a still afternoon and a pall of cigarette smoke hung over the spectators like a volcano that was about to erupt. This was a totally new experience for me. Mum, after her lucky escape on the cinder hills of Odsal, probably thought we would be safer there but within ten minutes of the start, our winger Ivor Watts, was tackled into touch and landed, with a Wigan three quarter on top of him, about 6 inches from my foot! It was a great game, but also, perhaps more importantly, my first real experience of that institution that I had heard so much of and that was to dominate my life for years to come, the Threepenny Stand.

Behind me there was a 'bear garden' of cheering, drinking, smoking, referee bashing, and swearing. My Mum, who incidentally, I never ever heard swear, seemed immune to it all, but oh boy did I learn some new words that day! There were profanities that even the lad from Chiltern Juniors, had never heard before. Finally I plucked up the courage to look over my shoulder at the wooden edifice that was soon to become my spiritual home. It wasn't the size of the crowd or the sea of faces that impressed me most though, it was the way that they all lived every minute moving from agony to ecstasy at the drop of a ball! These supporters were a lot different to those that stood with me in my usual vantage point over on the terracing on 'Bunker's Hill' at the Airlie Street end of the ground. These guys were allowed to shout "Bastard" out at the top of their voices, without attracting any attention at all from those around them. That smell of beer, cigarettes and just a hint of urine was one that was to indicate in years to come that 'I was home.'

For probably the first time in my life I saw real anger and real passion on display there and it was great, so much so that I made a mental note of the fact that the sooner I got myself into this stand the better! On Saturday afternoons in those days thirteen a side was a much different experience to the sanitised sporting day enjoyed by modern day crowds. There were no cheerleaders, no sponsored stadiums and no Australian coaches with their 'tactics' and 'sliding defences'. It was all pure drama for a young lad. Trawlermen swore and cursed at everything and everybody, grubby infant delinquents not unlike me pelted hapless shivering touch judges with half eaten pies and red faced Grannies turned the air blue, waving their meaty fists in the air and screaming "gerremonside!"

The game itself was an absolute classic with 'The Cream' coming out eventual winners by twelve points to eight with Kershaw scoring the winning try and Bateson slotting over the conversion. I was a bit too young back then to remember much more of the detail.

As the final whistle went the players hugged each other shook hands and then (like the Gladiators I had seen in those Roman epics on our new Rediffusion TV) they all turned to 'The Threepennies' to soak up the adoration of the crowd. As we filed out along the touchline and the last members of the team disappeared down the tunnel, I was bemused by the fact that most of those fabulous 'Threepenny Standers' just stood there, as if not wanting to go home and let the moment pass. It was always a big victory if you could turn over the 'Pies', as Wigan have always been known, but this was a cup game and they were of course the Cup holders. They had fielded a team with Bolton, McTigue, Sayer and Barton on show, who had all been instrumental in beating us so comprehensively in the final the previous year. Little did I realise then that I was going to be left standing on those pee soaked wooden steps, not wanting to leave the scene of a victory, on many, many occasions in the decades to come.

Vince, sitting at the other end, has just as strong memories of that day and he told me years later that he was sat there when Wigan's Norman Cherrington scored just 6 feet from him, only for the try scorer then to be congratulated right in front of him by the legendary Eric Ashton! He says that it was almost unreal to see those great folk heroes of the age there on the pitch before him. Vince incidentally says that to this day it was the most exciting experience he has ever had at a Rugby League game. Not bad for a Rover's fan, but your first big game as a kid is like that though isn't it?

Waving the losers goodbye

Train spotting was still very much on the agenda in those days and so having walked with my Mum back home, I raced to the level crossing at the top of the Boulevard to watch the 5 train loads of Wigan fans as they started their long journey home. There were quite a few of my pals who had the same idea down there and we stood with our faces through the barriers and booed and gave them the thumbs down as their glum faces peered at us through the grubby carriage windows! In all things there has to be losers and winners but that day we won, so it was a case of "Up yours Wigan" from us lot waving two fingers at them as they started their long trek back to Lancashire.

For those complete anoraks who have got this far in this catalogue of fanaticism, the trains were pulled by 5 ex London Midland Scottish steam engines, real rarities in Hull! There was one Patriot, two Jubilee's and two Black Fives. I guess to most of you reading this that means absolutely nothing at all! But, those were rare railway locomotives in these parts and back then to a ten-year-old, seeing them meant the end to a perfect day.

We beat Oldham 12-9 in a pretty none descript semi-final played at Station Road Swinton and we were back at Wembley again, for the second year running.

Wembley again and this time I'm there!

Saturday 13th May 1960   *Hull 5 – Wakefield 38*

The previous year when we were beaten by a record score, I watched the Final with my Mum in Aylesford Street and just to prolong the agony, a few weeks later Grandstand, the BBC's regular Saturday afternoon sports programme, featured our only try of the game, by Tommy Finn, in its weekly opening credits. This was something that survived to haunt us for many years to come every time we switched that particular programme on. There would be no TV for me this time around though because the moment we won the semi-final against Oldham at Swinton, this young fan was off to Wembley.

My first trip to the national stadium was to end again in a second successive record defeat for the Club, but that seemed a long way off as Mum and I headed off in a taxi to the station to catch the 6-00 am 'Train No 3' heading for London King's Cross. For a couple of weeks beforehand, shops had their windows decked out in black and white with large signs saying, "Good Luck Lads" and "Bring the Cup back Home for us Johnny", plastered across their windows. As kids it was all we talked about at school and at Chiltern Street, even Mrs Rutherford the head teacher had a 'Good Luck Hull FC' decorated table in the corridor outside the Assembly Hall.

Actually going to the game was a great adventure for a young northern lad and I was just amazed by the sight that met us at Paragon Station when we arrived. Everyone was in black and white, this included all the attendants, the guard on our train and even the people who had just finished cleaning the coaches out. Four trains were awaiting our arrival each with about 12 coaches and three trains, including ours were positioned in the old 'Excursion' platforms at the South side of the station. These crumbling platforms had seen some other memorable times in bygone years, none more so than when they were used many years earlier as the transit point for immigrants on route from Europe to the Americas. On this particular weekend the west side of the City was temporarily on the move on mass, to London.

There were trolleys, sack barrows and carts of beer everywhere. Crates of Hull Brewery Amber and Nut Brown were stacked in the aisles as we entered our carriage and pushed our way to our seats. I can still remember the strains of 'Old Faithful' ringing out around the train even before we had left Paragon Station. We were sitting with a friend of my Mum's Mrs Rogers who had the biggest rosette I had ever seen. She had also knitted herself an irregular hooped scarf that had Johnny

Whiteley embroidered on the white panels and Bill Drake on the black. In the early 60's it was a case of 'do it yourself' rather than any sort of merchandise being available to buy from the Club. Sheila Rogers was a really jolly heavily built lady who always laughed a lot between swigs from a hip flask she kept in her huge black leather handbag.

Everyone including me seemed to have a rattle. I had re painted mine in the Club colours, using some Airfix model paint I found in the shed and had stuck the names of the team, cut from the Daily Mail, all over it especially for the final.

The trip down was fantastic, with singing, laughing and drinking going on everywhere. It's a good job it was too because as was the case with excursion trains back then we were constantly stopping at signals and waiting on slow lines whilst the scheduled express trains passed, and the journey itself took over 5 hours to complete. When the train stopped at a signal for a while just outside Doncaster folks even climbed out onto the track to relieve themselves, it was mayhem but good natured mayhem. I was still spotting trains so despite all that was going on around me I spent most of the journey 'nose pressed to window pane'.

The trip from King's Cross to the Stadium, my first ever on a tube, was an amazing experience but for a young lad from Chiltern Street School whose idea of a day out was a trip to Hornsea on the train, Wembley was simply the biggest thing I had ever seen. It was massive! We found our seats that were just like the best stand seats at the Boulevard, on planking again divided by white paint lines with a number on each section. I joined in with the chanting and really enjoyed the community singing before the game got under way. Although most of these revelations will be a bit alien to younger readers, little has changed with the Cup Final's pre match rituals except that we didn't just sing 'Abide with me' but also several other songs that were printed in the programme including, 'She's a Lassie from Lancashire' and 'On Ilkley Moor Ba Tat'. Both Hull and Wakefield supporters sang along together and everyone seemed to get on really well.

Some things never really change, and as has become usual over the years, we went into the game without several first team regulars including half our mighty pack. So bad in fact was our injury crisis that we even gave a first team debut to Mike Smith who was, and still is, the only player to ever make his Club debut at Wembley.

Our pre match injury crisis was not helped when a week earlier in a Championship playoff game against the same team, our 'star' full back Peter Bateson was the victim of a stiff arm tackle from Derek 'Rocky' Turner and was ruled out of the final. Turner however 'got away with it', escaping a ban by the Rugby League and taking his place in the Wakefield ranks for the big game. We had therefore to switch our centre Kershaw to full back.

Neil Fox kicked an early penalty goal and that was followed by a try by Rollin and our worst fears seemed to be realised. But our depleted team battled on and nine minutes later Stan Cowen swerved and side stepped his way to a great try behind the sticks, Sammy Evans, our replacement hooker and king of the cauliflower ears, who was soon to become a wrestler, added the goal and at half time we went in with a respectable, if not surprising, 7-5 score line.

The second half saw Harris badly injured and hobbling about whilst Cowan suffered a cracked rib. As there were no substitutes we battled on gamely but were totally outclassed by the 'Trinity', who scored a number of long distance tries none better than Alan Skene's 60 yard dash towards the end of the game. Hull tried really hard but 5 tries in the last 20 minutes left us with another record Wembley defeat, this time of 38-5.

However disappointed I was at the result, I remember that whereas the post match reports the previous year had been embarrassing, this time they were full of praise for our patched up team, our battling qualities and never say die attitude. The score line did not do justice to our efforts and we left the field to a heroes' reception at the end of the game. I stood there in defeat and sung 'Old Faithful' with my Mum and I knew then, for the first time, there was certainly no escape, I was hooked.

Tommy Harris's performance won him the Lance Todd Trophy and was generally hailed as the bravest performance ever seen at the stadium. He was floored by several tackles that left him rolling about the pitch in agony but he still broke their line time and again. He eventually left the field, with 10 minutes to go, with severe concussion. In our ranks that day were some great players that I can still picture in my mind's eye because they were all heroes in a lad's eyes and it's still hard not to marvel at the performances of Kershaw, Cowan, Nan Halifihi, Broadhurst, Finn, Harris and of course Johnny Whiteley.

Some of the above detail, I have since become aware of from reading about that great occasion and in all honesty some of the stuff about my experiences that day is a bit hazy. I don't remember much of the journey back to Hull although Mum told me years later that it was about 4-00am before we finally got home to bed. 24 hours of excitement and I guess heartbreak for a young ten year old. The excitement and exertion, she also told me, saw me sleep right through the next day and the following night and it was Tuesday before I had fully recovered and went back to school!

Years later I came across a famous quote about Tommy Harris which was attributed to the Queen, who was attending her first ever Rugby League game that day. She is reported to have said to RL Council member Bill Cunningham, "It is amazing that such a small man can be at the bottom of a scrum and then be so active a short time later". HRH is a Hull fan!

Players that 'Take their bat and ball home'

As a footnote and considering the temperamental nature of some of our modern day sportsmen it was, looking back, a fine performance by 13 real heroes, however, even back then the game had its 'prima donnas'. The shock selection of twenty-two year old Smith to make his Hull FC debut meant that another reserve Colin Cole, who I think we signed from Hull and East Riding Rugby Union club, was left out. I knew Colin from getting his autograph at training but apparently he was so upset at not getting a place that he 'took his bat and ball home' and refused to play for Hull again.

After You Ivor!
Roy Francis makes way for Watts as he sets off downfield in the
1950/51 season.

The author in the backyard of number 23 with Abbie and Walter
and with Mum again on the beach at Hornsea.

Another Saturday night!
Dad on the left and Mum fourth from the left, join Ivy Mason and
the gang in Hull Supporters' Club around 1957

Johnny Whiteley (second left) and Roy Francis (second right) are joined by Directors at the annual Hull Supporters' Club dinner in 1953.

The team that beat Workington Town in the Championship Semi Final 1956

Standing: (Trainer) Watkinson, Drake, Coverdale, Whiteley, Bowman, Markham, Moat.

Sitting: Harris, Scott, Hutton , Darlington.

Kneeling: Finn, Cooper, Turner.

The Champions of the Rugby League 1957/58

Back Row: A. Holdstock (inset), P. Whiteley, S. Cowan, M. Scott, B. Saville, G. Sharpley (Trainer), G. Dannatt (inset)

Middle Row: B. Cooper, C. Cole, C. Sykes, B. Hambling, R. Francis (Coach), J. Whiteley (Capt.), T. Harris, J. Drake, W. Drake

Front Row: C. Turner, P. Bateson, I. Watts, F. Broadhurst, T. Finn, G. Harrison

The 1959 Wembley Team v Wigan

Back Row: Keegan, J Drake, Sykes, W. Drake, Cooper, Scott.

Middle Row: Saville, Harris, Whiteley, Cowan, Watts.

Front Row: Matthews, Finn.

A happy band of Rosamund Club regulars set off for Wembley in 1959. *(Courtesy of Hull Daily Mail)*

Girls on the Town.

Hull FC fans in Trafalgar Square before the 1959 final.
(Courtesy of Hull Daily Mail)

Queuing for tickets.

The amazing sight of some of the 16,000 people who queued for tickets on Sunday 13th March for the Wigan Cup Quarter Final Tie at the Boulevard the following Saturday. (*Courtesy of Hull Daily Mail*)

A week later and it's a full house at the Boulevard, as Chiltern Street School looks majestically over the ground with plenty filling those 'Ringside seats' where the author experienced his first big game that day, sat just in front of the Threepenny Stand (*Courtesy of Steve Wray*)

The great Wilf Rosenberg chases down John Moore with
Geoff Stocks behind. 27th March 1964, Hull 5 Hull KR 13
(*Courtesy of Hull Daily Mail*)

Revenge! 16th April 1965, Hull 12 Hull KR 10. Harry Poole looks for
support as Neale and Devonshire move in.
(*Courtesy of Hull Daily Mail*)

That was a hard lesson for the future for me having just seen the light and been converted to the cause. Temperamental players are occasionally an unfortunate hazard when you're obsessed with a sport's club. The rest of the 59/60 season was largely forgettable as far as the league campaign was concerned, although we did give a long service award known back then as a 'benefit year' to Tommy Harris, Brian Cooper and Ivor Watts our now retired Welsh winger, and of course my pal Mike's Dad who was then appointed assistant coach.

'Life's a gas', tripping in Mr Symonds class

As the first decade of my life closed and the 60's began I was looking forward to the 1960/61 season with great relish but unfortunately the great pack of those days was starting to diminish both in strength and numbers. Jim Drake went to Hull Kingston Rovers; Tommy Harris to York and others retired and moved on! That season was a poor one all round and we actually finished 16th in the league. No doubt for the seasoned fans it was a big disappointment although as a new convert to the cause, I loved every minute of it, but although I was captivated by all things Hull FC, in Aylesford Street life went on as usual. As I half heartedly prepared for my 11+ Examinations at Chiltern Street, I was being 'coached' in sums by my Dad whilst Mum helped with my English. At School I was now in Mr Symonds class, a nice bloke who was big in stature and who had distinctive ginger hair and freckles. He drove a Messerschmitt bubble car that led one or two in our class to say behind their hands, that he was probably a German spy. Even in those days I think that some of us kids watched too much TV.

Our classroom was at the top of the building at the Chiltern Street side of the school and looked out across the rooftops and over the Threepenny Stand. In fact when there was the odd rearranged mid week cup replay or special training session, you could when peering out of the window see the ball rise over the roof of the stand! However if old Symonds saw you looking out across the roof tops he would get you out to the front of the class and administer his 'Persuader', 'the Slipper'.

This was an old sandshoe that, having made you touch your toes, he applied to your backside with such force that you invariably shot across the room to fall in a crumpled heap against the wall. This display of discipline was usually accompanied with roars of laughter from the rest of the class and it was difficult at the time to decide whether it was the violent pain or the abject ridicule that hurt the most.

Old Symonds was preparing our raggle taggle band of academics for the 11+ Examination or our 'Scholarship' as some called it. This threat hung over us constantly in that last year at Chiltern Street. There was a bit of English and a bit of maths but basically it was an IQ test which in the end only proved who was good at....... doing IQ tests. We were just systematically programmed by the use of the 'carrot' and the 'slipper' to spot those differences, work out what was next in a certain sequence, see how quickly we could 'fill that bath' or decide which way the smoke was blowing if the train was going east and the wind blowing west etc. etc. etc. All this was just part of a process that rubber stamped every youth in the country as being either ripe for grammar school or subnormal for life. There were incentives though, Margret Andrew's Dad said that if she passed she could have a new bicycle; Billy Jackson's Aunt offered a racing bike whilst I was promised a bright future by my Mum and Dad, which I guess was great but not much good for getting to school on.

I remember that classroom was in fact above the boiler house, something you were actually aware of because you could see down through the gaps in the floorboards to the boilers below. In the afternoons, during periods of cold weather we all used to drop off to sleep as the fumes from the coke boilers oozed through the gaps in the floorboards and right up our nostrils! This was a sort of early manifestation of getting high on coke, but thankfully it was only the cinder variety! I can still recall that vinegary acidy smell today. Other than these brief, soporific trips to oblivion, life at school and home went on as usual.

No one was more surprised than me!

By that next summer, I was rugby barmy and eagerly awaiting the 1961/62 season, so imagine my surprise and utter amazement when a letter dropped through the letterbox at no. 23 telling me that I had passed my 'Scholarship'. In those days parents were asked to nominate in order the schools that they would like their children to go to. We had put Kingston High top of my list because Mum used to go there (with Amy Johnson, as she would always tell you) then opted for Riley High School because it was just down Anlaby Road and would save some bus fares and after that we were not that bothered. My parents must have put Kelvin Hall down next because I passed to go to my third option which was that self same Technical High School, miles away in 'Suburbia'on Bricknell Avenue in the north of the City, where, as Bill Jenks, who failed commented, "The nobs all live".

So pleased were Mum and Dad that they told everyone they met of my success, whilst I, never having thought of myself as the scholastic type, was a bit bemused by it all. They even rewarded me for doing so well, by investing 12 shillings and six pence of their hard earned cash, on a junior pass for the Boulevard! Not only was I a scholarship boy but I was also, much more importantly in my mind, a season pass holder for Hull RLFC!! Now it was official and who needed a new bike anyway. I have realised since then of course that as far as being a 'Loyal' supporter is concerned when you buy a season pass you are cranking up the 'belonging' a notch. I had my position on the Threepenny Stand, or on the Airlie Street end and that bit of card gave me the right to stand there and I would certainly glare at any big game casual fan that stood in it before I got there.

Looking back, all this new school 'stuff' must have been quite a sacrifice for my parents and it was only when they got a letter from my new school outlining just what was needed for me to live the 'Scholarship Dream', that the full impact of my success hit them. There was then much scratching of heads as Mum read out a list of uniform clothes, sportswear, pencils, protractors and plimsolls! The major problem was I guess that the majority had to be purchased from the schools registered outfitters and suppliers, Gordon Clarke's of Paragon Street in the City centre. The days of shopping at Boyes for my clothes were receding over our particular horizon very quickly.

Somehow they managed to get all the cash for the gear together and I found out that another Boulevard season ticket holder, Steve from down the street, was also going to Kelvin so at least there was someone going my way that had sensible interests! I remember the weekend before I started school I went to Sunday School (Yes I was still going) in my full uniform. I really must have looked a Wally (in the idiot rather than the Father sense) with my little cap sat on top of my head and my socks, for the first time in my life, pulled up my legs and being held there by elastic garters! They really dug into my legs and I can still clearly remember complaining to my Mum when I got home that my feet had gone numb! The uniform idea, I guess, was a good one and designed to bring some sort of parity to everyone who attended High School, presuming, I suppose, that those middle class kids from Anlaby High Road and 'the Avenues', would turn up in spats and knee boots if they were left to their own devices. The cap was the main problem though, because whenever you wore it, it became an icon of superior intellect which on the Boulevard meant that it was quickly destined to be snatched and deposited in the highest tree the 'urchin classes' could find.

An introduction to the fans of the other club in Hull

Saturday 12th August 1961   Hull 5 – Hull Kingston Rovers 14

The problem with a new school however was that although it was a harrowing perplexing and sometimes quite violent transition, there were more important things to worry about because by the start of September we had lost all 4 of our games in the new season. These included the traditional 'Curtain Raiser' to the season the Eva Hardaker Memorial Trophy game against Rovers at Craven Park! This was the first time I had been to 'That Place' and despite my Dad still working at the butchers on Holderness Road; it was the first time I had been allowed to venture that far into East Hull. I travelled there with Billy Jenks by Trolley Bus, firstly to the town and then on the Holderness Road service which dropped us at the Bus Sheds next to the ground. This was all uncharted territory for both of us. We paid our dues at the turnstiles and entered the enemy's stronghold for the first time.

What a strange place Craven Park was. I had been brought up with a distinct dislike of all things red and white anyway but the ground where they played really was a lot different to the Boulevard! There was a track all the way round that someone told me was used to race dogs, whilst at one end there was a massive score board which never showed the score, I was baffled! I later found out that this was actually the Tote Board, but what that was supposed to mean to a naive kid of 11, was anyone's guess! When the game began it seemed miles to the pitch and I was stuck at one end on wooden fronted muddy terracing behind, of all things, a privet hedge. Now one or two folks, including ourselves, had those in their front gardens back in Aylesford Street, but around a rugby pitch!! It was baffling! We lost the game 14-5 much to the incessant gloating of an old chap in an oilskin mackintosh stood next to me, who kept making snide comments about "Black and White rubbish" throughout the game; "What a moron" I thought, although his behaviour did at least give me a good indicator of what I could expect for the rest of my life from those of the same ilk.

Then, as is the case today in the 21st century, I was resigned to just being part of it all and I couldn't do much about it. We were facing another season and no doubt there would be more of this heartbreak to come. To this day my Club exploit me, disregard my views, sell my favourite players and move in a 'mysterious way and all I am left with is that age old conundrum for real fans that is the eternal conflict between reality and sentiment! At school and in the pubs and clubs of the City, most fans expound their opinions based on reality and steeped in pessimism but for me the start of a season has to be a time for optimism and hope; well it is until brutal reality kicks in and the season proper begins.

"What's happening at the Watersheddings?" Before local radio there was only … the 'Tannoy' system

With the exception of the odd safari to Craven Park we stuck to home games and anyway because of the lack of motorways, the shortage of available cars and the weather, travelling to most away games was almost impossible then even if your parents would let you go. So we would watch the first team one-week and the 'A' team the next. I really enjoyed 'A' team games even at that early age because they were so raw and basic and I loved the way that the abuse and profanities of the 'Faithful' few who attended, echoed around the old Threepenny Stand.

When I look back over all the years I have watched my Club I have come to the conclusion that there has always been an element of purity to Reserve, 'A' Team, Colts or Academy games. There are none of those fair weather supporters there, it's down to the truly committed fanatics. Back then at 'A' team games we used to get a first team score update at half time and that was usually it. However on very rare occasions we got "The latest score from Watersheddings (Oldham's ground) is..." but that was usually only when the Mail reporter was sat next to the only phone in the antiquated Press Box all those miles away across the Pennines. 'The Watersheddings', we thought, 'What must that be like?' It sounded like a wet dismal almost spooky place to us kids and of course a few years later we were to discover that it was just that.

Otherwise when the first team were playing away Jenksey and I just stood in our latest viewing position in the Threepenny Stand huddled together against the cold, learning new swear words and watched our second string perform. All the time we wondered just what the first team lads were doing all those miles away. The second team, in those days, was usually made up of young hopefuls, ageing heroes and a smattering of A.N.Others, (a name used to disguise Rugby Union trialists, who if discovered playing in the rival code would be disqualified from their game, for life). The 'A' team performed in faded shirts sometimes without numbers and were soon covered from head to foot in the famous, clinging Boulevard mud. This is probably, I guess, where the famous shout of "Up the cream" came from, because the shorts were just that whilst the shirts were actually faded grey and cream irregular hoops, not too much dissimilar to our away strip some 50 years later.

At the end of the game about 30 or 40 of us would, like beleaguered carol singers on some ancient Dickensian Christmas card, huddle together around the one tannoy speaker on the lighting pole that was situated on the very top of the "Bunker's Hill" terracing overlooking Airlie Street. There, lit by the yellow glow of the single light bulb, we waited for the final score from the first team's away game. We would often stand there silently listening to the static hum of the primitive PA system for up to 20 minutes, before at last it crackled into life, when whoever was left in the press box, over in the best stand, would announce "The final result from the Watersheddings is...." That was it, no scorers, no details and certainly no injuries update.

We knew nothing more than that until we had gone home, had our tea and the Green Sports Mail had dropped through the letterbox. There was no local radio and precious little coverage anywhere else except in local newspapers.

So, my new Technical High School beckoned and although we had already lost five of our first seven games of the season, a new era was starting. Academically it was a real culture shock, almost as severe as the one unfolding at the Boulevard as the Club was about to face the most difficult 20 years of its long history and this young impressionable supporter was about to endure it.

Chapter Four

'The whining school-boy ... Creeping like snail to school'

After that disappointing beginning to the 61/62 season at the Boulevard, my first Academic year at Kelvin Hall Technical High School started on 9th September 1961. I obviously didn't know any Shakespeare then, because it wasn't very Chiltern Street at all but had I been conversant with the works of 'the Bard' no doubt my demeanour that morning would have been best summed up with that extract from 'As You Like it' which states, "And then the whining school-boy, with his satchel and shining morning face, creeping like snail, unwillingly to school". It was just all that uniform stuff and the cap, boy I hated the cap, it just wasn't me at all. There was little doubt however that I found myself that day at an educational establishment that despite being just five miles from Aylesford Street and the Boulevard, was light years away from Chiltern Street Juniors.

The first morning that I stepped from the number 15 bus along with another dozen or so 'new kids', I was totally captivated, not so much by the school itself, that was just four years old and still in its infancy but by the playing fields that surrounded it on every side. As I walked through the gates, they were the only thing I could take in, they were gigantic, there was literally grass as far as the eye could see. I had never seen so much of the green stuff in my life and I remember making a mental note that this place was bigger than West and 'Picky' Park put together.

We were all immediately shepherded into the cloakrooms, where we deposited our hats and coats and were instructed to put on our indoor shoes. After a short assembly, where all the new recruits were read 'their rights' by our Head Master William Pattinson (or Bill as he soon became known), a roll call was read out and once this had been completed, we were marched off to our various classrooms. All this was done in utter silence because you simply knew no one, everything was new including your classmates. I was put into class 1DS: (the initials did not actually mean that they had already sussed my level of academic ability but rather that our form teachers were Miss Downing and Mr Stankley!) This was a modern school indeed, no streaming, no elitism and some girls that actually looked quite bearable, although everything to an impressionable young student was a completely new experience.

'Stinker' Stankley's name caused a few titters, which helped break the ice a bit and things were further eased when we found out our Geography teacher was a Mr Mann, our maths teacher a Mr Nutter and our English master a Mr Adcock!! The head teacher, Bill, was a fine figure of a man, standing six foot tall he always seemed to wear a light checked suit, well polished brown brogues and sported a shock of greased back white hair. Much to my relief Bill told us all in his 'Welcome' speech that he did not agree with corporal punishment which was quite a culture shock for me, particularly after what had gone on in the past with 'master spy' 'Herr' Symonds and that slipper, this, I concluded at the end of my first day, was maybe not going to be as bad as I had at first envisaged.

No Rugby League ... an introduction to 'kick and thump'.

Suddenly however, life was turned upside down as I quickly discovered that school was no longer a pass time to be endured between games of rugby and playing out, school days were now much longer and therefore more time consuming. I had to leave home at ten to eight to catch a bus to the town centre and then another to Bricknell Avenue. By the time I got home each night it was around five and then there was another new innovation to cope with, the dreaded homework! That didn't go down too well I can tell you, but I soon worked out which teachers demanded results next morning, and those who were not that bothered, so I just did what I had to. It made no difference of course to Mum and Dad who would still ask every tea time, when they caught me sat watching TV, "Haven't you got any homework to do?"

Every Thursday afternoon the timetable included a double period of sport with Mr Jones, a small but diminutive Welshman who insisted that there would be "No Rugby League played at his School" and so I was introduced, painfully, to a sort of kick and get thumped version of the game, that was apparently called Rugby Union or 'Ruggarrrr!' as Jonesey called it in his rich Welsh brogue.

I suppose when I look back now, considering this school was in Hull, there was certainly a modicum of snobbery about the place, and if like me you got into the school team, you would spend a lot of Saturdays travelling to faraway places in the East Riding like Driffield and Bridlington, where this strange game was also played by kids who spoke with very effected accents indeed. Old Chambers from Chiltern Street would have been pulling his hair out, if he had any of course. Strangely enough, I found that the more 'posh' the accents became at these schools, the more violent was the opposition. Soon, this quickly became little more than a weekly opportunity, to go out into the country and get my head kicked in and I soon decided that perhaps that was not for me at all. So, believing that discretion was the better part of valour, I quickly hatched a plan to stop getting beaten up every weekend.

When it came to Thursday's games lesson, I started to have attacks of amnesia when it came to remembering to bring my kit with me, an action which often led to me being given 'lines' by Jonesey which I studiously completed in the warmth of the changing rooms. However when we played touch Rugby League on the playground at lunch time, the speed and handling skills I had honed at Chiltern Street, ensured I was always the first to be picked to play by my new pals.

There are no grey areas; everything in our house is Black and White

Another problem with those Saturday morning Rugby Union outings was that arriving back at school in the early afternoon had started to effect my ability to get back to the Boulevard for those mid winter 2-30 kick offs. The Hull team in 1961/62, despite starting to disintegrate as the great players of the 50's began to age and move away, was reasonably successful and we won 23 games. As kids newly initiated to watching Hull FC we never thought much of it really but I guess that the older fans who had lived through that great period in the late 50's must have realised that things were on the slide. The problem was that we had a few young players mixed with some of the old guard, who were just hanging on, whilst diminishing financial resources meant that cash to replace our aged players was almost none existent.

If things were getting a bit difficult at school they were little better at home either as Dad was in a foul mood because for the first time in thirty years Hull had finished below Rovers in the league table. Back then, as is I suppose still the case to this day, that sort of occurrence certainly coloured the atmosphere in a rugby mad household like ours. As I said earlier some of the heroes of the fifties had departed, although some still remained, including Bill Drake, Tommy Finn, George Matthews and Malcolm Storey. Bill's brother Jim Drake became a real 'Turncoat' in this lad's eyes, when much was made in our house of the fact that after receiving a big benefit cheque from the Club, he had gone off to play for the enemy across the river. Dad had helped on his benefit committee too, so you will appreciate just how well his cross City move went down at number 23.

You see the thing you learn at an early age about being a fan is that you grow to find it incredibly hard to understand why players never ever feel as passionate about your Club as you do. You may sometimes think that they care that much, you always want them to and occasionally you really believe that they do, but trust me, after fifty years of devotion and loyalty to my Club the fact is players don't care as much as fans do.

Granted the players take all the physical stuff and injuries and I honestly believe that they give their all for their club, but it can never truly be their club can it? Well it can't when as a last resort, if all else fails, they can be transferred somewhere else whilst for us fans that is simply not an option. I don't believe that they make the personal, financial and emotional sacrifices that we as supporters make or indeed have to take the ridicule and hurt that us 'mere' fans do. We do all that in the end for a team that are to us the one and only club we follow, who are simply the best there is, and yet we know in our heart of hearts that they are never ever going to win that much 'Silverware' in any one fans life time. Although I was just eleven when I started to understand that fact, I guess back then in Aylesford Street with Jim Drake on his way to the Rovers, it was nothing new really for my Dad, and despite being furious about what had happened, he would have most definitely seen it all before.

Of course since then, as time has moved on, Jim Drake is remembered for what he was, a real hero, and a fantastic player and servant to the Black and Whites, but he had left us for the enemy and that's the way it was when you were a kid, there were no grey areas, in fact everything in our house was black and white! The season, which had threatened at times to trail away, amazingly ended with another Wembley appearance on the cards, well it did until we were walloped 29-9 in the Challenge Cup semi-final by St. Helens. It was a game that Mum decided we would not be attending, and when I heard the result I thought that she had probably made the right decision.

As well as Jim Drake moving across the City, Tommy Harris, one of Mum's big heroes departed for York and the day he left was another black one in our house. However despite a veil of gloom descending over number 23, I was still young and enthusiastic about the game and it all left me pretty unaffected, I just lived for going across the road to the Boulevard every week and during the long winter season it was the usual routine of 'A' team games one week, first team the next. During those long cold winters because there was no pitch side lighting at the Club at all, training was conducted at the local public baths in Madeley

Street. The junior pool was covered every winter with floor boarding, with just the 'big' pool left open for swimming. Incidentally this boarded and cavernous hall was also a regular venue for dances and of course Wrestling which was promoted there once a week by the famous Leeds promoters Relwyskow and Green and often featured the previously mentioned ex Hull hooker and 'now' professional wrestler, Sammy Evans.

Eventually Dad got over his depression and joined the committee formed to organise Jim Drake's brother Bill's testimonial in what was to be a joint benefit to honour the services to the Club of both Bill and Johnny Whiteley.

Enter Arthur Keegan; probably the best Full Back ever saw

Hull/Rovers Combined 17 – New Zealand 6

In the 61/62 season several of the old guard from the glorious 50's like Johnny, Mick Scott, Stan Cowen and a struggling Peter Bateson soldiered on in the first team, although, you'll recall, Peter had been badly injured in that Championship play-off game before the 1959 Wembley final, when Rocky Turner of Wakefield felled him with a late off the ball tackle and he had never really recovered. His confidence was shot and although still a great goal kicker, he was by now mostly restricted to plying his trade in the 'A' team, with his full back spot being taken in the first team by an up and coming hero in the guise of the great Arthur Keegan. We were trying to re build the team but lack of cash and some poor decisions on the signing of amateur players was making for slow progress.

We were still managed and coached by Roy Francis who was responsible for advising the Board on team matters and here it should also be remembered that it was not until the early 1970's, when Francis returned to the Club, that the board stopped picking the teams each week, a situation that is pretty hard to believe in these days of Super

League. Still despite our limited finances we did go out and signed Terry Hollingdrake, a prolific point's scorer from Bramley. Terry was well known in the game as a free scoring winger and he signed for the Club for the then substantial fee of £5,500. To this young and not easily impressed supporter though, he never really appeared to be that good and seemed to spend most of his time being pushed into touch! But what did I know because a glance at the record books shows that he actually was top try scorer that year with 21 touch downs, so I can only presume that he scored a lot of those away from home.

That 1961/62 season of Rugby League started much as the previous one had finished but little did I know that it was to contain a fundamental milestone in the life of this young supporter and something that would see me introduced to my first two real heroes of the Boulevard. The team plodded along in the first few games with the highlight of the early season being a win for a Hull and Rovers Combined team against the New Zealand Tourists. This was a great game to watch containing as it did some fantastic end to end rugby which was crowned by a 17-6 score line in favour of the 'City' team.

Two heroes for the price of one. The Flying Dentist and A. N. Other

Saturday 9th December 1961   *Hull 28 – Bramley 9*

However that December, just as things were settling down for another average season, the news broke in the Hull Daily Mail that Hull had put in an audacious bid for the Leeds star Wilf Rosenberg, or as he was widely known in the West Riding, 'The Flying Dentist'. Dad brought the paper into number 23 that night and immediately called me away from my home work and into the kitchen as he spread The Hull Daily Mail on the table, sending the carefully arranged knives and forks crashing to the floor. There must be, I thought, something pretty dramatic in the news today. He turned the paper to the back page and announced triumphantly, "Look at that Son, now he is a great player". The 'flyer' from South Africa had signed!

I was so excited and could not wait for his first home game that weekend against Bramley. On the days leading up to the game I desperately needed to find more out about this new 'Star' that we had acquired but with only a local paper to rely on, information was in scant supply. So in desperation I resorted to asking our Physics teacher Mr Bell, who hailed from Hunslet on the outskirts of Leeds, (but supported Bramley) just what he knew about 'The Flying Dentist'. I stopped him in the corridor at school before General Science that Wednesday morning and he willingly related all that I needed to know to ensure that, for me, a hero was about to come into my life.

He told me that Wilf was indeed a Dentist with a practise in Leeds, and that fact and his amazing speed with ball in hand, was the reason that he had been given his nick name. 'Belly' went on to tell me that Wilf was a real 'old fashioned' flying winger, whose speciality was to end his runs with a spectacular dive as he crossed the line. He also said that a lot of the Leeds fans over in the West Riding were 'Up in arms' about his leaving and added that he was amazed that Hull FC had got such a sensational player to move over to the Boulevard at all. I simply couldn't wait for Saturday to come. I ducked out of homework on Thursday night and went with Jenksey and a few of my pals to Madeley Street to see if I could catch a glimpse of Wilf at training. Sadly once we got there, and watched the players going into the building it was hard to decide whether he was there or not. One of my mates Steve said, "They all look the same with their clothes on" which I guess summed it up really.

Well over a thousand more spectators than usual turned up at the Boulevard that Saturday as Jenks, Steve Dyson and I watched the game from our most recently adopted vantage point, in front of the Threepenny Stand laid on the roof of the home teams trainer's hut. It was a great view, although you had to keep quiet or the coaching staff would pop their heads over the roof and tell you to "Clear off". For games to be really memorable back then and to send me back home buzzing with the overall experience of it all, I had to have fish and chips for dinner, meet my pals on the car park and watch from the Threepenny stand side of the Boulevard. I was meticulous in my planning that day and everything was set fair for a memorable game.

The Hull team that kicked off at 2-30 that afternoon was I suppose the usual mix of 'has been's' and youngsters, who were, none the less, still all big stars to this young supporter. Hollingdrake was missing because of a leg injury and as that made us short of 'Backs', Loose Forward and Captain Johnny Whiteley played in the centre for one of the few times in his career. This was probably, as one wag said behind us in the Threepenny Stand, "To bloody well make sure we get some value for money out of that bloody Dentist"

There was another surprise in store though because on our wing was a rare sight in those days, a black man. There were hardly any playing in the RL and it was a really unusual sight for us all to see this lean, fit muscular black guy, shining with embrocation, running straight out of the tunnel to take up his place in front of us. Looking on the team sheet in the programme he was down as A.N.Other, which seemed a really strange name for anyone, let alone a rugby player. Thankfully, someone in the know behind us explained that he was probably a "Trialist", 'moonlighting', from Rugby Union. Back then if you were found playing League by the other code's authorities your career was over, so aspiring converts reverted to pseudonyms such as A.N. Other, S.O. Else, Winger, Trialist and even, A. Newman. In fact when international sprinter Berwyn Jones who was probably the fastest man in the country at the time, had a trial for Wakefield in 1964, because he had already played Union, he was given the rather ironic alias of 'Walker'.

No one down at the Boulevard that afternoon had to wait long for some action because the first time 'Mr. Other' got possession of the ball he was off down the field at great pace and it took a brilliant last ditch crash tackle by Wilson the Bramley full back to stop him from scoring with his first involvement in the game. Then, the moment we had been waiting for arrived as Wilf at last got in on the action. Scooping up a loose ball about fifteen meters from his own line, he set off down the field, 'hugging' the whitewash that denoted the right touch line. As he passed level with us scorching down the far Best Stand side, everyone from the trainer's benches in front of us were on their feet. He looked like he would go into touch at any minute, (just as Hollingdrake seemed to do every week) but he handed away three potential tacklers in a thrilling dash to the line. Then, from what seemed like at least five yards out, with just one player left in pursuit, he took off for that famous dive Mr Bell had described so graphically the previous Wednesday. Rosenberg literally flew over the line parallel with the ground to complete his first touchdown for the Club, much to the pleasure of the posse of photographers eagerly waiting behind the dead ball line. As their flash bulbs lit up the dull afternoon for this fan a star was born.

That try and dive will stay in my memory forever, and I was not on my own because one of those photographs even featured in a couple of Rugby League annuals that Christmas!! Wilf scored 2 tries on his debut, whilst the trialist Winger Mr A.N. Other scored three, the last one a magnificent 50 yarder that saw the coaches and bench officials from both clubs applauding the effort, and so, almost as an aside, we won the game 29-9.

It wasn't all about our wingers though because impromptu centre Whiteley, had a great game that afternoon too, he even supplied the passes for one of Rosenberg's and two of the trialist winger's tries. As we sang 'Old Faithful' with the rest of the 'Threepennies' at the end of the game, little did Steve, Jenks and I know that we had just witnessed the birth of a star and the beginning of an era.

Getting 'coined'; the things you do for charity

As an aside and a footnote to that monumental moment in my life as a supporter, it should also be mentioned that at the same match, we witnessed a ritual that was seen as a regular tradition in the 60's and 70's. That year as I have already mentioned it was the joint Testimonial season for both Bill Drake and Johnny Whiteley and a collection for their benefit fund was taken at half time. This saw four members of the players' Testimonial Committee holding a bed sheet at each corner and tilting it towards the crowd. They then walked round the touch line inviting the spectators to throw coins into the sheet. It was all a very orderly affair as the group passed in front of the Best Stand and round the end terracing with folks moving to the front of the crowd and tossing coins into the sheet.

However, when they paraded down the touchline in front of the Threepenny Stand, all hell broke loose. We three lads watched in glee as the regulars magnanimously threw handfuls of coins, not into the sheet, but at the four characters carrying it. A cheer went up every time someone was hit, and a group of young lads followed up behind the procession picking up any coins that had missed the collecting sheet, no doubt on a 'one for you one for me' basis. It was certainly a fact that many a Committee member went home as battered and bruised as the players after these collections, and I bet Dad was glad that he had to work that Saturday.

Sullivan signs and we have the best pair of wingers in British Rugby League.

Saturday 6ᵗʰ January 1962   *Hull 30 – Bradford Northern 6*

After the Bramley game our Directors retired to the Board room to pat themselves on the back after the signing of Rosenberg and to consider what to do about signing their 'trialist', Mr A. N. Other. All of a sudden the whole place was thrown into turmoil when it was reported that three Halifax directors had been sat in the Best Stand and were so impressed they were looking for the young black winger to sign him up for the West Yorkshire club. However he had completely disappeared and fearing the worst our directors instigated a search of the City in which all the hotels were contacted but there was still no sign of the player. Had he just walked off or worse still been 'abducted' by the Halifax Directors? It was a mystery. A catastrophe was eventually averted when it was discovered that our coach Roy Francis had been worried about the rival club's officials as well and taken the player home with him for some tea.

The paper work was done on Sunday Morning and on Monday the Club announced that we had signed the young black winger, who apparently hailed from Cardiff's Tiger Bay area, and who was of course

Clive Sullivan. Thus began an era, which was one that few in Rugby League will ever forget, 'The Sullivan Years!'

I remember just two games later after a freezing cold Christmas that saw most matches in the league cancelled, we played Bradford Northern in a game that I watched in the Best Stand with Steve and a pal of his called Kenny. In that game the scoring roles were reversed, with Rosenberg crossing for three tries and 'Sully' scoring two. We won a famous and unlikely victory by 30-6. There were about 7000 hardy fans who braved the elements that day as the west of the City of Hull began to warm to these two flying wingers that were starting to set the Boulevard alight. As young supporters we loved it. In the remaining half of the season those two players terrorised defences and scored 28 tries between them! I also remember that year we signed two young forwards John Edson and Jim Macklin whose progress we lads followed in the 'A' Team. Of course on top of the try scoring list was, for the second season running 'my mate' Terry Hollingdrake, he had been moved to the centre after the arrival of the two new boys but still did nothing to impress me, although in more recent times my research has led me to believe that he was a fine player, and that I as a young and impressionable youth had got it terribly wrong.

The First team, the 'A' team, the football team

Saturday 31st March 1962   *Hull 'A' 12 – Featherstone 'A' 10*

Looking back on that 1961/62 season I guess that one particular weekend in late March sticks in my memory as a good example of what life at the Boulevard was like back then. We were in a bit of a poor run of form having lost 5 of our last 6 first team games, most recently to Oldham and Wakefield at the Boulevard. Much of the fans discussion and that of the media centred around Peter Bateson, the full back and goal kicker who had been the mainstay of our successful side in the late 50's. As I previously mentioned, Peter had never been the same since he got battered by Wakefield's 'Rocky' Turner and was now regularly described as 'Windy' by certain elements of the Boulevard crowd.

This particular weekend a few of us lads used our season passes to watch the 'A' team take on Featherstone 'A' in the Yorkshire Senior Competition. It was quite a nice day and as always for these games we took up our place on the Threepenny Stand with another 430 diehard supporters. Transfer listed Bateson was playing for the second string that day, whilst Arthur Keegan played in the first team away at Bramley. As is often the case in these situations, Bateson showed up really well in what was a dour game against the Colliers, who were always packed with big brawny forwards straight out of the coal mines, but who were usually short of speedy creative backs.

That day 'Hull 'A' ran out in faded shirts, some of which their wearers obviously found to be badly fitting, with Prop Malcolm Storey's so tight it looked like anytime it would split open down the middle. Tries for Storey and Clive's younger brother Brian Sullivan saw us lead 10-0 at half time but the tough uncompromising West Yorkshire men fought back in the second half, with two stars for the future Tonks and Morgan blasting over the line to score, whilst a young Eric Broom, who was two years later to sign for Hull, brilliantly converted a couple of long range penalty goals.

For Hull FC both Terry Devonshire, a young off half/winger who was to become a future hero and Keith Macklin had big games as did Peter Whiteley and Storey. The main action though took place in the last few minutes when our big trialist prop Wiles was felled by Morgan and a classic brawl in the mud broke out, (something that happened every week in 'A' Team games, in fact if it didn't you felt that you'd been cheated), in the end the referee had to physically wade in to sort things out. As I indicated earlier, in the end Bateson was to prove the hero, and whilst both Hollingdrake and Keegan were missing critical goals for the first team over at Bramley, Bateson stroked over the last minute 52 yard penalty, that had followed the punch up, to make the final score an exciting 12-10 victory to the Hull 'A' Team.

We all trooped down to the front of the stand and away round the ground for the usual ritual of congregating around one of the old 'Tannoy' speaker poles on top of Bunker's Hill at the Airlie Street end.

Here we awaited the result coming in from the first team's game at Bramley. After about ten minutes the speaker crackled into life with the announcement, "The final score from Barley Mow is Hull 8 Bramley 16." Another defeat and more disappointment as we trudged off for our teas chuntering and moaning about the state of our current form.

Later at home at number 23 the Green Sports Mail dropped through the letter box at around six thirty and indicated that the away game at Bramley had ended up 2 tries a piece but ironically for us lot who had marvelled at Bateson's late goal for the 'A' Team that very afternoon, the lack of a successful goal kicker meant that Bramley in the end took the spoils.

Apparently the first team were experiencing problems at half back and so we tried Dick Gemmell at number 6 instead of in his more customary centre spot, but this hadn't worked at all although my hero Wilf Rosenberg, who was Man of the Match, scored two great tries to see us level at half time. The first was after just 4 minutes when he scooped up a loose ball 40 yards out and charged down the wing to finish with his usual spectacular dive in the corner. We missed the conversion but then just before half time Wilf scored again after a 20 yard run that followed a rare flowing move from the Hull backs. Much of what we tried as a team, the paper indicated, was hopelessly out of time and we had dropped the ball regularly, in a game that featured 36 scrums.

The report went on to inform us that Trevor Whitehead was the pick of our forwards and although in the last ten minutes Keegan kicked a penalty goal, four goals in the second half by Bramley's Smith saw them home. The Sports Mail headlines said, "Hull may have to recall Bateson" but those who had made the coach journey to West Leeds told us next day, that Keegan despite his wayward goal kicking, had otherwise had a fine game at full back.

So in what was just another weekend of supporting Hull FC it was another defeat for the first team and a close win for the 'A' Team, however the action was not quite over yet as next day, Sunday, saw us all back at the Boulevard for a special charity event for the Johnny Whiteley Testimonial Fund. It was a football match between a 'Johnny Whiteley

11' and a 'Freddie Trueman 11' (the Yorkshire Cricketer was also having a benefit that year). I went with Dad and stood in the well of the Best Stand. An amazing 6000 people paid admissions totalling £1000 to watch the game and after expenses both beneficiaries received £350 towards their testimonial funds. A half time collection realised £31, and was conducted in the previously described tradition, when once again four brave souls carried that sheet round the ground again, running, as usual, the gauntlet with the marksmen in the Threepenny stand! This time Dad could not escape and took a corner of the sheet 'copping' a cut on the forehead for his trouble. The score ended 4-4 with David Bell (Hull and ER), Johnny Whiteley (2) and Groundsman Ron Tate scoring the home team's goals, whilst Yorkshire Captain Brian Close scored a hat trick for Trueman's 11. Three games and a lot of good fun it was just a typical weekend in 1962 really.

Hull FC on Tour and having to borrow some goal posts

During that hot summer of 1962, we went off to the converted railway carriage at Speights Farm in Mappleton, for what was to be our last summer holiday there. New regulations about both the condition of static caravans and the basic requirements of caravan parks dictated that the site and our 'railway carriage' were to be condemned. However whilst we whiled away the six weeks summer holidays on the sunny east coast, Hull and Rovers embarked on a promotional tour of the South West of England. Even then the administration of the Rugby League favoured these 'missionary' excursions into the heart of Rugby Union territory and as I believe is still the case these days, usually they failed to reap any real rewards. The two deadliest of enemies played each other 3 times in games at Cambourne, Falmouth and Penzance. Hull FC, we were all pleased to learn, won all three matches.

I seem to remember reading in the Hull Daily Mail that 5000 people attended one game where the Council had to provide some goal posts because the Rugby Union club who were tenants of the council stadium, took theirs down and refused to let the rugby league lads use them. For some reason, unknown to most at the time, the Union boys really feared Rugby League back then and tried at every opportunity to belittle and talk down our game. Still a lot of the players really enjoyed the experience and David Doyle-Davidson told me years later, that someone in the crowd at one of the games yelled out, "When are you lot going to start fighting then". I guess they looked upon our thirteen a side code of rugby as one that was played by northern upstarts, who more often than not let their fists do the talking. However this tour actually heralded the start of Arthur Keegan's permanent reign as full back and banished once and for all the spectre of Peter Bateson from the Club. At one of these tour games, when Arthur dropped a towering kick a voice in the crowd yelled "Bring back Peter Bateson". He related later that he thought, "Bloody Hell you travel 300 miles to play a game and there is still a Threepenny Stander waiting to bollock you in the crowd!"

Five 'Half Crowns' for a Season Pass

Saturday 11ᵗʰ August 1962   Hull 28 – Hull Kingston Rovers 11

The 1962/63 season saw me getting my usual season pass which was once again priced at 12/6d, a princely sum that was as usual provided for me by my Mother and Father who always encouraged my attendance at the Boulevard. I remember each year proudly presenting the man at the ticket office the five half crowns that secured the small piece of white card that I used to get into every game at the Boulevard that year. Mum used to cover it in cellophane paper to protect it and kept it 'in a safe place', but there still always seemed to be a scramble on match days to find it. When all the lads met up on the car park for the first game of the season we all agreed on a change of vantage point and decided to try a switch of our preferred viewing position to the Best Stand at the south end of the ground where, back then, there were terraced steps behind a whitewashed wall! The season started with a brand new competition called the Eastern Divisional Championship which was introduced to make up the number of games, following the decision in the close season to create for the first time for over 40 years, a competition which featured two divisions.

As usual the Eva Hardaker Memorial game was first up and we actually beat Rovers 28-11 in a really entertaining encounter. It's always great to beat the old enemy and although the match was deemed a 'Friendly' between the two clubs, we all knew then that there was and still is no such thing in Rugby League and every game against the old enemy is all out war. A great day out though was marred by a real catastrophe for the FC fans, when our 'lucky charm' and Club Captain Johnny Whiteley, went down in a heavy tackle and broke his leg, an injury which saw him miss the rest of what was to turn out to be a pretty poor season for the Black and Whites. We actually went on to meet Hull Kingston Rovers twice in that Eastern Divisional Trophy and twice in the League, so we got used to playing them that year. In fact, as our form was pretty atrocious by the end of the season we were sick and fed up of meeting them and of the fear and dread that derby games bring.

Luckily we had managed to finish in the top half of the league the previous year, so we started in the new First Division in 1962. Of course this format reduced the number of games and so that clubs were not short of income, the RL introduced these new Eastern and Western Divisional Championship Competitions. They were played as mini leagues at either side of the Pennines, until the Division One campaign kicked off on Hull Fair Saturday 6th October 1962.

If the season was disastrous as far as results were concerned it was none the less an eventful campaign for the Club and the fans. We played Halifax, Castleford, Rovers, Huddersfield and Bramley in the Eastern Divisional Competition winning just three of our eight games.

I have found that as you get older you remember more and more of days gone by and less and less of what you did last week. However the recollection of that season when at just 12 years old, I saw every home First Team and 'A' Team game, is still a vivid one and at least my parents got good value for their investment in my season ticket that year. It was a significant season in the British game too, as everywhere gates were plummeting and clubs were finding it hard keeping going at all.

The 'new' First Division campaign ... and a bottle for the linesman!

Saturday 13th October 1962   Hull 25 – Workington Town 25

That was a strange season indeed that featured some low scoring games, a home drubbing by 45-0 from Wigan at the Boulevard, a 4-2 victory at Craven Park and the coldest winter on record that saw us playing no games between Christmas and early March. There were however two games at the start of that first Division One campaign that really stand out for me.

We opened up on 6th October at Wakefield who were one of the strongest teams in the country at that time and we just failed to get a result losing 21-20. Then the following weekend, it was time for the home opener against a strong Workington Town team. As I indicated earlier I had learned very early in my supporting 'career' that all the Cumbrian teams were renowned for a no nonsense approach to the game and for possessing giant packs of forwards. Never the less Workington also had some handy backs and it was to turn out to be a thrilling encounter between two evenly matched teams. The game saw my 'new' hero, Wilf Rosenberg joined on the other flank for only the second time that season by Clive Sullivan, who was still in the forces and having difficulty getting time off for matches.

If this game proved one thing though, it was that if we could get them both on the field at the same time, we had probably the most potent wing attack in the country. Although no one could be faulted for the effort the Hull team put into that game, we didn't play that well at all, but Rosenberg scored two tries both right out of the blue. After ten minutes he took an interception on his own 25 and juggling with the ball he shot off to the corner for one of those spectacular dives that were his trademark. The second try by the South African flyer came late in the second half and brought the house down. We were trailing 18-20 as he gathered a loose ball up with one hand and accelerating away from the immediate challengers, he stepped round the full back on the outside, beating him completely for pace before touching down (with another dive) near the posts. Two minutes later he was robbed of his hat trick by the linesman who stood, flag raised, whilst Wilf dived in at the corner at the Gordon Street end of the Threepennies.

He was seen by everyone in the ground to be yards away from touch and had received the ball well back and inside his centre, so no one knew why he had been penalised but the referee ruled the try out. This caused a rumpus in the old stand directly next to the incident as the linesman got it from the partisan crowd and this led to the inevitable bottle flying onto the pitch and narrowly missing the official involved in the incident. He immediately appealed to the referee and was allowed to swap touchlines to get away from the wrath of the crowd who then threw another empty beer bottle at the new linesman just for good measure and possibly as a warning as to the level of decision making the fans expected from him.

Of course these days that sort of behavior is not tolerated or indeed wanted but in 1962 it was just part and parcel of the culture and legend that was that world famous viewing gallery. Every time it happened the police would march down the touchline to the incident usually accompanied by a chorus of the 'Laurel and Hardy theme' from the massed ranks of the 'Threepennies'. Sometimes a sergeant or overzealous bobby would climb over the fence to try and arrest the perpetrator but this usually caused such a deafening roar of laughter from the supporters that more often than not the local constabulary would just stir menacingly at the crowd from the safety of the touch line. Bottles flying out of that area of the stadium were not a rare occurrence at all back then and were always hailed by the rest of the crowd with a cheer that ran right round the terraces like some verbal 'Mexican Wave' before stopping short at the more cultured spectators who occupied the seats in the 'Best Stand'.

The game ended in a 25-25 draw after Sullivan, despite playing with a knee injury, also scored two tries. More interesting to us lads was our number 6 who we had never seen before. He was hailed in the programme that afternoon as 'yet another' A.N. Other who we found out a couple of days later was in fact Charlie Nimb a South African Rugby

Union half back of some repute. We weren't that impressed with him at all though particularly when on his debut he dropped a ball which was snapped up by the Cumbrians, who then went on to score from the next play the ball. There were however some great performances in the Hull pack with hooker Ralph Walters and Brian Clixby at loose forward showing up really well against the mountainous Workington six. Clixby in fact scored Hull's other try after a neat piece of play from scrum half Tommy Finn. At full back 'Mr. Dependable' Arthur Keegan was 'Man of the Match' and kicked five goals from five attempts but scores to the visitors from Glastonbury (2), O'Neill, Ferraria and Pretorus saw us share the spoils. The following week I watched the 'A' Team beat Batley at the Boulevard, whilst the first team were losing at Wigan and then we were back home again to face Warrington still searching for our first win in the new top division.

Charlie Nimb signs in and gets the Flu!

Saturday 27th October 1962   *Hull 28 – Warrington 15*

This game was to be our first success in the league campaign, with our lads beating the 'Wire Pullers' in a blood and thunder game using a mixture of guts and determination. Charlie Nimb was reported to have showed up well in the Wigan game and so the Club had signed him up on full contract terms and he had relocated to this country and a little rented property in Hawthorne Avenue. This match was therefore his 'Official' debut for the Club (although he was to catch flu the following week and miss the next three games). Despite being a convincing win in the end, it was a close game in many ways and although they made a few costly mistakes in the end Warrington were just 3 points behind us at one point in the second half before we pulled away to win 28-15.

In what was a 'Bottle free' game, our centres George Matthews and Jack Kershaw proved the difference, although Nimb had a great match behind the scrum as he produced some excellent field kicks deep into the opponents half which pinned the Lancastrians back. The first try was a vintage bit of play from the evergreen Bill Drake who rumbled through a gap and went over near the posts with three forwards on his back. But once again it was out wide where we punished the opposition and Wilf Rosenberg ran in for two great scores, the second a blistering touch line hugging 90 yarder, straight from a scrum on our own line.

Arthur Keegan had been injured at Wigan but stand in full back 'that man' Terry Hollingdrake made no mistake with five conversions from five after Nimb had started the first half by missing three attempted penalties on the trot. In the second row Malcolm Storey showed the speed of a centre when he went 40 yards to score after picking up a loose ball and another debutant Terry Devonshire, on the wing for Sullivan (who had not been released from work again), also gathered a Warrington fumble to score a try, which countered three by the visitors from Delooze, Glover and Gilfedder. It was just a relief to get a win and the crowd clambered over the fences and ran onto the field to congratulate the players as the final whistle went. Once the team had disappeared down the tunnel and the strains of 'Old Faithful' had started to drift from the dressing rooms, my pal Steve ran home to get his rugby ball so that we could have a game on the pitch, 'Just like Hull had done earlier' until the groundsman threw us out.

As part of his latest 'economy drive' Dad had stopped having the local newspaper delivered and so I went down the street to Benny Allgoods newsagents at about 6-00pm and waited till the 'Green Sports Mails' were delivered and I think it was apparent even back then that the obsessive behaviour that has followed my supporting Hull FC over the last half a century, was already starting to manifest itself. You see if we had won at home I would religiously go and buy the paper, then take it home, spread it out on the table and accompanied by a bottle of Tizer and a bag of Golden Wonder crisps, I'd read every word about the game I had just seen. When we'd lost I just saved my money!

Mutiny in the Cinema

Saturday 17th November 1962   *Whitehaven 5 – Hull 0*
(match abandoned after 28 minutes due to snow on the pitch)

There was much excitement after that win as we looked forward to playing Wigan next up at the Boulevard, however first we had to negotiate a difficult looking trip to Cumbria for a re match against that team of giants up in Workington. Our players went all the way to this northwest outpost of Rugby League only to have the game abandoned because of heavy snow. At the time that the game was called off the score stood at 5-nil to Hull FC. The following week my Dad heard a great story about the trip in the Supporter's Club. This featured the fact that the Hull FC Board of Directors had decided to 'push the boat out' and arranged for the team to stay over in Cockermouth on the Friday night before the game, in a large 16 room Bed and Breakfast establishment. Once they had all settled in, (the story continued), Ivor Watts who was now our Club masseur suggested that they all go to the local picture house, where Marlon Brando was starring in 'Mutiny on the Bounty'.

Now 'Wattsey' was a big Marlon Brando fan and so to humour him the rest of the team reluctantly agreed, as long as someone else paid. Eventually it was the Chairman who coughed up and paid for everyone to go in. Quite what it looked like with 15 or 16 burley rugby players sat together in a row across the cinema one can only guess but at the interval they spread themselves around the auditorium which was anyway, poorly attended and freezing cold. At least Ivor enjoyed the film but when the lights went up at the end he looked round to find the place empty, as all the FC players, accompanied by the rest of the audience, had sneaked out of the side emergency exit and 'legged' it to the pub!! To crown that, as I have already mentioned the game next day was abandoned when the 50 or so Workington supporters who had brought sweeping brushes from home, could no longer keep the lines on the pitch clear of snow. Finally to top off a troubled couple of days, on the way back the team coach got stuck in a snow drift near Scotch Corner.

'Grandstand' and 'Our Eddie' come to the Boulevard

Saturday 24th November 1962   *Hull 0 – Wigan 34*

So the scene was set for our first televised home game for some years, against Wigan at the Boulevard on 24th November.

In those days the BBC used to broadcast a Rugby League game every other week and on this occasion the 'Grandstand' cameras and of course the ubiquitous Eddie Waring, were heading for the Boulevard. The lorries and vans started to arrive on the Wednesday whilst we were all at school, and the BBC staff spent the next two days erecting a scaffolding rig for the cameras over the top of the Threepenny Stand. My pals and I followed this construction work after school, and got friendly with the BBC production crew. One particular scaffolder called Sid, was usually stripped to the waist whatever the weather and displayed on his torso a relative 'art gallery' of tattoos. He was a real Wigan supporter, and he told us every time we went to talk to him that the Lancashire club would absolutely thrash us that weekend, but we just laughed and said, "No Chance". However our portly tattooed new found friend from Lancashire was soon to be proved frighteningly correct.

A massive articulated lorry carrying a 60 foot hydraulic arm with a broadcasting dish on the top arrived on the Friday afternoon and was parked opposite our house. Looking back it was pretty exciting seeing all this happening particularly when it was right on your own doorstep.

On the day of the game we all tried to get a glimpse of Eddie Waring before he made the long and humiliating walk along the front of the Threepenny Stand to climb to his commentary position on the scaffolding that Sid and his workmates had erected. I discussed earlier in this tome the relationship that Waring had with the diehard supporters of the game and so it was no surprise that when he walked the touchline and climbed the ladder to the gallery poor old Eddie really came in for some stick from the local comics, and for him that day there was just no escape at all. He had quite a sad demeanour in many ways and on that cold November day after the game, whilst with autograph book in hand

I awaited the emergence of the Wigan players, I watched him sneaking out of the ground un-noticed with his collar turned up and his usual trade mark 'pork pie' hat pulled down over his eyes.

That game might have been one of the first Saturday afternoon televised league games at the Boulevard. I say that because, I lived so close to the stadium and yet, as far as I could remember it was the first time I had seen the TV cameras arrive. I decided to watch the first half in the ground, mainly because the BBC only screened the second half of games back then and anyway I wanted to enjoy the banter as the crowd baited Eddie as he sat up there above the Stand. Then during half time I climbed back out over the turnstiles and ran home to watch the rest of the game with my Mum on the TV. It was a strange experience indeed hearing the cheers from the ground across the street and watching the action there in our own front room.

Billy Boston a real legend

Wigan was 'the team' back then and although the Hull side had started their first division campaign reasonably well, Wigan 'took us to the cleaners' that day. By half time I was returning home to watch my favourites trying to come back from a 31-0 deficit. The game was of course shown in black and white and Eddie was at his usual controversial best as commentator. His turn of phrase and choice of words was no different to what we had come to expect although one thing that he said in his commentary that afternoon stayed with me forever.

Waring stated that, "This man you are watching is a phenomenon the like of which you will probably never see again this side of a Sheffield Flood" and later he added his usual, "He's a big lad but his Mother loves him", which as a twelve year old I cringed at then, just as I do now as I write it here. The player that was the centre of this praise was alas not Wilf Rosenberg or Clive Sullivan from my beloved Hull FC. However he was a big lad and not only his mother, but thousands of Rugby League fans did indeed love him, for he was of course, the great Billy Boston. Now for anyone who doubts just what a significant part Billy plays in

RL history, it is worth for a moment considering his pedigree, which in my opinion ranks with anyone you care to mention in the history of the game.

Boston joined Wigan for £3000 in 1953 when they beat off eight other clubs to his signature and he joined the Lancashire club with a massive reputation for scoring tries. Ex. 'Squaddy' Boston signed from the then Army Rugby Union Champions, Catterick Royal Signals and he could certainly cross the whitewash as his Union record of scoring 126 tries in 30 games certainly proved. That's an average of around 4 a game and when he signed for the 'Pies' eight thousand spectators turned out to see him score another four tries for Wigan 'A' on his debut at Central Park. After only six first team games Billy was chosen to tour New Zealand with Great Britain, when in 14 games he broke the tour scoring record with 36 tries.

By the time Boston made his last appearance for Wigan at Central Park in April 1968 he had in 14 seasons amassed almost 600 tries and everyone who saw him play during that career, marvelled at the style and ability that went with the fearsome strength of this iconic winger. For me, a one club supporter, there was still nothing in the game back then that could equal the sight of Billy heading down the wing and going for the line. In defence too, there was never a more forbidding prospect for a centre or winger than to know Billy was after you, intent on a crash tackle. At 15st and 5ft 10ins he was still agile enough to beat his man by 'sleight' of foot but there was no catching Billy once he had the ball on the run, as his hands were like dinner plates and packed amazing power to brush off the opposition as they closed in to try and affect the tackle.

That reputation of strength is further borne out by popular folklore amongst the 'old timers' which claimed that during that great Wembley final, that was featured in the last chapter when we came up against Wigan and Boston, he actually ran down the wing with our diminutive winger Ivor Watts tucked under his arm!! He didn't of course, but as is usually the case with sporting folklore that was soon the story that everyone down the years, who had not seen the game, swore was true.

Billy was one of the only players I have seen who had the ability to make those two heroes of mine Clive and Wilf, look pretty ordinary. It is easy to see how over 50 years later the Chairman of Wigan hailed Boston's signing back in 1953 as "The greatest signing we have ever made" and it's hard to imagine anyone in the modern game playing for 14 years and scoring 592 tries isn't it?

In his book, 'On Rugby League', that man Eddie Waring summed it all up really when he said, "I know that Billy Boston cried the day he quit Rugby League, and everyone in the game should have followed suit, for this was the end of an era, the retirement of one of the greatest personalities our great game has reared" I certainly cherish having seen Boston play at the Boulevard, I remembered him from that great Cup game a few years previously and from this latest drubbing too, when he scored two tries. He was a real hero of mine and is, without doubt, one of the few players who has not pulled on the Black and White shirt that I can say that about.

The coldest winter since 1947; Saved by some chemicals in Widnes and 'An electric blanket' in Leeds

The abandoned Workington game the week previously was certainly a warning of just what was to come in the infamous and deadly winter of 1963. We managed to play on until Christmas with mixed fortunes but a loss at St Helens on 22nd December was to be the last game we played until 7th March the following year. During that time I would watch through my frosted bedroom windows at number 23 as lorry loads of hay were ferried into the Boulevard in a vain fortnightly attempt to warm the pitch up, and us kids went into the stadium when we were not at school to 'help' the ground staff spread it. That was great fun but there was a serious side to it too because clubs depended solely on gate income for their survival and it was imperative that everything that could be done was done, to ensure games took place.

Early in February one hundred and fifty braziers were deployed on the pitch the week before a scheduled game against St. Helens but a blizzard and freezing conditions on the Thursday and Friday prior to the proposed fixture saw that match become just another cancellation in the ever growing backlog of games. The only club that was able to play in that period, besides Leeds, who had an electric under soil heating system, often referred to (probably originally by Eddie Waring) as their electric blanket, were Widnes. These two teams featured on alternate weeks on the TV throughout the big freeze. Widnes, managed to play their home games by living up to their nick name of the 'Chemics', which was originally attributed to their being situated in an area on the banks of the Mersey which was festooned with chemical plants and refineries.

The boffins at one ICI plant came up with a substance that, when spread on the Naughton Park pitch, thawed the surface and left, they claimed, the grass intact, thus allowing them to play their home fixtures when all others were called off. The actual details of this substance was top secret, however as us rugby starved fans watched the games on the TV and the weeks went by, we all noticed that the magic potion, although de frosting the ground, was also slowly but surely removing every blade of grass from it. By early March there was not a bit of green or even brown grass to be seen at Naughton Park and whilst other clubs were getting back into their season and playing on pitches that had benefited from a two month rest, Widnes played it out on a pitch of rolled sand!

Whilst almost the whole national sports programme was abandoned during the first two months of the year the Challenge Cup draw went ahead as usual. However with regional TV not starting till 1968 and no local radio, it was not until we got the Daily Mail next day that we realised we had been drawn against the form team of the season Wigan, (again) at home in early February. That game was of course postponed, with three more aborted attempts to complete the fixture soon following in its wake and despite the best efforts of dozens of volunteers, hundreds of braziers and lorry loads of straw it was just not possible to stage the lucrative fixture.

'Twagging' from school for the Cup!

Thursday 7th March 1963   *Hull 0 – Wigan 7*

We were all totally starved of live rugby when finally the Wigan game was scheduled for Thursday 7th March with a 2-30 kick off. Thursday was early closing day in Hull, and with no floodlights it must have seemed a good afternoon to stage the fixture. That, of course, suited my Dad, (the Butcher) down to the ground, it was his afternoon off but no one it would appear told Bill Pattison our head master at Kelvin Hall about early closing day!!! As the hay was spread on the Boulevard in the week preceding the game, Steve and I, plotted just how we were going to 'twag off' school to see the match without our school or parents knowing about it.

That Thursday we left school after afternoon registration and walked all the way from Bricknell Avenue to the Boulevard arriving at about 2-15. We thought things would be relatively quiet, but the queues were amazing, snaking across the car park and out onto Airlie Street. It seemed everyone was starved of the game we all loved, and it was no surprise when the final attendance was announced as 10,329 (paying £1,355).

The kick off was actually delayed by five minutes so that everyone could get in through the turnstiles and when we finally got a position on the terracing at the Airlie Street end the teams were already out on the field. The remnants of the straw, that had been cleared to form massive piles around the touch line, were strewn all over the pitch, but who cared? We were about to witness our first game of rugby for months. Sadly our mercurial winger Clive Sullivan could not again get time off from the Army and Bill Drake our Captain who had pulled up at training on the beach at Bridlington the previous Tuesday, was out too with an injured knee. Otherwise we were at full strength against a Wigan side that read like a 'who's who' of Rugby League.

Referee Lawrenson blew the whistle and we attacked the Gordon Street end furthest away from our vantage point. A quick check of a programme, over the shoulder of a short guy in front of me, indicated that Wilf Rosenberg was playing, so that was really all that mattered to me. I was really up for this one and so I was pretty despondent when Arthur Keegan who was usually so dependable with the boot, missed three penalties in the first ten minutes. The first half though was all Hull as we mounted attack after attack in their twenty five yard area. Both Matthews and Jim Macklin fell to desperate last ditch tackles by the Wigan full back Bolton as we pressed their line. Then Dick Gemmell got the ball and quickly side stepped Davies to send out a peach of a pass to Rosenberg who shot down the wing towards the advancing full back. As he approached Bolton, Wilf kicked ahead and it was 'try on' as the ball stuck in the mud over the try line where the tractors that had cleared the pitch had been turning, but he was blatantly obstructed by the Wiganer, who stuck out a leg in his direction and brought him crashing down. The resultant penalty was again missed by Keegan.

Scrum half Tommy Finn and young Terry Devonshire on the wing then linked on the other side with only an ankle tap on the youngster by Billy Boston saving the day for the visitors. Pitchford, McTigue and Collier in the Wigan pack were really 'fired up' and charged into our lads but they were well matched by Mick Scott, Hockley and Sykes in the Hull engine room. At half time Wigan led by a solitary Ashton goal which he added to straight after the break following a foul by Walters on Wigan's Pitchford. But at 4-nil we were still in it and without doubt the best team and with Ralph Walters at hooker winning the scrums 16-11 there was plenty of ball for our backs to play with. Two great breaks by Finn and Matthews just lacked the necessary backing up and then Rosenberg was just tackled into touch in front of the Threepennies, as he was about to launch his dive for the line.

With just ten minutes to go it looked like we had scored. Keegan joined the attack and shot towards the line, he beat their full back and was about to cross the whitewash when from nowhere winger Carlton hammered him to the ground and he dropped the ball. With two minutes to go and the game evenly poised all the accolades were going to the brilliant Hull defence when the inevitable happened. After all the Hull pressure and valiant defending, Wigan got the only try, as a break by Lyon saw his wayward pass fall into the arms of that man Billy Boston who charged down the touchline and right over Devonshire and Keegan to score in the corner, Ashton missed the goal, but shortly afterwards the whistle went and we were out of the Cup.

In the end, the much fancied Wigan outfit, in keeping with their 'Favourites' tag, had scraped home 7-0 but we had really put up a great fight! The whole day was an adventure which not only included a great match, and the first I had seen on a Thursday, but also the first and only time I twagged off school. My day however came to something of an ignominious end when on the way out of those big Airlie Street gates, I bumped into Dad, who was not too impressed at all with the 'bunking' off school idea, something that I seem to remember resulted in a few nights grounded at home! Still what a memorable occasion it was and if you're going to skip school there is hardly likely to ever be a better reason to do it!

As the milder weather continued the Club managed to get an 'A' Team fixture played across the road that weekend and once I had persuaded Mum to let me go out without Dad's knowledge, Jenksey and I were entertained by a full complement of hopefuls in their faded irregular hooped shirts playing out an entertaining encounter against Huddersfield 'A', that unfortunately we narrowly lost. Our team that day included Keith Barnwell, Brian Sullivan, Eddie Wanklyn and David Doyle-Davidson as well as the ubiquitous trialist's A.N. Other and S.O. Else.

The Beatles and the Police

Around that time the Club, blessed with a host of promising backs, transferred my arch nemesis Terry Hollingdrake to Bramley, and in an effort to improve a playing surface that was in a poor condition after that awful winter we took on a new groundsman Fred Daddy, who I got to know quite well. He would frequently chase us kids out of the ground when we climbed over the wall from Airlie Street to retrieve our rugby ball but on occasions we also helped him with moving straw and pulling that big concrete roller he used every Monday in a vain attempt to keep the pitch level.

At this point in my story I should also mention an incident involving a lad called Lenny a gangling youth of about 17, who always wore jeans and engineers boots and who I had got to know simply because we both frequented the Threepenny Stand. He used to join us young lads for a kick about on the Club car park and it was on one of these occasions that he told us about a pop group he had been to see at the Majestic Ballroom on Witham a few nights earlier. They were called the Beatles. Lenny was a friend of lots of the local bands that played at the Church Hall dances around the area and according to him the Liverpool band wore 'superb' leather outfits but their music was "nothing special". Over the years I reflected that Lenny was probably never destined to make a name for himself as a music critic.

The group that were to change the face of popular music forever actually became a little more famous in the area a couple of nights later when the Hull Daily Mail reported that their guitarist a certain George Harrison had appeared at Goole magistrates court. He was charged with running the group's van off Boothferry Road and into a ditch on the way back to Liverpool from that self same concert. Little did we or Lenny know, just who he had seen at the little Dance Hall in Witham although he's probably 'dined out' on that story ever since.

Chapter Five

Mum and Dad go to 'The Pictures'

School was still a pretty unpalatable experience as I continued to consistently underachieve but it had to be done and so each morning during term time I either walked to school down Walton Street and caught the bus to Bricknell Avenue or did the two bus bit and went round through the City centre. It was still though a long way to go each day, however in those days of Grammar schools, Technical High Schools and Secondary Moderns, everyone was on the move at 8-00 each morning and it was just something that you did.

The buses around school times were just like a menagerie, lads threw missiles out of the open back doors and deposited the contents of less fortunate kid's satchels out of the upstairs windows as the bus sped along. Cliff and Elvis songs were sung at the top of our voices and more often than not the conductor would turf us all off the bus a long way short of school! They were great days, when nothing really seemed to matter besides rugby and having fun, and despite the constant tirades of our teachers, school didn't bother us much either. The teachers at Kelvin did their best and I guess looking back we tried ours too but despite the lack of streaming and all the modern ideas it was still literally us and them. Them being the swots who sat near the front and soaked up knowledge like sponges and us the 'thickos', who sat at the back studying for a 'degree' in gazing out of the windows.

It was about this time too that I remember my Mum and Dad made a very rare visit to 'the Pictures'. This was an outmoded means of entertainment back then, Steven Spielberg, 'Star Wars', 'Indiana Jones' and the renaissance of the cinema, were still almost 20 years off and most establishments in the City were experiencing dwindling attendances and being run down or shut altogether, something that seemed to be brought on by the increasing popularity of TV. We all referred to them as the 'local flea pit' and I guess like many who lived around us my parents were just in essence the casual 'Sound of Music', 'South Pacific' 'West Side Story' type of movie goers.

This particular visit to the Carlton Cinema on Anlaby Road was a little bit special though and was in the form of an organised 'Outing' for the members of the Hull Supporters' Club. So what was so special? Well it was the showing of the new Lindsey Anderson film, staring a young Richard Harris, called 'This Sporting Life'. I was packed off to Martin Tomlinson's house in the Avenue across the road, where I spent the evening with him and his parents as this was definitely, I was told, not a film for 'youngsters'. I have watched it several times since and really rate it as a great period study of our game back in the early 60's. It is I accept certainly dated; that's part of its charm, but it's definitely a really good study of the adversity and struggles endured by the average Rugby League player in the 50's and 60's.

Whether the administrators of the game like it or not, ours is a northern sport and always has been, so for me this is the definitive movie about Rugby League in those 'bad old days'. It was filmed in and around Wakefield in the early part of 1962 and had several titles before 'This Sporting Life' was finally settled upon. Produced in glorious Black and White (is there any other colour?) it tells the story of an injured ageing player, Arthur Machin and his reflections on his life. Richard Harris starred and it is widely reported that he at first found it a nightmare filming with the Trinity players.

Popular folklore in the West Riding of Yorkshire indicates that he had any pretence of impending stardom knocked out of him on the first day of filming when Rocky Turner ran round a scrum and 'administered' a trade mark stiff arm tackle, the sort that 'did' for our Full Back a few years earlier. Turner was, you will remember, the player that just about finished Peter Bateson's career, so I guess roughing up a 'softy' film star would be no problem. Most of the filming was done at Wakefield's stadium, which was then known as Belle Vue. If for nothing else it is worth watching the movie just to see that famous Stadium as it was then, with its pergola like West Stand, a fantastic feat of architecture which had four wonderful brick chimneys on the top and which can be glimpsed in all its former glory.

The film succeeds, where so many sporting films fail, in that it gets the atmosphere absolutely right. There are some great performances too, from Leonard Rossiter as the 'weasely', 'Rigsby' like reporter, and Arthur Lowe (developing his character for the future Capt. Mainwaring in Dad's Army), as the club Chairman. The good people of Wakefield were paid the princely sum of £2-12 shillings a day to act as extras standing on the terraces and cheering to order, whilst script writer David Storey brought some authenticity into the plot by drawing on his previous experience of paying his way through Leeds Art College, by playing for Leeds 'A'.

For real film buffs there is also a cameo by Glenda Jackson, making her first ever, nonspeaking, film appearance as the pianist in the fictitious Dolphin pub during a bawdy player's night out. This fact only came to light a few years ago when she sent another extra in the film, Wakefield legend and ex referee Albert Raynor, an 80th Birthday card! Anyway Mum and Dad seemed to enjoy it too, and they talked about nothing else but 'This Sporting Life' with the neighbours for the next few days.

Taking the salute at Craven Park

Saturday 17th August 1963   *Hull 15 – Rovers 11*

On the rugby field there is little doubt that 1963/64 was probably the worst season the fans had been asked to endure since well before the Second World War. After another hot summer, things for Hull FC started reasonably well.

For the traditional Eva Hardaker Memorial Trophy opener, four of us travelled down to Craven Park in 'Bully' Spriggs's Dad's new Ford Anglia, and we all felt very important as we parked on the 'Official Car Park' in front of the Holderness Road Ground. Bully, who was driving, was not named because he was one to push folks around or anything, his sinusitis caused him to snort a lot and I guess looking back he simply really did look like a Bull! For the first taste of rugby that season there was certainly a good attendance that day and as it was raining and Bully was feeling a bit flush after getting his regular bonus from work, he treated us to seats in the Main Stand. We watched the game in the seating blocks adjacent to the side of the Stand, which back then had glass panels so the spectator's view of the try lines was not impeded. We all really enjoyed the match and the banter and experienced a great victory over the old enemy. Despite being just 'a friendly' (as I have said before there is simply no such thing between such bitter rivals) it was always good to beat the Rovers particularly at Craven Park. In the end after a close game it was the trusty boot of Arthur Keegan that converted the two decisive penalties to send us home happy.

We won 15-11, and buoyed by that feeling you get of not wanting to flee too quickly the scene of a 'special' victory, we remained in our seats after the game talking rugby and what we were all going to do that night to celebrate. When we finally left the stand and went back to the car the Car Park was practically deserted. In jubilant mood Billy drove around the perimeter of the cinder concourse with me sat on the bonnet of the car, waiving my scarf and singing 'Old Faithful' at the top of my voice. This drew a few abusive shouts and gestures from the remnants of the Rovers crowd that milled around the player's entrance waiting for autographs but I retorted with a 'Winston Churchill salute' in their direction, whilst Billy shouted back from the car that he would be surprised if any of the Rovers players could write anyway! Then, with shouts that questioned our parenthood ringing in our ears, we beat a hasty retreat down Holderness Road and back towards the relative safety of West Hull.

Rugby was everything back then, and I suppose that's when I even started dreaming about it. The dreams were usually muddled and fraught with desperation, although I particularly remember one of those anxiety dreams that you have when you're young (well actually I still have them to this day) where I would have a ticket for the big game, probably a final in Leeds, and was leaving Hull in plenty of time for the kick off. I get on the train and it's going to Scarborough, then onto a motor bike which loses a wheel, then into a taxi that gets a puncture and a bus that runs out of petrol, in fact every attempt I make to get on with the journey to the West Riding sees me travelling further and further in the opposite direction. By ten to three I am in somewhere like Selby desperately trying to hail a cab, it gets a puncture and so it goes on until I wake up in a cold sweat with the sheets round my neck safe and sound at home in bed. Most fanatical sports fans have dreams like that but few admit to them. I've sadly endured them, from time to time, all my life!

Hello Johnny, bye, bye Roy!

The following week of that 1963/64 season started with the visit of Leeds and we got the usual 'stuffing'. Next up though was the long trip to Widnes and we somehow came back from Naughton Park with a very creditable win. This was a complete surprise and gave everyone connected with the club tremendous heart for the season ahead. How wrong we all were to be proved, as what it actually heralded was a fourteen game losing run! That ended with an away win in the Eastern Divisional Championship to Keighley, but in the league by Christmas we were stuck at the very bottom of the table with just that Widnes victory to our name.

That situation sadly led in the autumn to the end of Coach Roy Francis and his position was taken by Johnny Whiteley, who was still struggling with injury. It was in fact a busy board meeting on 29th October that saw Francis resign to take up the coaches job at Leeds, Johnny appointed as his successor, Bill Drake placed on the transfer list at £5000 and the announcement of the debut for young Bill Pickersgill the following weekend, a player who had only signed from the amateur scene three weeks earlier. As a young supporter this was for me my first real experience of just how fickle sports fans can be, as Francis went from a hero, to someone that everyone on the terraces wanted to see the back of. That was my first managerial casualty as a fan and because Roy had always been there in the background rather like a surrogate father figure looking after my team, his leaving hit me hard.

Francis had always been our coach I had known no different and even though I was only a young lad I would miss him. Over the years you realise that the most intense relationship you can have is between coach and fan. Supporters have of course a great affinity with players but they can rarely change the whole feel of our lives like coaches can. When things are bad they get the blame and we all lay into them, although rarely are they hailed as the players are, when things go well. When some are sacked you're just relieved, whilst others, like in more recent times Peter Sharp, depart leaving a sense that you're losing an old friend. On the other hand when a new coach is appointed you are allowed to dream even bigger dreams than you did before and I should know because to date, I estimate in 50 odd years of watching Hull FC I have seen around 26 incumbents in that coaching role.

However, on this occasion, although a new broom is expected to make a difference, with limited resources and diminishing attendances, Johnny Whiteley had no magic wand and under our new coach the Club fared little better. We won only two competitive fixtures before Christmas, in fact between the Widnes game in late August and early February we won just once, in that game at Keighley.

New blood!

So despite a new coach, the current two division system coupled with our poor form dictated that we were doomed to relegation, it had looked that way from about November but thankfully our position in the First Division was saved by the RL scrapping the two tier system at the end of that season. To even get through the fixture list though we desperately needed some new faces because along the way some players just disappeared, whilst others retired and the quality of youngsters coming through to replace them had suddenly become poor to say the least. In the sixties of course you could have as many players on your books as you liked because they only got paid when they played, so Johnny decided to go on a recruitment drive. The Board found a bit of cash in the form of signing on fees to waive under the noses of potential targets and into the Club came Eric Broom a reliable goal kicking Prop from Huddersfield, Jim Neale a real 'hard man' back row forward from Cumbria, Geoff Stocks a high stepping winger also from Huddersfield, and a lad called Davis, again from the same club, who was a half back that never really made the grade.

With the exception of Davis, the others went on to make a total of over 450 appearances for the Club, so that was good business. Chris Davidson and Alan McGlone also joined from local rugby and soon started to make their mark. It was all good trading by Whiteley but it did little, at first at least, to turn the tide. Jim Neale was a great bloke: as hard as nails on the pitch and always the centre of any scuffles or fights. However away from the game he was a real nice guy, I should know because he lived in a club owned house at number 11 the Boulevard and I used to deliver his paper! Our pack was considerably lighter than the all conquering six of the 50's and although more mobile they had, like our speedy backs, a real problem getting any joy on a muddy Boulevard pitch that often resembled that Chocolate Pudding you got served up for school dinners at Kelvin Hall. To try and improve the surface of the playing area our new grounds man Fred Daddy deposited copious amounts of sand on the pitch which, when it rained, just made it worse. In winter it was like treacle, and in summer you had to protect your eyes from what resembled a dust storm in the Gobi Desert.

Heading for academic oblivion

As for my life, well school was panning out to be an unmitigated disaster and my Mum was already preparing folks for the worst by announcing to everyone that "Academically he's 'finding it tough' but will, turn out to be good with his hands". That didn't really bother me as my interest in music, railways and of course my rugby team, were surpassed almost overnight by a sudden developing interest in girls! They had always been a hindrance and if you like, an occupational hazard of mixed schooling. They, I remember, always seemed to me to have a strange aroma about them that was far removed from the liniment and chewing gum that I loved around the tunnel at the Boulevard, and I guess that was about the time that things started to go downhill big time. Still my trips to St Matthew's youth club on a Sunday after Church certainly started to become a deal more interesting! 'Good with my hands' I was proving to be!

That October at Kelvin we were all herded into the Assembly Hall to be addressed by Bill, the headmaster, where we were lectured long and vociferously about the evils of young lads working on an evening at the Hull Fair. Now here, I thought, was something to consider, as I had never thought of that one before!! So that year at Hull Fair, for £1 a night, I was employed on Doubtfire's Bombers, helping young ladies in and out of the tiny jet planes that whizzed round expelling compressed air. Mum and Dad thought that I was just going to the fair with my pals every night, but between 6-00 and 10-00 I got my first crude introduction to the world of work.

Travels with my pals … my first International and the great Reg Gasnier!

Wednesday 16th October 1963   Great Britain 2 – Australia 28

It was during that season too, that the Aussie touring team came to this country for the first visit that I, as a fan, had really been aware of. To this day I am still a one team guy and always have been. My Club comes first and Rugby League in general at both club and international level is a poor second. I think though that I am also pretty patriotic, although to this day I find it hard to get really excited about any international game simply because it doesn't feature Hull FC. The international side is OK and worthy of support as long as we as a Club have some representation in it, but Hull FC is the only team I have ever got really passionate about.

However back in 1963 all the talk in the papers was of the impregnable Australian Tourists that were to visit this country to play both club and international games. This hyping of the unbeatable Aussies got us all talking one night at youth club, where despite my age, (I was still too young to be a member) I was allowed to attend, and Barry Johnson, 'Bully' Spriggs, Mike Day and a couple of the other older lads decided that they would make the trip down to London to see the first test match as it was to be the first ever to be played at Wembley Stadium. The touting of the game in the press had reached unprecedented levels and it was billed that morning in the Sunday People as, 'The British Lions against the 'Invincibles'.

I went home that night and begged my Mum and Dad to let me go with the lads, but Dad said, as Dads do, that I was too young and it was much too far for me to go without my parents! Mum winked, as Dad left the room and whispered that she would, 'Work on him'. Next night 'surprise, surprise,' it was 'homemade' meat pie and mashed potatoes with gravy for tea, followed by Mum's 'special' rice pudding, Dad's favourite!! And so it was that a couple of days later Dad reneged on his original decision, and I was off to the game. One thing that my father had not however realised was that the game was in midweek, and as the club had a small amount of tickets on sale, I made sure that I had been across the road to the Boulevard to get mine, before he had chance to realise. So not only was I going to the match but I was also getting a day off school to do it too!! Things could not have been better.

The match took place the week after Hull Fair, on 16th October 1963 and just 4 days after I had watched the Tourists fielding their second string players at the Boulevard when they took on a combined Hull and Rovers team which they beat 23-10.

The lads and I aimed to get the 6-45 train to Doncaster and change there for an express to King's Cross. It was still dark at 6-00am that Wednesday when 'Bully' called for me, only to receive a right ear full about looking after me from my Mum and Dad, the latter standing at the front door wearing those obscenely 'gaping' pyjama's he seemed to save especially for such occasions. He told Bully to take care of me and that he 'Knew where he lived' if he didn't, and at last, with my illicit Hull Fair earnings in my pocket, we set off for the station where we met the other chaps from the youth club. The journey to Doncaster was pretty uneventful although there were about a dozen or so rugby supporters from Hull all travelling to the same destination as ourselves. There was certainly none of the high jinks on the train that I had seen that year Mum and I had gone down to the 'smoke' to watch the Cup Final. I was well occupied though with my train spotting, whilst the other lads, who were all around 16-20, produced a couple of bottles of Hull Brewery Amber and passed them around. I refused a swig and concentrated as it got light, on looking out of the window and tucking into the first of the banana sandwiches that my Mum had packed me up.

The connecting train at Doncaster was late by about an hour, so whilst they went off to the Station Buffet I continued collecting the numbers of the 'Streak's', 'Pacific's' and 'A1's' I saw whilst sat on a porter's trolley at the end of the platform. We eventually arrived at King's Cross station at around 11-30 and as we got off the train, the general melee and hustle of that great terminus and the capital itself smacked an impressionable 13 year old, straight in the face. I just could not believe how many folks there were milling about, and being a lad from a City with a small ethnic community, just how many of them had black, yellow or brown faces. This was only my second visit to the City of London and Wembley, and I was still totally overawed by it all.

Johnny, one of the lads in our crowd who I did not know very well, had an uncle who had a pub in the centre of the City, and so it was decided we would go there. I'd never been in a pub before so this was a real adventure, but I was reassured about the whole thing when Bully said "Don't worry about it, we'll sneak you in, but don't tell your Dad or he'll kill me!" After changing tube trains twice we arrived at our destination and once back out in the daylight, we quickly found the public house, which as the second part of this story unfolds plays an important part later in this supporter's life! The Prince of Wales in Drewery Lane was, even back then, a smart black and white half wooded building, with a welcoming and quite serene atmosphere. It was a real oasis when contrasted with the goings on outside in the street where everything was racing twice as fast as it seemed to do in Hull. I had a bottle of pop and a very strong Cheese and Onion sandwich, we sang a couple of chorus's of 'Old Faithful', much to the disdain of the hostelries regular lunchtime custom, and soon, clasping my ticket in my hand, we retraced our steps to the tube and headed for Wembley. It was just starting to pour with rain!

I might have been one of the youngest in our group, but I was still one of the only ones who had actually been to Wembley before, so I knew the ropes. When we arrived it was 'chucking' it down and as I lead the lads from Wembley Park Station down Wembley way to the ground I triumphantly pointed out the turnstile that my Mum and I had used for the final in 1960. The whole place overawed us, although I guess looking back it was getting a bit tatty for a National Stadium. Our seats, despite being quite a way up the terracing, were still out in the rain and even before the game had kicked off we were soaked to the skin. The attendance I remember was poor and the fare on the pitch, as far as the Great Britain team was concerned at least, was little better.

The touring team that year contained one player that I could just not wait to see in the flesh, Reg Gasnier, he was the player that everyone in the media and the game in general were talking about and there had even been a four page spread about him in last Christmas's Rugby League Annual. Reg was, and still is I guess, the best centre to ever pull on the green and gold shirt, and despite the weather, his display did not disappoint anyone. At just 23 he was the youngest ever captain of Australia and in a dream centre partnership with Graham Langlands he terrorised the British Lions from the outset. In an amazing display against the elements and what you could only call, a mediocre Great Britain Team, Reg scored a hat trick of tries, whilst Langlands landed 5 goals, with a soaking wet leather ball, from difficult positions, usually against the wind.

As the game wore on the rain got heavier and heavier and in the end a sad and bedraggled British 13, trooped off the pitch following a 28-2 trouncing. I didn't care though, even at an early age, I knew that as it was not a defeat for Hull FC, it just couldn't hurt so much, although I did realise that I had seen someone in Reg Gasnier that was really special. I remember thinking that perhaps Trevor Carmichael and Keith Barnwell, my heroes in the centre for Hull still had a bit to learn!! The 'Gas.' though was not the only star of the team because the tourists also boasted other household names like Muir, Hambly and Irvine. It was a great 'milestone' in my young life and one I guess you can understand has stayed with me to this day.

The journey home is a bit of a blur really, although I think that Bully and Mike got me safely back to Aylesford Street by midnight and then it was up for school at 6-30 next morning!! Trainspotting, my first pub visit, the Tube and Reg Gasnier; what a memorable outing to the capital that was.

As for Gasnier well, I am just honoured to have seen him play, he continued his rich vein of form throughout the tour which went from bad to worse for the British team. The next Test in November was televised from Swinton's Station Road ground, and I watched at number 23 with Mum, as even Eddie Waring ran out of superlatives; the Tourists trouncing us 50-12. This was a real low point for British International rugby and although we came back to win the third test 16-5, the Ashes went back to Australia with the tourists. Gasnier went on to play a total of 39 tests for his country scoring 26 tries and is still probably the best centre I have ever seen. He was certainly good at amassing points, as in a career which ran from 1959 to 1967 he scored a total of 219 tries and kicked 31 goals!! Not bad for a bloke who developed a serious knee condition and had to retire at the 'tender' age of 28.

'With The Beatles'

Whilst all this rugby stuff was going on, the rest of life was just all school and bed really although the weekend fix of Hull FC or Hull 'A' just about kept me going despite it being the worst season in decades. However for everyone who was around in those days something else was happening that was to change all our lives. Across the Pennines in Liverpool the four mop topped lads that Lenny had so quickly dismissed a few months earlier were leading the Merseyside music revolution and everyone you met was a fan of the Beatles. Looking back, it's hard to know now what music was around before the Beatles, although I guess there was plenty of it. Mum and Dad liked anything from Bing Crosby to Cliff Richard and quickly took the stand of most parents describing The Beatles, Mersey Beats, Gerry and the Pacemakers and the Searchers as "just a row". Especially, that was, when I was glued to the TV every Saturday night as they all appeared on the BBC's only pop music programme, 'The 6-5 Special.'

That same autumn, after much persistent pleading I was officially admitted to the St. Matthew's youth club, I had been allowed to go in the past because I was always hanging out with the rest of the older lads, but I was still 2 years under the official age for joining. We had to raise some funds because the Church Hall badly needed some repairs to the roof and so we decided to put on a show in there one Sunday after Evensong.

That night was a real culture shock for me because after singing the Magnificat and Nunc Dimitus in the Choir across the road at St Matthews I rushed straight to the Hall to grab my Beatle Jacket and Cardboard Guitar to pose with three of the other lads Dave, Barry and Mike, as the Beatles. All the old timers from Church came along to a show that included a couple of short plays, a monologue or two, someone playing the piano and us lot. We went down a storm, from the first bars of 'She Loves You', we mimed and mimicked along with the music as all the girls from the youth club screamed out "John" and "Ringo" and the old folks put their fingers in their ears and grimaced. We raised lots of cash too, although the vicar did receive some rather cutting comments from the neighbours down the Boulevard about the noise levels disturbing their viewing of 'Sunday Night at the London Palladium'. Still those who went seemed to enjoy it; church halls back then were real 'community centres' and the place was packed that night when some much needed funds were raised.

The real Beatles 'live and inaudible' at the ABC Regal

The mayhem continued when the actual Beatles made their second trip to the City to play at the Regal Cinema on Ferensway, on 24th November. Two weeks prior to that the tickets had gone on sale and there were queues of teenagers twice round the building 24 hours before the ticket office opened. In the end on Police advice, they had to open up early, for fear of a riot breaking out. Jenksy and I went to town that day just to see the crowds in the queue, something that several hundred other spectators had also done. We earned a bit of cash too, running backwards and forwards to Mackman's the Bakers for sandwiches for the queuing fans, who were famished but dare not leave the line in case they lost their place. It was an amazing scene. Girls sang Beatle songs and danced, whilst the boys tried to look 'hard' in their Beatle Jackets and winkle-picker boots. The whole place, which was right next to the bus station, was in complete uproar.

Sammy 'Jonno' Johnson who had just moved into number 16 in Aylesford Street was a member of the St. John Ambulance Brigade and was regularly seen at the Boulevard on stretcher duty. He was, along with just about everyone else in the Brigade, on duty at the Regal on the night of the concert and described the scene he found there on many occasions afterwards. He related with great dramatic gestures that the whole place went berserk and apparently you could not hear a word or a note that the band played for the noise from the audience. But no-one seemed to care. Sammy said that they had over 300 'cases' that night as people fainted and were trampled and crushed as the crowd went mad! With over 1200 inside there were another 2000 outside trying to get a glimpse of the 'Fab Four' who were smuggled, Jonno said, in and out of the building in a van through the back staff entrance!! It was the talk of the City for over a week and the Daily Mail had a field day on both the letters and front pages. The front page had graphic descriptions of the concert augmented with even more graphic photographs of girls crying and screaming. Whilst the letters page of the paper was reserved for the rather disapproving comments of the older generation. We as kids though were having none of the latter and were all converted over night as 'Beatlemania' swept the Country. It was then that I thought I might just have a bash at the guitar myself, but more of that later.

So it's come to this? We rejoice at beating Bramley

Saturday 15th February 1964   *Hull 12 – Bramley 8*

1964 was a year when we saw the end of a real institution if you lived near either the Hessle or Anlaby Roads. It was that year that Hull Corporation finally scrapped the trolley buses which were the stable method of transport backwards and forwards from the town. On rugby days there used to be a special service which augmented the usual 69 Anlaby Road trolleybus, which was numbered 169 and actually ran down the Boulevard to Malm Street to deliver fans to home games and then they queued up at a temporary bus stop outside St Matthew's Church Hall to take them back afterwards. As young lads we used to go down there to watch the conductors turning the buses around using the long bamboo pole that they stowed underneath the chassis. With these they detached and re-attached the electric terminals that connected the bus to the over head supply.

However back to the rugby and the game that stands out for me that season was our twelfth home game against Bramley on 15th February 1964. This was once again an Eastern Divisional match but by the end of it we had a win, so who cared? Although only about 4000 people attended the match we actually managed to come out on top after weeks of failing miserably. I guess I remember it particularly because Wilf Rosenberg scored one of the tries, whilst one of the Bramley efforts was scored by Terry Hollingdrake the ex FC player, who Wilf replaced. I watched the game from the Threepenny Stand and remember it was a cold afternoon with squall's of sleet lashing down the pitch towards the Gordon Street end.

For the first twenty minutes we came out and played like a team possessed as, with the wind at our backs, we scored two tries one by Wilf and a memorable solo effort by our centre Mountain. A strange story surrounds Mr Mountain because if I remember rightly he joined the Club in the late 50's and was then called Ali, but he changed his name because of "the abuse he was getting!" How times change, however I really don't know just why he chose Mountain but he scored a great try that day. Still I digress, the game flowed quite well in the rest of that first half but in the second with the sleet in our faces the 'Cream' were dragged into a dour forward battle and all we could manage against the elements were two penalties by Keegan. Hollingdrake's try for Bramley and a 'roly poly' forward effort from Morgan brought 'the Villagers' back into it, but we hung on for a memorable, if not scrappy, 12-8 victory. We had won at home for the first time in almost a year! Never to be understated the headlines in that evening's Sports Mail read "Hull break the Boulevard Hoodoo..... at long last". We had broken it and we were pleased, but in reality it was only Bramley.

One hundred years of Hull FC

In 1964, there was not much to shout about at the Boulevard although a run of six straight wins did give the crowd some hope and with all our new players settling in, it was a better season, but gates were falling and ended up at a level that was to prove to be a post war low. This was a shame because it was the 100th anniversary of the founding of our Club and a special brochure, to commemorate this most significant of years was produced by two Directors Albert Saville and Reg Lee. Benny Allgood's sweet shop in Airlie Street was selling them and Dad brought one home along with his evening paper, the first day that they were on sale. It was, as I remember, a glossy document of about 120 pages and sold for two shillings and six pence. It had a very prestigious forward in the form of a typed letter from The Right Honourable the Earl of Derby who was back then the President of the Rugby League. Within the pages of the Centenary Brochure were articles by luminaries ranging from The

Chairman of the Rugby League, to Mike Ackroyd who was Dick Tingle's predecessor and FC reporter at the Hull Daily Mail back then. There were Club photographs of teams and players from the past, and at the time it was a real 'collector's item' for a young FC Supporter.

Johnny Whiteley however continued his recruitment drive and Ken Foulkes, who had been international scrum half Keith Hepworth's understudy at Castleford, Mike Harrison a fantastic prop forward and two local lads Shaun O'Brien and Nick Trotter all signed on for us that year, as we tried desperately to build a competitive team. A young RU convert David Doyle-Davidson made Rugby League history that season too, when he was the first Club substitute to ever be used. He came on from the bench to replace Terry Devonshire on 5th September in a game at the Boulevard against Batley. It was also the year that our coach the battered and battle worn Johnny Whiteley finally retired from playing, to concentrate on his 'off field' duties.

It was a sad time too at number 23 because one of my Dad's old friends, his doctor and the Club's former honorary Physician, Ian Innes died suddenly. Doctor Innes had a surgery on the Boulevard next door to the St Matthew's Church Hall and was a real local character as well as a big Hull FC fan, Dad missed him a lot really, probably because he had become a good friend who had helped him with his 'Sand Fly Fever' legacy from the war, a complaint that sadly still bothered him, whenever the summer weather got a bit hot.

'March of the Mods'

Friday 16th April 1965   *Hull 12 – Hull Kingston Rovers 10*

Life in Aylesford Street mirrored the changes taking place across the country. I was just fourteen of course but even back then fashion played a big part in a teenager's life and it was about that time that Mum had bought me a brand new 'Fish tailed Parka' coat. I was into all sorts of music from the Beatles to the Who, and like most kids I loved Bob Dylan although for most of the time I had little idea what the hell he was on about. The fact remained though being a mod at Easter '65 was back then simply the only thing a young lad could be.

Everyone but everyone over the age of sixteen seemed to have a scooter which were invariably festooned in mirrors and adorned with chrome side panels and monogrammed paintwork. Every Sunday they would go to Bridlington to posture with the 'Rockers' on the beach and frighten the old ladies on the Prom, whilst during the week there would be regular 'rumbles' in the Kontiki and Gondola coffee clubs in the City centre. We lads were just too young to get a scooter, but we did our level best to look the part.

However that Easter when all the headlines on the TV and in the papers were being made by the 'Mods and Rockers' battling on the beach at Brixham, Clacton and Brighton, this FC fan had other things to do with a busy Easter programme for the Black and Whites, and two home games on consecutive days. In fact in 1965 we played three games in four days backing up a Good Friday fixture against the old enemy at the Boulevard with another home game against Wakefield and an away game at Bradford two days later on Easter Monday.

We had already lost 14 games that year and were well behind Hull Kingston Rovers in the League table and so as I made my way across the road in my new Parka (which I did everything but sleep in) for a noon kick off on Good Friday, I was fearing the worst as we had now got the unenviable record of having been beaten in the last ten League meetings against Hull Kingston Rovers.

The Rovers' fans had, as usual, been gloating over this record and the fact that they had finished higher than us in the last two seasons. The fact that we had finished above them for the previous 28 seemed to have been missed completely but as we all know, sports fans and particularly local rivals, have pretty selective memories when it comes to historical facts. However although I was still only 14 years old that awful feeling was already starting to grip me! I was already churned up physiologically by the magnitude of these Derby games and felt it in the pit of my stomach in that horribly sickly way that only the ardent fan who has suffered heartbreaking defeat at the hands of the 'infidels' understands.

The Match turned out to be a really tough and bruising forward game but Derby's always were back then, however on this occasion the massive Rovers pack full of 'big names' came up against a Hull team that was really 'pumped up' by the occasion. We battered the ball carriers in the first few exchanges and despite a Kellett penalty putting them 2-0 up we opened our scoring after just eight minutes. A great pass from Cyril Sykes found Keegan who ran up from full back and split the defence wide open as only he could do and as Moore and Blackmore closed in, he turned back inside and found David Doyle-Davidson, who was making a rare start in the centre and he ran in untroubled for the easiest of tries. That gave us a 3-2 lead but then the Hull defence squeezed the opposition into the middle of the field and would not let tricky scrum half Dave Elliot get the ball out wide to the fast and impressive looking Rovers back division.

This action meant that a lot of niggle and tension crept into the game as the 16,500 crowd created a cauldron of atmosphere as both camps exchanged 'compliments' and taunted each other. Several 'face offs' on the pitch had threatened to boil over as old scores came to the fore and Kellett who was really on form with the boot landed three penalties, (which stemmed from these skirmishes), to put the opposition in the lead again. Then at last Elliot moved the ball wide. A great pass to Burwell was shifted onto Blackmore un-marked on the wing, Brian Sullivan and Stocks tracked back across to try and nail the Rover's winger but in the end it was scrum half Kenny Foulkes that hammered him to the ground just ten yards from the try line. Up sprung the Rover's player to exchange blows with Foulkes who was still struggling to regain his feet and immediately referee Ernie Clay sent Blackmore from the field. Although they were down to 12 men, some real battling defence from the Rovers pack saw them still in the lead at half time.

Kellett landed another goal just after the re-start but after that it was all Hull. A high tackle by Poole saw Eric Broom fire home a great 40 yard penalty and then after Flanagan had been caught off side, he got another from a lot closer in. Then we saw the try of the weekend. Terry Devonshire picked up a loose ball in his own 25 yard area and started off down the field. With such short legs he seemed to be moving a lot faster than he actually was but despite the best attempts of Mullins, Moore and Burwell he got to the line and touched down just to the right of the posts. Broom landed the conversion and with 20 minutes to go we led by the slender margin of 12-10. They were nervous times indeed for a young fan and the last quarter was certainly not all plain sailing as Rovers threw everything at us to try and get a result. They had us rocking at times as Poole, Holliday, Fox and Foster tore into the heart of our defence. On one particular occasion, Rovers who monopolised possession from the scrums broke away and Flanagan stepped round Keegan and on toward the line before he was caught inches short by David Doyle-Davidson. In the end our half backs Foulkes and Devonshire had been just too good for Rovers and thanks to our brilliant defence in that second half we came out winners 12-10. The good sports amongst the FC fans shook hands with the Rovers' supporters and wished them well, whilst us 'Airlie Street Mods' just posed in our parkas pulled faces at them and laughed!

A busy weekend for Terry Devonshire

Saturday 17th April 1965   *Hull 16 – Wakefield Trinity 13*

Next day, Saturday, we were at home again and 7,500 people paid £925 to watch us take on Wakefield Trinity who were having their first game of the holidays. Despite a crunching encounter just 24 hours previously we made just one change from the team that played Rovers, with Trevor Carmichael coming in for Stocks at centre. This was surprisingly a game where our players showed no ill effects whatsoever and before the kick off Terry Devonshire received an award from the 'Programme Club' for being young player of the year whilst Arthur Keegan as usual received the fan's player of the year award.

This was another really exciting game for us spectators crammed into the Threepenny's as after two penalties by Eric Broom we went on to score the first try when Carmichael sent that man Devonshire in again under the posts. However Wakefield were soon back on terms by half time with two goals from Fox and a try from Hopwood. In the second half Devonshire shot in from a short ball on the inside from Foulkes and although both Fox and Broom exchanged penalties we came out winners 16-13. With almost the last play of the game Devonshire punched ex International sprinter, turned Wakefield winger Berwyn Jones, and was sent off by 'Sergeant Major' Ernie Clay who was officiating his second game in 24 hours at the Boulevard. So with three tries, two winning pay packets and a sending off it was an eventful two days for young Terry Devonshire.

We went to Bradford on Easter Monday and lost 15-9 but we had four points from the weekend and we had won the game that really mattered to the fans, the previous Friday. That's what you called a 'Good' Friday!'

Bert Wheedon's 'Play in a Day'

It was around that time that my latent interest in guitars came to the surface again and I decided to ask my Mum and Dad for one for Christmas. Barry from the youth club already had a solid electric one and was quite proficient. He was a bit of a retro fan really, and was still keen on the 1950's and big on Elvis and the Rock and Roll Years. Although I had lived through these, I never really realised just how good Gene Vincent, Eddie Cochrane, Buddy Holly and of course Elvis 'the King' really were. Barry took time to introduce me to this genre of music and I was soon hooked on hillbilly rock, as well as the obvious Beatles and 'Mersey Sound', and there was actually a distinct similarity in influences between the two styles of music that was to become apparent in some of the Beatles later LP's when they included some of the material they had played in the Cavern Club in Liverpool, and no doubt when Lenny went to see them in Hull.

Mum and Dad did not have a lot of money, although Mum had just started her first job since she was married, working on the school dinners at Constable Street School. Anyway, to cut a long story short, it transpired that the father of 'Ginger' Higgins one of my pals from down the Street, had bought his son an electric guitar the previous year, but

'Ginge' had soon grown bored of it, so my Dad bought it, and gave it to me for Christmas!! It was the first of many such instruments that I would own, and was a Hohner 'cut away' just like Hank Marvin's first guitar and I thought it was fantastic.

Barry lived with his two aunts in Ena Street just off the Boulevard and we used to practise every night in his front room. He played guitar so much better than me, and I found it really tough keeping up. Everyone seemed to be in groups back then and the success of the Liverpool scene certainly appeared to have got most kids 'star struck' and belting out the obligatory three chords! Good old Dad, who was working for Ross the Pork Butchers in Savile Street by then, bought me a 'Burt Weedon, Play in a Day' book from Gough and Davey's the music shop just across the road from his shop. However, I had to get rid it after 3 years, because I still hadn't learned anything. It was a good job that there was no trade descriptions act back then.

It's a good job too, that I got my guitar before Christmas because our first booking was on 2nd January 1965. Barry's Mum and Dad always had a New Year's party at the Conservative Club on Beverley Road and they asked Barry if we were good enough to play, 'Bazz' said we were although we definitely weren't, well I certainly wasn't anyway. So the date for our first performance was set. We had a repertoire of 5 songs including strangely enough (although no-one knew it at the time), the two songs with which Paul McCartney auditioned for the Beatles, namely 'Blue Moon of Kentucky' and 'Twenty Flight Rock'. There was also another one by Elvis entitled 'I was the One' and the Gene Vincent standard, 'Be Bop a Lula', to keep Barry happy! For my part we learnt a song that had been released about 3 months earlier by the Nashville Teens, called 'Google Eye'. I could barely play any of them and spent most of our 'Performance' 'John Lennon style' with my back turned to the audience, just so they couldn't see me fumbling about! Great fun, although even if our guitars were the same, Hank Marvin really had nothing whatsoever to fear.

On Thursday 21st March there was a very important end of season game at the Boulevard to honour scrum half Tommy Finn who was receiving a well earned benefit year. The game saw 'Past Hull' play Hull FC and it finished 31-26 to the current Hull team. 23 ex players lined up for the opposition and acquitted themselves really well and a crowd of 4,600 was in attendance. Steve, 'Spriggsey' and myself watched from the Threepennies behind the players' benches, which had to be extended that day to accommodate all the ex players. Two long distance tries by Terry Devonshire won the game in the second half but everything was played out in a really good spirit and the players 'chaired' Tommy Finn from the field at the end.

That season as our new acquisitions started to bed in at the Boulevard we finished in a respectable 13th place out of 30 clubs in the league. Eric Broom took over the kicking duties from Arthur Keegan and kicked 75 goals whilst top scorer was once again Clive Sullivan with 18 tries and that Centenary Brochure that I cherish so much was listed in the annual accounts as having made a profit of £169.

Perhaps things will improve if we get some new drains?

That summer, just after the season had finished and Mum had marched me down to Town to get some 'sensible' school shoes I remember Bill Jenks stood at the end of our back passage eagerly awaiting our return. I had worn holes in my favourite Chucker boots and Mother had therefore decided that drastic action was needed. Billy was going through a 'Cool' faze and nothing seemed to ruffle his 'Beatle cut' back then, but he was obviously keen to relay something to us as we walked towards him down Airlie Street. "Hey just come and look at this" he said as he dragged me across the road towards the open gates of the Boulevard ground. Once inside I could not believe my eyes.

I knew that the pitch had been like pudding all season and everyone had been complaining that it was stopping us playing fast open attractive rugby, but it was still hard to believe that there in front of the great old stand was a tractor with a plough digging up the pitch and turning it over. I doubted there and then, that it would ever be ready for the start of the season but after another 'mile and a half' of new drains had been added and the whole thing re seeded, it was back to a lush green sward for the pre season games. It was certainly a memorable day for us both as the green grass disappeared to be replaced by a sight that looked more suited to the sowing of some winter wheat.

More of Arthur Keegan, probably the Club's most popular player ... ever!

The return to school in September 1965 heralded the start of my GCE year and the chance for me to get some 'Certificates', as my Dad called them but although my parents were hopeful, I knew 'deep down' that it was already too late. Scholastic achievement that had been way behind girls, rugby, guitars, rugby and the Beatles.........and rugby, for the last four years, was still in its traditional position and that situation was unlikely to change any time soon. I was heading for disaster exam wise.

Across the road at the Boulevard 1965 saw Arthur Keegan made Club Captain and a popular one he was too. As I said earlier towards the end of every season, as you went through the turnstiles at the main entrance of the Boulevard, you were handed a voting slip for the fan's player of the season something that was rewarded at a special presentation evening that none of us lot could go to, in the Supporters' Club. Then the whole thing was repeated by the Chairman on the pitch at the last game of the season. Me and my pals always tried to choose someone different but it made little difference as Arthur Keegan was voted the fans' player of the year for the next 7 seasons and that's probably a record that will stand as long as the Club exists.

John Maloney makes his mark

That season Eric Broom and Keegan were relieved of the kicking duties when one of the greatest goal kickers I have ever seen John Maloney, signed from Shaw Cross amateurs in Dewsbury. John was an interesting character as well because although he could mix it with the best of them out on the pitch, he used to turn up for games and training in a Rolls Royce. His Dad owned a major engineering company in Dewsbury and

John was the Managing Director. As kids we used to go over to the car and marvel at it as it stood on the car park amongst the Vauxhall Victors, Ford Prefects and Morris Oxfords of the other players. Lenny who was always one for a 'quick return' even offered on several occasions to 'guard' it for him! John was of course to become one of the greatest point's scorers the Club had ever seen with a career that spanned 9 seasons and saw him kick 674 goals and score 38 tries. In fact his total points tally for the Club of 1462 was only beaten by the great Joe Oliver way back in the 1930's.

All the fun of the fair and the Kiwi's

Saturday 9ᵗʰ October 1965   *Hull 8 – New Zealand 11*

The second game that John Maloney played for Hull FC was a big one indeed because it was against the visiting New Zealand Tourists. It came 11 games into a season where we had lost 6 and won 5, so as usual back then, things were nothing if not 'average'. The game against the Kiwis took place on Hull Fair Saturday 9ᵗʰ October. It was a misty dank day best described back then by most folks who lived around the Boulevard as typical 'Hull Fair Weather'. Attendances were still dropping and the fact that Hull City were starting to put a good team together down the road at Boothferry Park did little to help our cause either.

Of course as usual with visiting touring teams we were definite underdogs and the fact that NZ put out 10 of the side that had just won the first Test against Great Britain at Station Road Swinton did nothing to raise our hopes of an upset. I watched the game from the well of the Best Stand with a couple of good mates Steve from Kelvin Hall and Kenny. The game kicked off with a reasonably good attendance to cheer on the Black and Whites. The opening exchanges saw some dour stuff with a lot of 'Incident' and niggling in the tackle. Both teams dropped the ball at regular intervals and a slippery pitch did nothing to encourage open rugby. However then the visitors flashed the ball along the line straight from a scrum and winger Reidy took a smart pass from loose forward Hammond and scorched down the wing with Sullivan in his wake. Just as Clive caught him about ten yards out he swung a great inside ball to Bailey who scored a spectacular try that the partisan but knowledgeable home crowd roundly applauded.

Then we went onto the offensive and firstly Sykes made an opening for Foulkes who knocked on and then Alan McGlone carved out a gap in the Kiwi's defence for Sykes to exploit but again the ball was dropped. Finally McGlone who was having what was to turn out as a career defining game, put Club Captain Arthur Keegan clear only for the popular full back to be held inches short of the line.

If we were not that good at most things back then, we were certainly good at goal kicking and John Maloney made sure with two penalties to give us a 4-3 lead. In fact just on half time Maloney was at it again converting a great 50 yard effort from half way to send us into the changing rooms with an unlikely 6-3 lead. The second half opened with Hull playing their best rugby for two years and only a great last ditch tackle by the Tourist's full back Tait avoided another score that could have seen us take control of the game. Then Terry Devonshire who was playing in the off half berth, shot through a couple of poor tackles and drawing two defenders passed to Arthur Keegan. He drew the last man to put Sullivan clear only for our usually reliable winger to juggle the ball and drop it as he crossed the line.

If the rugby was getting hot the exchanges in the tackle were reaching boiling point, as half way through the half, a massive fist fight ensued. Let's face it, if you went down the Boulevard back in the 60's you wanted your money back if you didn't see a good scrap, and no one was disappointed that day. Broom (and as usual) Jim Neale were pulled out and lectured by the referee who awarded the opposition a penalty in our 25. They pressed and pressed but we somehow held out mainly due to a great 'ball and all' tackle by David Doyle-Davidson which effectively stopped a two man over lap on the left. The Tourists were then awarded a penalty for some sloppy high tackling on Hull's part and full back Tait converted the penalty to put the Kiwis just one point behind.

Then from the kick off (with that old trick I have seen time and again) Kenny Foulkes sent the ball sailing straight into touch. Tait again opted to kick at goal this time from the centre spot and as the ball literally crept over the posts we were a point behind. On we battled, with Pearson our prop going close and Terry Stocks (who streaked down the wing running with his knees almost to his chin) just failing to squeeze in by the corner flag at the Gordon Street end of the Threepennies.

However that was it and despite a big pull possession wise in the last ten minutes the fitter and more polished NZ defence kept us in our own half and a late penalty to the visitors left the score at 8-11. As has so often been the case we created some great opportunities to score, but could just not convert them and after playing their best rugby for the last two seasons Hull FC came up just short. No doubt that night having read again about the game in the Sports Mail, I would be, as usual, off to the Fair to work as a spare hand and money collector on Doubtfire's Jets, where I was now a regular employee.

Clive Sullivan who continued to play well throughout the season scored 23 tries that year. No one was paid that well in the game in those days, something that was borne out by our balance sheet that year that showed players' wages amounted to a total of just £8,147. But, the 'A' Team, packed with young local hopefuls from the City's junior clubs won the Yorkshire Senior Competition Challenge Cup and we were there to watch them accept the Trophy, and then drop it, before an 'A' Team game at the Boulevard.

Leaving the Boulevard behind and to this day the biggest upheaval of my life

As my fifth year at Kelvin Hall Technical High School continued the run up to the examinations, it became clear to this particular scholar that the best I could hope for was a couple of GCE's and a couple of CSE's, but in any case, I told myself, University was certainly not for me, I wasn't clever enough for that. More worrying though was the fact that despite being in my last year at school I still had no idea 'what I wanted to be' although in six months time I would be jettisoned from the education system forever, and would need to find a job.

There then came a big change for all three of us living at 23 Aylesford Street and something that, looking back, I guess changed my life forever. One grey October Thursday afternoon in 1965, I had just got home from school, when Jessie my Father's Mother made her weekly visit! You will remember from way back in the early part of this tome that Thursday was 'Granny day' but this visit was somewhat different. There was much whispering and discussion which stopped every time I entered the little front room of number 23, and it seemed to me that something was definitely going on. When I left at around 7-00 with my guitar to go to St Matthew's Church Hall for 'band practise' with Barry and the rest of the guys, they were still at it. The 'pop' group was coming along well and we were starting to play a bit at the youth club on Sunday nights. These musical interludes certainly appealed to me much more than revising for examinations and the way some of the girls took notice of the band when we played on a Sunday night acted at that time as much more of an incentive than 'Getting some qualifications behind me!'

Anyway, the intrigue I had experienced at home was soon clarified when the reason for all the whispering was explained to me by my Dad over breakfast next day. It transpired that Granny knew a women from her days at school who owned a house way over the other side of the City in Sutton. The property in Potterill Lane was one that this Mrs James had rented out to one particular family for years but recently her long standing tenant had died and she was looking for someone to take over the tenancy. Granny had told Mum and Dad that it was theirs, if they wanted it, but they had to move quickly, and after doing their sums and realising they could just about afford it, they did want it ...badly.

I guess for them it was the chance to move on and get out of the Boulevard and into the country. Sutton in those days was just on the edge of the City of Hull and Bransholme, Spring Cottage and the other estates that now encircle the area, were still about 10 years away! When they told me all about it, despite the hard exterior I tried to portray, I could feel my eyes filling up, as things like the band, St Matthew's, the local girls and the closeness of the one big love of my life that was, so conveniently positioned just across the street, all meant that this move spelt disaster for me. At the time I was 'Going out' with a girl called Rita whose Dad was one of the very first Mr Whippy ice cream van drivers in the City. She would, I thought, have to go too, Sutton was miles away and I could get back for rugby, but not for a girl friend as well. I bet that this was a development that pleased her Dad because he didn't like me and I didn't care much for him either but at least you could hear him coming.

Mum and Dad had their minds made up on the move, and so, just 4 weeks after Granny had dropped the bombshell, Hardaker's Removal van pulled up outside Number 23 and the first chapters of my life and everything I knew as home was loaded into it. We all went off to Sutton to start a new existence, deep in the 'Red and White' heartland. In reality, there were actually a lot more Hull FC fans than 'Robins' fans in the village, but before I actually knew this it was a daunting prospect relocating to the heart of enemy territory. There would be no more popping across the road on Tuesdays and Thursdays to watch training, and no more leaving for games on Saturday afternoons at eight minutes to three either. As the big maroon removal van rumbled up the Boulevard with us lot sat in the front, it was if I was leaving for another country and I now knew how those blokes who join the army in the war and were then drafted abroad felt about leaving home.

Living with the enemy

10 Potterill Lane, Sutton was like another world compared with that little 'sham four' in Aylesford Street. There was a garden for starters and a long one at that, with apple trees, bird tables, a Larch lap garden shed and a chicken house (minus any chickens) at the bottom of the plot. The front gate had a yellow Laburnum tree growing over it and there were three bedrooms and a bathroom and a toilet upstairs! Mum and Dad had ordered some new furniture, two rocking type armchairs for the back room and a leatherette suite for the front and because Rediffusion did

not extend its wired vision service that far; they bought a 'new' second hand telly which obtained its signal from an ariel on the roof! One of our first visitors after moving in was Granny Allen who, taking a lot of credit for the move herself, asked me what I thought.

I must have said something about the distance it was to the Boulevard and even to Boothferry Park, (where I had on occasions taken to watching a game when it did not clash with Hull FC's home matches or an 'A' Team game), because what sticks in my mind was her announcement that I could, "Always pop onto Holderness Road and watch The Other Team." I can't remember my answer but it was probably something like "I'd rather cut my own head off". Jessie, bless her, just didn't get it at all.

I either had to go to school on my bike which took around 40 minutes, or take a seventy minute bus trip on two buses through the centre of Hull. It was all very inconvenient and I remember one wet windy morning suggesting to Mum and Dad that perhaps they had not thought all this out properly. Still it was too late now and number 10 was our new home although the first few times I travelled back to the Boulevard for home games I always went to the front of No. 23 Aylesford Street to pay silent homage to a place that was to this lad at least, a sort of shrine to everything that was happiness and Hull FC. Other people had moved in by this time of course and it all looked very strange through the faded net curtains that they had put up at the windows but this ritual continued and became a sort of fortnightly pilgrimage really.

The long trek back to my spiritual home

Saturday 11ᵗʰ December 1965   *Hull 25 – Hunslet 5*

I think the first game I travelled across town to see was a home encounter against Hunslet which we won easily, but the following week we played a dour affair in driving rain and clinging mud against Castleford which despite a rare Doyle-Davidson try, we lost 6-3. The journey home sat on the bus in soaking wet clothes was endless that day. Then of course we faced our first festive season in our new home and I celebrated on Christmas Day as you do, by catching the first no 34 bus from Sutton to Hull to get to the Boulevard for an 11-00am kick off and the annual Christmas Day fixture against Hull KR. The pitch that day was an absolute morass of mud but that did not seem to affect the supporters who turned up in their droves to watch the game. I believe there were over 12,000 there that day for a Christmas Day institution that was for me part occasion, part tradition, part pilgrimage and part purgatory. Why do they always schedule Derby's at times of celebration?

What did you get for Christmas? ... I got a defeat and a long walk home!

Saturday 25th December 1965   Hull 0 – Hull Kingston Rovers 2

For me, the lasting memory of watching those Christmas Day matches in the Threepenny Stand was the camaraderie and friendship that was everywhere as the hip flasks were passed round and the 'Wife's' mince pies handed out. In fact to this day whenever I smell Rum and cigar smoke it takes me back to those great Christmas lunch times at the Boulevard. That day the game was a really hard affair which we lost 2-0 to a solitary Cyril Kellett goal. It didn't seem to matter much to the rank and file of fans if you lost to the old enemy back then but I know that I will have been totally 'gutted' by the result. After the game I called on Barry in Ena Street and he showed me the new Selmer Amplifier he had got for Christmas. It had reverb and an independent switch pedal, however before I knew it, the time had crept onto 3-00pm and I decided to head for home. The buses on Anlaby Road that Christmas Day were certainly few and far between and I eventually arrived in the City Centre at five minutes past four. To my horror the last bus to anywhere that Christmas Day went at 4-00pm, and so I set off to walk back to Sutton via the heavy industrial areas of Bankside and Wincolmlee. I got home around six, and after a defeat to the old enemy and a six mile walk home, as you can imagine, Christmas spirit was at a premium for this fan, and as I ate my warmed up Christmas dinner and congealed sprouts the prospect of having to live in the midst of the Rovers imbeciles meant that I was not that keen on 'Decking the Halls with boughs of Holly' either.

Its official, I'm educationally subnormal

With the return to school after Christmas my GCE's loomed large and you know, it's a fact that there is something really strange about the year that sees the end of school and the prospect of life at work. It's the period of your life when you realise that at this time next year you won't be here, safe in the confines of Bill Pattinson's 'Home for the educationally challenged', but instead you will be out there expected to earn a living. It was miles too late for me to change anything now though; well it was as far as GCE's were concerned anyway. It was a fact I had come to accept but it was one that was certainly hammered home to Mum and Dad when a letter from school dropped through the letter box in late January. This piece of official correspondence was from Bill Pattinson himself and indicated that I would only be entered for the GCE examinations in Maths and English (which were compulsory for even the 'village' idiots amongst us) and a rather bemusing Biology plus two CSE's in German and General Science.

'OK, OK, I ain't gonna be a brain surgeon!'

There was a state of shock in our house in Sutton for several days. Dad tried shouting at me, but that didn't seem to make me suddenly more intelligent, so he then went into a silent mode, which in the end lead me to favour his first option because at least I knew what he was thinking. I even turned on him at breakfast one day and said, ' OK Dad I think you had better get prepared for the fact that I ain't gonna be a brain surgeon' Mum, just said that perhaps, 'I was good with my hands', (Ah that old chestnut) and that, 'Not everyone can be brainey'. I was however, in an effort to 'get out of the house', spending more and more time in the garden weeding and digging away my frustrations. The prospect of Study Leave from March till the exams in May certainly appealed to me, although it was not so much the 'study' as the 'leave' that was attractive.

Still there was always rugby, and I was thankful for what appeared to be the one stable thing left in my life, you could always depend on it. Well you could in as much as it did at least offer you either a First Team or an 'A' Team 'shelter' from the pressures of the world for at least an hour and a half every Saturday afternoon. For me over the years it has always been there in the hard times as a sort of 'Comfort Blanket' to use against the worst that the world could throw at you. You can get absorbed in it, and a great try or a massive tackle can render you totally elated and numb to an extent that makes you just for a few moments forget everything that's going on in your life. In fact with all the nervous illness and stress there seems to be in the 21st Century I am surprised that you can't get an obsession for your sports club on prescription.

There is a certain consistency about being fanatical about Hull FC even when on the field the team are anything but consistent because most times it's just good to be part of it.

'Sully' and 'The Doyle', 'Brothers in arms'

Saturday 26th February 1966   *Hull 11 – Salford 2*

As a team we were certainly not 'consistent' that year as, for the third year running, the papers described the 1965/66 campaign as yet another 'transitional' season. However as always there are a couple of games that spring to mind from that period, the first was a home game against Salford when Clive Sullivan scored a memorable try, with which he sealed a win by 11-2. That afternoon I remember 'Sully' raced in from 30 yards, eluding defender after defender to score under the post, which added to the two unconverted tries that John Maloney had already scored. Two weeks later it was David Doyle-Davidson that shone out in a game against Batley that we won 23-10. It was Maloney that got all the plaudits in the media with 7 goals from 12 attempts but 'The Doyle', as he was starting to be known by the fans, stamped his authority on the game with four or five massive tackles and some creative centre play. I also recall that Charlie Booth and Brian Clixby played well on that particular day, in a good forward performance.

However that year did at least see dependable, week in week out hero, Arthur Keegan made Club Captain and a popular one he was too. He had now developed into a masterful full back with a great attacking style and a wonderful step, whilst both under the high ball and as the last line of defence he was the best there was. His last ditch tackling style which involved a grab round the legs or him smothering the ball and pushing the player to the ground in one go, is a lifelong memory burnt onto the brain cells of this fan. He was just a fabulous player who was becoming a sort of 'Captain Marvel' character too, as he took most of the penalty kicks for touch and could still double up on the goal kicking if asked to do so.

In addition to Arthur another top performer that year was again our international winger, 'The Black Flash', (as certain members of the media had taken to calling him) Clive Sullivan, he again continued to play consistently well scoring 23 tries. Times were hard though but the 'A' Team, was a joy to watch and Steve, Kenny and the rest of the lads who went often talked more about them than the first team. The squad still full of promising local youngsters was destined to again raise the Yorkshire Senior Competition Challenge Cup that year and this time they kept hold of it.

In examinations it's generally accepted that those who know the most usually finish last.

The time of my Exams finally arrived before 'I'd had any time to revise' and I entered a couple of weeks that were for me an absolute nightmare. However hard I tried to cram a few morsels of information into a brain that was stuffed with try scorers, league tables and guitar chords, in the actual examinations I always seemed to finish first and write the least, and I guess I knew in my heart of hearts that the eventual outcome was to be disastrous. Still I gave Mum and Dad glowing reports of how I was getting on with them, and how I had 'revised all the things that they were asking in the questions', but as soon as I had managed to get through the actual ordeal of the examination process, I started to dread the results and prepared for the fateful day by planning how I could ambush the postman before he arrived with the 'glad tidings'. It was time I decided to think about getting a job.....quickly.

I was still spending a lot of my spare time helping out at home in the garden. It was a long thin expanse of land bordered by low hedges on each side, which had originally been reclaimed from an old orchard that had once been behind an imposing house owned by local entrepreneurs the Sewell's. It was good fun getting my shirt off and being out in the sunshine and as I had absolutely no idea what I wanted to do as a job of work, I decided to find out about the possibility of doing a bit of gardening to earn some money. One night in mid June, whilst on my way through the paper in search of the sports pages, I noticed an advert in the 'Situations Vacant' column which invited applicants for 10 posts as Apprentice Gardeners at the City Council, the wage was the princely sum of £2-15s- 6d a week and so I applied, and soon got an invitation to an interview on Tuesday 25th June at Ferens Chambers, 79 Ferensway in the centre of Hull.

My 'googly' gets me by

I bought a suit, well Mum bought me a suit from Johnsons on Holderness Road and I presented myself as indicated at 2-00pm. The office of The Parks Cemeteries and Allotments Department of the City Council was on the top floor and I was quizzed by the receptionist about my name and age before I was ushered into an office which announced on the door that it was occupied by A.T. Hawksley Assistant Director of Leisure Services. Tom, as everyone knew him, was a really nice guy and completely different to the executive I had expected to meet for my interview. He sat, with his feet on the desk as the sun streamed through the attic style windows of his office. I had tried to best guess what I would be asked but his opening gambit certainly caught me completely off guard as he asked, 'Now then lad, do you play cricket'. I nodded and added just what Mr Jones at Kelvin Hall had told me; that I was a 'Right arm slow medium bowler and a middle order batsman'. 'Great', said Tom, 'The Parks Department's Works Sports cricket team is struggling for players'.

We chatted a bit about my experiences in the back garden at Potterill Lane and my studying Biology at school (although I omitted to mention that I only answered two of the five questions on the exam paper) and then it was agreed that I would start work on 1st August 1966, at East Park. Of course Mum and Dad's reaction was a cross between ecstasy and relief, as they greeted the news with a big hug and a handshake, and the announcement of how much my 'Board' would be from week one.

I got washed and changed and headed off for a pint. After a few drinks in the 'Duke' around the corner, where there seemed to be a rather lax regime when it came to the sale of alcohol to 'juniors', I went home and probably slept easy that night, safe in the knowledge that my career until the day I retired was now 'In the Bag' and that when the dreaded results arrived in mid August I would be secure in my chosen profession. The Postman was safe again!

The World Cup, 1966 and all that

Of course the big sporting event in that year was the staging of the World Cup in England and in Hull, like everywhere else across the country, World Cup fever was taking hold. I watched most games with Frank Robinson and a load of my other school pals who lived on the Bilton Grange Estate about ten minute bike ride from my home in Sutton. I had meandered down to Boothferry Park from time to time with my pal Barry from Ena street and watched a bit of football but it had always been something of a slower game and the lack of physical contact meant that it was, for me at least, never to be in the position of eclipsing my love for Rugby League and my beloved Hull FC. My girlfriend at that time Jenny lived on Ings Road Estate and her father had bought a massive TV for the World Cup. He used to invite all the street round to watch the games, but threw me out of the Argentina game when he caught me and his daughter celebrating an England goal with a crafty 'snog' in the kitchen. Football fans eh? No sense of occasion.

Of course as the World Cup unfolded I got wrapped up in the drama too and when we won I was as excited and proud as any Englishman, but it would never ever turn my head and with me 16 years old and about to set out on the journey into the world of work, the die was cast, the decision made and the obsession that started all those years ago sat in my pram in Airlie Street was destined to dominate the rest of my life. For this lad there was only one team and one game, you could keep your Bobby Charlton's, Nobby Stiles' and Bobby Moore's because for me they simply couldn't 'black the boots' of the Chris Davidson's, Arthur Keegan's and Clive Sullivan's of this world, these were my heroes and that's how it would stay for the rest of my life.

Chapter Six

A working man ... adventures with Billy and Sid

As I stated previously 1966 was a big year for soccer, not just because of England's victory in the World Cup but also down on Boothferry Road where Hull City, (under local millionaire and gravel pit mogul Harold Needler), were 'buying' their way towards some really big gates. They never really achieved the ultimate success that they craved, First Division football, something that was to take another 40 years to arrive, but with signings like Wagstaff, Houghton and Butler, this ongoing team rebuilding had certainly captured the imagination of the local sporting community.

These happenings up the road certainly made it difficult for Hull FC to attract anything like the attendances that they had enjoyed at the turn of the decade and the Club found themselves down to, if not the bare bones of support, then struggling to maintain attendance levels year on year. As the bulk of the City's floating sports' fans were gravitating towards Boothferry Park, our situation wasn't helped by the fact that we played in the same winter season as the football club and their Saturday afternoon fixtures were often in direct competition with our games. Often I remember you could stand in the well of the Best Stand watching some dour game of rugby and see, quite clearly, the 'Tigers' new floodlights in the distance as they twinkled and shined over the rooftops of the houses in Division Road.

However, attendances apart, coach Johnny Whiteley, the Board and the players did quite well and we finished a very commendable ninth in that 1966/67 season, with Sullivan not only once again topping the Club's try scoring charts, but also with 28 touch downs being crowned for the first time as the top scorer in the British professional game. Another national accolade was gained when Arthur Keegan, who was our Club Captain, and again Player of the Year, was picked to tour Australia with Great Britain.

Despite us rugby fans trying to dismiss it as a passing phase the World Cup was the big news across the nation and football was a sport on the up, although at 10 Potterill Lane in Sutton the talk was all about my new job, which was to start at East Park on the first day of August. As I have already stated, I was destined to be employed for the next five years as an apprentice gardener with the City Council and it was on that Monday morning that my journey to manhood started in the leafy and verdant surroundings of the City's largest park.

On that morning it was with some trepidation and a deal of nervous foreboding that I rode my bicycle down Summergangs Road and into the service yard in the Park for a 7-30 start. On arrival the place was in turmoil, with bales of straw, piles of rubbish, discarded tables and chairs, and paper everywhere. It was the first working day after the Hull Show, a 'Town meets Country' sort of event that was staged every year in the park and attended by thousands. Despite therefore my dreams of digging and pruning, it was pretty inevitable that my first couple of days as a trainee horticulturalist would be spent picking up paper and other rubbish as an army of council workers executed what was called 'The Big Clean Up'. I managed to get through the first day without any of the initiation ceremonies my pals had warned me about, until, that is, I arrived back in the service yard at 4-30 to find my bicycle had been hoisted to the top of the flagpole at the front of the park.

If the work was tedious and the surroundings strange it only took me a couple of hours to recognise a few friendly faces from the Boulevard as I quickly reacquainted myself with two familiar characters from my spiritual home. Sid and Billy were in their early 60's and Billy was poorly sighted, wearing what were then affectionately referred to as 'bottle bottomed glasses'. On the Threepenny Stand everyone knew Billy as the always laughing, dumpy little guy who stood on the fence on the touchline at the very front of the terracing giving the match officials the benefit of his thoughts on their parenthood not that he was a loud guy because he certainly wasn't. He had sat for years in the best stand at the other side of the ground in seat H32 above the players tunnel, but moved over to the 'Threepenny's' when his eyesight worsened. Still he was a real fixture at every home game and just one of literally dozens of characters that the game attracted in those days. Before moving to Greatfield housing estate in the east of the city, he had been a lifelong resident of Gillett Street on Hessle Road, deep in the bosom of the fishing industry and in the heart of Black and White territory.

Sid was less well known, although I still remembered him from home games at the Boulevard. At work he wore faded blue overalls and a flat cap that he never seemed to be without. It was like that with folks who wore flat caps in the 60's you either had one or you didn't, but if you did you just about slept in it! Sid though always referred to Hull FC as 'We' and not 'They'. I instantly loved him for this because to this day, anyone who speaks about my Club as 'We' shows that extra caring and belonging that I feel myself, so Sid was fine in my book.

Both these stalwarts had been watching Hull FC since well before the Second World War and throughout my stay at the park, as soon as work started, whether it was digging in a wintery shrubbery or sweeping leaves on the perimeter roads in autumn, the conversation soon got onto Colin Hutton, Bruce Ryan, Bob Coverdale or any one of dozens of ex Hull players about which they both seemed to have an almost encyclopaedic knowledge. Billy seemed to be on first name terms with many of the current and past players, so the stories were many and varied and the days flew by in those first few weeks of my working life. My pay of £2 15s 6d, meagre though it was, seemed to cover amply all my needs and after the rigours of Kelvin Hall, East Park was a happy introduction to the world of work.

Encouragement to work and learn; wellington boots, latin plant names and 'snickling'

Although I am sure when I look back now the outcome of my first steps on the road to being a working man may not have been as my Mum and Dad had hoped when I passed my 11+, they were still tremendously supportive and at the end of my first week my Dad returned home from work with some new wellingtons and gardening gloves for me to use at East Park. However being an apprentice meant there was an element of learning to the process and so, no doubt believing I was enjoying myself too much, Percy Brown the Park Foreman 'attached' me to the 'Rock Garden gang', where I met my new supervisor Harry. He didn't like rugby, or football for that matter, and was completely steeped in his gardening. He seemed to know the Latin name of every plant there was and once he had told you them he expected you to remember them forever. He used to march me down into the rock garden every morning and give me six botanical names of plants which I had to memorise and repeat next morning before learning the next six.

His main teaching aid was a swift clip across the back of the head if you didn't get them right and believe me whatever the politically correct 'brigade' of more recent times would think about this incentive scheme, I became a fast learner. Harry was certainly a dour character, with a round weather beaten 'gardeners' face, who didn't smile much unless I fell down a muddy embankment, or into the fish pond in the rock garden, which I did manage to do on several occasions. I certainly learned a lot from Harry and not all of it was about gardening.

One day I remember some young 'urchins' (as Harry called them) had been fishing in the lake and caught a smallish pike. They had run all the way with it in a Keep Net to the lily pond in the rock garden where, unknown to any of the parks employees they triumphantly liberated it! Of course at that time the fish was only about two foot long but it was about to get bigger.

As the weeks went by, slowly but surely, the Koi Carp, Rudd and Chebumkins that Harry cherished so much, started to disappear from the pond. This baffled him no end until one day he spotted the culprit lazily basking in the sunshine on top of the water, no doubt licking his chops after eating another fine specimen of my bosses celebrated fish collection. Next day at my supervisor's request I brought an old steel guitar string from home and after looping it and attaching it to the end of a long bamboo cane, he settled down behind a bush next to the pond to await the appearance of his quarry.

Sure enough as the sky brightened out came 'Pikey' and as he basked after his breakfast in the warm spring sunshine, Harry deftly dropped the circle of steel into the water and slowly slipped the loop over the back of the Pike. I watched from a distance in quiet admiration as, quick as a flash, he tugged at the cane, the wire tightened round the fish and with a flick of the wrist it was catapulted clear of the water and through the air, to land in an instant, high up on the rockery besides the pond. Harry was up there in a flash and as I scrambled up the rocks behind him he was bashing the fish's head against a big flat stone in manic fashion, whilst muttering curses of celebration under his breath. He had soon bashed the living daylights out of what had grown to be a 40" Pike. This sort of cemented in my brain the fact that perhaps it was wise for me to remember that, whether you were a young lad who was slow to learn plant names, or an unsuspecting predator, it was not advisable to mess with Harry.

Who killed all the fish?

Talking of fishy tales and those first few months on the Parks Department, I remember that they always used to put some sort of preparation into the big boating lake every spring to retard the growth of pond weed so that the rowing and motor boats that were there for hire, could operate across the whole expanse of the water throughout the summer. Pond weed used to wrap itself around the screws of the petrol driven motor boats and rendered them inoperative usually, I found, in the middle of the boating lake with a couple of young girls aboard, if I was lucky!

That year, the ritual of applying the 'Aquacide' was the responsibility of the character who looked after all the boats on the lake, an Irish guy called 'Duffy'. His job was to disperse the diluted herbicide into the water, something that he did with a watering can whilst stood up in a rowing boat. The boat was specially equipped with a large galvanised tank which held the solution that was to be applied. Now Duffy, a handsome looking character who always wore a red neckerchief, had an ear ring in one ear and was never seen out of wellingtons that were turned over at the top, liked a drink or two, and had on several occasions according to the parks popular mythology, fallen out of the boat and into the lake whilst performing this task. He should really have been taken off the duty, but because the stuff they used was rather heady and the fumes could burn your arms and face, there was only Duffy who would attempt it. The year I was at East Park though, this often inebriated Irish 'mariner' went a bit too far.

Although he vociferously denied it afterwards, his 'state of health' that morning dictated that he had probably put too much of the neat solution into the lake that February and within two days of the application, hundreds of fish were being washed up dead! I remember going into work at four o'clock one morning to shovel dozens of dead Roach and Rudd into an antiquated dumper truck, before we secreted them in a big hole we had dug in the nursery plot in the service yard. We had, for obvious reasons, to complete this task well before the public were about in the park! Duffy got the sack for that! However my best recollection of the whole episode was of the bigger fish that survived. They may not have been killed outright but they were severely anesthetised by the deadly solution and for a couple of weeks after the mass genocide of the smaller fish, if you looked carefully you could see Pike sometimes up to six feet in length floundering or just laying there on the surface of the lake, stunned.

'The Hearth Rug Karma Sutra'

Saturday 1ˢᵗ October 1966   *Hull 21 – Bramley 6*

Back at the Boulevard the Hull FC fans suspected that all was not well in the board room, although to their credit the members of the executive did their best to project a united front. However barely six months after his appointed new chairman J.L. Spooner announced his resignation and at the same time Cyril Fowler was appointed as Club Secretary. Reg Lee was then appointed as Chairman but the rumblings behind the scenes continued and although it was hard to find much out, to the average fan it appeared that at the very top the Club opinions were divided. Clive Sullivan had a good year again and possibly the most memorable game for our flying winger was the only one he missed against Bramley on 1st October 1966. Hull won the game 21-6 but more importantly it was the day that Clive married his girlfriend Rosalyn and the whole team went straight from the game to the reception. What a night that must have been. The Welsh flyer that was now a fixture on the wing saw his year culminate with selection to the Great Britain World Cup squad.

Although I had already had a good introduction to strange folks, at Chiltern Street, on the Threepenny Stand and on 'Bunker's Hill' there was never a more diverse, or odd, collection of guys than those I experienced at East Park. The mechanisation of farming and the demise of small holdings meant that many farm labourers from the surrounding countryside had moved into town to work in the parks. The head 'Flower' gardener, who whatever the weather was another that seemed to live his whole life in Wellington boots, was the spit and image of a character called Uncle Fester from the popular American TV comedy, 'The Addams Family'. He was short, tubby, and balding and always had a big toothless grin for anyone he met. Every lunchtime in the mess room, he used to wait until everyone had settled down with their sandwiches, before regaling us with his stories of his sexual exploits with 'The Mrs' on the hearthrug in front of the fire the previous night. These graphically described acts, even more bizarrely, were apparently carried out to the accompaniment of 'Criss Cross Quiz', on the TV.

My first chance to bring home the fish and it cost me ... big time.

As well as gardening and learning my 'Latin' there were other duties for a young man in the first throws of his apprenticeship to worry about too. It was my job to go for everyone's Fish and Chips on a Friday and so early in my stay at the Park I was duly instructed about the location of the fish shop, what everyone wanted, who wanted salt and vinegar, pickled onions, Cod Roe etc etc. My final instruction was to ensure that when I got back I put the fish and chips in the oven to keep them warm until the lads got in for their lunch. I followed these instructions to the letter, and triumphantly that first Friday brought my first dinner order back to the Mess Room in two big bags on the handlebars of my bike. I remembered my peer's instructions and duly deposited the various lunches in the Oven, turned it on and went off to wash my hands. Ten minutes later as I walked out of the wash house shaking my hands to dry them, I witnessed a strange sight indeed. There were blokes running about hither and dither waving their arms, or carrying buckets of water, in the general direction of the mess room. A couple were shouting about 'Fire' as they passed me to disappear into the dining area.

My step quickened, as I thought about the fish and chips, let's face it after all that work, I didn't want my efforts to be scuppered by a fire. However in the end it was my fault anyway. No one had told me to take the outer news paper wrapping off the fish and chips before I put them in the 'gas' oven had they? I was popular that day I can tell you, it cost me half my weeks pay to reimburse everyone for their ruined lunches and if that humiliation was not bad enough, I knew having burnt his Cod and chips it was only a matter of time before I got another clip round the head from Harry. Perhaps that was the first signs of my apparent lifelong inability to tackle anything that could be loosely described as culinary.

Christmas in East Park

If a few months in the midst of these 'hair arsed gardeners' was full of surprises for an impressionable 16 year old, Christmas was a revelation. Days before the big day arrived these hardnosed, traditional 'Sons of the Soil' would show a real change of character, carols were whistled by some whilst they worked, whilst others decked out the Bowling Green Pavilion with holly, yew branches and paper chains. Even 'Uncle Fester' entered into the spirit of the season, and substituted his usual extracts from his 'Hearth Rug Karma Sutra' for licking a few paper chains after his lunch.

On Christmas Eve, things took an even stranger turn. At around 11-00 everyone finished their work, washed their spades and marched to the highly decorated Bowling Pavilion which by then resembled a 'full blown' Santa's Grotto. This was the East Park staff Christmas Party for which the lads had been saving all through the year by weekly subscriptions collected by Sid. It was an unbelievable sight as what looked like hundreds of bottles of beer were spread out in the corner of the room. Soon members of the staff who usually rarely said a word, were all singing 'O Come all ye Faithful', plus standard 'Pub' songs like 'Pal of My Cradle Days', and 'Dear old Pals' (all of which, this youngster who preferred the Kinks and Beatles thought, were sickly sentimental twaddle). Then 'Uncle Fester' smiling with his toothless grin through a tatty cotton wool beard, appeared as Father Christmas and gave everyone a present, although even in his brightly coloured outfit and freshly washed and polished Wellingtons, I still found it hard to dispel completely the terrifying vision of the hearth rug, the 'Mrs.' and Criss Cross Quiz. However, as the afternoon wore on, things just got stranger and stranger.

Being 'A lad' I was only allowed two bottles of beer, so I remained reasonably sober, whilst all around me got 'wasted' as the conversations got louder and louder. At 4-00pm with everyone legless, and several asleep, the lights were switched off, and by the illumination of the Christmas Tree, we all sung 'Silent Night' Some hummed, others mouthed the words but they all swayed in tune with the music and to this day it was probably one of the most bizarre situations I have ever been in.

As I was the apprentice and the only person left who was in a fit state to get onto a bicycle never mind ride one, I was sent off with the foremen's big bunch of keys, to lock all the gates around the Park. When I got home Mum asked me what Christmas Eve in the Park was like but frankly I just didn't know where to start.

I'm obsessed, (with not being obsessed), with the enemy across the river.

Friday 24th March 1967   Hull 13 – Hull Kingston Rovers 12

As for the rugby, well one game in 1966/67 that held fond memories was against Rovers at the Boulevard when we beat our illustrious neighbours 13-12. The Robins had already beaten us at home in the Yorkshire Cup and were well fancied to do so again at the Boulevard. However in front of 14,000 fans the unfancied under dogs produced one of their best performances of the decade, which saw the game won by a drop goal from David Doyle-Davidson. Stranger still, in a total of 158 appearances for the Club it was the only drop goal 'The Doyle' ever kicked. Even though I was just 16 it is the sort of thing I will remember forever. I always have vivid memories of the games when we beat the old enemy and conveniently forget completely the detail of the times that we didn't. Nothing changes over the years and for me, if you're a fan of Rugby League in Hull you find it hard to tolerate anything that is printed or spoken about the other side, it's simply just part and parcel of the mindset of being an obsessive fan. The word fan itself must be a shortened version of fanatic anyway and therefore hints at least to some tenuous links to mental health and for me that probably explains a lot.

Although, having said all that perhaps I am still a little interested in hearing about 'them' at times. Some people, who simply don't understand all this stuff, criticise me because I have a go at Hull Kingston Rovers at times but why shouldn't I? I used to be one of those folks who would tell everyone that, as far as I was concerned, "if they were playing in my back garden I would have to draw the curtains"; they could do what they liked because I didn't give a toss about them, unless they were playing my team and then I only cared if we won!!!! But that's not strictly true if I'm honest, because when they are the mortal enemy, however you try to ignore them you simply can't resist finding out what they are up to.

Perhaps, and as a brief aside, I can illustrate this situation best by coming back up to date for a moment and looking at an incident that happened only a couple of years ago in a Super League game at Wigan. It was Friday night and there I was sat in the away end watching the best outfit in the competition taking my beloved Hull FC apart, as we presented them with penalty after penalty from which, every time, they seemed to score! Put yourself for a moment into this situation, you're dejected, frustrated and wondering, after battling the traffic on the M62 for 4 hours, just what the hell you are doing there in the first place. Then there is the goon three rows back sat with his phone pressed to his ear catching up with everything that is happening at Craven Park and giving everyone, whether they want to hear or not, a running commentary from a game taking place 120 miles away in East Hull. Rovers are beating Wakefield easily and quite frankly I wish this sad soul would just shut up.

Then all of a sudden, through my attempts to ignore him, in drifts a claim that Wakefield are fighting back. Still not interested? Well not really. Then they are level and all of a sudden you hope he speaks up a bit and as the final score and the news of a surprise defeat for the old enemy is confirmed, you sit back safe in the knowledge that however bad the last five minutes of your own personal hell at Wigan pans out, Rovers have lost and so perhaps it's not quite so bad. Many sports' fans reading this will now be saying, "Nah that's not me" but many others know that it is them to a 'T' but perhaps like me you just don't want to admit being interested at all. Quite frankly, as I am being honest here, since those days back in the 60's I have actually grown to dislike games between the two Hull clubs, particularly the away ones! I don't go to Craven Park very often, because it's a place where the hostile territory, brings out the worst in our fans, and therefore in me as well.

However whether we like them or not and I certainly don't, Hull Kingston Rovers are part of it all because if you love Rugby League and want to live in a cauldron of emotion and passion about the game, there is no doubt at all that Hull is the place to be. It's a place where despite their affiliations to other sports everyone but everyone claims to have a leaning either to the red and whites or the Black and Whites, rather like the clans of Scotland, it's in their families and their lineage.

'The Sherriff of Fractured Jaw'

Still enough of the present and my failed obsession with not being obsessed with the old enemy, let's go back to the mid sixties and to my career as an apprentice gardener. I spent 6 happy months in total in East Park, finishing in late March and then moved onto tending the verges on Holderness High Road between Ings Road and the Ganstead roundabout where I worked with a new set of 'horticultural' friends. It was certainly a dangerous business because you not only had to be aware of the traffic flying by your backside as you bent over to weed the flower beds on the intersections, but also of the passing Councillors who seemed to be always watching you as they drove by, no doubt on their way to the Guildhall. Although there were certainly some perks too, with the young girls walking their prams up and down the road being just one of them.

The foreman this time was a cockney named Dave who was again a character. He didn't have a TV set and would talk endlessly about the radio programmes he listened to and the two films he had seen at the pictures. These were an American version of Robin Hood, from which he imitated Americans trying to speak in an English accent, and 'The Sherriff of Fractured Jaw' which was a Western staring Kenneth Moore, the British actor. How I wasn't killed in those shrubberies alongside the road I don't know because Dave would sneak up behind you whilst you were bent over weeding and shout "Go for your gun" which usually saw me fall out of the flower bed with shock. Another work mate called Bill, whose hobby was writing poetry, was really intelligent and used to accompany rose pruning and leaf raking by singing Gregorian chant and Handel's Messiah at the top of his voice. I might have moved locations but there was no doubt at all that as far as characters were concerned it was 'Business as usual' on Holderness High Road.

After my time out on 'the road' I was moved to the Council's central nursery about a mile from where we lived in Sutton. There I was introduced to propagation, greenhouse management and even a bit of flower arranging. The complex produced all the plants that were to be used in the City for both the summer and winter bedding schemes so it was to be an interesting year. One of the regular and most memorable jobs that I was employed on was going with the tractor driver Tom, riding in an open trailer to the central abattoir in the town centre to get the weekly load of manure. There always seemed to be tons of the stuff (but then the nature of their business down there dictated that there would be) which we loaded with pitch forks onto the trailer. The load was then tied down with a tarpaulin sheet and I rode back from Hessle Road in the City Centre to Sutton 5 miles to the north, sat on top of the load, hanging on for grim death, as the manure slopped around under the sheet I was sat on. The advent of the Health and Safety at Work Act was still some years away, and for me it was just part of the working week and I was certainly blissfully ignorant as to just how dangerous it probably was.

Let there be Lights!

In the sporting world of 1967 the live spectacle of Rugby League was being eclipsed by televised sport in general and football in particular. This was not just happening in Hull, where Hull City were still doing well and mopping up any 'floating support', but across the heartlands of the game in general until that was, someone thought of the BBC 2 Floodlit Trophy. This was a competition the Rugby League and the Broadcasting Corporation manufactured to meet the needs of TV, (something, sadly, that seems to have happened countless times in our game since then). BBC 2 was the corporation's new second channel, which had started two years earlier in April 1965 and since its launch it had gained something of a high brow reputation.

This had not pleased a section of the licence payers, particularly those of us who lived north of Luton. In their search for programming that would popularise the channel in the north of the country, the Governors of the BBC decided that sport should be introduced to their programming and so the then Controller, David Attenborough, came up with the idea of incorporating a bit of 'Northern Culture' in the form of a Rugby League tournament, which I guess in their 'southern' eyes at least, fitted the bill exactly.

A typical Arthur Keegan last ditch tackle. 1964 and Arthur grabs Rovers winger Graham Paul (The Cornish Express) just in time, as the crowd in the Well at the Boulevard gasp with amazement.

(Courtesy of Hull Daily Mail)

1965, and the old boys rally round.

Past Players v Present Players who turned out for the Tommy Finn Testimonial game.

Back Row: Markham, W. Drake, Whiteley, Hockley, Sutton, Dannett, Halifihi, Cole, Gemmell, Hollingdrake, J. Drake and Sutton.

Front Row: Scott, Coverdale, Bowman, Saville, Harris, Broadhurst, Finn, Evans, Holdstock.

Where's the ball?

Hull Loose Forward Clixby buries Rovers Harry Poole whilst everyone else seems to have lost the ball. *(Courtesy of Hull Daily Mail)*

3rd September 1966; Geoff Stocks passes to a young Chris Davidson who heads off towards the line. Just 7000 people attended this Derby, as the sparsely populated terraces testify.
(Courtesy of Hull Daily Mail)

24th March 1967, Hull 13 Rovers 12, Hull's Joe Oliver side steps
Stan Fleary with David Doyle-Davidson in attendance.
(Courtesy of Hull Daily Mail)

We always enjoyed a pitch invasion and the end of that Derby game
was no different. *(Courtesy of Hull Daily Mail)*

It looks like that was an awkward question!

Chairman Ernie Hardaker addresses the Annual General Meeting
on 30th April 1968. On the top table are Directors Joe Latus,
W. Downing and P Rose. No wonder Hardaker looks a bit shocked
he and Downing were about to be voted off the Board.

Wednesday 27th September 1967; Hull 31 Leeds 6

Back row: Brown, Whiteley (coach), McGlone, Broom, Macklin, Sullivan,
Harrison, Johnson, Neale and Booth.

Front row: Stocks, Devonshire, Keegan (Capt), Carmichael, Huxley and
Foulkes.

1968 Hull v Hull KR. The Eva Hardaker Memorial Trophy game at
the Boulevard sees Howard Firth and John Edson set off in pursuit
of Phil Lowe.

Clive Sullivan is a blur and too fast for the cameraman, as he flies in
to score against Hull KR at Craven Park in 1970.

Good Friday 1971 Hull 26 Hull KR 12. The great Terry Kirchin, master of the released ball and big hero of the author, scores at the Boulevard as Coupland takes a seat!

The Hull team of 1972 line up in the Directors' Lounge for an 'amateur' photograph the origin of which is unknown.

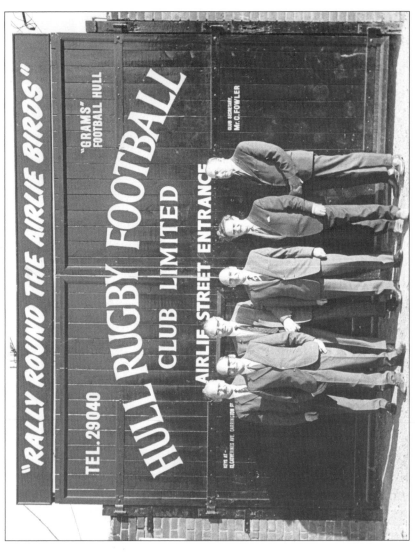

Chairman Charlie Watson and the Directors of Hull FC admire the Club's new gates in 1972.
(Courtesty of Hull Daily Mail)

Ironically enough, the idea was one that had been tried by the fledgling ITV networks ten years earlier when eight clubs took part in a tournament that toured football grounds in London. The City of Hull was not represented and in the end Warrington beat Leigh in the final at Loftus Road the home of Queens Park Rangers Football Club. Rugby League recognised the fact that they needed to raise the profile of the game nationally, but having decided that it was a good idea to work with the BBC they suddenly realised that few Rugby League clubs actually had any floodlights.

Many clubs and supporters had reservations when the BBC's idea was first muted and there were several strong letters in the 'Rugby Leaguer' which was the game's only weekly newspaper back then. However so successful was the exposure the tournament gave to participating teams, it caused no fewer than twenty-one clubs to install floodlights in pretty quick time. In 1967 the competition experimented with limited tackles for the first time, and this proved to work so well that a 'four tackle and a scrum' ruling was adopted for the full League programme the following year.

The series of games were staged in the autumn and each week at least one match would be played under floodlights, on a Tuesday evening; the second half of this match would then be broadcast live on BBC2. Non-televised matches were played at various times, depending on clubs' fixture lists and quite ironically the only condition for inclusion was that the club had to have floodlights.

In typical Rugby League fashion and quite bizarrely, the rules did not stipulate that these lights had to be good enough for TV cameras to be able to film the proceedings and so despite the title, many matches in the early rounds didn't even take place under floodlights and when they did it was hard to see what was going on out on the pitch. Clubs such as Barrow and Bramley, whose lighting was sub standard still took part in the competition but their games at home could not be televised. It was just another outlandish chapter in the catalogue of such shambolic happenings that litter the history of Rugby League and its administration.

So it was in 1967 that floodlights first arrived at the Boulevard being introduced solely to allow Hull FC to compete in the new competition. The then chairman J.L. Spooner and our Board decided, along with a lot of other clubs, that they wanted a piece of the TV action and so some floodlights were ordered and paid for by a loan from the Rugby League. The new lights were housed on eight columns four in front of the Threepenny Stand and 4 in the well of the Best Stand where holes had to be cut through the asbestos roof to accommodate the pylons. The total cost of the installation was according to that year's account's £7,138. Ironically Hull lost their first game under floodlights 8-12 to Rovers, at Caravan Park, in the preliminary round of the BBC competition. However nine days later we beat Leeds in a Yorkshire Cup semi-final in our first home game under lights, but more of that in a moment.

I have a vivid memory of that first Floodlit Trophy game which saw 14,000 fans packed into Craven Park to see their new lights for the first time. The incident concerned was a tackle by David Doyle-Davidson on the Robins new hero the dynamic scrum half from Castleford Roger Millward. Although afterwards all the players agreed it was an accidental tackle from where I was stood at the Tote End of the ground it looked horrendous, as Roger fell to the ground pole-axed and had to be stretchered off the pitch.

Years later David related a story about how the referee realised straight away that it was an accident but as the Rovers fans went wild and demanded blood, he called our player over to him to have a word. Doyle-Davidson had only been moved to number 6 that day to mark the mercurial Millward because he was accepted as being Hull FC's best tackler at the time and so understandably the crowd suspected foul play. The referee told 'The Doyle' that he realised it was an accident but as he could see how the crowd were taking it he would point to the Dressing Rooms several times and David would nod his head, he added, 'If you do anything else you will be off'. So, as the crowd screamed for him to be sent off our player stood hands behind his back nodding as the refereeing motioned towards the dressing room and the situation was defused. How times and referees in particular have change!

Several years later in 1974, under player coach and ex Hull hero 'Mr Reliability' Arthur Keegan, Bramley beat Widnes in the final of the Floodlit Trophy and it was to be the only senior cup competition the famous old West Yorkshire club would win, however, with another twist to the story of the competition, that final had to be played in the afternoon because of power cuts and the three day working week that was introduced throughout a period of national industrial unrest.

I would, no doubt, have been taking a great interest in the day to day work taking place at the ground to install the lights, had I still lived at number 23 but as I was now living in Sutton, I felt a bit removed from all that was happening down at my old stamping ground. If I was perfectly honest although Mum and Dad were happy living in the rural surroundings of Sutton my heart was still in Airlie Street and I missed the nearness of the Boulevard a lot.

Annie Robson's curtains

Although there was no indication as to just how much electricity these new lights actually used one thing is for sure and that is that when they were switched on they lit Airlie Street, Carrington Street and Division Road with an eerie sort of half light which created a strange and perhaps spooky effect for the folks who still lived around the stadium. A lady who lived in Carrington Street, Mrs Robson, actually wrote to the Hull Daily Mail claiming she felt she needed reimbursement for the cost of having her front room curtains lined, because she claimed, when the lights were on she couldn't see her television properly.

Despite the new attraction of the floodlights, times were hard for the Club and good gates hard to come by particularly with football still the talk of the country and the growth of the popularity of other distractions like television, pop music and motor cars. Whilst my pals and I were wearing beads, hipsters and caftans, and growing our hair to ensure that we complied fully with Hull's own version of the 'Summer of Love', it was the season in which Clive Sullivan scored 5 tries in one game away at Doncaster. This feat was heralded in the media the next day as, "Five of the best from the Black Flash". It was also the year that we lost to Rovers in the Yorkshire Cup Final at Headingley when, as a rare honour for the losing side, Chris Davidson was awarded the White Rose Man of the Match Trophy. I didn't go to the final for reasons I can't now recall and I guess feeling as I do about Derby games that was probably a blessing in disguise.

The first match under floodlights at the Boulevard

Wednesday 27th September 1967   *Hull 31 – Leeds 6*

As I alluded to earlier the first game that was played under our new lights was not actually in the Floodlit Competition but a really memorable semi-final game, on our way to that Yorkshire Cup final defeat. The game itself saw us produce a wonderful performance as that night we ran Leeds off their feet and we as fans absolutely loved it. Although the chants of 'We All Hate Leeds' were still some 40 years away, there was no doubt that back then, we still did!

The game took place on 27th September when we came out winners by 31-6 in an epic match in which once again, Chris Davidson shone. The Leeds team, packed with quality players like Bev Risman, John Atkinson and Mick Shoebottom, were red hot favourites to march on to the final, but our little scrum half took them apart with a marvellous display of terrier like tenacity, to which the much fancied 'Loiners' had no answer.

I enjoyed every minute of the game as did the rest of an amazing 14,000 crowd, many of whom it was suggested had been attracted by the novelty of the new floodlights rather than the anticipation of a good game of rugby. Any victory over Leeds was always massive for us kids back then, there was a pitch invasion at the end and we 'chaired' our victorious heroes off the field that night! Looking back to being a supporter in those days Leeds were in fact the one team with the exception of Rovers that we classed as our 'arch nemeses'. What it was that motivated our players so much when we played Leeds, is something to his day that still confuses me but there is no doubt that even in the darkest days of the 60's and 70's we always had a real go at Leeds when they visited the Boulevard. Their fans were always portrayed as a little 'superior' when compared with the working class core of FC supporters, an image that their apparent arrogance certainly perpetuated. They were also a club that always seemed to have pots of money to spend on players as well and the 'Threepenny Stand Choir' liked nothing better than to chant (to the tune of Camp town Races) "Spent a Fortune won f*ck all Leeds, Leeds" as invariably we overcame our West Riding adversaries in the Boulevard mud.

A busy Christmas? Father Christmas has nothing on the FC players

Saturday 23ʳᵈ December 1967   *Hull 22 – Castleford 6*

As I said we lost the final of the Yorkshire Cup that year against Rovers and before we had, as fans, really got over that embarrassment the year was drawing to a close. The festive season was always a busy time for players and fans alike and at Christmas 1967 it was no exception. Whilst the Beatles were in the middle of a seven week run at number one in the charts with 'Hello Goodbye' and 'Spirograph' and 'Action Man' were the top toys in most kids stockings, it was a great time to be living close to the Stadium. However, now I was based in Sutton there was a lot of travelling backwards and forwards involved in any busy yuletide fixture list. At least this time I manage to avoid getting stranded by the Christmas bus time table but looking back there is little doubt that particular festive period certainly emphasised how much different the game was in the late sixties.

Players worked full time and only trained when they could and because many of them needed the money they played whatever the circumstances, often despite suffering bad injuries and sometimes playing several games in a week. These situations driven by the need to earn as much money as possible may have led to the health problems some of them experienced later in their lives. That festive season was no different either with the FC playing a staggering three games in four days and all of them at the Boulevard. Can you imagine that happening now? OK some folks will say that it's more physical and intense these days, but it's all relative because modern professional players are fine tuned sporting machines, whilst back then I would describe them as 'hard as nails' part-time heroes, who gave their all every time they pulled on the Black and White shirt.

Thankfully at least the festive period was milder than the previous three had been but the Boulevard pitch was a real mess before we even started and of course that frequency of games did little to improve it but it was just the way the fixtures fell, because that year Christmas Day was on a Monday. The previous Saturday the 23rd, we played an 'awkward' looking game against Castleford and a good gate of 6,500 gave the Christmas shopping a miss and despite an East Yorkshire Bus strike, there was a great festive atmosphere in the Boulevard that afternoon.

The game started at 3-00pm and the new floodlights were on again but if I remember rightly they were always on back then, whatever time the kick off, something that was probably down to the novelty value of our new equipment. Still this was to be our best performance over the holidays, Jim Neale won the Man of the Match accolade after a masterful display in the second row and Keegan put in a great stint at full back joining the line in fine style whilst at scrum half Chris Davidson scored a great try. He was put through the Castleford defence by Nobby Oliver who cut in from the wing to feed a perfect ball inside to our scrum half. John Maloney could not get the day off work and so Davidson took on the goal kicking as well and landed four beauties from wide out. Willett the Castleford stand-off half kicked three goals in the first half, but tries from Terry Devonshire, Nick Trotter and Arthur Keegan saw us home, as we came out winners 22-6.

Then on Christmas Day, despite a skeleton bus service and no trains at all, 11,800 attended the local Derby against the old enemy which kicked off at 11-00am and turned out to be a ferocious game in which there were no fewer than 7 fights as a few old scores were settled. A brilliant first 17 minutes by the Rovers in which Flash Flanagan scored and Holliday kicked 4 goals saw the Robins put themselves in an unassailable position on what was a really heavy ground. Dick Gemmell our centre was mysteriously unavailable and we really missed him and as the cigars were smoked and the brandy swigged on the 'Threepennies' we finished on the wrong end of a 15-9 scoreline. Davidson had three skirmishes with Bill Holliday the last of which saw him land a 'pearler' of a right hook on the Rover's second rower's jaw for which he was immediately ordered off the pitch near the end. Alan McGlone 'planted' a brilliant left hook on Barry Cooper who was carried off the pitch in the last minute and in spirit of Peace and Goodwill the final whistle saw skirmishes break out right across the field. Joe Oliver pulled back a try for us and Maloney who replaced Gemmell kicked three goals, but in the end we lost. The game had promised a lot but as one 'hack' said after the game, "it had promised so much but ended up a damp squib".

Next day, Boxing Day, there was no let up as we played our third game but the time of year, the 1/9d admission fee or maybe even Cool Hand Luke and Dr Doolittle premiering at the Cecil and ABC Regal meant that just 3000 turned up to see what should have been an easy game against lowly Doncaster that in the end turned out to be anything but easy. Two really hard games had taken their toll and as we made just two changes, it was certainly hard going. The men from Tattersfield 'stuck it to us' in the first half and it was 30 minutes before John Maloney got a penalty to open the scoring. Gemmell was back in the team and broke several times but tired legs meant that there was no backing up and several chances were lost.

Otherwise the only other player to do his reputation any good at all was Arthur Keegan who had another fine game at full back but then again he always did. Devonshire and Davidson got tries for us and we were cruising toward victory, when in the last quarter of an hour the unfancied visitors roared back inspired by the try of the game, a brilliant 75 yarder by winger James which led to a 'jittery' last few minutes, but in the end we came out winners by 10-3. So it was 4 points out of 6 but the one we lost was as always the one we the fans were most interested in winning. We played at Bramley four days later and lost again but that was what the game was like back then and you have to wonder just how the players managed to keep going.

The biggest disaster of them all

As for the rest of the 1967/68 season it was by and large a quiet affair really, although I do remember that we signed Ken Owens an Aussie hooker who was not that good at rugby, but who the ladies really seemed to take to. However in the City of Hull and the fishing community in general the winter was to feature one of the worst tragedies that our brave, resilient people had ever seen. Hull FC being based in the heart of the fishing community was closely allied to the trawler industry and many of those who stood on the Threepenny Stand and 'Bunker's Hill' back then worked either off shore on the trawlers or in the ancillary industries which ranged from the fish houses and ice factory to net mending and trawler repairing. Everyone it seemed was involved in some way and before just about every home game the announcer at the Boulevard would read out telegrams sent from the crews of Hull trawlers wishing the team good luck that afternoon.

Then on 11th January 1968 disaster struck with the news that the Hull trawler the St Romanus had gone down in the North Sea just 110 miles off Spurn Point, with the loss of all 20 crew members. No sooner had everyone started to come to terms with the shock of that loss then on 26th January the Kingston Peridot sank off Skagagrunn on the Icelandic coast, again with the loss of all 20 men. A sombre minute's silence before the Wigan game on 3rd February was followed almost immediately by a further disaster. The final tragedy of what was to become known across the world as the Triple Trawler Disaster was the sinking of the Ross Cleveland on the 4th February as it sought refuge from a storm in the natural inlet of Isafjord in Northern Iceland. The three trawlers sank with the loss of 58 lives, with just one person surviving the disasters.

The whole City went into a state of mourning. Jenksey my pal lost two cousins on the St Romanus and an uncle on the Ross Cleveland

and Jim a lad who always stood with us on 'Bunker's Hill' at the Airlie Street end of the Boulevard, lost his Dad. The Hull Daily Mail was full of the grief and sadness that the City felt at the time, and at the next home game at the Boulevard another immaculately observed minute's silence was conducted before the matches began, grown men cried, and afterwards the usually bumptious and animated fans on the Threepenny Stand were strangely subdued and quiet.

Fighting Back!

The residents of the area were not prepared to just sit back and wait for more deaths to occur and the fantastic community spirit that pervaded the Hessle Road area back then led to a campaign for better safety at sea being launched by the wives, sisters and daughters of trawlermen. The campaigners met with trawler owners and government ministers, and some wives picketed the dock and even jumped onto trawlers as they went through the lock pit, in an effort to make sure no ship left without a radio operator.

These determined women, led by Lil Bilocca, affectionately known to everyone on Hessle Road as 'Big Lil' also travelled to London and met ministers to discuss better safety and fairer working conditions in the fishing industry. The campaign really seemed to capture the nation's interest too and it was strange to see images of Hessle Road and the Fish Dock featuring on the six o'clock news as we watched back home in Sutton. Nationally this action became known as the 'Headscarf Campaign' after that phrase was used on the front page of a national newspaper. Whether conditions improved that much is I suppose hard to say as already at this time the industry was starting to decline, something that was going to hit the community surrounding the Boulevard hard in the coming months and years.

The Curse of 'Mudball'

After Great Britain came back from the Mexico Olympics with 5 gold medals, the start of the 1968/69 season was a quiet affair on the rugby field, whilst for me as an 18 year old it was still largely a question of all work and rugby with the odd girlfriend, (many of my pals would say that my girlfriends were usually 'odd') and a few nights out with the lads, drinking, dancing and flirting with the ladies. I also attended 'Night School' at the Hull Technical College on Queen's Gardens in the town centre two nights a week, and went on a pleasant bus ride out to Bishop Burton College of Agriculture every Tuesday afternoon, to train for my City and Guilds Examinations in Horticulture. As I continued as an apprentice Gardener, I was still regularly moved around the City by the Council gaining experience and meeting more characters on the way. It was around that time that I worked a couple of three month 'placements' in Eastern Cemetery on Preston Road and at Sutton Golf Course on Saltshouse Road. They were interesting places to work and both hold special memories of a time when things at work were a bit more basic, and certainly a lot more relaxed than they are today.

There are stories too numerous to relate from this period of my life but I have selected one from each establishment, to give a flavour of the times and the backdrop to a life supporting the team I loved.

Firstly I was sent to work at Eastern Cemetery, where I was employed to cut the grass and look after the flower beds. Working in cemeteries, I soon found out, attracted a wide and varied set of often strange and morbid people, the most unusual I encountered in that cemetery being a grave digger called Harold, who was known on all occasions except when he was actually present as 'Mudball'. He was a giant of a man, totally bald, who was usually covered from head to foot in mud and seemed to arrive at work in a morning as muddy as he had left the night before. Folklore had it that once when working down a deep grave the walls threatened to collapse and as they started to crumble he held the clay up with his back whilst his pals escaped up the ladder and out of the grave.

He was certainly the strong silent type. He would work in all weathers getting sometimes soaked to the skin, and was always the one that the boss asked to dig the 'difficult' graves, particularly those in 'Swamp Corner' which was a particularly wet end of the burial ground. Funerals in this area were known to the staff as 'burials at sea', because the ceremony often had to be performed quickly before the grave, that had been pumped out right up to the cortége arriving, filled up with water again. It was all very serious stuff but there was great humour in those places too and a good camaraderie amongst the staff, let's face it there had to be, because if you couldn't laugh they were dour places indeed.

Everyone got on pretty well with each other except for 'Mudball', who kept himself very much to himself. I was often advised by the other gardeners to, "Keep away from him, he's bad news" and although I tried on several occasions to make conversation, all my efforts failed miserably. That was until one particular day!

On this occasion he had just finished opening a deep '10 footer' and was sitting next to the hole about to finish cleaning his spade and go to lunch. I was walking by and heading in the same direction, when he asked me if I would do him a favour and just pop back down the ladder to the bottom of the grave because he had left his 'baccy tin' down there. I, seeing an opportunity to strike up a repoire with the grubby giant, shot down the ladder only to find to my horror, that the bottom of the grave was actually the pierced top of another casket that had been buried there years earlier. There were bones, shroud and a skull to be seen through the broken coffin, and the sight of this turned me white with fear. I had heard a lot of horror stories from the other guys working in the cemetery, but this was, at just 18 years old, my first experience of something that the rest of the workers took as commonplace.

Then, before I could even let out a shriek, Mudball, had pulled the ladder out of the hole and left me down there. He then took one of the big sections of boarding that they used to cover open graves to ensure that no one fell in, and put it over the hole. I was immediately bathed in darkness with only the rotting remains of a long dead decomposing citizen of East Hull for company. I could hear 'Mudball' laughing as he walked away, and so there I sat for the next hour with just a skeleton and an empty 'bacca' tin for company! To my horror the hole then slowly started to flood until there was about a foot of water with bits of bone floating in it, lapping round my legs. He let me out without saying a word when he returned after his lunch, but as I walked off to find some dry socks I just laughed it off, because if I hadn't, it would surely have happened again and again.

Making money was par for the course at Sutton

Sutton Golf Course was of course a much jollier place to work and I was there, according to the 'Movement Letter' I received from the Council, to learn 'green keeping and fairway maintenance'. My mentor was a chap called Lenny Hunter who was a hyperactive, slender individual who always wore blue overalls and who had a friendly word for everyone. He had been Head Greenkeeper so long he seemed to know everyone who played the course and would share a joke with most of them as we met them around the fairways.

Within days of being there, the staff presented me with a battered golf bag with a shoulder strap, an old driver, a putter and a 'two' iron, and every lunch time after we had eaten our sandwiches we played the first five holes. I had never hit a golf ball in my life but believe me by the time I moved on, I knew every blade of grass on those first five fairways and had an almost mechanical knowledge of the lay of the greens. I always remember that it was quite a lucrative time too, as we all used to make a bit of money selling golf balls back to the golfers. The ironic thing was that often these were their own balls that they had lost but they didn't seem to mind. There were two ponds on the course and once balls had gone in there the players used to give up on them, and continue with a new ball.

Unbeknown to them we had large wooden rakes with 12ft handles secreted in the bushes and trees near these water features, and early in the morning when it was quiet, we would dredge the ponds, and retrieve the lost balls, before cleaning them up and selling them back to the golfers. We would have been in trouble if we were discovered, but we never were, and at 6d each we were happy, as were the golfers who got a supply of balls much more cheaply than buying them from the resident Golf Professional. However one incident does stick in my mind, which I will relate here as a cautionary tale about how it's not always a good idea to help other people.

Worm killer is something strictly for the worms

Today because of the rules and regulations of the EU there are few proprietary brands of worm killer on the market; in fact there are only a couple of industrial remedies, and none at all available to the amateur gardener. Of course, back then as now, the one thing you don't want on the velvet sward of a pristine golf green are worm casts because they can ruin the run of the ball. Indeed in 1968 it would not have pleased the mixture of local businessmen and 'un hired' Dockers that used the course every day, if their long putting game was spoilt by the remains left by some itinerant nematode.

Luckily for Lenny and the hundreds of other Green Keepers around the country back then the EU was still a way off, and the problem was easily solved, because in those less cautious days the accepted method of ridding the greens of worms was to use large amounts of arsenic. This was just one of several deadly poisons that the gardener had in his armoury back in the 60's and when used twice a year as far as killing worms was concerned, it was terminally effective. We always warned the golfers with signs at the gates telling them that there was poison on the greens and Len used to jokingly shout 'You're not a dog, so don't lick your balls', which always got a laugh. The deadly stuff, in the form of a white powder used to be supplied in big black drums about two feet high that carried a large white label with a skull and crossbones motif on it.

On one particular day in the late afternoon when Lenny and I were busy cleaning the grass off the blades of the gang mowers we used to cut the greens, we were interrupted by a regular golfer and eminent local businessman who we will call Rob. He put his head round the half closed door of the Machinery Shed at the side of the first green, and after an exchange of pleasantries, bemoaned the condition of his garden at home which was located at the more affluent end of West Hull in Kirkella. My ears pricked up as I thought that perhaps here was an opportunity for me to get myself a lucrative 'Govey' job, doing a bit of private gardening to supplement my wages. However, the talk quickly switched to his lawn and putting green, and the trouble he was having with worms. He said to Lenny, "Can you let me have some of that white stuff you put on the greens Len, the little blighters are driving me mad".

Now Lenny would help anyone, he had a great disposition, and often decanted small bottles of weed killer etc. to help folks out and I could see that he was tempted to oblige Rob. However having thought for a few minutes he refused to supply any worm killer, alluding to 'Council Rules' as an excuse to avoid the request. That was certainly a surprise because it was possibly the first and only time he had ever been anything but obliging. With that Rob got really upset, saying something like, 'Bloody typical, don't expect anything from me Hunter', before storming off. Lenny looked at me, shrugged his shoulders, and said, "I don't think he has anything I need really" and grinning got back to cleaning the mower blades. As for Rob, well the next we heard about him was in the Hull Daily Mail when the headline, "Bankrupt West Hull Businessman Commits Suicide" informed us that he had finished his life by gassing himself in his garage two weeks later. I don't know to this day why Lenny refused to supply that worm killer but at the time as you can imagine it made us all think a bit.

At last we see a few more new faces at the Boulevard

The 1968/69 season at Hull FC was as always full of expectation from this fan, although logically it has to be said that our poor financial state and transitional team meant that major success was highly unlikely. Still we had a new Chairman, Reg Lee, in place, and had signed Len Casey, Don Robson and Keith Boxall from local rugby, and Howard Firth from Hull and ER the top Union club in the City who were based in Berrisford Avenue. Howard was an exciting player who played at the opposite side of the field to the great Clive Sullivan in the position once occupied by my hero Wilf Rosenberg and as a try scoring winger Firth really looked the part. He was a teacher by trade, and had a physique built for speed; sleek and angular, with a shock of flowing blonde hair. He soon settled in and proved to be an elusive winger who could score the long range efforts but was particularly potent from 20 yards out and when stepping inside the defence. The media often described him as a 'mercurial' winger which pretty much summed him up.

Filling your face at half time and devouring the 'Pies'

Saturday 5th October 1968   *Hull 20 – Wigan 9*

Keen to move with the times, that season our Board introduced a new culinary experience to us gullible followers of Hull FC when they accepted a hot dog franchise for the first time, which the accounts for that year show raised £250 in concession payments to the Club. As for the season on the field, well it's safe to say that my usual initial optimism was predictably short lived and we fared poorly in all competitions, being knocked out of all the cups and the league play-offs in the first round.

The team was, some of us thought, just starting to emerge a little from the doldrums of the previous years and although we lost a lot of games we seemed to be starting to play a bit of decent rugby. The most memorable game in the early part of the season saw Wigan, the then elite of the league, visiting the Boulevard in early October 1968, for a game that came just one week after we had secured a tremendous 25-6 win away at Widnes. That campaign, as I said previously, was in fact destined to tail off badly towards the end but in those early weeks that rare victory at 'The Chemics' certainly raised our hopes for the visit of Wigan to the Boulevard, a fixture that always got everyone talking.

That 5th October it was once again 'proper Hull Fair weather' but in front of a crowd of around 9000 we gave 'The Pies', who were accepted in those days as one of the greatest exponents of flowing open rugby, a real lesson in how the game should be played. In fact by the end they could only look on and admire what was a tremendous display from the Airliebirds. Our coach Johnny Whiteley's attempt to beef the team up a couple of seasons earlier was starting to pay off and the new forwards we had gained like Jim Neale and Eric Broom coupled with some great local youngsters, like Macklin and Edson, were starting to lead the team around the field whilst the backs certainly had the speed to capitalise on some better organised play and score the points.

That misty Saturday Brian Hancock kicked off into a light breeze and just two plays later Chris Davidson felled Johnny Jackson with a real haymaker of a high tackle that got our scrum half penalised and set the tone for the early exchanges. Jackson in fact spent the next ten minutes staggering around in a daze and was soon replaced by Keith Mills coming off the bench.

Our backs were faster than the Wigan outfit and with Firth on one wing and Sullivan on the other, our centres got the ball out wide at every opportunity with Dick Gemmell having a superb game and scoring our first touchdown. Interchanging passes with stand in Hooker Jim Macklin he used Firth as a foil before dummying and outpacing the Wigan cover for a superb score out wide in front of the Best Stand at the Airlie Street end. The 'Pie eaters' didn't like that at all and tried their best to use some muscle to get back into the game but as Terry Foggerty dropped the ball on our 25 yard line, Arthur Keegan was on it in an instant. He accelerated away from the Wigan defenders and drew the full back Tyrer, before a looping wide pass released 'The Mercurial' Firth to run, hugging the touch line, to score in the same corner. Once again Maloney converted and we were 10-0 up.

There then followed Wigan's only real period of pressure and they scored a try themselves when Maloney missed a tackle on Ashton and he released Foggerty to score under the posts a touch-down that was converted by Colin Tyrer and so despite more pressure from our forwards and John Edson dropping the ball over the line as he stretched to score, we went in just ahead by 10-5.

The second half was all Hull. Hancock and Davidson taunted the Wigan forwards and opened the game up at every opportunity whilst prop Jim Macklin, playing as a make shift hooker, thrilled us all with some barnstorming runs down the middle. It was one such excursion into the heart of the Wigan defence that set up the next try. Macklin drew several tacklers before releasing the ball to Jim Neale who ran straight back into the heart of the Wigan resistance before passing onto Maloney. He turned inside to find the now released Macklin again and the big prop rolled over the line next to the posts. Macklin's tenacity and persistence won him a standing ovation from the fans in the Best Stand seats as he walked back from scoring the try, just as the Threepenny Stand broke into a resounding chorus of 'Old Faithful'. We were not finished yet either and Joe Brown made a break from the kick off which left Wigan's centre Ashurst grasping thin air. Joe was finally tackled by full back Tyrer but got up, played the ball forward to himself, and ran in to score another try which he also converted.

Wigan 'huffed and puffed' but just got more and more frustrated with our solid defence and in the end resorted to kicking the ball, usually straight to our full back Keegan, who returned it 'with interest'. There then followed some rough treatment by the Wigan front row forwards on Howard Firth when the winger moved inside, and then right in front of us, Ashurst stood on his hair in the tackle which prompted Man of the Match Dick Gemmell to race in and drag the Wigan player away.

However for this fan, enjoying the game from the Airlie Street terracing the most memorable part of the match came ten minutes from the end when the 'Big time Charlies' of the league decided that they had experienced enough of trying to beat us by playing rugby, and Ashurst once again took out his frustration on young Howard Firth. This time he dragged him back by his long blonde hair and 'all hell' broke loose. Edson, who had looked like 'losing it' on a couple of occasions already, ran straight to the melee and tried to punch Keith Mills, he missed completely but connected with Chris Davidson's elbow and fell pole-axed onto the grass.

Rather than calming things down this just made the whole situation worse, and to the cheers and goading of the 'Threepennies', Macklin crowned a brilliant game with a superb left hook that laid Fogerty out cold. As both he and Edson laid side by side on the pitch unconscious, several scuffles broke out and at one point referee Naughton waded in himself to try and separate both sides.

As it eventually calmed down, the two comatose players received the 'magic sponge' from 'trainer' Ivor Watts and the Wigan staff, whilst the referee lined both sides up facing each other and went down both lines of players shouting in their faces and wagging his finger at them. It was all very school boy like and comical, and the fans loved it. Sending offs for fighting were still very rare occurrences back then and all that eventually happened that afternoon was that both captains got a warning and we got on with the last few minutes of the game.

In the end the final score was 20-9 and we all went home happy. The tries scored and general play from the Black and Whites was great, but it was always something special when you beat Wigan, and there was no doubt what was the topic of conversation in the pubs and clubs of Hull, that night; Jim Macklin, (who left a few years later for Bradford), was long remembered at the Boulevard for that left hook!

Chapter Seven

Sunday ... bloody Sunday!!

Sunday 20th September 1968   *Hull 28 – Huddersfield 14*

The 1968/69 Rugby League season contained a very special event in the history of my great rugby team when, along with several other 'hard up' clubs, Hull FC decided to give Sunday rugby a try for the first time. The first game we ever played on the Sabbath was at home to Huddersfield on 20th October 1968. The game was certainly a success as far as the Club was concerned and reflecting on the actions on the field the headlines of the Hull Daily Mail next day described it perfectly when they stated 'Sullivan Try Highlight of First Sunday Game'.

A big crowd of 8,600, (who paid £2059), stood clasping their match day programmes, (which they had purchased at an inflated rate to compensate for the fact that it was illegal to sell tickets for any sporting event on a Sunday), and watched a bit of history being made at a sunny Boulevard. On the car park before the game we were greeted by several people from the 'Lord's Day Preservation Society' who stood sentinel like holding up banners that announced, 'Keep the Lord's Day Sacred' and ' Repent ye the Kingdom of Heaven is nigh', but just queued round them, and paid little heed as we made our way to the turnstiles. It was quite 'tight' standing on the Threepenny Stand that day, with the most memorable aspect of that tradition breaking afternoon the first try, after just five minutes, by Clive Sullivan, which the local paper referred to in that headline.

The try unfolded like this. A move on half way saw Gemmell, Hancock and Davidson inter pass for the ball to go out to Clive who was well covered by three Huddersfield defenders. He swept past two of them and then hared down the touchline hugging the whitewash for about 40 yards with what was left of the visitor's defence trailing in his wake to touch down in the corner to great celebrations all round the ground. Next up it was Dick Gemmell's turn to go on a run. He picked up a loose ball about 30 yards out and ran for the line. He checked back inside a couple of times but by the time he got to the white wash he was met by a wall of Huddersfield defenders, that had tracked back to cover, but Dick just ploughed into them and stretching an arm out of the ruck to place the ball over the line for our second try.

Huddersfield scored next with a try for ex London Saracens RU player, John Kersey-Brown. He followed a kick through from Gordon Wallace, to harass Arthur Keegan into a rare mistake. As our full back dropped the ball, Kersey-Brown kicked ahead and touched down in the corner just before the ball trickled over the dead ball line. It was only a small setback for Hull though and before half time we were on the score board again with a try that was simplicity itself. Shaun O'Brien took Chris Davidson's short ball on the charge and shot through under the posts to reinstate our lead. O'Brien had a great game and was awarded the Man of The Match accolade, although he was closely followed by Joe Brown who had recently switched from centre to loose forward with great effect.

The second half was played in bright sunshine as the Hull team stretched their lead this time with a try by the 'ubiquitous' Howard Firth who somehow got in at the corner after a sweeping move involving Keegan, Charlesworth and Chris Davidson. Kersey-Brown forced Firth out of play but the touch judge decided that our winger had got the ball down and the score stood. Next as we started to take control, Keegan and Charlesworth put Davidson away. He passed to Sullivan who drew three men towards him before turning the ball back inside to the trailing

Davidson who scored untouched by any Huddersfield player. Jim Macklin who was then playing the best rugby of his career at Hull, took umbrage at a loose arm and repeated his party piece from the Wigan game by laying the Huddersfield hooker out cold. However the referee either decided to ignore the offence or missed it completely and just waved play on.

Finally a sweeping move involving Macklin and Edson put Gemmell into a gap, he drew the defence and passed to Firth who once again managed to beat the Rugby Union convert to the corner but only just, and he received a clout on the head after he had scored that saw him have to leave the field with blood streaming down his face.

When the game was won in the last minute Kelsey-Brown finally got in as he caught our defence flat footed and probably already thinking about a celebratory drink, and the visitor's winger swept down field and scored next to the posts. We won the game 28-14 to record our biggest victory of the season so far. The fans loved the idea of playing on a Sunday and no doubt some City supporters who usually watched their games down the road at Boothferry Park came along for a look too! So all in all our first sortie into Sunday rugby was a great success, and despite his mistake Arthur Keegan who was once again crowned the fans' Player of the Year that season, got the Man of the Match award.

Transfer talk; it's what kept us going

That season we signed several players in an effort to try and continue rebuilding the team, as back then there were no embargoes on signings, quotas, salary caps or indeed rules on poaching staff. Players changed clubs and were signed up throughout the year unlike more recent times when all transfer and contract business is done well before the season starts and mid season changes are a rare occurrence.

Back in the sixties although classed as a 'Professional' game, Rugby League was to all intense and purpose a 'semi professional' set up and there was always a vast amount of movement of players between clubs during the season. Players were even 'tapped up' after games or visited at home mid week, by grey men in long coats with turned up collars, for clandestine meetings, to offer an extra few bob to move clubs. This of course led to a healthy level of interest in the game here in Hull, not only on the field at a weekend, but also between games, because local speculation was always rife about who we, or Rovers, were about to sign.

In part, our geographic isolation was a problem when trying to bring new team members in, because it was difficult to get players to relocate to Hull. In fact in hindsight I suppose that Johnny Whiteley did really well to attract players like Eric Broom from Huddersfield and Jim Neale and Terry Kirchin from Cumbria. If our position at one end of the Rugby League heartland meant it was hard to get new recruits it also worked in our favour as it was also hard for other clubs to poach our home grown stars and get them to leave the City as their employment was usually here, and back then with no motorways, travelling was a time consuming experience. It's amazing that our Dewsbury based captain Arthur Keegan never ever learned to drive and if he couldn't beg a lift from Ken Huxley who lived just down his street, he used to travel three times a week to training and home games on the train. When you consider he played for Hull for 13 years that was certainly a feat.

The lack of expensive full time contracts also meant that players could get released more easily and transfer fees were commonplace. Chris Davidson, Joe Brown and Alan McGlone all, from time to time, asked to be put on the transfer list, usually when they had a grievance with the Club but in the end stayed at Hull because they could not afford to move to the West Riding. There was always a great buzz around the national media when a 'world record' fee was placed on a Rugby League player's head. I well remember back in the early 80's, when we signed Steve Evans from Featherstone for a fee of £70,000, the national media were ablaze with speculation as to where he would go for days before the deal was announced. We of course were ecstatic when he signed for Hull FC.

Sadly, these days, all players at Super League clubs are under contract until at least the end of the current season, and no movement is allowed, officially, (unless the players' current club gives permission) until the end of August. That, for me, is a shame, and I feel not only contributes to the lack of exciting speculation and fervent gossip in the media, but it also adds to some of the ridiculous rumours that circulate at all clubs during the season. A glance at any of the independent club message boards on the Internet will soon show that some of the stories and speculation would often be better attributed to Hans Christian Anderson than the clubs or players themselves!

The demise of transfer fees in general is I feel a little sad, if not (bearing in mind the large salaries clubs have to pay out these days and of course the salary cap) very understandable. Back in 1901 there was, I am sure, great excitement when Bramley's Jim Lomas was transferred to Salford for £100! And the media profile for the game was further enhanced when Mick Sullivan was transferred from Wigan to St. Helens in 1916 for a world record £11,000. Not to be outdone, more media frenzy followed when Oldham signed Ike Southwood for £11,002 and ten shillings two weeks later. The steadily rising tide of transfer fees finally came to a head in 1991 when Martin Offiah left Widnes for Wigan for a fee of £400,000, but with clubs struggling to make ends meet anyway by then things really had started to get a bit out of hand.

Back in the sixties, you always got a morning paper to read in your break at work and we all used to comb it for news of our club and possible signings. Most of the national morning newspapers, particularly those printed in Manchester, contained speculation about these imminent moves and players often used to contact the media themselves to generate their own rumours to help improve their options. There is nothing like an odd rumour or two to get clubs a bit twitchy about losing their best players! In fact the Sunday tabloids such as The Mirror, The People and The News of the World had gossip columns by John Huxley and Co. about Rugby League every Sunday. We used to pour over them every week, but more importantly this exposure meant that the uninitiated fan or the casual observer could get interested in what was going on in the world of Rugby League. Just try and find any coverage at all in these Sunday papers in modern times and you'll see that rugby coverage is usually confined to three pages of 'Yawnion', followed, if you are lucky, by a single match report from a Saturday league game on the previous evening.

It is important as the spectacle and excitement of our great game increases that we make the most of it in the media, but I think it is about time the national media had a good critical look at their football dominated sports pages. I'm sure that the inclusion of a bit more Rugby League particularly on weekends would increase their readership considerably, at least in the north of England. Perhaps the Rugby League should also look at their rules on contracts etc and see if there is a way by which there could be more movement during the season, as the inclusion of a bit of transfer speculation, and news, throughout the year, would I think probably help interest in the game no end as it did back in the 60's, 70's and 80's.

A guitar hero is born and I was there ... well sort of!

When I left Lenny and Sutton Golf Course I had experienced three of the most enjoyable months of my apprenticeship thus far. In fact when my movement letter from the Council offices in Ferensway dropped on the mat at 10 Potterill Lane, it was a big disappointment indicating as it did that next I would have to peddle my bicycle a bit further along Saltshouse Road onto the Bilton Grange Estate.

My next place of work was to be Alderman Kneeshaw Playing Fields or AKPF as it was known to all on the Parks Department. The park was a windswept place with a cinder running track, which was the home of East Hull Harriers and this part of my apprenticeship was aimed at developing my skills in maintaining these kinds of athletics facilities. The boss Ronnie was waiting outside the mess room to meet me on my arrival that first Monday morning and immediately appeared to me to be a stern individual. He was clearly unfit (something I found out quickly was down to his inactivity during working hours) and the way that his brown smock coat only fitted where it touched meant that he could best be described as portly. He was never seen without that coat, which I quickly found out was referred to by the rest of the staff as his 'Bulling Smock'.

All this paled into insignificance though for a young apprentice because all I really noticed on our first encounter was the fact that Ronnie had really strange eyes. One was fixed straight at you whilst the other was scanning the skies! This condition which was referred to as being 'Wall eyed', was like club foot, cleft pallet and stuttering, a deal more common back then but still took you back a bit when you encountered it full on! I was now getting used to meeting new people and I quickly settled into the routine at what was a relatively new park.

The work was interesting, if not a bit boring at times, although Ronnie didn't hold back on using the experience I had gained on the bowling greens of East Park when Harry Clappison, the regular green keeper, won the football pools and just walked off the job one Wednesday afternoon! For a couple of weeks I was in charge of the bowling greens and at the mercy of the Veteran's Bowling Club, who I found very quickly were difficult, if not impossible to please. The game of rink bowling or 'old man's rugby' as it was affectionately known to many who didn't play, was taken very seriously indeed and often arguments would break out on the greens as one bowler or another was accused of measuring the distance from the bowls to the jack utilising 'an elastic handkerchief'.

The best memory from that period of my life though concerns the other gang of parks department workers who shared the mess room facilities with the permanent staff at AKPF.

They were a group of gardeners and labourers who looked after all the verges, playgrounds and gardens surrounding the 'Pensioners Bungalows' in and around Bilton Grange Estate. All of them were real comedians and thoroughly good blokes, if not a bit 'laddish' in their behaviour. They didn't work directly for Ronnie and so they used to give him some real stick, in fact I guess they were a real wild bunch at times and would often play the card game brag for big stakes during the lunch hour. Amongst them was a tall, good looking guy with flowing blonde hair who wore the tightest jeans you ever saw and always had a smile on his face. He was, I was soon to discover, the late great Mick Ronson the world renowned guitarist who formed the Spiders from Mars with David Bowie. He then went on to play with Ian Hunter and Mott The Hoople and to produce records for hundreds of artistes before he tragically died of Liver Cancer on 29th April 1993, when he was just 46 years old.

Back then (and probably to the day he died) he was just an ordinary guy with ambitions that at times did not seem to match his obvious talents. He was a smashing bloke and a real friendly character as well as being a brilliant musician. Mick and I got on from day one. He lived on Bilton Grange, with his Mum Minnie, his Dad George, sister Maggie and much younger brother Dave. From the day I met him I made it my business to take every opportunity I could to go and see him and his band the Rats wherever they played. Looking back I am so glad that I did. I was completely taken with Mick indeed I think I was a little over whelmed by him and spent hours talking to him and listening to the stories he told about his adventures out on the road with the band. He was so easy going and of such a generous nature I think to this day he was one of the nicest people I have ever met.

The amazing flying guitarist!

One of his favourite stories was usually precluded by him showing a small scar on his stomach which he gained one night when he was playing in the local band the Cresta's, before he joined the Rats.

The band were, (he related to a packed mess room), performing a Beatle's number and Mick was singing harmonies when he reached out to hold the mike whilst keeping one hand on the strings of his guitar. Who Knows? Perhaps the equipment was faulty or wasn't earthed properly but there was a mighty explosion and Mick flew off the stage and ended up across a table out on the floor amongst the surprised dancers. One of the other band members had to prize the guitar off his body where it had burnt itself onto his stomach. Well that's what Mick said anyway. He was rushed to hospital as he was out cold and was told by the doctor in charge that he was, "A very lucky young man". Mick was almost paranoid about checking his equipment after that.

He also had lots to say about a period in 1966 when he had taken his guitar and set off to earn fame and fortune in London playing in two bands 'The Voice' and 'The Wanted' and he told tales of freezing cold bed sits, begging for food and playing at the Marquee Club. It was just great to be around such a lovely bloke who radiated stories about a world we had only read about in the papers.

Whenever he went out onto Bilton Grange with the old four wheeled cart full of gardening tools, all the girls, young and old would shout, "Hiya Mick" whilst the lads would usually shout "Ronno" at the top of their voices and wave to him. Every time a Co-op mobile shop van passed there would be a great laugh amongst the lads too, because it was in one such mobile shop that Mick first worked after he left school. He was without doubt a real local hero. Mick was always the rock star even back then, and could be seen constantly stroking his long platinum locks whilst he inevitably had a supply of combs in his inside pocket.

Following the Rats

The Rats certainly were a great band with Mick Bolder on Bass, Woody Woodmansey on drums, (both of whom went onto play with Mick in the Spiders from Mars) and Benny Marshall on vocals. Their repertoire was bluesy and featured a lot of Mick's favourite music of the times by Jeff Beck and the Cream. Some of the songs I remember seeing them perform include Beck's, 'You Shook me', Cream's, 'I'm so Glad' and Hendrix's 'Hey Joe'. Whilst at times they would throw the odd bit of more mainstream stuff in, like, when it was released, the Beatles 'Paperback Writer'. Mick 'worshipped' Jimmy Hendrix though and I remember his favourite album of the time was, 'Electric Ladyland', which he always laughingly referred to as 'The Electric Landlady'. He had a strange taste in films too and was severely ragged when the lads found out that he had been to see the musical 'Mary Poppins'.

There was a strong music scene in the City then and as well as the Rats (or the Treacle as they were known for a short while) there was a great 5 piece who specialised in Tamla Motown music called the 'Variations', and a couple of good bands that used to come over from the Scunthorpe area called 'The Peighton Cheques and 'Gospel Garden'. I used to travel quite a bit on a weekend to see these bands and the Rats, and despite not owning my own car I managed to get there somehow, either by a lift, the train or the bus. I occasionally travelled a bit further afield, travelling to venues such as Brough Village Hall, Beverley Regal, Hornsea Floral Hall, Withernsea Pavilion and South Hunsley High School.

Although it goes against popular perceptions with regard to Mick's unflagging ambition to be a big star, my chats with him left me with the memory of someone who was, at that time, a bit disillusioned with the national music industry and really happy playing with his pals in the Rats on the local scene. I had moved on to Pearson Park and lost contact with Mick by the time Woody Woodmansey sought him out as he marked out playing fields on Greatfield Estate and persuaded him to leave his marking machine and go and join him, Mick Bolder and David Bowie in the Spiders from Mars, the rest as they say is history.

Mick was as I said, tragically taken from us in 1993 but, despite everything that came after in his illustrious life, I will never forget my brief encounter, at Alderman Kneeshaw Playing Fields, with a real 'guitar hero' and a really top guy.

In out of the Cold

Sunday 23rd March 1969   *Hull 11 – Leeds 11*

So, after that short excursion into the world of popular music it was back to the 68/69 season at the Boulevard which turned out to be one of mixed fortunes with a run of 9 games undefeated in August and September. In the New Year however the snow and frost descended on the Boulevard and we only played one game between 27th January and 23rd March when we 'Came out of the Cold', as Mike Ackroyd of the Hull Daily Mail put it, with a massive game against Leeds the old enemy from the West Riding. This time it was the League game, against a team that I already realised always magically brought the best out of my team.

It was a Sunday match and with City doing so well down the road (although the official switch by the Rugby League to playing all games on a Sunday was still some five years away), this change of day for the big games was the only way our Board of Directors could attempt to entice the 'floating' sports' fans of the City back to the Boulevard. At that time, as I said before, it was still illegal to charge for games under the Sunday Observance Act. This piece of outmoded legislation dated back to 1780 and prohibited public entertainments in England and Wales on a Sunday for which an admission charge is paid, although apparently you were alright if you played in Scotland. So as I said previously, you paid your money as usual and to get round the law the programme that was usually fourpence 'suddenly' cost you 'half a crown' and of course your 'admission' was then free.

That year the whole league programme had been decimated by the freezing cold weather, but Leeds, because of that underground 'electric blanket' at Headingley, had kept their home games going and were, when they arrived at the Boulevard, sat at the top of the League and certainly 'match hardened'. Of course we always played well against them but on this occasion the Boulevard was heavy and quite devoid of grass in the centre third and you had to fear for our lighter pack against the big mobile forwards of the West Yorkshire club. I was still watching my rugby from the Gordon Street end of the Best Stand and it was pretty busy in there that Sunday when, starved of the game they loved, 7,400 fans turned up to 'buy a programme'. There was a strong rumour after the game which inferred that so many people attended, the Club ran out of programmes and in desperation sold beer mats as a means of admission. However I have to say I never met anyone who actually owned up to buying one of those costly coasters, but it's a good story. It was a big day too for local hooker Alan McGlone who returned to the team for his first game for over a year.

It was a dank misty afternoon when the teams ran out dead on 3-00pm, and with the floodlights already on everyone stood about waiting for the three officials. For some unknown reason it was a full two minutes before the referee Mr Manley appeared with his touch judges, but at last they ran out and we were ready to start.

The game was destined to be one packed with spectacular rugby and great attack and defence from both sides. Leeds with that famous half back combination of Seabourne and Shoebottom took the early exchanges, although a couple of great tackles by first Dick Gemmell and then Howard Firth twice stopped Sid Hynes when he looked like crossing the line. However, after some robust tackling the first touchdown came on the 15 minute mark and it went to the Airlie Birds. Alan McGlone was a good solid local player who had clearly decided that as he had got his place back, he was keeping it. Finding himself with the ball in midfield he produced one of those great trade mark side steps where his floppy sandy hair went one way and he went the other, as he opened up a massive gap in the Leeds defensive line. He shot into the opposition's 25 yard area before turning the ball inside for Joe Brown to crash in under the sticks. John Maloney stepped up to stroke over the conversion and added to it with a penalty after 27 minutes, and we were 7-0 up and looking pretty good.

Leeds was a classy outfit and it was taking all our guile and tenacity to keep them out. After that penalty Arthur Keegan tackled both Cowan and Bill Ramsey inches short of the line and it looked like we would hang on to our lead until half time when we lost concentration momentarily and the mercurial Bev Risman shot through a gap near half way. Again Keegan tackled him but the big, mobile Leeds forwards carried on the move and second rowers Ayres and Ramsey presented hooker Tony Crosbie with an easy try which Risman converted.

We were all preparing for half time, but just on the whistle we missed a great chance to stretch our lead. Chris Davidson who was having a great game keeping Seabourne quiet with his terrier like tackling hit the diminutive half back head on and as he dropped the ball, Chris fell on it to regain possession near the Leeds 25 yard line. Hancock handed onto Eric Broom who carved out a great opening before sending Jim Neale trundling towards the line. He could probably have scored himself but he turned the easiest of passes inside to the unmarked Edson who dropped the ball in front of him. The whistle went and although we only led by the slenderest of leads, we all agreed that the quality of the rugby after such a long lay-off was great to watch and more than we could have really expected.

The second half started late again, this time we were all in 'fits of laughter', as the referee came out with his two officials but both teams held back and to chants of 'Why are we waiting', from the Threepennies, they made the officials stamp their feet for two minutes before emerging from the tunnel. Coach Johnny Whiteley's half time talk must have been on the subject of 'What you have you keep' because the Hull team obviously had decided to ditch some of the flamboyance of the first half and concentrate on defence, and counter attack. Leeds on the other hand stepped it up a notch, and threw the ball around like those Harlem Globe Trotters who had graced the Stadium all those years earlier.

For the first ten minutes we held Leeds at bay but lacked field position and found ourselves constantly pinned back in our own 25 by the probing runs of the big Leeds pack. When we finally got out of our territory on the end of a great run by Edson, we were awarded a penalty for off side and despite a following wind an audacious 40 yard attempt from just in front of the Threepennies saw Maloney's kick hit the left hand post and bounce dead.

We scrapped our way back up field again and this time Davidson tried a massive 48 yard drop goal which hit the right post and bounced back in play and into the arms of a startled but relieved Bev Risman. In the stands the opinion was that we were not having too much luck at this point. Then Joe Brown picked up a loose Cowan pass and wrong footing the attacking Loiners set off down the pitch. Risman came across to attempt a 'ball and all' tackle and in doing so smacked our loose forward across the face. Maloney made no mistake with the penalty and stretched our lead to 9-5.

Only three minutes later Leeds struck again. This time it was their stand out forward Mick Clarke who got the ball wide out and headed towards the corner. As the Hull cover hesitated, expecting him to pass to winger Smith he dummied, then kept going and as our cover realised too late to do anything, he was over in the corner. Risman narrowly missed the goal but our lead was reduced to just one point and it was 'panic stations' both on and off the field. As we all looked on nervously, Leeds threw the ball about and Hynes went close before Risman shot through to the line only to drop the ball as he crossed the whitewash.

We were certainly hanging on, but once again it was Man of the Match Chris Davidson who came to the rescue, as he dummied out of the line from a scrum, breezed past Shoebottom and made about 40 precious yards down field before Cowan caught him from behind. From the play the ball McGlone brilliantly delayed his pass and then switched play to the open side and almost as soon as he had received the ball, Joe Brown dropped an amazing goal on the run. He ran forward stepped round a Leeds tackler stopped dead in his tracks, looked up and dropped a 30 yarder from slightly to the left of the posts. With just 10 minutes to go and a three point lead we scented victory and our tackling really stiffened up, causing the Leeds forwards get a little upset and concede penalties when they were in good positions.

Then after Keegan had fielded a deep kick from Risman on our line, Harrison passed onto Maloney who would have been better driving in and 'dying' with the ball in the tackle. However in the heat of the moment our centre dropped the low pass and with just 5 minutes to go Sid Hynes picked up and touched down in the corner. To everyone's relief Risman missed again and although it was 3 tries to 1 in Leeds favour the scores were tied 11-11. Still the excitement had not finished. Stung into attacking action, the Hull side finally came out of their shells and twice brought Howard Firth into the game down the wing. The first time he 'Scored' only to be brought back for a forward pass and the second time, the last play before the final whistle went, he was forced into touch just 5 yards short.

Hull had looked likely winners until that late try, and despite only drawing the game no one left the ground before the final whistle, after which the reception the home lads got would have led anyone entering the ground at that moment to believe Hull had actually won. In the end it was all down to goal kicking, Maloney got 3 from 5 whilst Risman only got 1 from 6. However after such a great performance it would have been a total injustice had either side lost. Everyone had a fantastic time that afternoon, a fact that was emphasised by the 'gallery' of empty beer bottles left on the ledges at the back of the Threepenny Stand as the crowd departed. I felt truly elated again, so much so that for once I even enjoyed the long bus ride home to Sutton.

Bishop Burton College and back in a band

As I indicated earlier, as an Apprentice gardener part of my training required that, as well as going to night school in Hull, I attend the East Riding College of Agriculture and Horticuture at Bishop Burton one afternoon a week. Night class on a Monday and Friday was alright, in fact I quite enjoyed it really, something that I suppose looking back was mainly down to the lecturer on the course, Fred Fletcher, who was the head of the botanical gardens and grounds maintenance side of the University of Hull. He was a real fanatic and loved everything about gardening. He was a small guy with a wicked sense of humour who always wore the shiniest shoes you have ever seen. His lectures spanned all aspects of the subject from detailed elements of Botany to how to construct a rock garden from the debris of an old air raid shelter.

He talked about everything mundane or otherwise with great enthusiasm and a relish that seemed to rub off on all his students. If College on a night was great, Bishop Burton College on 'day release' was all a bit bizarre really. Firstly you had to get to the City Centre, and then there was a long bus ride out into the country. The students at these sessions were not only drawn from the apprentices of the Hull Parks Department but also from other areas of horticultural work and there were tractor drivers, botanists, hedge trimmers, glasshouse workers and gardeners. If the range of careers was wide, then so were the personalities.

There was the head lecturers son John, Colin from Ellerker, Ted from Brough, Kevin and Mary from Skirlaugh etc. etc. etc. Dick Robinson who, a few years later, was destined to become a real personality in the world of local radio, and even made it onto Radio 4's Gardener's Question Time, was the senior lecturer. What a guy he was, small diminutive with a weather beaten florid face, a neat tweed suit and (again) well polished working boots. Dick, who had worked his way through the Hull Parks Department himself years earlier, was also an accomplished Church Organist, and he certainly did not stand for any messing around in class. In fact on a couple of occasions he threw me and my pal 'Fritz', out for fooling around and cracking jokes at the back of the classroom. Dick though knew his stuff and I think he eventually forgave me in the 80's, when I was City Hall Manager, and I let him have a couple of goes on the City Hall Organ. He really enjoyed those sessions. He's still around at the time of writing, and since retiring lives in Rudston.

My relationship with Barry back on the Boulevard had waned somewhat because of the distance between where we now both lived, so the band stuff had all fallen by the wayside, and although I was still playing my guitar at home, that was about it really. However my brush with 'Ronno' and love of attending live gigs meant that I still had ambitions in that direction and this led to me receiving a proposition, during a pruning session in the walled garden at the College, by Colin who hailed from the village of Ellerker. Col was, I found out later, an accomplished bass player who wanted to form his own band. He worked at Beans, the commercial lettuce, cucumber and tomato grower in Brough and was without doubt a real 'country' character. He had long frizzy hair, was around 5ft tall and always wore really high Cuban Heeled Boots. In addition he usually wore a tatty green parker coat and smoked a curly pipe stuffed with Old Holburn!

Colin invited me to his house way out in the country one Sunday, and I took my guitar on the bus and jammed a bit with him and his pals in an old Air Raid Shelter in their garden. I was doing OK, and they were I think all quite impressed until we were joined by a lad from Liverpool called Denny who arrived with a Burns guitar which he plugged in and then commenced to blow us all away. Colin lived with his Mum who was known to everyone in the village as 'Ma' and Denny was a lodger with them. Denny who spoke with a rich 'scouse' accent was a real wide boy type of character, who I took to immediately. If you saw him on the street he was a pretty none descript sort of guy in his mid twenties with freckles and wiry black hair, but put a guitar in his hands and he was a star.

The rise and fall of the Clockwork Chicken

Denny was certainly a cultured musician, not as good as Mick Ronson, but light years ahead of me and so it was decided, there and then in the block house in Colin's back garden in Ellerker, that we were to form a group with Colin on Bass, Denny on Lead Guitar, a lad called Howard on drums and me, (as I seemed to be the only one who could sing), on rhythm guitar and vocals! The 'Clockwork Chicken' was born!

I returned home excited about the chance to play in a band again, and on the long bus journey back to Sutton I frantically tried to work out how I could persuade my Dad to lend me the £120 I needed to buy a PA system. We had plenty of amps and speakers but nothing to sing through. Mum, (good old Mum), thought it was a great idea, and helped persuade Dad, as usual, with a few of his favourite teas. Finally he succumbed and about three weeks later I had bought a pair of Selmer Speakers, a Carlesboro amp and a Shure Unisphere microphone from Johnny Pat at J.P. Cornells Music Store on Spring Bank in Hull. The band practised in the little Church Hall in South Cave, and although mainly a singer, I was still allowed to play a bit of rhythm guitar on some numbers. However, soon, under the guidance of Denny, we honed a couple of dozen songs and were ready for the road.

After a few pretty ineffective performances at the local youth club that mainly featured power failures, exploding amplifiers and the smell of burning, we managed to get ourselves an agent and the bookings started to roll in. The problem was that we only had two old Ford Anglia vans to ferry everything about in, so everywhere we went we went in convoy. That was fine at the Regal Ballroom in Beverley, but our so called 'agent' continued to get us bookings at places like the Greyhound in Louth in Lincolnshire and the Lincoln City Supporters club. At £20 a night for four of us, we were never going to be millionaires at this rate. In addition to this rather worrying drawback I was also often found the next day by my foreman on the Parks Department, asleep in a shrubbery after those long hauls to darkest Lincolnshire. We got some gigs in Hull though, and one memorable evening we played the Humber St Andrews club on Hessle Road. At the interval I was just about to get a pint to calm my nerves after a set in front of what could only be described as a 'hostile' crowd, when a giant of a man came over and pinned me against the bar. He said, "Was you looking at our lass?" to which I replied, "I certainly was not", to which he retorted, "Why, what's wrong with her?" That was an interesting night!

We played all sorts of stuff from the Byrds, 'So You Want To Be a Rock and Roll Star' to Crazy Elephants 'Gimmi Gimmi Good Loving' and from Cream numbers like 'Sunshine Of Your Love' (everybody did that one), to Cupids Inspirations 'My World', the programme was as varied as the response we got from the crowds. There is no doubt that it was great fun, although I am afraid to say it was also very short lived. Denny was an obvious talent and was soon poached by a top club land Country band and the rest of the Clockwork Chicken just fell apart. So as Mick Ronson went from strength to strength, after about twenty odd gigs, me and my PA system returned to Sutton, and my career in gardening.

A tragedy at home!!!

It was a good thing that I was not too preoccupied with becoming a travelling troubadour or a 'Rock Legend' either, because I was needed at home, as it was around that time then that disaster struck when Mum had a lump in her breast diagnosed as Breast Cancer. No doubt many people reading this will have been there either themselves or with loved ones but there is simply nothing that prepares you for the news and no one that can quite explain just what you are about to go through as a family. Why us? Why my Mum? She was taken into Hull Royal infirmary within two weeks of discovering the lump for a small 'Lumpectomy' but as was so often the case in the sixties, once they got started with the operation it was a lot worse and she was in the Theatre for about 5 hours. She left hospital three weeks later sadly minus both her breasts.

Mum and Dad had always smoked cigarettes, it was an accepted thing with most of their post war generation and it was that habit that was just twelve years later to lead, in part at least, to the demise of them both. After three weeks in hospital Mum's initial recovery was slow, starting with two weeks at the local Health Authority's convalescence hospital at Withernsea. Dad and I made the long haul on the bus to the coast to see her just about every night and it was a lot easier once she was home again. She was in a terrible state for someone who had such a flamboyant and happy outlook, but she battled on and the support she got from her new friends the congregation at St James Church in Sutton, where both my parents now worshipped, was particularly helpful. It was hard to come to terms with the change in circumstances we were all experiencing but Dad and I tried our best to get things back to some sort of normality. They were tough times for Mum though, not just physically but psychologically and she was sadly never to be the same bubbly person she was before the operation.

Meanwhile the only thing I had time for after work and helping look after my Mother was rugby and at the Boulevard the season was drawing to a close with three wins on the trot and a final weekend defeat at Wheldon Road Castleford by 10-14. For us fans it had been a mediocre season under Chairman Reg Lee but at least he had started to sort out our finances and at the annual shareholders meeting the Club were able to post a small profit of £1530.

Terry Kirchin, simply a magician!

Saturday 9ᵗʰ August 1969   *Hull 30 – Castleford 4*

Now as an aside for a moment I would like to take a little time to talk about one of those forgotten heroes that stick in your mind as a fan for your entire life and yet are never mentioned in the annals of our great Club in the same breath as say Knocker Norton, Dave Topliss, Clive Sullivan or Peter Stirling. They are the players that have that special quality, be it skill, character or just plain toughness that all real fans love and that helps keep the player's memory alive in their thoughts forever. I guess, for this fan, there are just one or two who fall into this category which Americans call their 'Hall of Famers' and second row forward Terry Kirchin would always be in the ranks of my all time great players along side the likes of Kenny Foulkes and Chris Davidson for their loyalty, Wilf Rosenberg and Clive Sullivan for the sheer spectacle and excitement, and Knocker Norton and Peter Stirling for their absolute genius.

Terry is one player that I just cannot forget and any catalogue of my life, or the history of my supporting the Club I love would not be complete without him getting a special mention. On Thursday 7th August 1969, the Club announced in the Hull Daily Mail that we had signed a gangly, tall second row forward on a three game loan deal from Barrow. No one had heard of the player who we were told was called Terry Kirchin. His debut that Saturday against Castleford in the first round of the Yorkshire Cup saw us beat the West Riding club, 30-4, and Kirchin was simply amazing. Time after time he ran the ball in hard, 'sucked' in the opposition forwards to then reveal what was to become his trademark move. Wherever he was on the field he would keep on his feet in the tackle, a hand with the ball in it would appear from the ruck and it was out of the melee to whoever wanted it.

For the first few times this happened that day against Castleford, the ball just went to ground, but once Davidson and Hancock had 'Got the Idea' they took the ball every time and Kirchin's trickery led to three tries that day. The man was a marvel and by today's standards he is probably best described as a cross between Paul Sculthorpe and Paul Daniels, so good was his second row play and so magical were his repeated off loads. In fact the more that Castleford tried to stop it the more he did it. At the end of the game the crowd gave him a standing ovation but our Board, cautious as ever, said that he would play out his loan spell before they made a decision on his future.

However after he had reproduced exactly the same form and trickery at York the following week, and as other clubs were starting to take notice of his stylish play, action had to be taken and he was signed on for a career that lasted three seasons, during which Terry made 118 appearances for

Hull FC. As a slight aside it would not be right not to mention that game at York which we won 22-15, without including details of an incident from that game which showed just how things have changed from those days back in the 60's.

If Terry Kirchin played well that day it's a game that Arthur Keegan will never forget because half an hour before kickoff he thought that he was going to miss the match altogether. He didn't travel with the rest of the team from the Boulevard in the bus but instead got a lift from his home in Dewsbury straight to the Wiggington Road Stadium. With just half an hour to kick off he was stranded hopelessly in a traffic jam and still three miles from the ground. Arthur had been named on the team sheet and therefore had only one option. He abandoned his 'lift' and ran to the ground arriving just five minutes before the start of the game. In fact if that was not enough in the dying minutes of a gripping Cup tie, with his pre match exploits unknown to the one thousand Hull supporters in the ground, Arthur pulled off a brilliant try saving tackle on York player Rippon when a match winning score seemed certain. Running three miles to a game and then playing....those were certainly the days!

We won the Cup, we won the Cup!!!!!!

Saturday 20th September 1969 Hull 12 – Featherstone Rovers 9

As Mum struggled to recover from what was viewed as a major operation back then, Dad and I worried and I tried my best to do everything I could to help at home, whilst continuing working and attending College but after that there was precious little time left for much else. Well not for much except of course rugby and the 1969/70 season was one that holds for me some pretty great memories. With no M62, away trips were of course limited to big cup games and therefore most of what I remember features First Team and 'A' Team games at the Boulevard, but that last season of the decade was the one that the Club at last managed to secure some silverware.

The Yorkshire Cup still featured as an early season competition back then and that year we had beaten York and Castleford at home in the early rounds and then beaten Leeds 20-17 in the semi final under the lights at Headingley, which meant for the second time in three years we had got through to the Yorkshire Cup final.

So it was that on a drizzly September morning I made my way from home in Sutton to Paragon Station to catch the 9-00 o'clock train to Leeds for our appearance in that Final where we were to play Featherstone Rovers. Two years previously we had come up short in the same fixture against Rovers but this time with new signing Terry Kirchin on board we had high hopes of getting our first final win in the competition since 1924. It's hard to believe that with all our success in the second half of the 1950's this trophy that was probably (because of the competition format) the 'easiest' to win had still alluded us and although we had been in the final eight times in recent years we had still fallen short on each occasion and lost out when it mattered most.

The train was packed with Hull FC fans starved of success and once we got off at Leeds City I went for a few beers in the Scarborough Hotel which was just round the corner from the station where the juke box blasted out the Beatles 'Come Together' and 'Sunny Afternoon' by the Kinks. At about 1-00pm, a little the worse for wear I got some fish and chips and then boarded the bus for Headingley where we alighted right outside the Cricket Ground turnstiles in Kirkstall Lane. Once inside we took up our position in the South Stand amongst another 6000 high spirited Hull fans. Rugby League was going through a torrid time back then and that was reflected in a gate of 11,089 which was the smallest to ever watch Hull FC in a Cup final. I suppose as we were three places above Featherstone in the League table at the time, we just started the game as favourites.

The day before the match coach Johnny Whiteley had announced that Club Captain Arthur Keegan would miss out through injury. There were few times in his thirteen year reign as Club full back that Arthur missed a game and so it was to be ironic that 'Mr Reliable' was missing when we won the only piece of silverware we got during his entire career at the Club. His place was to be taken by youngster Malcolm Owbridge who was playing in only his seventh First Team game. The other big pre match worry was the fitness of Centre Dick Gemmell who had taken no part in the cup run having been out for the past eight games. He had suffered with a bad ankle injury, but with Keegan out it was decided that Hull would risk him with his ankle strapped up.

He took over the captaincy for the day and said afterwards that the large wad of white strapping was actually on his good ankle to fool 'would be' tacklers in the Featherstone ranks. He had two pain killing injections in the bad ankle before the game which by the end appeared to be wearing off a bit. Just how brave Dick was that day can I think be gauged by the fact that after the match, so badly had he aggravated his injury, he couldn't walk to the bus and because of this injury he was then out of the game for 12 weeks. Still cometh the hour cometh the man and Dick led us brilliantly that day.

The game was played under the four tackles and a scrum rule that was introduced three years earlier and the number of scrums this generated (39 in all) saw us given a big advantage throughout the game by hooker Alan McGlone who won 29 of them. Sadly at times poor handling and 'option taking' meant that we wasted that advantage somewhat.

We kicked off playing towards the current score board end, although back then it was on the opposite terracing which these days accommodates the new Carnegie Stand. In our first set of four plays 'Mr Magic' Terry Kirchin managed to release a ball from a five man tackle to the supporting John Maloney. This play eventually saw a 50 yard flowing move thwarted on the line by the 'Colliers' full back Cyril Kellett. Next it was the turn of Alf Macklin who took a great inside ball from Dick Gemmell to again be held just short. Featherstone then threatened through Newlove and Nash but Hull's defence, with particularly Harrison and Forster repeatedly stamping on any power thrusts by the Featherstone stars Thompson and Mick Morgan, stood firm. One player that was literally sparkling though was our loose forward Joe Brown, who was by far the most creative player on the field having the Featherstone defence mesmerised at times. The rest of the half was really a stop start affair with Hull taking the lead through a Maloney penalty and Kellett kicking two more for the opposition leaving us trailing 4-2 at half time.

The second half started with a 'nice little' punch up when Smales went for Gemmell and three or four FC players piled in. From the resultant 'tap penalty' Hartley the 'Colliers' scrum half 'scored' only to be brought back for a forward pass. Then we took the lead. A flowing move started with some great slight of hand by Kirchin this saw Brown carry the ball down field before releasing it to Dick Gemmell. Now I don't know if you ever saw Dick play but if you did you would remember the way that he took the ball into the tackle and being such a tall guy he was able to somehow pass over the top of the opposition player to release the ball with a bullet like wide pass. That is just what happened that day and Sullivan gleefully took the ball and cantered in for a try which Maloney converted.

At 7-4 up we had a golden opportunity to put the game to bed but we then witnessed the one piece of action that anyone who was there back in 1969 will remember to this day. Alan McGlone broke free from a tackle and fed Gemmell who was by this time limping badly. Three would be tacklers saw his distress and decided to pounce but once again out came that wonderful, powerful pass over the opponent, and Sully was away and heading for his second touchdown. We all cheered with great relief as he crossed the whitewash but stood open mouthed as he just kept going. He then turned to go to a position closer to the posts but before he could get the ball to ground he slipped and shot over the dead ball line. We just could not believe what we had seen, and neither could Clive who said after the game, 'My feet just shot from under me, I felt like crying'. So did the crowd who were momentarily reduced to a stunned silence.

Still we only had to wait a few more minutes before Joe Brown set up the winning score. Once again, vindicating Whiteley's decision to risk his dodgy ankle, it was Gemmell making the initial break before he passed onto Joe. Brown ran straight at the heart of the Featherstone forwards dummied once and then twice before slipping a wonderful inside pass to Prop Jim Macklin who ran in to score unchallenged. Maloney kicked the goal and despite a Steve Nash try in the dying minutes causing a few hearts to flutter, the whistle went and we were home and dry, we had at last won the Yorkshire Cup.

We all ran onto the field to congratulate the lads and then congregated around the central section of the best stand to watch the trophy presentation. Joe Brown got the 'Man of the Match' award that day but the whole team, resplendent in their white shirts with the black V, looked so pleased with the victory. The fans went mad singing and chanting as it took Dick Gemmell all his time to crawl up the steps to lift the trophy. But for me personally it was a defining moment because we had won a Cup, the first since I saw the light and became hooked on Hull FC and it was a brilliant feeling. A few more beers with the players and a round or two of 'Old Faithful' in the bar under the Stand, made for a pleasant journey home although it was a good job that the trains from Leeds terminated in Hull back then, because by the time we reached Paragon Station the guard had to wake me up as I was fast asleep clutching my programme and no doubt dreaming of more silverware.

If you're a 'proper' fan there is little doubt you'll have suffered a lot for your team and you'll also 'benchmark' your life with their exploits. Some fanatics seek assistance by keeping programmes, scrap books or press cuttings, others continuously talk about the past as if in fear that they forget it. We all have statistics and Club and player records in our heads too. These days in the 21st century I can't remember what I did last Saturday, but I can tell you exactly where I was stood on the pitch at Headingley when Dick Gemmell raised that trophy. That in the end is what it's all about for me!

We're so lucky as Hull supporters to have the greatest battle cry in the whole of the Rugby League World

It was, funnily enough, during that game that I remember looking across to the Featherstone fans who had regaled us with their chants of 'Featherstone Featherstone' throughout the game and seen the look of envy in their faces as we belted out 'Old Faithful' back at them. It's a look I have seen literally dozens of times as I travelled the country watching the team I love because it is without doubt the greatest battle cry there is in the game and most other supporters know in their heart of hearts that it is simply unique as anthems go.

Why do I say that? Well Leeds have more recently adopted 'Marching on Together' Rovers have their 'Red Red Robin' and Saints 'When the Saints go marching in' and I guess that's about it really as far as bespoke anthems go. But the 'Loiners' song was written specifically for Leeds United Football Club, whilst the Hull Kingston Rovers and the Saints 'anthems' see them adopting a song because it has their club's nickname in the title. 'Old Faithful' though is different, it is a one time popular song that has no mention of Hull, our ground or even our nickname in it and so as an adopted song that has lasted for 80 odd years it is very special. In fact, it's just an otherwise little known popular cowboy song, sung in the mid thirties by Gene Autrey to his horse.

It is said that it was first sung by a single voice and then taken up by the crowd, in a game against Wigan in 1936 and was directed to our most faithful of servants and absolute icon of the game Joe Oliver. Whether this is true we will probably never know, but there will no doubt be Hull fans everywhere who claim a different origin for this most famous of battle cries. All I know is that it is heard at grounds across the game as well as at funeral services, wedding receptions and even in one case around the font at a Christening I went to! We are so lucky to have the unique anthem that is 'Old Faithful' and that along with the most original strip in the country really does, for me, set us apart from all the rest of the clubs in the game. But then again I am a bit biased! Still it is debatable what effect 'Old Faithful' has on the team that Hull are playing at the time that it is sung as well, because a lot of folks I know feel that it also inspires the opposition to greater things, but that's again something that we will probably never know.

It was that season that the diminutive figure of Charlie Watson took over as Club Chairman. He was a mild mannered, dapper, well dressed man who was always seen smoking his pipe and it was not long before he had granted Arthur Keegan a well deserved Testimonial Year, in recognition of our full backs service to the Club. We all bought raffle tickets and entered into the spirit of the benefit campaign because Arthur was now just part and parcel of the 'furniture' at the Boulevard, and despite being of West Yorkshire heritage most certainly one of our own.

That's Hubert over there; he's the one peeing on the Chrysanthemums

As I navigated the world of work my next port of call as a garden apprentice saw me sent for three months to work in the old Conservatory in Pearson Park. The foreman down there Frank Bates took me that first Monday morning to meet the guy in charge of the old Victorian edifice that was the giant greenhouse in the middle of the Park. There I was introduced to Hubert who was probably the cleverest gardener I ever met. He was a short fat guy with an infectious smile and an opinion on everything. He wore a traditional gardener's apron, trousers tied up with string and rode everywhere on a rickety old delivery bike with a metal basket carrier on the front.

I was to serve under his guidance, and learned everything there was to know about growing hot house flowers and plants in deepest West Hull. The heating system was powered by two massive cast iron boilers in the cellar and it was my job every evening before I went home to stoke the boiler so it stayed warm through the night. Next morning even before the kettle was on I had to rake all the clinker out of the foot of the furnace and barrow it out up a steep ramp before re-stoking the boiler for the day ahead. That was back breaking work and I was also, once every two weeks, spending all day shovelling the latest supply of coke from the path (where Rafferty and Watsons the Coal Merchant tipped it), into the massive coal bunkers next to the boiler house.

Hubert it was said could, 'Root a broom handle' and he certainly used some unique methods to get the best results. He collected rain water for his African Violets which he grew on corrugated iron shelves over the heating pipes, ground bones that he had delivered from the local butcher for fertilizer and used human urine as a secret additive in his Chrysanthemum watering, "to make up for the lack of trace elements". It was not unusual at all for a member of the public to open the big white front door of the Conservatory to find Hubert relieving himself into a watering can!

He had a wicked sense of humour too and I remember one day a rather suave gentleman entering the Conservatory and enquiring as to the availability of a 'gardener' to give him some advice. I called Hubert and the businessman then related how he was worried that his next door neighbour was growing, "that 'Marijuana' stuff they are always talking about on the TV". He said that he had tackled him about it but his neighbour had assured him the plants were in fact sprouts but he was, he said, "Terribly worried." Hubert thought for awhile, stroked his chin and then said, "Well, If I were you I would climb into his garden whilst he is out, take some of the leaves home, boil them, let them cool then eat them and if your still worried in half an hour, then I think I can assure you that they're definitely Sprouts". Hubert was, like so many others that I met on the Parks Department, simply a great guy and a real character and it was a sad day when after just three months my stay at Pearson Park came to an end. But I was a much wiser gardener for the experience.

Leeds Again ... I bet they're getting fed up with us lot beating them!!

Sunday 23rd November 1969   *Hull 9 – Leeds 8*

Next up in the League was the mighty Leeds. Back then for every other Rugby League team 'big spending' Leeds was the outfit that everyone wanted to beat. Between 1968 and 1973 they reached the play off final four times and won it twice. They had some great players included in their ranks like that 'sparkling' halfback pairing of Seabourne and Shoebottom, who were still going strong and the 'mercurial' Bev Risman who seemed to be always hitting the headlines in the 'Rugby Leaguer' newspaper. This game was probably the best that season if you exclude that wonderful Yorkshire Cup final win and was played on 23th November 1969 at the Boulevard on a cold, cold day in front of 7,500 spectators. The visiting 'Loiners' provided us with a stern challenge having lost just once in the League in 14 games. We on the other hand, were in turmoil with the players in dispute with the Board over pay and threatening to go on strike.

On top of that, two of our best players, Dick Gemmell and the great Arthur Keegan, (the latter still in his benefit year), were both missing through injury. Gemmell was still injured after his heroics at Headingley in the final, whilst Keegan had been back playing since that game but had received a back injury in training in the week leading up to the game. We had actually already beaten Leeds on the way to that Yorkshire Cup Final triumph so the fans all hoped against hope for another upset. I watched the game from the Threepennies that night and although it was only November there was frost in the air and I particularly remember that the old ground looked really run down, something that was hardly helped by the fact that although they were musically a thing of the past by then, you could still hear The Bachelors crooning 'Diane', 'Ramona' and 'I Believe' as their nasal tones crackled out of the Rediffusion 'tannoy' speakers around the ground like some scratched and worn out 78rpm record. If, that was, the speaker near you was actually working at all!

Stood there in the old stand, amongst friends and amidst the smell of beer and cigarette smoke, we were all still discussing the possibility of a players' strike when that greatest of goal kickers John Maloney, kicked us into a seven minute lead and slowly but surely the confident Leeds outfit started to buckle under the threat of a well marshalled Hull pack. Players like the soon to depart Jim Macklin, and Mick Harrison, Alan McGlone, Joe Brown and Chris Forster ripped into the Leeds pack whilst Terry Kirchin again mesmerised the opposition's tacklers by always being able to sneak the ball away before the tackle was completed. It was almost a challenge every week for the opposition to stop it, and in one incident he was surrounded by no fewer than 6 Leeds players, but still managed to stay standing, before handing the ball out to Ken Huxley to start another attack.

Then right in front of us Clive Sullivan, with the embrocation that he lathered his body in before games shining in the floodlights, sped in at the corner following a superbly smuggled pass out of the tackle by Kenny Foulkes. Back came Leeds to 'pepper' stand in full back Owbridge with a series of high kicks, the third of which resulted in a dropped ball and Leeds regaining possession. The ensuing play the ball caught our defence flat footed and the speed of the Leeds backs saw Bev Risman sending Mick Shoebottom flying away for a converted try. So we went in at half time just two points behind on the scoreboard but full of heart for the rest of the game.

The second half was just as intense as the first, and Hull went back in front with two more Maloney penalties one for a foul on Kirchin whose magical ball skills in the tackle were by this time starting to rile the Leeds players. As the clock ticked on, Leeds suddenly seemed to realise that they were about to lose only their second game in the League that year and 'cranked everything up a notch', but try as they may they could not break our defence to score. In the end they had to be satisfied with a solitary try far out on the right by Atkinson after a last ditch tackling effort by Alf Macklin just failed to nail him. Risman could not convert and as the final whistle went the sound of 'Old Faithful' ringing through the rafters of the old Stand heralded a famous 9-8 victory for the FC.

It was a fabulous win and a great 'backs to the wall' performance that saw our Directors, coaching staff and players out on the pitch at the end. As we jumped the fences and chaired the players from the field we all thought that the Cup game followed by this great win had seen us turn the corner. As always seemed the case back then, it was another false dawn, and we fell away badly at the end of the season. However one thing that was good was team spirit and the players could often be seen out and about together around the town. There were plenty of jokes around as well, with Alf Macklin and Terry Devonshire the Club jesters who were always playing tricks on the rest of the team. One great story saw Terry Devonshire and Clive Sullivan admiring one of the other players' newly born baby in a carry cot. Clive said to Terry, "Look at her poor little mite she thinks we're the Black and White Minstrel Show".

Now everyone's talking about Terry Kirchin

Saturday 8th March 1970   *Hull 17 – Huddersfield 3*

By the time we got to the New Year and a new decade everyone it seemed was talking about my new favorite player Terry Kirchin and his ball releasing and handling abilities. Since he arrived at the Club his reputation was growing and he had become quite the local hero. The thing was back then he was a completely new phenomenon, because in those days forwards just didn't release the ball. Before I leave that season and indeed the decade of the 1960's I must just report on what was probably the best game I saw Kirchin have in the famous Black and White hoops. It was a match that took place at the Boulevard later that season on 8th March 1970 when the opposition was Huddersfield, a team who were just one place behind us in 9th position in the league.

Throughout the game we were much the better side but for all our efforts it took us a long time to get the better of the 'Fartowners' that day. Huddersfield who had taken an early lead with an opportunist try by their loose Forward, Davis in the 26th minute took everything that we threw at them and were assisted, I remember, by a glue pot of a pitch which was in places ankle deep in mud and that made turning quickly nearly impossible. Just before halftime however in the south corner of the ground, Terry came to the rescue when he plunged through a ruck of players at the play-the-ball, to score and Maloney tagged on the points for us to go in 5-3 in the lead.

The second half was the memorable part of the game for me and it was Hull all the way, as we belied the conditions and threw the ball around to play some great rugby. Hancock fed Eric Broom who put out a deft little 'reverse' into the path of Kirchin. This time Terry just charged at the Huddersfield forwards as one after another they attached themselves to him. As players tried to get his legs he just stepped out of the tackles and ploughed on. He shook off the tacklers and started striding into a gap about 20 yards out and could have probably scored himself, but instead the rangy forward gave the ball to John Maloney who went on an arching run round the defence to touch down in the corner. Maloney himself converted from a difficult angle and we were on our way.

About ten minutes later, Loxon the Huddersfield scrum half tried a short kick out of his own twenty five but it went straight to Dick Gemmell who drew the defence before giving an inside pass to Brian Hancock to score another. Our forwards were now on top and Kirchin was in the thick of everything we did. His driving runs had Huddersfield players showing a distinct aversion to getting involved in the tackle and he was matched for most of the time by Mick Harrison who ground into their pack time and again. There were, we found out later, two of the Rugby League's International selectors present and no doubt Harrison's form that day would have caught their eye. The other forwards got involved too with both Roy Firth and Shaun O'Brien following Mick's lead.

Huddersfield 'Hard Man' Ian Van Bellan then decided that he had experienced enough of the constant hard tackling that he was being subjected to by the Hull pack and hit out at Mick Harrison felling probably the toughest player I have ever seen in a Hull shirt with a perfectly executed right hook to the face. The referee had an idea as to what had happened but was obviously confused and as Mick was helped to the side lines by our coaching staff, he just had a 'Stern word' with the Huddersfield captain for the night, Senior.

As we looked on from the terraces and with blood pouring down our prop forwards face the doctor administered about 5 stitches above Mick's eye whilst he just stood there hands on hips staring at the action going on out on the field. Immediately after the physician had tugged at the stitches to tighten them and washed his face with a sponge, Mick went back onto the field. Still bloodied all over his face, he stood in the line and as the referee followed the play as it swept to the left, he walked out of his position and hit Van Bellan so hard with an upper cut that the St John Ambulance stretcher bearers were onto the field before the referee had chance to blow the whistle. Apparently after the game the referee commented that he knew Harrison had hit Van Bellen but he, "Hadn't actually seen it!"

With around five minutes to go to the final whistle, Kirchin got the ball on his own 25 and ran straight at giant Huddersfield prop Stephenson, who crumpled to the ground as three more would be tacklers moved in, but Terry just took the tackles standing up and while the opposition tried to rough him up he wrestled his ball handling arm free and handed the ball out to a grateful Ibbotson in support, he ran on another twenty yards before being stopped in a great last ditch tackle by Huddersfield second rower Bob Taylor. That last play of the game has stayed with me all my life and despite watching hundreds of games and players involving our great Club that vision of Terry Kirchin is for me one of the easiest RL memories to recall.

Just to put the icing on the cake Terry eventually left us for Rovers after three seasons for a handsome transfer fee, but he decided that after a couple of games he did not like it over there in the East and he quickly disappeared back to a job in the petroleum industry and relative obscurity! Anyone who has watched rugby in Hull for over 40 years will remember Terry Kirchin and for those who don't, believe me, you missed a treat!! The great times of Terry, Arthur Keegan, Clive Sullivan and Dick Gemmell gave a glimmer of hope for the all the fans of Hull FC at the end of the sixties but it was a glimmer that the first part of the next decade extinguished completely.

So the seventies started with me at twenty and continuing to ply my trade as an apprentice gardener, Hull FC were doing reasonably well when you consider our difficult financial situation whilst Mum continued to struggle to recover from what was back then a long process of convalescence. The future was beckoning, as was probably the toughest decade I have had to endure both as a fan and a person and it was going to be pretty shocking for my rugby team at times too.

Chapter Eight

Hard times are on the way

As the 1970's arrived, back at the Council new employment legislation deemed that the minimum age for a worker being paid as an adult was to drop from twenty one to eighteen and so although I had not completed my full five year apprenticeship, at the age of twenty I was moved back to East Park to take up the position of Assistant Gardener. My wage shot up to over £20 a week and I felt like a millionaire. In fact it was to transpire that those of us actually caught in the gap between eighteen and twenty one were to be the last ever apprentices in horticulture at the Authority, and so I guess I was really lucky to actually come out of this period of work with a 'Trade' as a 'time served' gardener, a profession that was to be something, as far as local authorities were concerned, that would be a thing of the past.

On a weekend I continued to travel to dances at South Hunsley High School and Brough Village Hall, where I enjoyed some great local bands like the Strollers, Mandrake and The Amazing Blondel, there, in addition to listening to excellent music there was also a bit of dancing and a deal of fraternising with those beautiful East Riding girls too. At Boothferry Park Hull City under their new manager Terry Neill were doing well, although the banter between the football supporters and us rugby lads was as fierce as ever. We did all have a laugh though when two City fans were prosecuted by the magistrates in Sheffield for throwing oranges at Ian McKechnie the City goal keeper at a Sheffield United v Hull City game. It was an accepted part of the tradition at Boothferry Park but a tradition that was obviously completely alien to South Yorkshire Police.

As far as rugby goes little was changing, well not for the better anyway. Saturdays (or increasingly Sundays) were still spent down at the Boulevard although times were hard and destined to get harder. In fact looking back it's fair to say that those first seven years of the 70's were some of the toughest we had ever seen at the Club. I accept there were some good times and some great wins but they were borne out of the principle of passion and determination overcoming adversity and ability, for we were certainly far from being a great team or likely to get anywhere near the top of the league. Despite the undying passion of us fans and the efforts of the administration at the Club the latter scenario was simply never going to happen.

Admittedly in that period Hull FC broke lots of records but sadly they were always for plumbing new depths in the level of our attendances, for larger than ever losses of income, overdrafts at the bank or for the number of points we conceded. The Boulevard itself was looking really run down as well and most weeks when the floodlights, (which had been lit with such pride a few years earlier), were used, there were as many bulbs that had failed as there were those that were lit.

However despite dwindling interest on the terraces, and a rundown Stadium, Hull FC did reasonably well at first. Money was in short supply and there were few new faces coming into the team. But despite that we still had 'Sully' and Arthur Keegan, Chris Davidson, Brian Hancock, David Doyle-Davidson, Terry Kirchin and Eric Broom and we finished in a very creditable 8th position in 1970/71, a standing that owed much to the determination of these senior players and a great start to the campaign. The problem was possibly our forwards who were lighter than most in the League that year, so when the pitches were hard we were fine but we faltered when the going got heavy.

However despite the poor wages that the players received, falling attendances and dim floodlights we started the season reasonably well winning seven of our first ten games. That bright start was followed by four straight defeats and that lack of weight, some injuries and poor form in mid season saw us sliding down the league table when the grounds were heavy, before 8 wins in the last 10 games, when the pitches got hard again, saw us finish in the top half of the table and so we finished on a positive note. My main memory of that year was of the two derby games, in these we managed to beat Rovers twice and one of those wins saw us pull off a fantastic 26-12 victory at the Boulevard. There was also a massive blow for all the fans however when after rumblings that there were problems between the Board of Directors and the coaching staff, Johnny Whiteley departed as coach. The distress of the supporters was further heightened by the fact that our greatest hero of the last 20 years did the unthinkable in crossing the river to take up the reins at Hull Kingston Rovers. Even though my parents rarely ever attended games it was a real blow for Mum and Dad and it was the first time I had ever heard my Mother have a bad word for Johnny, and safe to say, when the move was announced in the Hull Daily Mail, in Potterill Lane we ate our evening meal in silence.

Ivor Watts: the rise and fall of the 'Magic Sponge' man

The demise of Johnny however did give our 'trainer in waiting' Ivor Watts the chance to take over the coaching duties and he certainly deserved what was to turn out to be a bit of a 'poison chalice'. Ivor who has featured a lot in my story already had been with the Club since the early 50's and after retiring from playing he had done just about every job off the field at Hull FC with the exception of tea lady. In fact it was normal in the late 60's to see Ivor who was then assistant trainer, running onto the pitch with that battered enamel bucket that contained some freezing cold water in one hand and that 'cure all' 'Magic sponge' in the other.

He was always there when someone was injured, it was the most privative of treatments but the effect it had on every player whose face came in contact with the freezing cold water was miraculous. If the sponge did not work then the loyal, and somewhat aging members of the St John Ambulance Brigade that sat crouched with their stretcher, vulture like, ready to pounce from the touchline, would be called into action. The Threepennies used to whistle and sing the 'Laurel and Hardy' theme as they enthusiastically stumbled across the field to load the injured player onto the old canvas stretcher and carry them off. On one memorable occasion the usually 'boisterous' Jim Neale was 'pole-axed' by a 'stiff arm' from a big Whitehaven forward and as he didn't move after the sponge treatment Ivor summoned the St John lads. As they carried the comatose Neale off the field with Ivor administering the sponge to his face, all of a sudden the old fabric rent asunder and our second row forward dropped straight through the stretcher and landed still out cold on the pitch. One wag in the Threepenny's shouted out immediately "If the stiff arm didn't quite finish you off Jim, that stretcher certainly will have!"

Speedway, Doyle-Davidson and Hot Dogs to the rescue

Saturday 21ˢᵗ February 1971   *Hull 7 – Featherstone 7*

In early 1971 the Boulevard became for the first time in many, many years a multi use stadium. In the distant past its illustrious history had seen greyhound and cycle racing and athletics held at the ground, and so, once again, prompted by the lack of finance coming into the Club, the Board took the controversial step of sharing the place with another sport for the first time since the greyhounds were there back in the 1920's. Keen to increase revenue our always resourceful Chairman Charlie Watson had talks with Workington Speedway bosses Ian Thomas and Wally Maudsley and as the season ended the sides of the pitch were ripped up, the touch lines moved in about 5 yards and a shale Speedway track laid around the perimeter of the playing area.

The new club, the Hull Vikings, started really well with a couple of attendances of over 7000 and even when things settled down and the novelty wore off a little, they regularly got more fans through the turnstiles than the rugby ever did. In that first year the Club got a well needed £510 from a 'part year' of that speedway franchise, which was in the next few years to realise thousands of pounds that probably saved Hull FC from bankruptcy. All credit to the Club as with the American craze of Hot Dogs sweeping across the country, the Board also invited tenders for the right to sell them on match days and made another much needed £300 from the franchise in that first year. Westler's hot dogs were a real experience in the seventies and were already sold on most street corners in the City centre by vendors with illuminated hand carts.

The sausages used in these hot dogs were slimy in appearance, briny in flavour, and served with or without 'rubbery' onions. This gastronomic delight was completed by being served wrapped in a finger shaped bread cake which was invariably the best part of the deal. As soon as it was possible to get these wonderful examples of early 'Fast Food' at rugby, it was hot dogs and Bovril at every game for me and my pals on the Threepenny's. That season also saw David Doyle-Davidson granted a benefit and a name that was to feature as both a hero and a villain at the Club in future years, Mick Crane, joining as a young player from local amateur rugby.

In the spring of 1971 we played Featherstone at Post Office Road in the Challenge Cup, the date was 21st February and it was always a tough game at the home of the 'Colliers' but on this occasion Hull had several injuries with Arthur Keegan, Clive Sullivan, Terry Kirchin, Brian Hancock and Chris Davidson all missing from the starting line up so it appeared that it was going to be almost impossible to get anything in the way of a win that afternoon. Back then we had a 'Super sub' who was regularly on the bench in the form of David Doyle-Davidson. He had throughout his career at the Club been a good ball handler and runner and a great tackler. He had played in every position in the backs and so his versatility had made him an ideal candidate for the 14 or 15 shirt. On this occasion as our injury jinx struck again David came on from the bench after about 20 minutes when we were already 7-2 down. 'The Doyle' then commenced to literally tackle everyone on the Featherstone side at least three times and his 'one man show' of defiance was such that we fought back to attain an unlikely 7-7 draw. A truly 'one man performance' is actually almost an impossibility at any level in Rugby League but on this occasion the media hailed David's efforts as just that, and having been there myself I will vouch for the fact that it was a worthy accolade.

David was cheered from the pitch at the end and carried off by his team mates. This was a good thing for the hero of the day as Clive Sullivan and Arthur Keegan had to take his boots off in the changing rooms after the game because his 'Super Human' effort meant that he simply couldn't stand up. At the replay, which we won 12-8, word of his amazing performance at Post Office Road had spread through the ranks of the Hull supporters, and no doubt we gave David Doyle-Davidson a standing ovation as the teams entered the field of play at the Boulevard, but despite all his efforts three days earlier……. he was still on the bench!

Back with Sid and the gang at East Park

Having spent three months in my new position in East Park I was working regularly on the flower gardens when l started to get moved around the City as new projects were launched. It was around that time that I was sent to work on Queen's Gardens to help with planting out the summer bedding that always adorned the area around the Fountain. One lunchtime I remember watching as a big transit van pulled up on Queen's Dock Avenue and from it climbed two men dressed as women, who then went through a bizarre comedy double act, watched by an ever increasing group of inquisitive office workers who were out on the gardens to eat their sandwiches. Little did I know then that the organisation was a recently formed theatre group called Hull Truck who were soon to climb to the top echelons of British independent theatre and carry our City's name around the world. Hull in 1971 was a developing place with Boothferry Road the approach to the town centre from the West, receiving an award for having the best entrance to a City in Great

Britain. I did my bit too being regularly sent there by the Council to help with planting new rose beds and trees.

They caught me dribbling in the chapel

In winter, when there was little to do in the Park, I was often sent to help out wherever there was work. You can therefore imagine my dismay when I was drafted back that winter to Eastern Cemetery to help with some drainage work, however I was relieved to learn that 'Mud Ball' had taken exception to someone in a public house and was currently spending some time at 'Her Majesty's Pleasure'. When I got down to Preston Road it was obvious why they were having drainage problems as most of the Cemetery was flooded. The first day I was there it poured and poured and after about an hour working in a trench in the torrential rain we were all saturated. Frank the foreman at the Cemetery then gestured to us all and we retired into the chapel at the back of the burial ground.

Once inside the regular workers cleared the chairs to one side and someone produced a football from behind the pulpit and we had a great game of 5 a side football. Great that was, until there was a loud knocking on the front door. "It's the area Foreman" said someone, "No he's in the big meeting in town this morning" said Frank, "Come In" he shouted. With that the big oak doors flew open and there outside was a full funeral cortége, (black top hats the lot), headed by the Chief Mourner who had knocked on the door to gain entry. Although the Council managed to keep the incident out of the local paper, there were a couple of disciplinary hearings and warnings issued after that adventure, but luckily as the new comer I was not one of them.

Wet days in the Bowling Pavilion

As for the tempo of life back in East Park, well little had changed and although Billy had retired, Sid and the other FC fans were still there, as were 'Thick ear' Harry and 'Big' John Hatfield. The FC crowd were still talking about their adventures supporting the Club they loved and although Sid's retirement was looming, he still seemed to be the one person that had more Hull FC stories than anyone else. It was becoming a tradition that when it rained it would be time for one of Sid's now famous stories. Sid always seemed to be able to denote different games in the past by remembering that he had his bike stolen whilst he was at one game, or lost his cap when he threw it up in the air to celebrate a score at another.

There were so many tales which were usually related on wet afternoons in that same Bowling Pavilion where I attended my first East Park Christmas Party six long years earlier. When you got 'rained off' everyone descended on the Pavilion and sat around on old crates and piles of seed boxes drinking tea and talking. Then Sid, sat in an old rocking chair in the corner, started with his usual introduction of, "Did I tell you about the time that.........?" These tales ranged from the unlikely to the absurd but as the story ended there was always an impromptu round of applause from the gathering of gardeners as Sid sat back in his chair with a contented smile on his face. It was certainly great to hear these stories of 60 odd years of supporting Hull FC and what Sid related was just the sort of folk law that surrounded the rugby Club back then, there was always rumours and stories which was all part and parcel of following 'The Cream'.

Talking of Sid I once remember him being caught returning from the barbers at around 11.30, one Tuesday morning, when he was supposed to have been digging a shrubbery. Unfortunately 'Norman the Foreman', caught him sneaking back with an obviously recent short back and sides and a clean shaven neck. Usually Sid would have denied any knowledge of having his hair cut but this time he was caught red handed. However when asked if he had been to get his hair cut and realising that any 'fabrication' of the truth was futile, Sid said straight away, "Well it grows in works time so I thought I would get it cut in works time too."

Saturday night with Ricki Dodds

At 21 my social life revolved around rugby and my Friday and Saturday nights out in the town. I still spent a lot of time watching live music but there was a gang of us from Sutton and a couple, including Jenksey, from the Boulevard area, who used to 'go to town' and as well as enjoying the same sort of music and pubs, we were all Hull FC supporters which helped no end when the conversation died a bit. Fridays were usually reserved for some serious drinking in 'The County' in Charles Street, 'The Manchester Arms' in Scale Lane and 'the Black Boy' in High Street.

Saturdays were a different matter as resplendent in our latest 'trendy' outfits we would hit the town. These fashion accessories usually consisted of a Ben Sherman shirt, Fair Isle jumper, Stay Press trousers, brogues and a Levi jacket. 'Hitting the town' usually entailed a few beers for 'Dutch courage' in the 'Corner House' and then onto a night club, either Bailey's on top of the Co-op in Jameson Street or the Locarno Ballroom in Ferensway.

That August a new night spot was added to the City Centre scene in Hull when 'Malcolm's' opened in George Street. This was a plush place indeed and became our regular venue for meeting girls and having a few beers and a lot of laughs in our Saturday night 'finery'. Often we would see Hull FC players in there sporting black eyes, bandages and the scars from that afternoon's battle. The music provided by resident DJ Ricki Dodds and his crew was engineered to create a great atmosphere but even though it included David Bowie and T Rex we all definitely drew the line at sporting anything 'Girly' like these icons of the time were wearing.

The Club itself was well furnished and the height of luxurious surroundings back then although licensing regulations meant that it was only open between 7-30 and 11-45 on a Saturday. Malcolm Backhouse who owned the place often used to pop in for a chat and just four months after he had opened what was now the City's top night spot, he and the owners of the other two city centre clubs applied to the Courts for an extended license to stay open until 1.30am on Sunday morning. There was a massive uproar and letters a plenty to the Hull Daily Mail but Mally was successful and so at last 'proper' nightlife came to Hull and we loved it!

Malcolm's was also used a lot for mid week concerts and I remember going to see amongst other bands of the day, The Sensational Alex Harvey

Band and Vinegar Joe (who featured Elkie Brooks and Robert Palmer ex of the Mandrakes from back in the South Hunsley concert days). For four years most Saturdays were not complete without finishing a night out at Malcolm's. Of course after a few beers there was no better a way to finish proceedings than to partake of a good 'carpet' burger from the caravan outside and a long walk home to Sutton to sober you up!

The return of 'Father Christmas'

That summer and after just one unsuccessful season in charge, coach Ivor Watts, had his contract terminated by the Club and he retired to run his sweet and tobacconist shop in Woodcock Street, not too far from the Boulevard where his loyalty had seen him 'part of the furniture' for over 20 years. He was always rumoured to be a fiercely passionate employee who hated fans wearing replica shirts, believing them to be the 'privileged uniform' of the players. He also disliked any player who switched allegiances and moved across the river to Hull KR and when Whiteley went to be their coach it was always said that Ivor refused to talk to him, but that was maybe just an urban myth of the time. Then, in a surprise move by Club Chairman Charlie Watson, Roy Francis returned from Leeds to coach us. Again, as has so often happened at our Club across the years, this came as a complete surprise as far as the fans were concerned although looking back I suppose it was all planned before Ivor was relieved of his duties. Roy brought a lot of discipline and some rugged training methods with him and did his best to strengthen the team despite the meagre finances available.

The playing side of things was certainly struggling and one of the first things that Roy had to sort out was the situation surrounding our scrum half and local hero Chris Davidson. His plight illustrated the state of the game back then as he threatened to quit the Club because he had been injured for around six months and although his right knee, which had been 'pinned', was getting better, he was trying to manage financially on sick pay of just £6 a week.

He had been unsettled for a while and had asked for a transfer before he was injured. After that request he had been placed on the transfer list at the end of the previous season for £10,000, but now with the State paying him £4 a week and the Club just £2, Chris was on the breadline and finding it hard to survive. He said at the time, "No one is going to pay £10,000 for me in this state and I have to get some money from somewhere, so I might as well throw the towel in as far as rugby is concerned and head off to London to find a job" Whether this was just a threat, or a real plea for help, is hard to know but somehow Chris soldiered on until he got back playing again and eventually came off the transfer list to continue starring for his home town Club. He was in fact to play some pivotal roles for the Black and Whites in the coming years. Still, looking back it's not difficult to see how so many players found it hard once they were injured and why many played on despite bad injuries, (and suffered for it in later life), because they quite simply needed the money to survive.

What the hell is a 'Ginger Group'?

If things on the field were tough then the Hull FC Board of Directors appeared to be in a bit of turmoil too and had to fight off a 'takeover bid' from Joe Latus and his 'Ginger Group'. Joe the proprietor of a Socialist bookshop in Hull City centre formed the group out of concern for the falling gates and lack of interest that there was in the Club from the fans. The groups name is a strange one but was probably derived from the expression to 'Ginger things up a bit' or revitalise them. Joe was a tremendous supporter who really loved Hull FC and was I guess, like all of us, worried about the state of our beloved Club at the Boulevard. This takeover attempt took place at Dad's last meeting as a shareholder, but he came home that night talking of a real battle that had seen 17 potential board members vying for just nine places. On this occasion, Watson and the current board had gained enough votes to keep going, although Dad made it clear that he had voted for Joe. The current Board of Directors won through that night but changes were just around the corner.

The shock of this opposition to the current Board, which was certainly popular with the fans, saw Charlie Watson and the Directors trying hard to support their new coach and a young prop from amateur rugby Keith Tindall followed in his father's footsteps and signed for Hull FC, this was followed by the capture of Full Back Mike Kendal, Centre Steve Portz and Welsh wingman Ron Cowen. Sadly we lost some of the 'old guard', and although neither Mum or Dad made the journey from Sutton to watch the lads anymore, there was a deal of sadness and more silent meals at home in Potterill Lane when Arthur Keegan asked to be released to became assistant player-coach at Bramley, he was quickly followed by ace goal kicker John Maloney who went to York, (he did however return a couple of years later for two more seasons), and Forward Chris Forster who left for Huddersfield.

It was particularly sad to see Keegan go and my Dad and many others at the time said that they believed Arthur had hoped to get a crack at the coaching job at the Boulevard but when Roy Francis was brought back in he started to look elsewhere. The travelling every week to training and games at the Boulevard from Dewsbury was certainly another factor in his decision as it must have been tough travelling three times a week from the West Riding often on the train. In fact in the end it was a great move for our captain and full back as he was by early 1973 promoted to the West Yorkshire club's Head Coach and was to become the only coach to take the great little West Leeds club to a final victory, when at the height of the Miners' Strike they won the 1973/74 BBC Floodlight Trophy Final against Widnes.

More tough times

The hard times really started to bite at the Club once the 71/72 season began and the Boulevard was starting to look a real mess with the shale for the Speedway track covering all the seats in the Best Stand with a thin layer of red dust after every meeting. Several season ticket holders complained and there were a couple of letters in the 'Sportsman Say' column in the Hull Daily Mail so the Club reluctantly bowed to public opinion and employed someone to wipe all the seats before home games took place. The famous stadium, despite being run down was still a valuable asset which the Club clung to, and no doubt borrowed money against. It was valued in the annual accounts that year as being worth £30,000. Shortly after his appointment Roy Francis was named Team Manager which meant that it was he and not the Board who was responsible for 'all team matters', which included for the first time the actual selection of the team. We fans didn't realise it at the time but this was a fundamental change to the way that things were done at the Club.

Surprisingly enough Roy had only been in post a short time when he requested and was granted four weeks off for 'Family' reasons during which time, as Johnny Whiteley was also away on holiday, Ivor Watts was ironically called back from the Old Holburn, Park Drive and Arrow bars to look after things. It was thought by all us fans that the return of Roy to the Club after his success at the Boulevard in the late fifties and a great spell at Leeds would perhaps turn our fortunes around but despite his obvious charisma and technical knowledge mistakes like bringing over nine 'hopefuls' from Australian rugby, (which proved costly particularly as only two played any games at all in the first team), were to see Roy just lasting in the job for a short time.

Breaking records ... but all the wrong ones!!

The Speedway was doing well in 1971/72 and made the Club £3213 with TV income from the Floodlit Trophy raising another £3673, which in the end saw the Club make a profit of £3,699 but despite this the playing side of things was literally haemorrhaging money. On the field itself it was a poor season when we finished 19th out of 30 teams. There cannot be a worse sight than to see someone who is healthy, happy and fit slowly deteriorating before your eyes. The same can be said of your rugby team. Our attendances reflected this slow demise too and as the Hull fans voted with their feet Speedway regularly generated bigger gates than rugby and it was possibly only that Speedway franchise, the TV money and perhaps those hot dogs that kept the club afloat. In August just 1243 turned up to watch a game against Dewsbury and two months later the visit of Huyton attracted only a slightly better 1450.

These were the lowest gates ever recorded at the Boulevard in our long history of playing there, but worse was still to come. There were many forgettable games at the Boulevard that year but we did have a couple of memorable wins over Warrington in October and Huddersfield in March and we beat Hull Kingston Rovers twice, at home 7-5 in February and at Craven Park 10-9 at the end of March. There were I remember a lot of close games that season mainly down to the fact that the shale from the Speedway track was starting to block the land drain's under the rugby pitch and it was at times in mid winter like playing on a swamp.

Four games in eight days and a bag of chips for Craney. It's just another November at Hull FC

Tuesday 16ᵗʰ November 1971   *Hull 15 – Huddersfield 7*

There was one particular performance which just shows what adversity we were in and indeed how the fixtures used to pile up for our part time heroes in those hard cold winters. The game I refer to was a televised BBC 2 Floodlit Cup game away at Huddersfield.

I will try and retell the happenings on the field a little later but it was the circumstances surrounding it and indeed the build up to the game that was so different to anything we see in Super League rugby these days. November that year was a particularly wet month and pitches around the league were in general like 'pudding'. Often matches were played with standing water on the pitch, but it was necessary to make sure you got games played because the revenue they generated was critical to the cash flow situation at all the clubs. So, despite it being relatively early in the season Hull had to play 4 games in eight days that November. On Saturday 13ᵗʰ we played away at Dewsbury in the Players No 6 Trophy and after a sterling backs to the wall defensive display we came away with a 5-5 draw.

The following Tuesday we played the game I refer to away in the BBC Floodlit Trophy at Huddersfield and then two days later there was the replay against Dewsbury at the Boulevard which we won 22-10. Then finally two days further on, at the Boulevard on the Saturday, we got beaten by Wigan 20-8. 320 minutes of Rugby League in 8 days with just two substitutes allowed at each game and all our player's semi professional with most, with the exception of Chris Davidson, working full time as well.

That brings me to another difference in our game 40 years ago, and that was the ability of some players to get time off work to travel to away games mid week, whilst others found their bosses less understanding. This particular game was played at the Fartown ground in Huddersfield with the second half broadcast live on BBC 2. However on the eve of the match disaster struck when Alf Macklin our regular winger cried off with a thigh injury. He had been injured at Dewsbury in that drawn game and although he had reported fit to play in the West Riding three days later, he broke down at work 24 hours before the game.

His obvious replacement was our speedy winger signed from local Rugby Union Howard Firth but he was a school teacher and could not get time off to travel or indeed miss a night class he was to take that evening. So the replacement fell to Terry Devonshire who had been dropped from the first team 3 weeks earlier to allow Ken Huxley to play. The problem was though that Terry was working out of town in the West Riding and staying over there in a boarding house throughout the week. It was long before the luxury of mobile phones and it was virtually impossible to get hold of him. The Club Secretary Cyril Fowler, tried everything and finally got hold of Terry's boss at 11.00 on the morning of the game. The bus picked 'Devo' up in Leeds in his work clothes and in borrowed boots he played that night.

That was not the only problem that Hull FC had that evening either because they were also twenty minutes late setting off from the Boulevard. At 4.00pm the coach was parked next to the Club house on the car park in Airlie Street with as usual the Directors sat at the front and the players at the back when a head count indicated that we were one player (plus Devonshire) short. It was quickly apparent that new young 'sensation' Mick Crane was missing and no one seemed to be aware of why. He had been at training the previous night and passed fit to play, so there was a bit of panic amongst the Directors when it looked like he was going to be a 'no show'. The talk got round to who they could call up at short notice when thankfully Mick came into view sauntering down Arlie Street with his kit in a paper bag, smoking a cigarette and eating a bag of chips.

As anyone who saw 'Craney' play will tell you he was a fantastic rugby player but could never ever have been classed as a 'Model Athlete'. In fact during a game he was not averse to wondering over to the Threepenny Stand and 'cadging' a few puffs of a fan's cigarette whilst a conversion was being taken. Still, onto the bus 'Craney' climbed giving a casual wave to the lads at the back and muttering something about "getting stuck in the bookies", before sitting down to finish his chips. Meanwhile the Coach driver started the engine and set off to search the West Riding of Yorkshire for Terry Devonshire. All I would say, a bit different to the slick, well organised and sanitised workings of a Super League club today. Only 40 years ago, and yet light years from modern Rugby League.

So to the match that I believe may well have been Dick Tingle's first reporting on Hull FC. We had already attained an unlikely win at Huddersfield that season in the League but the 'Fartowners' were a formidable outfit on their own ground and it was 'a big ask' to go there and win, although a victory would have meant a place in the semi-finals of the BBC Floodlit Trophy, and some much needed income, so the match was certainly an important one. It was thankfully one of those games where that master of the art of releasing the ball, Terry Kirchin, had a blinder.

Unconcerned about two more games coming up in the next 4 days Hull ripped into the fancied Huddersfield outfit from the first whistle. Hull took just two coach loads of fans and at a game that had only attracted 3000 spectators that night, we probably looked lost in what was a cavernous ground. After Devonshire had been fouled by Senior and Pickup in the 5th minute, from around 30 yards out Kendal coolly stroked over the kick and we were already two points in front. After 16 minutes however Eric Broom tripped Loxton and the home side's kicker Hooson levelled the scores. A faultless piece of cover defence by Devonshire when he tracked back to flatten Senior, was followed by our stand in winger (in borrowed boots) breaking away after darting through a pack of Huddersfield players. He ran 30 yards and fed Huxley who was just held short two yards out from the try line by a brilliant last ditch tackle from full back Bedford.

Then Devonshire was at it again this time having a try disallowed for a debatable forward pass from Hancock. From the resulting scrum we won the ball 'against the head' and Kenny Foulkes broke from behind the collapsed pack to feed Kirchin, (who had been instrumental in collapsing it in the first place) who peeled away from the second row. With three players on his back he crashed in near the corner, but Kendal missed the goal. Then came the best try of the game as Kirchin our man of the match, made some space and from a knot of players he somehow smuggled the ball to Harrison, he passed to Ibbotson who fed straight onto Hancock. Our captain sped away and using the strangely 'quiet' Clive Sullivan as a foil to his left, he dummied and roared in to score under the posts. This time Kendal made no mistake and at half time we were in the lead by 10-2.

As Hull ran out for the second half the wind had stiffened considerably and we had to play into it. The little band of FC Faithful huddled together on the massive terrace behind the sticks were then treated to 40 minutes of great tackling and solid defence as the home side charged towards them and our line. Huddersfield tried everything to break our defence and half backs Chamberlain and Loxton worked hard to break through the middle and get their big forwards running.

Time and again these two tried that old scissors movement favoured by half backs in those days but not once did Hull's defence 'buy it', however a period of intense pressure finally bore fruit and after ex Hull Forward Chris Foster had made a break, Evans shot onto the ball to score and Hooson converted. It was then just 10-7 to Hull FC. A string of scrums with head and ball to the home side could have sunk us, but some inspired 'shovelling' against the head from our hooker Roy Firth kept the ball away from Huddersfield's attack although Bedford did try two rather desperate drop goals, (worth two points that season), both of which he screwed narrowly wide.

As the home side pressed again we needed the last score and one final effort saw us take play down field with a tremendous run from 'that man' Kirchin who having handed off three players sidestepped one way then the other before releasing Doyle-Davidson (who had come on as usual from the bench), on the other side. After running about ten yards David took the tackle and got up to play the ball quickly enabling Foulkes to spread it wide the other way to Huxley, who switched it back inside for supporting full back Kendle to dive over with just three minutes to go. He missed the kick but made up for it in the last minute with a late penalty goal. As the game finished it was the Hull heroes covered head to foot in Fartown mud that were celebrating as they all leapt in the air on the final whistle and then walked off to the bath, steaming in the cold November air. It was a great victory in a hectic period for the Club and after a bath a couple of drinks and a sandwich it was back on the bus and home to Hull for work next morning and Dewsbury the day after! How things have changed.

I become a Shareholder

I just cannot emphasise really how depressing these times were for the average Hull FC fan and of course there was nothing average about me, I was fanatical if not a little despondent. At the start of the 1972/73 season they were tough times and the incidence of a win was something of a rarity at the Boulevard. We did however witness a brilliant Man of the Match performance by a young 'Chip eating' Mick Crane in the season's 'Curtain Raiser' the Eva Hardacker Trophy game against Rovers on 12th August which we actually won by a staggering score of 43-5. It wasn't so much that we were good but Rovers were shocking, still it gave us the bragging rights over the old enemy until they beat us at Craven Park on Boxing Day.

It was a sad time though for FC fans in general and Mum and Dad in particular as we lost ex Chairman and architect of the great team in the late 50's and early 60's Ernie Hardacker, who died in a car crash and not long after that the deaths also occurred of two other hard working ex Directors Frank Giblin and Reg Lee. Mum and Dad attended all three funerals.

I still saw my boyhood pal Bill Jenks a time or two on the Threepennies where it was a case of everyone being on first name terms with everyone else, because there were so few fans who continued to turn up. Bill's Dad Bert had started going to games with us but as a Docker he missed quite a lot early on in the season because he was travelling daily on the Humber Ferry to picket the unregistered wharfs on the Trent. This was because there was a massive Docks dispute going on between the Trade Unions and the National Dock Labour Board. They were certainly militant times, and on 18th August 1972 Bert and another 2,500 Dockers packed the Best Stand at the Boulevard for a mass meeting about the Dock Labour scheme and the 'Strike Breakers' at the independent wharves on the Ouse and the Trent.

The season started badly and before a ball was kicked we had 12 players sidelined with injuries, a situation that led to the worst start (four straight defeats) for 40 years. We didn't play that badly but it was the constant mistakes that our young stand in players made that really let us down. A defeat at Doncaster was the last straw for my Dad who, now that we lived in Potterill Lane, only went about once a season, if that. One night as we sat gloomily at home talking about the position our Club was in he left the lounge to return a short time later with an old tin Pears Soap box that he had, for as long as I could remember, kept under the bed.

With great ceremony he lifted the lid and handed me a faded dog eared envelope which had obviously seen better days. "There you are son" He said, "There's your inheritance!" What was this I thought, "He's only given me his life savings to buy Hull FC", which even when you consider the value of the ailing Club and his circumstances, was a pretty unlikely scenario. I opened the envelope and there was something he cherished almost as much as his savings; it was his shares in Hull FC and he promised next day to get them transferred into my name.

These were of course worthless in monetary terms but just like the act of purchasing a season pass every year, here was something that saw me 'buying' even further into my Club. These bits of faded folded paper were of no value to the average person but to me they were priceless because of one very important fact: They got me into the annual general shareholders meeting that Dad had spoken so intently and interestingly about since I was a lad. These meetings were to be something that I regularly attended for years after that, but I will never forget the first one I went to on Wednesday 23rd August 1972.

I witness a boardroom coup d'état

That night I presented my share certificate to the man on the door at the meeting, which was held at the Central Library Theatre in Albion Street in the Hull City Centre. The room was buzzing with conversation as shareholders huddled together in 'pre meetings'. I waived at Sid in one such 'confab' at the other side of the room, that was now thick with the smell of the dense clouds of cigarette smoke that rose from each small gathering. For the previous two weeks I had been receiving telephone calls from prospective board members, most of whom I had never heard of, who called me Mr Allen and asked if they "Could rely on my vote". Quite frankly, it was all pretty confusing. The meeting itself started well with an immaculately observed minutes silence for the three ex directors that had died during the year and then Charlie Watson the current Chairman lit up his pipe took two long draws on it and opened the preceding. Thereafter however the whole thing descended into farce as the voting and movement of motions was constantly questioned from the 'Floor'.

It seemed too that other shareholders were tired of the proxy vote system that the Club used because like me they had been constantly hounded for their vote over the telephone. Accusations flew back and forth and I just sat back and enjoyed every minute of it.

In the end Charlie Watson the Club Chairman was voted off the Committee as he along with Albert Walker got the least amount of votes out of the 11 candidates. When the announcement was made it was first met with abject silence and disbelief before mayhem broke out with papers being thrown across the room and oaths a plenty being aimed at some of the successful directors. Apparently one holder of a stack of proxy votes had thrown them behind everyone but Watson and in the wake of this action, Joe Latus, who had a year earlier formed that 'Ginger Group' to criticise the administration and 'Ginger' them up a bit, was again a Director. Mr Latus said he was against Proxy votes whilst Watson retorted that "Well It was you who started them when you were last on the Board" and so it went on! Utter chaos but great fun.

Fans of the modern game at the KC would find it interesting to note at this point that there was also a long debate about a motion from one shareholder that suggested that the fans would prefer to watch their rugby on a Friday night, rather than a Sunday afternoon. Some things it would appear never really change! In the end a fan's ballot was suggested to solve the match day issue which actually in the end saw a massive majority plumping for games on a Sunday.

Still at least some of the news from the meeting was positive as the Club had finally managed to pay £6000 off the 'Floodlights loan' they received from the Rugby League in the previous decade. All in all as I left the meeting and walked into the street with the shouts and accusations still ringing out from the room behind me I thought that one thing was certain and that was that these meetings would be a must in the future. As a foot note I would add that Charlie Watson was soon back on the Board of Directors, but Joe Latus did not survive long at all although the bookshop owner was soon to leave his mark on the history of our great Club by penning a book on the life of Clive Sullivan entitled 'Hard Road to the Top' which is still a good read to this day.

Almost immediately after the meeting new Chairman Charles Clegg announced in the Hull Daily Mail that the Club would look to sign some new players and after four defeats 'on the bounce' they were certainly needed. Francis went after the first of his Aussie targets a full back, winger and loose forward whilst it's a little known fact that Hull FC also went after 'Big' Jim Mills the ex Bradford Northern Forward who was at the time playing in Australia, and who was to become the most sent off player in British Rugby League. Sadly we missed out on him.

After the 'light relief' of the shareholders' meeting the quality of our rugby was starting to really get me down. I well remember being out on a date at Malcolm's one particularly gloomy Saturday night when even the party atmosphere of my favourite club could not lift my spirits after we had lost again. Out of the blue my 'companion' said, 'If it bothers you so much when they lose why don't you stop going?' Needless to say I ditched her pretty quickly; she just didn't get it at all! Whilst I am on the subject of girlfriends another, a few years later, told me that "I should not let rugby get to me and learn to manage my emotions". Have you ever met a true rugby fan who could manage his emotions? "This is not life or death", I told her "This is Hull FC you're talking about, it's a family thing". She didn't last long either. As I have said in here before some probably lucky people, just don't get it do they?

'Bad Finger' at the Locarno.

Music was still a real sop to the indifferent rugby I had to endure every week and I remember that the occasional concert certainly acted as a temporary distraction. One great night out was on 6th November when a packed Locarno Ballroom in Ferensway greeted Liverpudlian Band 'Badfinger' who were just back from their victorious American tour. The band, of whom I had always been a big fan, played a great concert which included hits like, 'Come and Get It', 'No matter What' and 'Day after Day', and that night I particularly remember them returning to the stage to do three encores which including the Beatles 'Love me Do' and Little Richards 'Lucille'. It was certainly a memorable night.

I need a car, so it's a 'crash' course in driving

In April that year my Mum and Dad encouraged me to learn to drive and so I enrolled at Quick Pass school of Motoring who were based next to Furman's shoe shop on Queens Dock Avenue in the centre of Hull. The company was owned by a Mr Leech who took my £5 when I presented myself for my first lesson. Back then that payment secured six one hour lessons and it was considered that after about twelve lessons you would be ready to take your test. My Driving Instructor Malcolm was a big guy who barely fitted into the duel control Mini's that 'Quick Pass' used to teach you to drive in. With his massive frame squashed into the passenger seat I took my first tentative steps towards my driving licence, I suppose when I look back Malcolm was a good driving instructor although I would have got on a lot better without his horror stories of other pupils who had crashed into walls, rolled their Mini's over and collided with other vehicles. Mum described him as "A bit of a romancer" when I related Malcolm's tales to her and I think she was probably right.

After ten lessons I took my first test from the Park Street Test Centre at 10.30 on a Monday morning and despite giving it a good go, after about twenty minutes my examiner a Mr Christie said, "I think we'll go back to the test centre now Mr Allen". However four lessons and several more horror stories from Malcolm later, I took a second test this time from a different centre in Salisbury Street, in the leafy Avenues area of the City and despite reversing up the kerb in Alexandra Road and stopping over a double line at a junction, the examiner a nervous looking man called Mr Sellars, passed me and I had my licence.

Then of course there was the question of a car and with 10 Potterill Lane proving a costly place to run, money was certainly a bit tight at home. However as always when the chips were down, good old Mum and Dad somehow came up with the goods and lent me £200 with which I bought a great little 998cc Ford Anglia in Spruce Green. LAL 707E was my pride and joy and I had soon taught myself to change the plugs, tighten the fan belt, gap the points and adjust the tappets. Tight finances rendered garage services out of the question back then and so it was a case of if you couldn't afford it, you did it yourself. The world was now my oyster I had my own 'wheels' and I would cruise round the streets of East Hull with the window down and the radio on just like those American guys I had seen on the TV. I even rigged up a portable tape recorder to play through a couple of second hand speakers on the back shelf, and rode around the neighbourhood with my favourite Lindisfarne album 'Fog on the Tyne' blasting out till the tape recorder's batteries ran down.

Things were actually much tougher than I knew at home and whilst I was doing my best impersonation of 'Happy Days' in the Ford Anglia, Mum had found some lumps under her arms and behind her ear which were to prove that her cancer had returned, and there were to be a few tough years ahead for all of us.

A new Board at the Boulevard but for the fans little seems to have changed!

Down at the Boulevard there was a lot of talk about improvements on the field but talk was all it was and few came as the new Board and Chairman settled into the same old routine that we had seen from the previous administration and results went from pretty predictable to predictably disastrous. The quality of our playing staff was without doubt the problem but quantity wasn't and you couldn't say the Board and Coach didn't try to ring the changes as we used forty-eight different players that year. Mally Walker, Tony Wardell, Brian Waltham and Tony Salmon were amongst that plethora of players that joined the Club.

Sadly my big hero Terry Kirchin had gone in the early part of the campaign, signing for the enemy across the river Hull Kingston Rovers. Hull received a much needed transfer fee but his switch to the opposition was as I remember a bit strange, because although he was always upfront with Rovers and informed them from the off he was about to take up a post with BP, they still signed him. He subsequently lasted just a couple of games before he moved off to work, I think, in Scotland and that was sadly the last I heard of the big fellow with long arms who could release a ball like no one else in the game.

'Clive Sullivan.....This is Your Life'

For many Hull FC fans the high spot of that New Year's celebrations came when we tuned in, as everyone did, to BBC 1 on 3rd January 1973 to see the appearance of Clive Sullivan on the national BBC show, 'This is Your Life' hosted by Eamonn Andrews. This followed our winger captaining a GB team managed by Johnny Whiteley who had recently won the Rugby League World Cup. A few weeks previously he had been welcomed back from France with the Cup and paraded it with Johnny in a lap of honour around the Boulevard. I watched the show with Mum and Dad who were visibly proud to see our unassuming hero receiving all those accolades from famous sportsmen and people from within the game. My parents may have thought that all the distance they had put between themselves and the Club both mentally and physically had let them off the belonging and caring bit, but deep down in the end the passion was still there gnawing away at them.

Years afterwards at a benefit dinner I got the chance to speak to Clive about the lead up to the show which of course relied on the participating subject knowing nothing about him featuring until compere Andrews appeared with the big red book and said, "Clive Sullivan, This is Your Life". Clive said that the actual day had caused his wife Ros' some problems and the cloak and dagger goings on that actually got him in a position to meet Andrews with that book, were nothing short of hilarious. Clive was called down to London to participate in a 'Sports Forum' and once she had seen him off at the front gate at home in Brough, Ros had then to follow him down for the surprise in London, without Clive knowing what she was doing.

She waived him off in her working clothes and then had to race upstairs to change into the 'Glad rags' she had bought especially for the occasion and hidden away at the back of the wardrobe. Ros then left for Brough station to catch the train that departed for London twenty minutes after the one that Clive had caught. It was all tense stuff for everyone involved but the show was hailed as a great success and Clive became a national sporting personality overnight. However no doubt after all his celebrity status it was back down to earth with a bump as he returned to the Boulevard to continue the struggle that was our league campaign that year.

For those of us who were still very much involved emotionally, (possibly more by habit than anything else) in a team that appeared to be going nowhere, it was all pretty bleak but as always despite a poor showing that season, we could still find one or two pluses. These included beating Rovers in the Derby, and gaining a creditable 18-18 draw with Leeds in the John Player Trophy only for us to predictably lose the replay.

Even 'the Daleks' had seen enough!

Saturday 17th February 1973   *Hull 2 – Oldham 24*

With falling attendances, apathy amongst the fans and poor results, the new Board ran out of patience and in an effort to depict a show of strength Roy Francis was the fall guy and left the Club in February 1973 to be replaced in the short term by stand in coach David Doyle-Davidson and then national media personality Clive Sullivan. However we failed to fair much better for the rest of our games mainly due to a mountain of injuries and whilst Hull Kingston Rovers finished tenth and stayed in the top flight, we finished 24th out of 30 teams and well down in the bottom half of the table and therefore moved into the newly formed Second Division for the 1973/74 season.

Once again the Rugby League was tinkering with the competitions format and this time we were in the wrong place at the wrong time, without the resources or luck to get us out of it. Player coach Sullivan was next to go, despite struggling with no real financial backing, he had to take the rap for that poor season end. Administrators need scapegoats when the fans close in and Clive was handily placed to defect the flak from the Board, so before the next campaign was underway David Doyle-Davidson was back at the helm whilst ex player/captain Clive Sullivan was expected to revert to just a player again. It was a bad year indeed and with three coaches, dozens of injuries and relegation to the new Second Division, it is hardly surprising that the balance sheet that year showed a loss of £9,500.

Before I leave that season, there was one game that year that brought a particularly poor performance from Hull FC and which was perhaps a pointer to the general malaise of the fans and things to come. It was against Oldham in the Challenge Cup at the Boulevard on 17th February when we were beaten 24-2. For as long as anyone could remember the Club had allowed invalid carriages and sometimes supporters in wheelchairs onto the apron behind the goal posts and dead ball line at the Airlie Street end of the Boulevard and in 'Ryan corner' (named because the famous Bruce Ryan of the late 40's scored most of his tries there) at the Gordon Street end. That day things were so bad that the five light blue three wheeler carriages started to move off ten minutes before the end. As they slowly processed in single file along the dead ball line towards the exit one particularly disenchanted fan in the Threepenny Stand shouted out, "Bloody Hell we must be bad, even the Dalek's are leaving".

The return of the Spider from Bilton Grange

Although I hadn't seen anything of him for years I followed keenly the career of Mick Ronson and although finding the femininity of the Spiders from Mars's act a bit difficult to comprehend, I was really proud that a lad from Bilton Grange had done so well, and the Ziggy Stardust album is still one of my favourites to this day. He was one of the nicest guys you could wish to meet and although by now he was one of the most famous faces on the world music scene, I suddenly heard from him again.

If an indication of his kindness and consideration is needed, then it was amply displayed when around the beginning of June 1973 I was working on a project on Queen's Gardens which involved planning the planting of a new avenue of trees. One of the staff from the Guildhall sought me out and walked over and handed me an envelope which was simply addressed to 'Pete Allen, Gardener, Hull Council'. On opening it I discovered a ticket and a Back Stage Pass for David Bowie's concert at the

Royal Hall at Bridlington Spa on 28th June. It came with no explanation, except for a piece of torn white card with 'Mick' scribbled on it.

I of course attended the concert, that had sold out weeks earlier and after a fabulous performance, clutching my pass, I managed to get myself backstage. I never actually got to see David Bowie, but I did see Mick and we talked for about ten minutes about the old times at Alderman Kneeshaw Playing Fields. We were in the company of another guy who I think was called Mike Garson and who was, at the time, the band's off stage keyboard player. We had of course both moved on and the conversation soon dried up after a few 'Remember when's...', however my lasting memory of Mick was of a lad that never really let stardom get to him he was always the same and always just 'one of the boys'. That concert was for me a fantastic occasion and remains as a very happy memory, but however much I loved the music, all the camp glam stuff was not really for me, it was not really Mick either I didn't think, and it was certainly not 'Rugby League' was it?

Things had moved on and despite being pleased to see 'Ronno' again, I found it all a bit awkward really! Still, my backstage adventures meant that I managed to miss the last train home and so I slept, curled up, under a set of wooden steps that led onto the beach, before enjoying a brilliant sunrise over the North Sea, a pot of tea at an early morning cafe at the harbour and a ride on the first train back to Hull and the Council.

I never saw Mick again, and as I said previously, he tragically died of cancer in 1993. However as a footnote to this excursion into the world of 'Glam Rock', I was lucky to be in the right place at the right time some twenty-four years later when as a Senior Officer at the City Council I was able to help manage, with Maggie, (Mick's sister) and record producer Kevin Cann, the Mick Ronson Memorial concerts at the Ice Arena and on Queen's Gardens on 9th/10th August 1997. This weekend led to the creation of the Mick Ronson Stage which the City Council has treated so badly in recent years. Although there has been talk of a statue to Mick, at the time that I am writing this, nothing has been forthcoming.

Still as a lasting memorial there's always Ronson Close where he worked and lived on Greatfield Estate.

Enter 'The Doyle', an unlikely saviour?

Down at the Boulevard it seemed that the end of the Club was in sight as we moved from crisis to crisis, until that was, an unusual and unfashionable 'Messiah' came along in the shape of our latest coach, the ubiquitous David Doyle-Davidson, who took over the reins at the end of the 1973/74 season. After 3 years of wallowing in abject mediocrity in the doldrums of the Second Division, David took the Club by the 'scruff of the neck' and with our old second row hero Cyril Sykes as his assistant all of a sudden things started to look a little brighter. We were not much better in attack because we didn't have the class of player, but all of a sudden we became a lot harder to beat. Having made his last appearance as a player in a game at Castleford in 1972, David Doyle-Davidson had ended a playing career that spanned 11 years, during which he had made 184 appearances and since then he had helped behind the scenes at the Boulevard just waiting his chance to take over.

You'll no doubt remember that David had already etched his name in the history of the Club when in 1964 he was the first ever substitute to take the field of play in the game of Rugby League and he had already served as a stand in coach prior to Clive Sullivan having a go, before, probably as a last resort, he was officially made first team coach in May 1973. It turned out to be a very shrewd move on the part of Hull FC because 'The Doyle' had great man management skills and soon started to make a difference both in the passion and the discipline the players showed on the field. That year the team, despite consisting of basically the same core of players, were running on pride and passion again and although we were still way behind the standards we had seen twenty years previously, as fans we could ask no more.

Despite some poor results at first, the atmosphere in the changing rooms back then was excellent and there was a tremendous team spirit. David was renowned for his passionate motivational speeches, which he delivered at great length before each game. Sometimes, I remember, the team came out late because of the verbosity and passion of these 'Churchillian' speeches, which reminds me of one of the story's about David from the Hull Daily Mail's Correspondent at the time Dick Tingle.

He relates how before one game all the players waited patiently for David to deliver his speech. When he got into full flow, the joker of the team Alf Macklin said, "Don't worry boss there's no need for that I've got last weeks here". He then produced a portable tape recorder and played the previous weeks speech back to the assembled group. The place erupted with laughter and Dick said afterwards that it was probably the only time he had seen Doyle-Davidson lost for words. Of course the significant thing about that story is that it proves that instead of all the falling out and disruption there had been in the dressing rooms, the elements of passion and fun were back there now.

Be Bop De Luxe at the Duke of Cumberland in Ferriby.

So if the 1973/74 season started with a new coach and a bit more passion, then everything else was much the same. That same Alf Macklin still turned up for training on a bike with no doubt a tin of paint for one of the lads on the handlebars and the Speedway franchise was still doing really well. As the season got under way our coach was looking around to sign some new blood and we made an audacious approach for Salford's star player Bill Kirkbride which floundered on the usual problem of the distance Hull was from his home in Lancashire. Then we got a new winger for a month when a 'wayward' Mick Crane was allowed to go to York on loan, whilst their winger Clive Hill joined Hull for the same period, although he never made the first team. All the while Clive Sullivan was not too happy at the way that he had been treated by the board when coach and was looking for other options as far as his playing career was concerned.

That year, away from the rugby, there was still a thriving 'Grass Roots' music scene in the area and particularly out in the surrounding East Riding! I was still going to dances at Welton and Brough but there was lots of live music about and although by then I was not playing in any bands myself I loved watching these ensembles whenever I could. At that time it was usually the case that the lads and I would head off on Friday and Sunday nights for a few beers and then on to watch both local and regional 'breaking bands' at various clubs, pubs, village halls and schools around the county.

Some of my most memorable excursions were to the Duke of Cumberland pub in North Ferriby on Sunday nights, where there was a big concert room at the side of the hostelry and the band we usually went to see was Be Bop Deluxe a four piece outfit from the Selby/Pontefract area. Their blend of 'space pop' and a fantastic liquid gel light show created a great atmosphere and really captured our imagination and myself, Ted and Bill (a couple of my guitar playing pals) were actually there in October 1973, when the band were watched for the first time by an A & R man from the Derram record label. Bill Nelson who fronted the group was a tall skinny 'Bowiesque' guitar hero, an excellent song writer and a 'flash' guitarist. He was soon to lead the group to international fame and millions of record sales; although in fairness he ditched the rest of the original line up along the way to becoming that internationally acclaimed act.

Two years later in June (1975) the band headlined at East Park at one of the frequent free Sunday 'Rock in the Park' events that local musical entrepreneurs Rick Welton and the late Barry Nettleton promoted to vast crowds sometimes totalling over 8000 people. In the first few years of the decade we had seen bands like Juniors Eyes, Wishbone Ash, and The Edgar Broughton Band. They were fantastic times although that afternoon when Be Bop Deluxe performed was the last time we saw them around these parts for a few years as they soon hit the big time and toured the world. In fact the next time I saw them was supporting Cockney Rebel at the Mecca Ballroom on Ferensway where the shouts of 'Be Bop Deluxe' from the partisan fans drowned out the main act, and after that headlining their own 'Modern Music' tour at the City Hall in 1977. After those nights at the 'Duke' it was strange seeing them in such a big venue but with albums like 'Live in the Air Age', 'Modern Music' and 'Axe Victim' they were certainly a good band with their own unique sound that we found so distinctive when we first heard them in Ferriby years earlier.

Sully leaves for Rovers and dogs and cats across West Hull start to disappear

But back to 1973 and soon we were to read the terrible news in the Hull Daily Mail that Clive Sullivan had absconded to the 'Dark Side' and joined Hull Kingston Rovers. Most of us knew what had gone on and realised his unhappiness about the coaching position would probably lead to his departure but no one thought he would move across town, to the 'Robins'. Mum and Dad were devastated as once again their inborn passion for the Club came to the fore and all over West Hull dogs and cats called Sully started to mysteriously disappear. What Jenksey did with his cat I'm not too sure, although I can probably guess?

If that year was significant for rugby in Hull, it was also an important time for the game as a whole as it was then that the member clubs of the Rugby League finally agreed that the accepted regular match day should be changed officially to Sunday. The Sunday Observance Act was still a big hurdle to this progress though, and was still being circumnavigated by all us fans having to buy a very expensive programme to get in! No sooner had that decision been made, when back in Hull there was more significant transfer news at our Club as despite Doyle-Davidson's protestations Mick Harrison who I personally think is the best No. 8 I have ever seen in the Hull shirt, left for Leeds, in a £10,000 deal that just about kept our Club afloat.

It was hard for the coach but we as fans stuck with David because I suppose to us lot stood shivering in the stands, the team spirit was so much better than we had seen for years and in the end although it is always great to see expansive flowing rugby, all the average fan wants first and foremost is to see a bit of honest endeavour and pride in the Club shirt. The high spot I remember from a largely forgettable season, was when we beat a resurgent Bradford team, (who only lost twice that year), 11-2 at the Boulevard. As was always the case with night games under floodlights we played that match with a white ball. Chris Davidson launched a towering 'up and under' towards the wing and as Bradford's black winger Keith Barrends 'lost' the ball in the floodlights it swirled in the wind, hit him smack on top of the head and shot off into the Threepenny Stand.

Now it should be remembered that back then the outset of political correctness was still some way off and anyway the guys stood in the Threepenny Stand were certainly no respecters of anyone who had an opposition shirt on, whatever their colour or religion, and so quick as a flash someone near me towards the back of the wooden terracing shouted, 'White ball in off the black: seven away!'

So much more than rugby to be worried about, disaster strikes the community again

If things were difficult at the Club on the field for Doyle-Davidson and his charges, then February 1974 was a bad time for Hull in general and in particular the fishing community in the west of the City. It was then that the deep sea factory ship the Gaul sank some time on the night of the 8/9th February, in storm conditions in the Barent Sea off Norway. No distress signal was received and her loss was not realised until the 10th following the vessel twice failing to report in. An extensive search operation was launched but no trace of the ship was found, until a lifebuoy was recovered three months later.

Thirty-six crew members from Hull were lost in one of the worst peacetime disasters to befall the UK fishing fleet. Back then the conspiracy theories and espionage links that were to leave question marks hanging over the disaster for a couple of decades were still some way away but the whole city was plunged into a state of mourning and most folks who lived in the Boulevard area knew someone whose family had been touched by this unforgettable turn of events. At the next home game against Blackpool a minutes silence was immaculately observed. In fact I remember that the only sound that could be heard on the 'Threepenny Stand' that day was the occasional sob emitting from some of the toughest and most hardened members of that great fishing community with whom I was honoured and humbled to share the moment and that terrible sense of loss.

'Sportsman's Say', the 'message board' of the 70's

It was to take the local community a long time to get back to something like normality after those tragic days but as always many sought solace within their close knit families and some of course used their weekend trips to the Boulevard as a distraction and I suppose part of the healing process. Things were not going well at the Club though, mainly because our gates were nothing short of appalling and those who did go certainly gave the Board of Directors some stick both in the form of taunts from the terraces and also by way of abuse shouted from the well of the Best Stand directly at our officials sat up in the Directors seats. Others, like the anonymous message boarders of the present day fans sites, who didn't want to be so forthright, 'vent their spleens' in the 'Sportsman's Say' column of the Hull Daily Mail.

Every night there seemed to be a letter from some disapproving disenfranchised fan and ex Directors had a go too. In February 1974 so upset was ex board member and local scrap metal dealer Dave Bassett that he said in the paper that the current Board would never be successful because they would not get their hands in their pockets and finance some signings. In response our Chairman Charlie Clegg said that his experience of 'moneyed people' on the board was that they usually kept their hands deep in their pocket which was a strange comment indeed. Dave like many fans loved the Club, although hundreds had now just simply lost interest, something that was all the more galling because the football team down the road were still doing well and attracting good gates.

A close shave against Halifax

Saturday 23rd February 1974   *Hull 24 – Halifax 22*

For me, the game of that season was one against Halifax. I particularly remember this match because in the end it was not one that we deserved to win, in fact we were lucky to come out on top at all and it was against a team that over the past few seasons had started to become the 'new' nemesis of Hull FC.

The game was played at the Boulevard surprisingly on a Saturday in late Winter 1974/75 when although it was quite a barmy afternoon for the time of year, the Boulevard pitch was surrounded with great pools of water that had been cleared from the playing area following heavy overnight snow fall six days earlier and for most of the week the ground had been flooded. It was the 23rd February and we were as usual suffering with injuries and had fielding a 'cobbled together' team, but thanks to 'Mr Motivator' Doyle-Davidson we were still doing reasonably well and on the fringes of the promotion pack in the Second Division.

I was late for the game that day and all my usual pre match rituals and preparations had been thrown into turmoil, when as 'Stand By' Parks Foreman for the weekend, an outbreak of vandalism the previous night in Pickering Park had seen me out with the Police all Saturday morning, surveying the damage. So after racing down Anlaby Road and leaving my Council van in West Park I had a real dash to get to the ground, just arriving in time to see the referee blow the whistle to start the game. One 'Wag' who I only knew to 'nod to' shouted out across the Stand, "It's nice to see you could make it, can we get started now?"

The match kicked off in front of an abysmal gate of just 1,583 and as soon as I had collected myself and had time to scan the players we had out on the field I realised that we were missing another key member of the team, our captain Brian Hancock. Against Halifax I thought "This is going to be tough". However we started to pass the ball around crisply and after just five minutes a fine move between Casey and Hicks sent Davidson through a gap. As our scrum half brushed tackles away, he crashed into the open and ran 20 yards to touch down and open the scoring, before converting his own try. At 5-0 we were well on top and Davidson returned the compliment to his team mate when ten minutes later he sent Hicks in wide out on the left and added the two points himself from what was a tight angle over on the touchline in front of us in the 'Threepennies'. It was all Hull now with Terry Devonshire, (who was now approaching veteran status), shining at off half and young Stenton in the centre giving his best performance to date.

Chris Davidson then converted a penalty when Pitchford tried to decapitate Alan McGlone and although Brown scored a lucky touchdown for Halifax when the ball shot out of a tackle like a bar of soap and he cantered in to score, Wardell charged through on a typical run and using McGlone as a foil he dummied and dived in for Davidson to again add the extras. Wardell was everywhere for Hull and having a great game, with prop Jacklin not that far behind him for endeavour and running. Then 'The Fax' came storming back with a Burton try but at half time we were comfortably in the lead at 17-6.

We were all to say the least a little surprised at the ease by which we had attained that advantage but as usual things started to go wrong as soon as we re-started the game after the interval. After just five minutes Hicks threw out a speculative pass toward Hull winger Gibbons, the ball hung in the air and was intercepted by Hoyle, who ran 60 yards to touch down and give Halifax new heart. Then Len Casey, who sensed that the visitor's forwards were getting on top went for Mark Watson with a shocking head high tackle that left the Halifax loose forward pole-axed face down in the mud. Referee Ronnie Campbell had no hesitation in sending Casey straight from the pitch, which I guess meant that the following Thursday, along with both Wardell and Hick, he would at least make up a car load for the trip to the monthly Disciplinary Meeting in Leeds. Hull FC was usually able to fill a car for those meetings!

Fired up by Len Casey's departure, Hull roared back at the visitors and Chris Davidson with another FC try, this time straight from the scrum, re-established our lead but it was obvious with twelve men that the cracks in our defence were starting to show. The visitors brought on Phil Davis to play scrum half who immediately scored but another goal from Davidson made the score 24-14 and we looked home and dry. We were neither 'Home' or 'Dry' and as the rain started to fall, Halifax's Brown scored a try that looked like a knock on over the line, and then in the dying minutes Brown kicked ahead and touched down again and with a goal added from the touchline Halifax were just two points behind as the final whistle went. Another couple of minutes, and no doubt we would have lost, so stretched was our defence in that second half. Still we won 24-22 and got two precious points.

There was no doubt either who would be awarded the title of Man of the Match because with two ties and six goals the very player who had threatened to quit a few years earlier, our battle wearied scrum half Chris Davidson, had sent us all home happy that day. The players would no doubt get into the bath, sing a few rounds of 'Old Faithful', and then experience a bottle of beer or two and one of Ivy Mason's post match teas. These feasts were prepared by Ivy and a gang of volunteers after each game for many, many years, and their quality was famous throughout the Rugby League.

At Easter I remember proudly taking Mum and Dad to Bridlington in the 'new' car. Mum was really struggling by now and everything was becoming an effort for her as she had to go back to the hospital more and more for treatment. However one of her greatest pleasures was to sit and watch the sea rolling up and down the beach so that's what we did that Easter. Sadly even though she appeared to enjoy sitting there on the promenade and the fish and chips we ate in the car for lunch, it poured and poured with rain on what was later announced to be the wettest Bank Holiday of the century. In fact by the time we had got back home to Sutton it was apparent that certain places were starting to flood and later that night on the local news we heard that Chanterlands Avenue and Boothferry Road in Hull were under over a foot of water and in the village of Cottingham, King Street and George Street were flooded too.

Partings, ground improvements and a beer in the Boulevard

These memories of the 1974/75 season end for me with a chance meeting I had at an 'A' Team game with my old pal from Division Road Billy Jenkinson who had strangely been missing from the terraces of late. Never a fair weather fan, I presumed he must have been ill, but he informed me, as we watched the young hopefuls on the pitch get muddier and muddier, that following a short courtship and an even shorter and unplanned pregnancy, he had got married. Apparently Melissa his wife was from a rather well to do family in Hessle and her Mother and Father had set them up in one of those £5000 bungalows they were building up on the Sutton Park Estate, north of Sutton Road. Jenksey had moved to the very place where, he told me years earlier, all the snobs lived and although I said that they would have to come and see us in Sutton, somehow I knew that he wouldn't, because it was apparent at this point, that we had both moved on and in pretty different directions.

For the first time I could ever remember, Jenksey, the eternal optimist and FC fanatic looked sad and I could tell that he was not that enamoured with married life, Sutton Park, missing rugby or being a Daddy! I decided that the usual retort of "Why the hell didn't you wear one?" would have little resonance in this situation and I remember making a mental note that if ever there was a glowing endorsement for birth control Billy's face that day was probably it! Despite his new living arrangements, for Billy, who worked for the Yorkshire Electricity Board, money was tight and with another baby on the way, his season pass, had it seemed, disappeared over the horizon. Talk about a prize every time, poor old Jenksey must have been more fertile than the Nile Delta! I have only seen him a handful of times since and on each occasion, trailing a procession of kids, he still looked permanently depressed. However he always seems to become invigorated when the good old days at the Boulevard, with Sully, the Flying Dentist, Craney, and those Hot Dogs are mentioned. It was that day, in the divorce lawyers parlance, a case of irretrievable breakdown and the end of a long FC friendship with someone who had been through a lot with me. Together we had lived the dream and more often than not, suffered the nightmare and it was for me a really sad day.

Back at the Boulevard, the Board at Hull FC needed to raise more cash, and in May 1974 they managed to obtain a licence from the local Licensing Magistrates for a new bar to be built on the terracing at the Airlie Street end of the ground, just in front of the Speedway pits. Arthur Sanderson and Co the local builders were commissioned that summer to build a new Club house with a glass front overlooking the pitch, from which, I suppose, the Club hoped to make their fortune. Whilst for us fans the thought of getting a pint inside the ground was certainly appealing and helped to justify (if justification was ever needed) investing our money in a season pass and our time, energy and emotion in another season at the famous old ground!

Chapter Nine

The hardest season of all?

If the last Chapter found me in a despondent mood then there are few reasons to think that this next one will see my own fortunes or those of Hull FC improving that much, well not initially at least. The Seventies continued with the local and national music scene in what is called these days the 'pre punk glam rock era' that still saw men dressed up like women and wearing glitter and tight jumpers, whilst Mud, The Sweet and T. Rex dominated the national pop music charts. As always, whatever was happening out there in the wider world the Boulevard continued in its consistent, (if not depreciating) timeless state. We all felt that in David Doyle-Davidson we did at least have an inspirational coach who despite limited resources was trying to bring players in and changing things around as far as training and tactics were concerned. He certainly struggled at first but I detected a willingness in the fans back then to give him a chance and they seemed to have more patience with him than they had with Ivor Watts or Clive Sullivan.

Of course the Board's main priority was to make sure that the Club was kept afloat financially and so from time to time we had to sell what we, on the terraces, considered to be our best players and that didn't help our overall morale but with fans it never does. So I think despite the green shoots of optimism that could be found in the hearts and minds of the fans who were left on the terraces, it has to be said that

1974/75 season was probably the all time low for me as a supporter of the Club. It was arguably, in my life time at least, the worst season we've ever experienced.

In the end it's all about winning, 'If you want entertainment, then go and watch some clowns'

Still as a rugby fanatic and an average sort of guy in his twenties, back then and indeed now, hard times are all part of the ongoing learning process that is life and supporting a sport's club. In fact if there is one thing that being a fan of professional sport teaches you, it's that you never stop learning. It's at times like those grim days in the 70's when you realise that the relationship between entertaining rugby and the fanatic is a strained one indeed. You appreciate the entertaining stuff when it's not your Club you're watching, or when you're winning by a big score but when it is your team, in the end if you're honest, rugby that is pleasing to the eye is a bit secondary. When considered in its rawest state loving your Club is all about winning or at least not failing. Whatever happens you still attend, simply because when you're hooked there is nowhere else to go when your team is playing. There are a few lucky people who have chosen the club they support but most of us, for better or worse, have just had our club thrust upon us, or at the very least we have inherited it through our family's loyalties.

So as your team slips down to a lower division, gets knocked out of the cup by the 'little' club, or when your Board sell your best or your favourite player, you just turn up, curse a bit, grumble a lot, usually lose, go home and turn up at the next game to suffer it all over again. Don't get me wrong over the years I have lamented long and hard about the Board, the players, the coach and anyone else I can blame but deep down as a fan, entertaining play has always been the last of my considerations, in fact for me personally it's a bonus if we are winning and an added frustration if we're not! To this day I still go to rugby for loads of reasons but being entertained is sadly no longer one of them!

It's just the same now as it was back in the 70's, in fact when I look around me today during a game at the KC Stadium little in the crowd has changed. It's all very much like it was on the Threepenny Stand in 1974. The fashions, haircuts and shirts are different but I still see all those harassed and worried faces that make me realise that I am not a special case and certainly not on my own. I have to say though, that it was probably back then in the depth of the depressing 70's that I learned what that 'suffering for your sport' stuff was all about. Winning in the end is the important thing but as Alan Durban the outspoken football manager of the 80's once said, "I want to win but if you want entertainment, go and watch some clowns". However should I have met Mr Durban I would, as a lifelong follower of Hull FC, have respectfully replied to that statement by explaining that perhaps when you're a sport's fan who cares about his team, you realise that clowns are not exclusively reserved for circuses. He should have seen some of the players I have endured over the years.

Of course some folks are a lot luckier than the fanatics like me because some can walk away when the going gets tough and in those dark years in the mid 70's many did. It must be great if you are able to treat your weekly sport as some do their local pub, they love the place and the company but by and large if the beer goes off, you go somewhere else. When you love your team you simply can't do that because there is nowhere else to go and you suffer and suffer, until eventually the 'beer' that is watching your Club kills you, or at the very least it kills completely your will to have any rational thought about it. Strong words perhaps but over 50 years of following my Club leads me to believe that they are true ones, just the same.

Breaking records of the worst kind......again!

That season of 1974/75 we certainly had the worst gate we had ever seen at the Boulevard when just 983 turned up for a game on 16th March against Huyton. I won't bore you by telling you I was there, or that I still have the programme because by the end of the decade you could find at least 18,000 'loyal' supporters who claimed they had been there on that day. Not many of us are real fanatics but when the 'going is good' everyone wants to claim they have always been one! That game became part of Hull FC folklore and was widely used as a benchmark of your loyalty to the Club. Despite all the 'Sing when you're winning', 'Only here for the Beer' supporters that followed Hull FC and packed the Boulevard in the early eighties you were only really a 'Proper' fan if you had been to that Huyton game of which there is more a little later.

As fans, we were down to the last remnants of blinkered loyalty and those who attended games were either, like me, so conditioned in that it was 'just what you did' or completely numbed by years of disappointment and more often than not the latter was a prerequisite of the former. Our beloved Hull FC battled on with diminishing resources and often, it was rumoured, players not being paid at all. Our coach did his best in the transfer market too and had some limited success bringing the great prop forward Bill Ramsey to the Club from Bradford Northern and centre or winger George Clarke from New Hunslet. We also managed to do well in the early rounds of the Yorkshire Cup, but there was a glimmer of hope, if only a slight one, because it was becoming apparent to us all on the terraces that although the resources he had at his disposal were making it tough in league games, David Doyle-Davidson had that certain something when it came to 'lifting' our performances for the big matches.

Everybody off!

Tuesday 10th September 1974   *Hull 12 – Leeds 8*

Back then there were three cup competitions as well as the League to play for although we always seemed to get drawn against the same teams in the knock out tournaments and so there were few surprises for us as the draw was made for the second round of the Yorkshire Cup in 1974 because who should we come out of the 'hat' against? Yep you guessed it; Leeds again, as usual. We always seemed to be drawn against the 'Good time Charlies' from the West Riding and always gave them a good game, so much so 'The Rugby Leaguer' called us the 'Loiners' bogey team. The match was played under floodlights at the Boulevard on a barmy, late summer evening in front of a very respectable attendance of over 4000 people. That was certainly a good gate for that season and there can't have been too much going on in Hull that night! One wag commented to me before kick-off that, "Perhaps most of this lot thought it was Speedway tonight".

I watched the game from the Best Stand, which was a rarity for me, and quite why I wasn't in my usual position on the Threepenny Stand escapes me now. The souvenir programme's listings reflected Doyle-Davidson's efforts to build a viable team as it included a few youngsters that were the first green shoots of what was to be a great team in the later years of the decade. It was a game that I have to include here in this journal simply because of the amazing circumstances surrounding the referee that night Mr. Lawrenson. We were the team floundering in the Second Division whilst Leeds had won that same Yorkshire Cup for the past two years and were, as usual, the top club east of the Pennines and 'dead certs' to win it again. Their line up back then included familiar names like Langley, Holmes, Syd Hynes, Keith Hepworth (late of Castleford and soon to be of Hull FC), Mike Harrison (ex of Hull FC) and a great flying winger called John Atkinson.

The pundits had us down for a good hiding but we shot into a surprise 7-0 lead in the first half hour, however it was just before half time when the whole thing kicked off. Hepworth tackled our captain, the usually mild mannered Brian Hancock, and much to the delight of the fans a fist fight involving six players immediately broke out centred around these two. Referee Lawrenson sent Hancock straight off the field for what was the player's first ever dismissal. His Hull FC team mates crowded round the official to object and Len Casey must have said a bit too much because off he went too, as the referee again pointed to the dressing rooms.

Our blind side prop forward that day 'Big' Jim Macklin, who never had that much patience, had clearly had enough! The fiery front rower motioned to the players and pointed to the tunnel as most of them started to trudge defiantly towards the dressing rooms. Now this was a real surprise for the fans who had never ever contemplated seeing the players walking from the field in protest. It was simply unheard of and we all stood in absolute amazement. The official, who clearly had no idea what to do next, (nothing new there then) told Leeds to ignore our players and get on with the penalty, Syd Hynes tapped the ball and set off arrogantly jogging down the pitch towards the Airlie Street end, with a wide grin on his face.

Alf Macklin, Jim's brother who was stuck out on the wing and not part of the walk off, shouted to the lads and pointed to the Leeds player whilst mouthing "F*cking get Him" a call that was taken up immediately around the terracing. Our players turned round, and in a fit of rage ran back across the field and Jim Macklin and Don Robson sunk the now fleeing Syd Hynes with one of the biggest crash tackles I have ever seen!! The referee had by now completely lost control and the game continued to the break by which time the eleven players of Hull FC, playing like men possessed, had somehow managed to tough it out, and keep the marauding Leeds forwards from scoring any points.

However the excitement was not over yet because after the referee had blown the whistle for half time, a Hull fan, obviously enraged by the earlier dismissals, vaulted the hooped top fencing in front of the terracing at the Airlie Street end and ran towards the match official. Spotting this, referee Lawrenson, who obviously fancied himself a bit, set off toward the supporter to confront him, head on! It was all happening, and the crowd roared their approval as two policemen 'rugby tackled' the fan, whilst Chris Davidson, our scrum half, held back the referee and escorted him off the pitch. That was a real reversal of roles because with Chris it was usually the other way around. This unique occurrence was something that was not lost on the crowd who were buzzing throughout the whole of the half time interval.

If the first half was pure circus, then the second half was possibly the best display of 'backs to the wall' rugby I have seen on any field of play anywhere in my lifetime. The crowd, who had come along to watch an anticipated drubbing, were treated to the best dogged, gutsy exhibition of Rugby League most of them had seen, and in fact would probably ever see! The 'flash' Leeds team ripped into the 11 men of Hull from the kick off but the home defences somehow stayed intact and then when Davidson kicked a penalty and a drop goal to move the score line to 10-0, what we were witnessing was almost too impossible to believe.

Leeds numerical superiority brought them two quick tries, as they threw the ball around and after 60 minutes they were trailing by just 2 points at 10-8. For the last 10 minutes they bombarded our line but somehow we held out! In those days of unlimited substitution our coach rang the changes so many times in the last fifteen minutes that the referee stopped the game on a couple of occasions just to count how many players we actually had on the field. I have witnessed some great gritty and passionate performances since, notably winning at Castleford again with 11 men in the early 80's, but no display was greater than that one!

Looking at the record books for that year Hull finished the season 6th in the Second Division whilst Leeds were the first ever winners of the Premiership title! But I bet they and their fans remembered that September night at the Boulevard for a long time afterwards because it was simply unbelievable.

Ain't superstitious? Lucky steps, toilet breaks, Wagon Wheels and 'Adam's lucky conker'

After my brief excursion into the Best Stand I returned to watching games from my usual place on the Threepenny Stand. I loved it in there, because it had always been the 'Home' I returned to when times were hard but I also have some great memories of some equally great victories watching with my pals in there. We had a certain position at a certain height towards which we all gravitated before the kick-off. We all agreed that it was our lucky place on the Stand and was the only position that we would stand in. Later when I went back to watching games, from Bunker's Hill at the Airlie Street end of the ground, I adopted a 'Lucky step.' Why exactly it was 'lucky' is shrouded in the misty memories created by Hull Brewery and North Country Bitter, but it was lucky none the less and woe betides anyone who stood on it! I suppose I had once stood there when we won a memorable victory but despite its origins being beyond my recollections, standing there was a ritual that started when I left the Threepennies for ever in the mid eighties and it continued until we all left the Boulevard in October 2002.

Over the 50 years I have supported my Club there have of course been dozens of other similar bits of nonsense all designed to guarantee that we won, and that have come and then been discarded, usually when we have lost. There have been lucky socks, lucky hats, lucky scarves and even lucky underpants, and to this day I never wash my Hull shirt after a victory, my wife says that I'll smell but that's hardly likely with my team's record of wins on the trot is it?

Years ago, probably in the late 60's, I tried eating a 'Wagon Wheel' biscuit after our first try and even had some success after I realised that we had scored a winning try in the last minutes of the game whilst I was in the toilet. After that every time we were behind I was dispatched by my pals to the 'Little Boys Room' where I awaited the roar of the crowd that heralded a try. Amazingly this seemed to work for a while but I was glad when it stopped inducing tries, because whilst it was working, I was 'sent to' the toilet several times a game and subsequently missed some great scores. It seems that you're not really a sport's fan if you don't have a few rituals and superstitions. Listening to games on local radio is far worse though and sometimes I switch off altogether when we are just winning in the vain hope that when I switch back on again nothing will have changed. In more recent times I even stopped recording our televised games because we always seemed to do better when I had forgotten to record a match. It must have, by now, become obviously apparent that I am just an incurable obsessive when it comes to Hull FC.

If I am honest about these superstitions nothing has ever been any good but it is at least heartening to know others suffer the same way that I do. Take my pal Adam who sits near me at the KC stadium. He found that a lucky conker was the talisman that made us win and sure enough it seemed to work. Every time he took the conker to games we won, until that is, a fateful night at Wigan when in just 80 minutes it seemed to lose its magical power.

Two weeks later at the KC we were pressing the Bradford line with two minutes to go and I manically shrieked, "Have you got the lucky Conker?", to which he replied "No I slung it on the pitch after the game at Wigan". We lost that Bradford game and so we'll never know whether the Wigan experience was just a hiccup and whether that mystical fruit of *Aesculus Hippocastanum* could have won us that game against the Bulls. It's just superstition isn't it? Or is it, who knows, but there is a nagging doubt lodged at the back of my brain that perhaps that conker was after all the much sought after 'Holy Grail' of the world of sporting talisman but now we'll never know. However if there's a Horse Chestnut tree growing out of the pitch at the away end at the DW Stadium next time you visit, then you'll know who's responsible!

I would say as a footnote on rituals and 'lucky charms' that you might as well keep looking to find the one that works because what else can we do? As sports fans we spend our lives, month after month and decade after decade investing our time, money, energy and passion into something that we have absolutely no control over. We have no chance of changing things, picking the team, signing the players or even deciding on the flavour of the pies and what will be, will be. However we should never stop searching to find that one thing that might just give us that advantage and control over the outcome of a game, let's face facts here, it's only what primitive communities have, done from the year dot, to try and protect themselves from dark times.

The possibility that one person carrying out a specific act can change the course of a game of rugby is rather farfetched to say the least and goes against everything we would claim to be common sense, still it is not going to stop me leaving my shirt dirty till we lose! I once asked the Club Chaplain if he prayed for a victory during games and if he did, how did God decide between his prayers and those of the opposing club Chaplain. He said that if he prayed it was for 'An honest and satisfactory outcome'. 'Great' I thought, 'He must have been asked that one before, what he needs is a conker!'

Seven hours there and seven hours back; Barrow on a Friday night.

Friday 29ᵗʰ November 1974   *Hull 7 – Barrow 21*

When writing a journal such as this it is rewarding to be able, at times, to feature happenings that show how different sport and life was back in the mid seventies. One game of rugby that illustrates just that was played on Friday 29ᵗʰ November 1974 under the floodlights at Craven Park, Barrow.

I didn't go to this particular game, Barrow on a Friday back then was a fourteen hour round trip!! However the game did have some strange circumstances surrounding it! Friday night matches didn't happen back then, well not that often anyway, but Barrow had a major employer in the Vickers Ship Yard, with whom half the population was employed. The rugby club insisted that because of the strange shift system that major local employer operated, the game would have to be played on a Friday. I wouldn't have minded but in the end, only 1400 of the North West's 'Sons of the Sea' turned up anyway.

This was a major problem for Hull FC though, because many of our playing staff were in full time employment and would find it hard to get off work for a full day to take the long and winding bus trip to North West Lancashire. The pay for playing for the Club was way below what the players could expect for a day's work in their regular jobs and as match fees were performance related, that was particularly the case if you lost! No one could risk being sacked for not turning up for work either and although some employees were sympathetic to the demands of the game, others certainly were not.

The Rugby League Board of Management ruled that the game had to go ahead as they said that it was Barrow's decision as they were the home team and so seven of our first team players had to withdraw because they could not get released or afford to miss a full day at work. The squad we took all that way was certainly a strange one. Tony Banham, only half fit and just signed from Keighley was at prop, whilst the Club signed young Ray Butler from the amateur game to make up the numbers in the second row. Incidentally in the second row that night too was Barry Kear, a big name signing, who promised much, but who in the end had a poor game, (but then those who saw him play will remember, he always did).

Apparently Kenny Foulkes and Brian Hancock tried really hard at half back that night and Barrow's winning margin of 14 points flattered them but in the end our inexperience and a long bus trip the same day, meant that we were never going to win and we came home empty handed losing 21-7. Hull gave half back Steve Lane his debut that night and according to the papers next day, Boxall had a good game too. But with players like Alf Macklin, Len Casey and Howard Firth missing it was always going to be a struggle! Good old Chris Davidson was missing as well but he was in the middle of a six match suspension for scrapping, (nothing new there then) but that as they say is another story!

The lunatics have taken over the asylum: The Council put me in charge of the Boulevard!

It was around that time that gardening on the City Council changed forever as the authority introduced an incentive bonus scheme to improve the staff wages, cut the work force and make the cultured art of gardening into a mechanical process. For us horticulturalists it was a real change as we were followed everywhere by a man in a raincoat and trilby who would be incessantly scribbling on a clip board and timing everything we did. This procedure was aimed at having a standard time for every job there was, be it pruning a rose, tying up a tree or cutting a piece of grass. Once this time had been ascertained, the 'Time and motion' men then told us how many roses we had to prune and pieces of grass we had to cut in an hour, day and week.

Anyone who has done any gardening at all knows that it just isn't like that, every rose is different every piece of grass has varying amounts of rubbish and old arm chairs on them and every tree, a different amount of pruning needed. However the rewards were very good and if you did your fixed rate of jobs a week then you could earn up to half the total of your weekly wage again. I suppose I was quick to prostitute my beliefs because I really liked the money which increased the frequency of my Saturday visits considerably to my favorite record shop Sydney Scarborough's under the City Hall, but I didn't like the ideology at all. Still I got on with it which is more than could be said for many of the older gardeners like Hubert at Pearson Park and Lenny at Sutton Golf Course, for whom the change in methods was all too much, and so sadly after years of loyal service many of these old hands retired or left the authority.

In addition to this instead to having work place based gangs of staff in parks, playing fields and cemeteries the whole City was split up into nine districts and I was recruited to train for one of the new district manager's positions; they must have been hard up! This management trainee position meant me being based at the new organisation's offices in Pearson Park wearing a suit and riding around in a van all day. I was sent to check that the Gardeners were actually doing what they were supposed to be and not just booking jobs they hadn't done to make sure they got their full bonus. The first change this brought about was the fact that the lack of any sort of manual work saw me put a stone on in weight in just two months.

In those early days of being a manager I was never really suited to being 'A Boss' and took every opportunity I could to socialise with my old pals from the gardening staff. However they looked on me differently now and I suppose it was then that I realized that there was no going back, with all the change that these people had experienced they just didn't trust anyone from the 'Management' anymore and it was now a case of 'us and them'; those great days of hoeing rose beds, whistling at the girls and talking rugby had gone forever. In early 1975 I received my first ever salaried wage and was promoted to Area Manager for North Hull. By summer had arrived I was promoted again to the same position in the central area of the City which included Queen's Gardens and the City centre. Things were going reasonably well, the staff who I was now looking after were mellowing to me and my new position and the money

I was receiving for the job was good, however things were about to get even better.

One morning I was called into the offices in Pearson Park to be told by the Managing Director that we had taken on a new contract on behalf of a private company in my area. "So what" I thought, we were doing this sort of thing all the time. However I was then told that this contract was to reinstate and develop the pitch at the home of Hull FC 'The Boulevard'. "Perhaps you should go down there and familiarise yourself with the place" said the Boss, "I don't think that will be necessary", I thought out loud, "But I'll definitely go down there and have a look".

As I drove away from the offices I remember that I felt that it had to be an amazing co-incidence that I would not only be attending my spiritual home every other weekend through the next winter, but I would also be responsible for the upkeep of that most sacred of playing surfaces too. When I told Mum and Dad they were so happy about my new responsibilities back there in what was I suppose still the family's spiritual home just off Anlaby Road.

It was around that time too that I went to the City Hall in Hull again, this time I went with Ted my pal from the Parks' Management team to see Procol Harem in concert. The band, of whom I had always been a fan, had by that time moved on a long way from their initial hit 'A Whiter Shade of Pale' and were now touring and featuring songs like, 'The Devil came from Kansas', 'Bringing home the Bacon' and 'A Salty Dog'. It was a fantastic night when everyone sat in their seats and listened, which made a big change from more traditional pop concerts that I had attended when the fans went clambering over the chairs to get to the stage.

Rock bottom (with at least 18,000 fans in attendance)

Sunday 16ᵗʰ March 1975   *Hull 17 – Huyton 15*

So we now arrive at that very unglamorous game that is so significant in the history of Hull FC that it would be totally wrong if I were not to include it here. Any older supporter will know what is coming next because it's the Hull FC game everyone knows about and remembers, for all the wrong reasons. It was played on Sunday 16th March 1975 and what was so significant was the fact that we played in front of just 983 fans in a league game against lowly Huyton. This was officially our lowest ever gate at the Boulevard and although there didn't seem many there at the time, few if any of the fans that did turn up knew that they were about to make history. Before the 70's our previous lowest attendance was 1700 for a game against Doncaster in 1966. There were lower gates in the early seventies as I have already indicated, however this was the day when we were to plumb the very depths of rock bottom attendance wise.

Looking back it was probably only the Speedway Franchise and perhaps those hot dogs that was keeping us going. We had already played Huyton over in Liverpool in November and lost 32-10 in a poor game that had the national Daily Mail's rugby correspondent talking of "The beginning of the End" for our Club, however this game was to be an equally dire affair but for everyone at Hull FC it was not so much about playing well as about averting a second humiliating defeat. We found out after the match that over on Merseyside the media were claiming that this was Huyton's chance to get a very, very rare away win and their predictions almost proved to be right.

Anyone who was there (I've been through that already) will first of all remember the shocking condition of the pitch. The shale from the speedway track was now well bedded in everywhere so much so that it had started to silt up the land drains under the playing area. The whole pitch was a morass of mud, described pretty descriptively by the Hull Daily Mail the following evening as a 'gluepot of a Pitch'

The roar of the grease paint, the smell of the crowd

The Threepennies were so sparsely populated that day that when the team ran out onto the pitch several people were using the steps as seats just as they did for 'A' Team games. I watched from there because it was one of those games when you felt you needed to be amongst friends rather than isolated on the vast expanses of the deserted end terraces. It was our lucky spot and the place to be, particularly when the chips were down and everything was against your team, you could suspend reality for a while as you clutched your Bovril and drank in the unmistakable odour of cheap cigarette smoke, and that 'uriney', sweaty smell that said you were home.

Although the drama was usually reserved for the playing area, there were always plenty of characters about on the stand and at that time it often seemed that only they remained. A pair that were well known around where we stood went by the nick-names of Cuckoo and Graffiti. Why they had these titles no one really knew, but Cuckoo stuttered really badly and although able to sing 'Old Faithful' flawlessly, he was the constant butt of amateur impressionists across the stand, whilst Graffiti had an amazing ability to misuse words. He would say things like "I went out for a lovely meal and afterwards I gave my condolences to the Chef", and "On Sunday last week I took the neighbours 'Al Stat chon' dog for a walk down to Mini Vera Pier". However his best ever effort came one wet half time when we noted that he had been missing for a few games. He said this was because his wife had been in hospital for a serious operation which he described as her having had an "Hysterical Rectum". No doubt on that bleak afternoon these two kept us amused whilst we waited for the serious business on the field to start.

It was all so predictable and 'safe' in that stand back then, there was the ritual welcome for the team, the cheap jibes and resulting laughter for the opposition, the shapeless roar when we looked to be making a break, the bemoaning of the referee, the chanting when we scored, the round of applause as the scorer walked back up the pitch and of course the choruses of 'Old Faithful' just when the lads were flagging. It was always fun to spot a female new comer in the form of someone's wife or girlfriend who had obviously never been on the famous stand before, because the look on their faces when the regulars started their choruses of 'Oh, Oh, Oh, Oh, what a referee', with the string of expletives at the end, was simply priceless. Distress flares 'sneaked' off local trawlers were at times thrown onto the field stopping play, anyone in the ranks of the opposition with fashionably long hair would be instantly christened Marilyn or Freda, Rovers scarves were burned in the wooden rafters above our heads and linesmen religiously and mercilessly abused, it was all just a ritual really, but nevertheless it was 'Home Sweet Home' for the ailing FC fans.

If you're a 'real' fan, a wins a win, whoever you're playing!!

That particular afternoon, once we had eventually kicked off there was little surprise around me when we went behind to a 'shock' Huyton try after just 6 minutes with the score going to their star back Don Preston, who they were soon to sell to Warrington.

We needed a response and it came from a dependable source when some good work in the mud by Bill Ramsey put Tony Salmon through into the clear and he just managed to crash over the try line for Keith Boxall to add the goal. Back came Huyton and an offence against Salmon for 'laying on' too long in the tackle saw the visitor's goal kicker Watts make no mistake and it was 5-5.

It was then a case of dropped balls and crunching tackles from both sides until, the local hero of the day, 'The Rhino' Keith Boxall received an inside pass from our scrum half Steve Lane and in typical fashion he shrugged off two tackles and set off on one of those 'barreling' runs that made him such a big favorite on the terraces. He was caught but managed to just plunge over the line in the midst of a pile of Huyton players. So we were at least ahead at half time as the teams trooped off steaming and appearing, as was usual back then, to be playing in a strip that was brown shirts, brown shorts and brown socks. As my pal Steve commented after the game, it would probably have been more appropriate had the fans been supplied with brown trousers that day!

After the mandatory changing of shirts at the interval, Huyton stormed straight back with a try from Prescott and a penalty goal from Watts. With the scores tied we all thought that Huyton were to get that much desired away win as they mounted wave after wave of attacks in our half of the field. Then, as the rain lashed down, we watched as Mally

Walker, who had come on as substitute, stepped out of a tackle and gave a good 'switch' inside pass to Salmon who ran over three would be tacklers, American Football style, to end up over the line and with Boxall converting we were again in the lead. As you looked out at the pitch that day, it was a sad and depressing site. There were pools of water starting to form, whilst the half illuminated floodlights picking out two teams of steaming players, plodding about in muddy, faded shirts, on a bog of a pitch in front of a pitiful crowd!

Some really sloppy play in the visitors' half saw Hull knocking on 5 times in about ten minutes which put us under pressure again. Then we conceded another try, this time Trevor Lloyd went through three would be Hull tacklers and scored with some ease for Watts to kick the goal. The game was now all level at 15-15 and on 'a knife edge' with not much time left to go to the final whistle.

We did at least mount some pressure on the visitors' line in those last few minutes and a head high tackle on Brian Hancock, that was certainly lucky as it was caused as a Huyton player tried to keep his balance on the slippery surface, meant that Boxall got a late, late penalty to put us back in the lead. In those final minutes the visitors came back to pepper our line with forward runs, but by then it was almost impossible to tell who was who, so dark and dreary was the weather, the floodlights and the shirts and after what seemed like an age the whistle went and we had won.....just!!!! An almost ironic cheer went up from the supporters in the stands, whilst the steaming players' mud splattered faces grinned at us as they punched the air in triumph before tramping off for a few beers and one of Ivy's teas. It was a hollow victory in the bigger scheme of things and did little to cheer up this fan, although as many people said as they trudged out of the ground, the rain pouring down their necks, "A win's a win".

"When you're struggling in the League, if there is anything better than a cup run to get the fans' minds off what's really happening, then I've yet to find it!"

Sunday 23rd November 1975   *Hull 9 – St Helens 8*

As a 25 year old trainee manager surrounded at work by 'bandwaggoning' Hull City supporters clambering aboard the 'Promotion' train, it was tough being an FC fan in 1975. Still as a Club we continued to soldier on in ever depreciating surroundings, beset by despair, shrinking gates and a lack of finance. However we needed to get some cash together and in sport there is nothing like a good cup run to do just that, perhaps here it is worth trying to describe just what a successful run towards a trophy final is all about for success starved fans. The Players No 6 Trophy later to become the Regal Trophy was in its infancy as this was only the fifth year that it had been contested. The prize money saw the winners get £6000 and the losers £3000.

It was during that cup run that as fans we finally realised what a great coach David Doyle-Davidson was. He had come to power at a time when we were at rock bottom and despite being given little financial encouragement by the Club's Directors, he had slowly but surely cobbled together a handy looking team, full of guts, passion and spirit and probably in the end, although it wasn't pretty to watch and there were certainly still a few 'clowns' on show, his style of 'full on' rugby was pretty effective in the sudden death arena of a knockout competition.

In the first round of the tournament we had scraped an unconvincing win at Doncaster, then following a 9-9 draw at the Boulevard we went on to beat a highly fancied Leeds outfit in the replay at Headingley. That was a great game which we had not been expected to win but from which we came out victorious by 23-11. Then the draw for the quarter finals was made on regional TV and as I watched with Mum and Dad at home in Sutton we came out of the 'bag' to face Saints at the Boulevard that November. That day I was joined by another 4500 of the Faithful and what was estimated to be well over four million on BBC TV, to experience a truly great Hull FC performance. The fact that at the time

4500 was a good gate shows how our expectations had declined. But then again it was a step up from that attendance against Huyton and it was on TV, so I guess a few chose to watch at home and therefore at that time, this was as good as it would get.

We were certainly getting our share of exposure on the TV that year as only the previous Tuesday on BBC2 we had gone down by 36-13, to the Saints, this time in a televised Floodlit Trophy game, so this time around few neutrals watching at home gave us a chance. Our Prop Forward that night Alan Wardell once told me that Doyle-Davidson hammered on at the players before the game, saying that "After last Tuesday night everyone expects us to get a drubbing, so let's show those folks watching at home what we are really about here in Hull". It was even more of a surprise when it leaked out afterwards that the Board had also refused to pay a cup bonus to the players and they were playing just for the usual league winning pay. Our coach had somehow managed to watch the Floodlit game again, which was a rarity in the days before video and coaches' reviewing tapes and it was revealed later that 'The Doyle' and his coaching team had studied the Saints tactics and totally changed the FC game plan in just three sessions of training.

From the first play of the game we had the Saints tactically beaten. Every time they tried to move the ball wide our cover came up into the line and broke their play up. After about three set plays in which Saints dropped the ball a couple of times, they tried to change their tactics but visibly failed as Hull just drove on at them. Then, on 10 minutes, Keith Boxall broke through a three man tackle and set Alf Macklin haring for the corner. Alf was caught 5 yards short, but pushing two much bigger tacklers off, he dived in over the line. This battling action, by probably the smallest player on the field, was to set the scene for the rest of our performance.

Despite that tough game just four days previously our tackling was of the highest order but so too was that of the Saints and so the game settled into a 'slog' of big hits and crunching tackles. After 12 minutes when he looked to be covered by Pimblett, Kenny Foulkes dummied his way through the Saints cover straight from a scrum and as he stepped over the 25 yard line he found Hunter with a little inside pass. He ran for the line with three defenders chasing him and arcing towards the corner flag he just got the ball down before being hammered to the ground by Saints' winger Roy Mathias. Although Kendle missed both conversions it was a dream start and a lead we were not to relinquish.

The Saints' pack that day was five stone heavier than ours but our six, brilliantly led by the great Bill Ramsey dominated the exchanges, with Cunningham, Chisnell, Nichols and Mantle rarely breaking our defensive line and recent recruit from Rovers, Peter (Flash) Flanagan 'shovelled' the ball out for us, beating international hooker Liptrop 19-12 in the scrums.

The game settled down somewhat after that lightening start but just as Saints started to get a foothold in our territory, Hancock picked up a loose ball, spilled after a massive Ramsey hit, and set off towards the Saints' half. He was tackled some thirty yards out but two more forward drives, one a blockbuster from Boxall, saw Chris Davidson open on the left, and he dropped a perfect goal to stretch our lead further.

We went in at half time leading 7-0 but as the TV coverage went live, any thoughts of an easy victory were quashed when Saints came back with a quick Mathias score in the corner, which Pimblett converted and then we were under sustained pressure as the Lancastrian First Division team sniffed a win. Then on a rare sortie up field Mally Walker broke a tackle and panic reined in the Saints' ranks, until that was, centre Les Jones strode into the collision and punched our second rower in the face. After missing three pots at goal Kendle at last placed the resultant penalty between the uprights and despite an unconverted try by Wilson in the corner in the last minute we held on and recorded a memorable 9-8 victory.

It was a thrilling cup tie that I best remember for some titanic defending and 'last ditch' tackling. After years of struggling the fans loved it and I ran onto the field at the end as usual to congratulate our heroes. The fact remains for me and other 'old timers' to ponder that although much maligned in some quarters David Doyle-Davidson was certainly a good coach particularly in Cup matches, and in hindsight I guess, did a lot of the spade work and recruitment that Arthur Bunting was to capitalise on in those fantastic golden years of the late 70's and early 80's.

I then travelled across the Pennines with the Supporter's Club motor coach to watch a superb game at the Willows, when we took on the star spangled Salford side in the semi-final. Salford were just starting to crank up the off field stuff back then and had a wonderful club where you could get a top class meal and watch international artistes after the game. There was a lot of razz-a-ma-tazz about the old place back then! I know it's hard to believe it these days, but back then The Willows was quite a smart stadium. Their team was top of the League and full of household names being lead by that Welsh wizard and RL legend, David Watkins. To everyone in the game's disbelief, we won that semi-final by 22-14. I remember that Boxall, Tindall and Bill Ramsey ripped the Salford pack apart that night, and sticking rigidly to the Doyle's latest 'master plan', we ran out easy winners and were into the final!

"Misfits and under achievers." But heroes just the same!

Saturday 24th January 1976　　　　　*Hull 13 – Widnes 19*

As you can imagine the build up to our first final in almost seven years saw cup tie fever return to West Hull. You know even now when I look back at the team photograph taken on the pitch at Headingley on the day of the game I have to wonder how a Second Division team of such varying size and stature could ever expect to get to the last two in the competition never mind think they could win it. David Doyle-Davidson had put together a team of players of various sizes, shapes and abilities and we looked, if I am honest, like a raggle-taggle band of unlikely heroes. One supporter once described them to me as a band of misfits and under achievers and although I would not go that far, I think I appreciated his point. However once on the pitch their tenacity and passion for the Black and White shirt they wore was there for all to see. Why in fact should it not have looked that way because that year we were in the end the Second Division underdogs who were destined to not even finish in the top four promotion places in our League, and on that day we were facing the First Division 'Cup Kings'.

Still the Club certainly took advantage of the public relations opportunities the game provided and milked the situation for all it was worth. There were 'pull-outs' in the local paper and banners in the front room windows of houses around the ground. More bizarrely still the team even made a mid week personal appearance and photo call at 'Boyes' the department store on Hessle Road that features so heavily in my recollections of early life 'on the Boulevard'. The squad were also taken back in time by the coach, when he used Madeley Street Swimming Baths for two indoor fitness sessions before the final and there is little doubt his inspirational speeches and rhetoric in the dressing room was of great significance as far as Hull's performance on the day was concerned. Whatever else our current coach was, he was an excellent motivator.

For my final build up to the big game I met with a few pals and some of my work colleagues on the Friday night, for a good session of 'Hull Brewery's Best' at the County Hotel in Charles Street in the City Centre. To the accompaniment of rousing cheers we watched as the 10.30 regional news on the pub TV featured our squad and coach, who interviewer Keith Macklin described as the "undoubted underdogs". There were a few words from 'The Doyle' and Keith Boxall and then as the short news item finished a rousing chorus of 'Old Faithful' rang round the bar and saw the old pub shaken to its foundations. The scene was set for a big day out in the morning.

Obviously of course, Widnes were the definite favourites having already won two trophies in the previous ten months, whilst we had been in the doldrums and not won any sort of title for six years. So it was that on Saturday 24th January I made my way to Paragon Station to catch the 10.10am 'Trans-Pennine' train to Leeds City, which was, when I managed to board it, restricted to 'standing room only'.

Once in Leeds it seemed many of my fellow 'Black and White' travellers had the same idea and we all went round the corner to the

Scarborough Hotel for what was becoming our ritual pre-match drink. When I finally got to Headingley the snow was blowing in the wind and it was a bleak and cold afternoon which saw the bars packed so tight it was futile to even try and get inside for a drink and a warm. As we entered the ground the Players No 6 Promotions girls shivered in their high boots and mini-skirts as they distributed plastic bowler hats in black and white. Literally hundreds of these could be seen in both factions of the crowd, as of course both clubs' traditional strips are the same colour. In fairness the tournament had not really captured the public's imagination and although the final was televised and well publicised, the bad weather meant that only 9035, our lowest gate ever in a senior final, were in attendance, in reality of course at least 7000 of those were from Hull.

The FC fans already assembled in the South Stand amused themselves by singing along to the public address system as it blasted out 'Bohemian Rhapsody', the number one record at the time. When the record finished the massed ranks of the 'FC Army' re-sang the middle section through to the end unaccompanied, to the great amusement of the Widnes' supporters gathered under the score board, who gave a warm round of applause to the Hull fans when they finished. We took over the South Stand and 'Old Faithful' rang round the ground as the teams ran out.

As the snow flurries continued the pre-match predictions of an easy Widnes win seemed to be spot on as the favourites swept into a 7-0 lead in just 8 minutes. Firstly Walker was penalised when he got in between his own player and the Widnes' defence and Ray Dutton landed a penalty goal from 30 yards. As the opposition swept back down field, Mick Adams strolled in to score a try from a Jim Mill's pass. At this point the gulf in class between the two teams was really apparent. In that move I remember 'Big Jim' swotted off three Hull tacklers on his way towards the line, whilst Dutton added the conversion and then after twelve minutes in which we had hardly touched the ball, Bowden dropped a goal to extend the lead to 8 points.

Things looked pretty grim for the FC but we fans did not let up the continuous chanting and singing as slowly but surely the team got a bit more of the ball to play with. It was desperation rugby really but our willingness to keep the ball alive in such windy and cold conditions saw Widnes a little taken aback. The two players that stood out for Hull in that first half were without doubt veteran prop Bill Ramsey and the ubiquitous Mick Crane who always saved his best performances for the big games. It was these two who combined brilliantly to put our first points on the board as Ramsey made the break and slipped out a smart inside ball to Craney who romped in to score our first try, juggling with the ball as he crossed between the posts. Boxall kicked the goal and we were just 3 points behind. As we stamped our feet and sang our hearts out, Hull were level before half time!

This time a period of pressure for the FC saw a scrum formed 30 yards from the Widnes' line. Veteran hooker 'Flash' Flanagan shovelled the ball out against the head and the Hull three-quarters used 'fast hands' to move the ball and run it into the opposition's twenty-five yard area, before Jimmy Portz was stopped by a crunching tackle from Dutton. A quick play the ball sent the play down the 'blind side' and winger Paul Hunter just squeezed in at the corner for us to go in at half time drawing 8-8.

The second half began as the first had, with a confident Widnes' attack keeping the ball and pressurising our line, we were struggling to keep them out and eventually their mercurial Welsh winger David Jenkins shot in at the corner for two brilliantly executed tries and although Dutton failed with both conversions we were trailing again by six points. Widnes then settled into a period of 'Fancy Dan' type rugby no doubt in an attempt to emphasise their title of 'Cup Kings' and at 14-8 they would now surely run away with the game. Well they might have if it were not for that man Mick Crane. As Widnes rumbled out of their twenty five a try looked certain as Hughes opened the game up and flashed out a long looping pass towards their centre George who was well clear of his marker, but from nowhere, Mick was in between the two players intercepting the pass and galloping down the field to touch-down.

The Boxall conversion meant that with just a quarter of the game left we were just one point behind. This rattled the Widnes' side and the next fifteen minutes were played at a frenetic pace and a bit more guile and enterprise would I believe have seen us win the Trophy. However the loss of hooker 'Flash' Flanagan injured with fifteen minutes to go, saw Hull starved of possession at the scrums and unable to turn up the heat on the Widnes' defence as much we would have liked.

Victory to the gallant under dogs was not to be and as if to epitomise the class player that he was, from nowhere Reg Bowden shot out of the line and nipped in, as all great number 7's do, to score the decisive winner. As the final whistle sounded the 'tannoy' PA system announced that Bowden had been made 'Man of the Match' and so impressed were the sponsors with what was in hindsight a fabulous display, they had doubled his prize money to £100. We didn't care of course and as Widnes received the Trophy you would have thought that we had won, so loud and proud was the singing and chanting for Hull FC.

In fact it was only after the teams had disappeared into the dressing rooms and we were making our way round to the Best Stand bar that a feeling of melancholy, sadness and disappointment started to kick in. We had as a humble Second Division team, been so close to a magnificent win and yet we were leaving in the position that everyone expected us to be in as losers. It was a great performance by a team of real 'heroes' and to finish the day off the snow fell thick and fast as I travelled on the train back to Hull. However for me more than anything it's the memory of that feeling of pride mixed with despair that makes it a game I'll remember forever!

A less charitable affair as the 'Benefit' boys are short changed.

Sunday 1ˢᵗ February 1976   *Hull 30 – Blackpool 6*

Back at work that week it was all talk of heroes and near misses but in our heart of hearts all Hull fans knew that we had missed out. Having gone so close in a big game which could have been a famous victory, the following weekend it was back to the grind of the Second Division.

That next game we played was at least at the Boulevard and gave us a chance to welcome the lads home from the final. It was also the Testimonial match for two of our long serving stalwarts Alan McGlone and Eric Broom. We played Blackpool and in the end won easily 30-6 but there were other problems in the dressing rooms that day. The players had agreed to forfeit their wages for the game and the Board at the Boulevard had agreed to give the proceeds from the match, after expenses, to both players, who were having a well deserved Benefit Year, which was, with interest in the Club waning, proving to be a hard slog for their Testimonial Committee.

This situation was not made any easier by the actions of the players that day either. Eric Broom said afterwards that both players were extremely disappointed at the actions of some of their colleagues after nine came forward to be paid after they had all agreed to give up their match fees for the game. That caused some acrimony in the camp and the two beneficiaries ended up with just £95 each. At the end of the year they both received a cheque for £600 which was then a lot of money but perhaps scant reward for all the years of service they had given the Club.

Mum continued to find it hard to get about and Dad and I were obviously worried. She used to have a full window ledge of prescription drugs in the bathroom to keep her going and now stayed at home most of the time, whilst Dad was still working at Ross's the butchers in Savile Street with Bill Steeksma and a great bunch of lads. At work I was finding the management stuff pretty tough going and a couple of difficult 'disciplinary hearings' with members of staff at which I didn't get a lot of support from the senior management, left me pretty disenchanted with everything Hull City Council wise.

Adventures at The Hull Cheese

On top of that the lady with whom I had been spending some time with between games over the past year, had decided that perhaps we should be thinking of living together or even getting married and to raise some cash she got a job at the new Hull Cheese public house in Paragon Street.

This establishment used to be known as The Paragon and had been for many years a regular haunt of seamen visiting the City and of those infamous ladies of the night. It had recently however been purchased by the Gilpin Group from Leeds who had completely refurbished the place transforming it into a top quality and quite sumptuous lounge bar.

Having collected her a few times from work I got to know Doug Barnfield the Manager quite well, in fact after a while I started popping in and 'drinking our savings'. The Gilpin Group were not only well known for running a string of quality pubs across Yorkshire but were also renowned for running 'outside bars' at big events like race meetings, weddings and, private parties. I decided that as things were a bit tough at the Council and as a bit of a distraction, I would do a bit of 'Moonlighting' and work for the Gilpin Group driving their van to and from these events, setting them up and serving behind the bar. This was great fun, as well as hard work and I often turned up for the day job next day bleary eyed and exhausted.

The job involved loading the van up with copious amounts of beer, wines and spirits, bar sections, optics, pumps, gas bottles etc, then collecting waitresses and bar staff from various points around the City, before we all set off to the location of the bar we were to run that night. I promoted events in barns for Young Farmers barn dances, at people's homes, in church halls and even in a marquee at Beverley Race Course and at County Cricket at the Cricket Circle.

Arrested!!!!

At one particular party in the Village Hall in Bilton the celebrations were in full swing when, as ironically the DJ played 'Teenage Rampage' by the Sweet, the Police arrived, requested that the music be switched off and declared that it was 'a raid'. Several people who they thought were at the party had apparently jumped bail and so everyone was lined up against the walls and had to give their details and proof of identity. At this point, as we all stood and watched from the safety of the back of the bar, a rather officious looking sergeant who could have done to lose some weight, came over to me and asked me for my identification.

All the staff were of course in their 'Black and Whites' as waitresses usually are, but I was just in trousers and a jacket. I told him I was the bar manager but with the problems of my full time job's 'auxiliary work' contract clauses, I was reluctant to say much more. He looked at me suspiciously, glanced across the bar and said, "Well where's your licence then". Of course the occasional licence had to be displayed over the bar, at all times alcohol was being consumed and I suddenly realized that I had left it in the office at the Hull Cheese.

I thought at first he was going to handcuff me but he agreed to ring the Hull Cheese to ensure we had indeed obtained the document from the Licensing Magistrates. It was Friday night at 10.00 and the Hull Cheese was 'banging' so much so that no one could hear the phone ringing and so it was that I was carted off in a police car to Central Police Station. The bobby who took me was a lot less stubborn than 'porky' the Sergeant and agreed to go round to the Hull Cheese on the way to at least try to verify my story. You can imagine how it looked as I walked in the packed pub accompanied by a policeman. However to my relief the situation was soon sorted out and I picked up the licence and left the bar with the constable.

"Well Sir, you should be more careful in future but it seems that you're in the clear and you can go back to Bilton and continue with your business", said the PC, once we were outside, to which I victoriously replied, "Ok, great but don't say I didn't tell you!" However as I attempted to open the police car door to get back in, he said, "We have no further business with you sir and so you can get the bus". Great, I thought, typical Police, I dare not go back into the pub for fear of looking stupid in the eyes of Doug and there were just no buses going out to Bilton till the last one at 11.00pm. So I flagged down a cab and went back to work. The Taxi cost me almost as much as I earned that night but at least I had saved face and my most serious brush with the law to date certainly ensured that I never forgot the licence again.

The only thing that was leaking more than the roof of the 'Threepenny Stand' was the Boardroom

As sports' fans we all have one thing in common, one thing that we all share and one commonality that is simply universal. We don't like, or at least we don't often agree, with referees. That's probably because if you absolutely love your Club they never get it right particularly when you lose, well they don't as far as you are concerned anyway. It's rare though that in any fan's life time you see such a bad display by a referee that it becomes something you remember for the rest of your life. However, I've seen them and will now relate one such incident.

In February 1976 it was a time of 'Board Room intrigue' with rumors of unrest in the dressing room circulating the terraces, but it's a defeat at McLaren Field, Bramley, on a cold Sunday afternoon that I remember best of all that year, simply because it was there that I witnessed one of the worst refereeing displays I have to this day, ever seen. The game featured an abject performance by a second grade referee, who was ironically named Mr. A. W. Allen.

Our new Board of Directors headed by Charlie Watson were starting to flex their muscles a bit, which, as I said, made it an uncomfortable time for some at the Club. They were as a Board of course to oversee that great resurgence in the final years of the decade and those fabulous times in the early 80's, but back then they were a bit naive in some ways, particularly when it came to stopping what appeared to be a constant stream of leaks from inside the Boardroom. No one knew where they came from but the 'rumor mill' at every home game had gone into over drive as everyone seemed to know who we were about to sign, who got on with who at the Club, what our debts were etc. etc.

Dick Tingle the Hull FC rugby writer at the Hull Daily Mail was having a field day as he revealed that the latest rumor to come his way was about several of our Directors being unhappy with David Doyle-Davidson and looking to replace him as coach with our current Prop forward Bill Ramsey. All this was apparently being discussed just four weeks after we had been the toast of the RL as the first Second Division team to reach the Players No 6 Trophy final. But four weeks was a long time in the intriguing morass that was Club politics back then and this particular week it had emerged from 'Sources close to the Board' that there was also some unrest within the ranks of the players with several unhappy with the way things were going remuneration wise.

Trouble in the camp at (Mrs.) McLaren's Field

This particular weekend we were all heading off to McLaren Field Bramley for an away trip which was still for me anyway, a rare occurrence back then. The habit of vast numbers of fans travelling away to every game seemed to catch on in the great 78/79 season and before that, although we did go away, it was usually only to the West Riding based clubs and then only when we could afford it. That day I travelled with East Yorkshire Motor coaches on one of three bus loads of fans, and was looking forward to a few pre-match pints in the Barley Mow pub. All the way there the travelling fans were fascinated with the rumors of unrest which were discussed endlessly for the whole journey to West Leeds. It was said by the Mail that Bill Ramsey had been promised the coaching job, after he had turned down a recent approach to coach at Rochdale. Chairman Watson stated in the press that nothing was confirmed as far as the position was concerned but he did intimate that there were one or two other off the field issues to sort out at the Board meeting the following Tuesday.

These, we fans speculated, probably involved the fact that Malcolm Walker, having been dropped the previous week along with recognised goal kicker Keith Boxall, had refused to be named as substitute for the Bramley game. This action of dropping Boxall seven days before by Doyle-Davidson meant, that we had played Saints at home in the cup without our first choice kicker which led to some criticism when we only lost 5-3. This unrest, compounded by the problems I outlined at the Eric Broom/Alan McGlone Testimonial game certainly indicated that all was not well with the players.

I think looking back that there was a fair amount of internal 'politics' going on but I wasn't too bothered about that as we tumbled out of the coach and entered the newly built Barley Mow pub in West Leeds. This was a shrine to the Bramley Club, having dozens of pictures of players, teams and action festooned all over the walls. It had been built to replace the old hostelry of the same name that had once accommodated the changing rooms for the club's Barley Mow Ground which had been sited behind the public house and next door to McLaren Field.

This strange arrangement had come about as the Brewery who owned the original ground gave Bramley notice to quit in 1964 because they needed the space for a car park. This luckily (for them) coincided with the death of a Mrs. McLaren who owned the field behind the then best stand and who in her will donated that piece of land to the club. So Bramley moved next door and built a nice little ground with a new all seater stand and open terracing over most of the rest of the perimeter. The whole move was completed in just 10 months and so it was that on that Sunday in February 1976, we stood on the open terraces of 'Mrs' McLaren's Field overlooked by the stark outline of the Brewery's tall slender chimney, that was a well known local landmark right across Leeds.

'Oh, Oh, Oh, Oh, What a Referee' Mr. Allen shows his true colours!

Sunday 22nd February 1976   *Hull 13 – Bramley 14*

Bramley were an improving side but still one that we should have beaten and we put on a brave fight against the odds, the biggest of which was Mr. Allen the referee. The game started in freezing cold conditions with both teams trying to play a bit of rugby. In the first scrum our hooker Tony Duke was penalised for striking early and Hay kicked a penalty. Hull were pressing more than Bramley, and so Terry Dewhurst and Ian Johnson of the hosts decided it was time to try and disrupt our pattern of play a bit with some off the ball fisticuffs and although the referee completely ignored their often blatantly illegal tactics, we still battled on. When Boxall crossed for a perfect try, running onto a short ball from

In 1972 Coach Roy Francis brought in a host of Australian players for trials. Here Drew, Tommerup and McDonald, who made just three first team appearances between them are pictured with the Directors and sponsors after signing. (*Courtesy of Hull Daily Mail*)

Man the pumps the Boulevard is flooded! The melted snow left
thousands of gallons of water on the still partly frozen pitch. It was
22nd February 1975 and we played and beat Halifax the next day!
(Courtesy of Vera Campbell)

Another GOOD Friday: Boxall and Casey of Hull cover
John Millington in front of a packed 'Threepennys' as Hull
beat Hull KR 17-13. *(Courtesy of Hull Daily Mail)*

24th March 1978 Hull 24 Hull KR 10. Mounted Police stand guard in front of the Threepenny Stand as the fence collapses and violence breaks out during half time in another Good Friday Derby. (*Courtesy of Hull Daily Mail*)

The perpetrators are led away by the local constabulary!
(Courtesy of Hull Daily Mail)

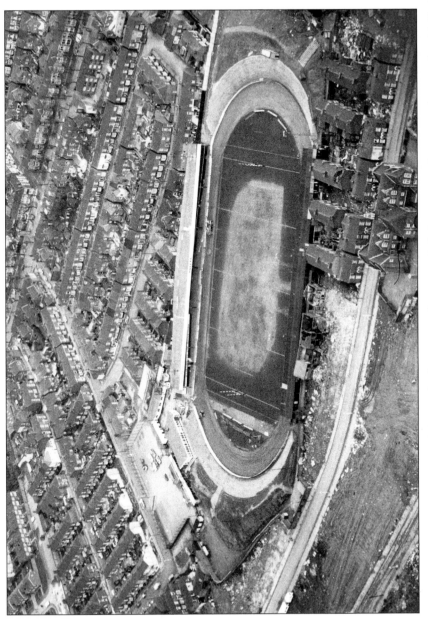

In this aerial view of the Boulevard from the late 70's the new club house on the terracing at the Airlie Street end can clearly be seen as can Chiltern Street School in the foreground still standing amidst the rubble of Division Road.

Steve Dennison, hero of the hour, proudly displays the BBC 2
Floodlit Trophy after Hull's famous victory over Rovers in 1979.
(Courtesy of Phil Arundel)

Two grainy but atmospheric photos taken from the terraces by fan James White

1978/79 and Huyton switched their home game to the Boulevard to raise much needed funds for the struggling club and here 'Knocker' Norton prepares to spread the ball wide.

In the same year, the day we won the Championship at Blackpool, as 'Knocker' comes in for some close attention whilst John Newlove passes the ball out.

He's There! Sammy Lloyd thinks that 'Knocker' Norton has scored but he is held just short. That Cup semi final against Widnes at Station Road Swinton in March 1980 which Hull won 10-5.

Lest we ever forget! 3rd February 1968. Always at the heart of the community, a minutes silence to remember those lost on the trawlers St Romanus and Kingston Peridot.

Hancock, referee Allen said he had bounced it, which as it was right in front of us, I can tell you, he certainly didn't.

Next Allen awarded a penalty to Bramley again under the posts and, although the poorer of two poor teams, a drop goal then saw them 5-0 up. Straight from the kick off Hull stormed back and Bill Ramsey sent Boxall in again, this time for the try to be awarded and Keith converted his own touchdown to level the score. In the next passage of play two fine touch finding kicks by Foulkes saw us down on the Bramley line where Portz was held inches short. Then after 29 minutes we scored again when Hancock shot between Naylor and Hay to score near the posts although Boxall missed a relatively simple conversion, leaving us with a slender three point lead. Mr. Allen's worst refereeing error however came just four minutes before the interval when Hull's half back Hancock kicked over the advancing Bramley defence and as he ran through to collect the ball he was flattened by a forearm smash from Steve Naylor the home side's second rower. This was such a blatant foul which left Hancock rolling on the floor clutching his neck in agony. Mr. Allen however, having watched exactly what happened, waived play on and ignored the incident.

Seeing this, fiery FC prop Alan Wardell, who had clearly had enough, went after Naylor and finally caught up with him seconds before half time, flooring him with a tremendous right hook; of course he was promptly sent off! It was certainly a blow because just ten minutes earlier we had lost our other prop Bill Ramsey with torn ankle and knee ligaments, meaning that in the second half both Keith Boxall and Jimmy Crampton had to move into the front row to cover the missing 8 and 10's, and just before half time, with the last kick of the half, after Wardell's dismissal, Bramley converted the penalty and we went in just one point ahead at 8-7.

With a reshuffled pack we dominated the start of the second half as the snowflakes started to fall across the ground. Then on a breakaway, against the run of play, the host's second row Johnson drew full back Robinson before releasing Bond who touched down and converted his own try. Trailing 12-8 and still the butt of some terrible refereeing decisions, we hit back again. This time Foulkes received the ball at first man, wriggled through the first tackle and then set off on an arching run towards the corner. Our centre George Clarke came back inside him and took a wonderful slipped inside ball, to go on and score, and with a great Boxall conversion from wide out into the now driving snow, we were a point ahead at 13-12.

Of course Mr. Allen was to have the final say and we were beaten by a penalty two minutes from the end. Under our own posts a Bramley player was held up by Crane and Hunter in a standing tackle and as he retreated Crane said something to the opposing player, who threw the ball at him as he retired to our defensive line. The ball hit Crane on the head and immediately Mr. Allen blew his whistle and penalized Hull for what he said afterwards was stealing the ball. Hay made no mistake and shortly afterwards, the official blew the final whistle and we had lost 14-13. Mr. Allen waited on the centre spot until his police escort arrived, and our indignation as fans was certainly vindicated when he failed to return to first grade refereeing that year. It was a hard result to take though in that it was so unfair, because our patched up pack had played magnificently and had we received a bit of 'even handedness' from the referee, we would no doubt have won a famous victory with just 12 men.

In the mean time David Doyle-Davidson, 'Quite rightly' survived the 'Night of the long knives' at the Board meeting the following Tuesday and Bill Ramsey with his several injuries and no coaching post, quit the Club, and signed for Widnes.

I become a 'cannibal'

I was still working as an area manager for the Parks Department and as the rugby season meandered to an end with Hull just missing out on promotion on points difference, the Council and the Club decided that it was the time to re-sow the centre strip of the Boulevard pitch with new grass seed. The grass had been so badly worn away during the previous hard winter that now this area was just made up of rolled mud.

The original arrangement between the Club and the Council was going well and although the Boulevard's ageing handyman and groundsman Fred Daddy marked out the pitch, my staff cut the grass and generally did everything else. What was needed though was a complete rebuilding of the infrastructure of the pitch itself and so twenty tons of soil were tipped across that central section and then levelled and fresh grass seed sown the length of the field. We then top dressed the whole playing area with fertilizer and left strict instructions to the Club staff, (who were prone to a bit of tinkering when the 'Council' weren't around) to 'Keep off the grass'.

A few days later I called in at the Boulevard and was horrified to see a long thin line of powder stretching out onto the field. As was the tradition with gardeners back then I licked my finger and took a small amount of the powder and tasted it. It certainly tasted like fertilizer and so I was off to find groundsman Fred for an explanation. Someone, I thought, had obviously fertilized the pitch against our instructions and if that wasn't bad enough carried a punctured sack, dribbling fertilizer, across the field to the centre area. I challenged Fred with what I had found and added that it looked and tasted like fertilizer to me which contravened the instructions that I had left the previous week. As a smile spread across Fred's face he said, "Oh that's not fertilizer it's just old Bill Stamps ashes, he left a final request in his Will for them to be sprinkled on the pitch". I apologized for my outburst and slunk away musing on whether my actions that day actually deemed me to now be a cannibal?

The night the shirts ran out!

Sunday 28th November 1976   *Hull 7 – Bramley 5*
(Match abandoned)

Although 1976/77 was the first really successful season of the decade, in which we had some good wins and a great finale, I feel I should here cover one of the most bizarre games I have seen in all the years that my life has been inter-twined with the sport of Rugby League. Great times were around the corner at the Boulevard, although we certainly didn't know it early that season, as we battled away with poor attendances and a deal of debt. Back then it was really difficult for most clubs to make ends meet with falling gates across the game still a massive problem. Despite the best efforts of the Club and the Council our pitch was still a mess, and although there was some nice new grass to be seen at the start of the season, as the drains silted up with Speedway shale, it soon left the usual morass of mud with very little of the new grass evident at all. In winter it was a mud bath and for the last few games it was as hard as nails, in fact on one occasion that year Castleford even tried to get an end of season game cancelled when they arrived to find the playing surface made up of rolled baked mud.

The game in question was another game against Bramley who our 'A' Team had visited and beaten the Friday previously, the significance of which you will see a little later. The weather that month was shocking and the general opinion in Hull was that we would be lucky to see a game that weekend at all. Still as game day dawned, our desperation to generate some cash to keep the debtors from the door dictated that the match was still on, and I watched from the Threepenny Stand with four of my pals that I had met in the 'Eagle' on Coltman Street for a pre-game pint. 4000 other hardy souls were in attendance that day which was a great attendance for us that year.

As we walked down Saner Street and onto the Boulevard the rain was coming down like 'stair rods' although by we had got through the turnstiles it had stopped again! The pitch was covered in small puddles and Fred the groundsman and several helpers were busy forking the pitch to ease away the water. It was a thankless task, as even the 'invalid carriages' that usually parked on the pitch got stuck in the mud well before they could get into position behind the dead ball line!

Bramley's player/coach was Peter Fox, a colorful character from the 'Fox' rugby playing dynasty of Wakefield. He always had something to say and where Hull was concerned it was usually derogatory. 'Foxy' got the usual rousing and abusive welcome from the Hull supporters when he walked out onto the pitch before the game, and although the conditions were dreadful, the game started on time. The match itself was a nail biting tussle with veteran scrum half Keith Hepworth playing a storming game for us. Bramley were, as I said earlier, a handy outfit back then and it was only through three great last ditch tackles by our full back George Robinson that we kept them from scoring in the first ten minutes! However then, on the eleventh minute mark, from our first attack, Hepworth, Hancock and Hunter linked to send 'Super' Alf Macklin in at the corner. We continued to press until a long looping pass by Hancock was intercepted by Langton and he scooted fifty yards down a thin track of green on the wing, to score for the visitors.

That mistake turned the game and with Fox's canny 'spoiling' tactics behind just about every move they made, Bramley started to dominate in the sludge down the middle of the field. In fact after Boxall had punched Jack Austin in the tackle, it was Fox their player coach that stretched their lead to 7-5 with a penalty goal. Try as we may, we could not get another score and with the ball like a bar of soap, mistakes were to the fore as we saw 24 scrums in the first 40 minutes. On three or four occasions the respective scrum halves dropped the slippery ball before they had even left the back of the scrum and the players left the field at half time, muddied from head to foot, with that same close score of 7-5 showing on the score board.

During half time as we went for a cup of Bovril and a hot dog, it poured down again and when we got back to our places on the 'Threepennies' we all had to move back up the steps to get out of the rain and avoid being drenched. Both teams changed their shirts at half time and as the rain eased no further points were scored before once again it became really dark and the heavens opened. It rained so hard that the referee had to stop the game at a scrum, as no one on the field could see. After 56 minutes so muddy were their kits, that both teams looked exactly the same, so the referee had little choice but to take both sets of players off the field to change their shirts again.

Unfortunately our Chairman, Charlie Watson, claimed that we had already gone through two full strips on Friday in the 'A' Team game, and now having used up two more strips that day, we had no more shirts left. Bramley had just brought two sets of kit and although the referee said he would play on if just one team changed, neither side had anymore shirts!

As we stood on the terraces stamping our feet the tannoy interrupted a very scratchy rendition of 'Morningtown Ride' by the Seekers, to announce that the referee had abandoned the game and we all trudged off chuntering about getting our money back and what a farce the whole afternoon had been. Peter Fox was most vociferous in Monday's Yorkshire Post though, saying that Bramley could have won the game and it was the responsibility of the home team to change their strips. He also refuted what Watson had said about changing strips at half time in the previous 'A' Team game and it all got a bit personal. However, the RL decided that the game should be declared void and it was replayed later that year when on a Wednesday night we beat Bramley 26-10. As you can imagine, "Foxy, Foxy what's the score?" was the chant that rang round the 'Threepennies' that night!!!

We the fans never liked Peter Fox really and he didn't like us either, something that caused a long running feud to develop between him and the fans in that famous stand. Later in his career when visiting as a coach, he returned a bottle (that had been thrown at him on the trainers' bench), back into the Threepenny Stand. The bottle hit a stantion support and shattered all over the crowd and as several supporters clambered over the fence to have a go, he was asked to leave the touch line by the Police, probably for his own safety. The next time he appeared at the Boulevard in charge of Bradford, he complemented his usual 'pork pie hat' with an immaculate, obviously new, sheepskin coat. One fan, probably fed up with his constant goading of the crowd and abuse of the Hull FC players, climbed over the fence and quick as a flash poured the trainers' bucket of water over his back. He was not impressed at all, but then again Peter Fox was never the most popular visitor to the Boulevard. It's not difficult to see why the trainers' huts were moved to the other side of the pitch at the end of that decade, because the folks in that famous Threepenny Stand were certainly no respectors of reputations and, as a player or an official, if you represented the opposition, you were in for it!

Man the pumps; the Boulevard is flooded

In January 1977 as the City was just coming to terms with a tragic fire at the Wensley Lodge Old people's home in Hessle which had seen 12 men burnt to death, sport was the last thing on a lot of people's minds. It was to be 1981 before Bruce George Peter Lee was to be found guilty and imprisoned for life after confessing 11 acts of arson including starting that fire, (in 1983, a public enquiry concluded that the fire at Wensley Lodge was accidental and that Lee was not responsible for it), but at that time it was seen as a tragic accident and a disaster for the City. The whole of Hull was in mourning. However as is always the case in times of local and national grief sport continued there in the background bringing some semblance of order and consistency to everything that was going on around it and so we looked forward to a game against Keighley at the Boulevard on Sunday 16th January.

It had been a strange start to the year really and in the Parks Department work had been severely interrupted by the coldest weather that the region had seen for 13 years, as frosty nights and heavy snow fall brought the local road and rail network to a grinding halt. As it seemed was always the case in our part of the world, the bad weather went as fast as it arrived and then the problem was melting snow and flooding, with Springhead Golf Course, The Cricket Circle and Oak Road Playing Fields all under water. That Wednesday I was driving my little maroon Council van between East Park and the City Centre when I received a call on my intercom to say that at the Boulevard the South West corner of the ground was under 'a foot of water', and that, only three days before the game against Keighley was to be played.

I went down there to be met by the sight of a lake of water spreading over a quarter of the playing area and Fred Daddy with a fork!! As Fred gave me a lecture about how that area of the ground was once a brick pond, I managed to hire some pumps and piping and eventually got all the water pumped away and into the drains in Division Road, so that he was able to mark out the pitch and the fans were able to look forward to an exciting if not soggy encounter with the team from Lawkholme Lane in the West Riding.

On the Sunday morning of the match it was still raining although local radio had informed us at 10.00am that the game was to go ahead and there was an appeal for fans to go down to the Boulevard with garden forks to help drain away some of the standing water forming on the touchlines. It was an important game because although we had experienced a run of four losses before Christmas since a Boxing Day defeat at York we had won the last two games and Hull were now back up there battling with Keighley to regain the top spot in the League table. Just over 4,200 people went to the game but as we stood on the Threepenny Stand and awaiting the 3.00pm kick off little did we know of the drama that was unfolding in the dressing rooms.

Where's Mike Stevenson?

Sunday 16th January 1977   *Hull 16 – Keighley 3*

We had suffered several bad injuries in a big win at Doncaster the previous weekend and our playing resources were already stretched to the limits. The previous night at training Ibbetson had pulled out injured and second rower Tony Salmon who was already expected to play on the wing was drafted back into the forwards with a young Terry Lynn coming in onto the wing and Chris Davidson returning to the bench. Then 15 minutes before kick off a head count in the dressing room revealed that Mike Stephenson our stand-off half was missing. He had simply just not turned up. This set the panic bells ringing. Brian Hancock switched back to off half, and Davidson moved into his centre spot but there was no one to play second substitute with Clarke. We then all realized that something must be wrong when there was an appeal over the Tannoy for any players in attendance at the game to go straight to the dressing room.

At one stage Steve Mallinson looked likely to make his first appearance but in the end 'A' Team coach Kenny Foulkes who had retired from playing, took the number 15 shirt. This must have buoyed a Keighley team who had won their last four games and as their players ran out it was clear that they were confident of getting some reward from the game. Before the match started Dave Bassett one time Director and lifelong supporter of Hull FC was presented with a scroll enrolling him as a life member of the Humberside Sportsman's Club. He was already Hull's first ever Vice President and this honour was met with a warm round of applause by everyone there, because Dave was that rarest of people back then, a popular Director.

From the kick off, no doubt due to the late changes, the team looked disjointed. Then Hull broke away but a good move faltered when a Jimmy Crampton pass destined for Lynne was easily intercepted by the visitors' winger Morgan. After that we started to slowly get some cohesion into our play and Jefferson the visitors' full back made a try saving tackle on Alf Macklin, before play was switched inside and hooker Tony Duke was held just short. Always alert to these situations Tony stood up played the ball forward to himself and ambled in for an easy try which Lynn converted.

Ten minutes later in the 34th minute Boxall broke out from deep in his own half and having made about 20 yards passed onto Crampton who raced to the line only for the pass to be adjudged forward and the try disallowed. Referee Naughton kept a tight grip on a game that was starting to get a bit fiery and with two minutes to go to half time their 'cheeky' scrum half Loxton was a bit too cheeky for the official and from the resultant penalty Lynne sent us in at half time leading 7-0.

The interval discussions amongst the fans were almost drowned out as the rain beat on the roof of the stand but by the teams re-appeared the rain had stopped again and the second half started much as the first had finished. Charlie Birdsall who was playing loose forward for the visitors' tripped centre Mick Crane as he carried the ball forward and another scuffle ensued. However we were now starting to play some better rugby, much of which came from loose forward Nick Trotter who held the makeshift pack together superbly and instigated a lot of Hull's moves. He twisted clear in a tackle after 45 minutes but Tindall dropped his pass when he should have scored. However we pressed again and Jefferson had to kick the ball dead as Hepworth threatened to score from a grubber kick through by Crane.

From the resultant drop out Hepworth who was now starting to run things, collected the ball and passed onto Foulkes who instigated a flowing cross field move that saw Alf Macklin score in the corner. Lynn failed with the conversion but we led 10-0. Then there was a concerted period of Keighley pressure but the visitors lacked much invention and their attacks proved too orthodox to break down what was developing into a resolute Hull FC defence. When we did get the ball back Macklin again went close before he took a great ball from Davidson to go wriggling and squirming towards the corner flag with three defenders in attendance. As a fourth joined the effort he popped out a great pass back inside to Mick Crane who ran in untouched.

The best move of the game came ten minutes from the end and it had everyone in the ground and indeed on both team benches on their feet applauding. Hepworth broke the line and passed to a morrording Boxall who crashed down field before Chris Davidson appeared from nowhere to grab a pinpoint pass and fly in to score in the corner with four defenders trailing in his wake. With a 16 point lead we relaxed a bit and Birdsall, who was easily the visitors' best player, sent Morgan in wide out from an obvious training field move. As referee Naughton blew his whistle for the end of the game we jumped over the railings and slipped and skidded our way across the mess that was the playing surface and as the Tannoy public address system let rip with a very unlikely rendition of Smokie's hit 'Living Next Door to Alice', the players left the field for a well earned plate of sandwiches and a beer or six to celebrate a 16-3 win. We then went on to win a string of good victories which consolidated our position at the top of the League.

Champions Again!!! Norman Collier does the honours

That Spring of 1977 the weather continued to be extremely changeable and on Easter Monday I took Mum and Dad for a ride out to Hornsea to have a look at the real novelty of snow on the Beach! Then at our last home game on 24th April the title of Champions of Division Two was officially bestowed on the Club as comedian Norman Collier presented

Club Captain Brian Hancock and Chairman Charlie Watson with the Trophy. After 'the ceremonials', in his own inimitable fashion and to a rousing cheer from us fans, Norman treated the crowd in the Best Stand to one of his famous trade mark 'Chicken Walks' as he left the field to the strains of 'Old Faithful'.

So it was a great season, at least for those of us who had managed to survive the trials and tribulations of the previous five or six, in fact Hull were even starting to attract some bigger gates for certain games and that made it all the sweeter for the rest of the lads in the Threepenny Stand who had, like me, seen some torrid campaigns of late. We had finished top of the Second Division and Doyle-Davidson had successfully rebuilt the team bringing in players like veteran half back Keith Hepworth, Dave Marshall, Graham Bray and Mick Sutton, whilst Tony Banham left for Doncaster, Len Casey for the Robins, Barry Kear to Oldham, and Nick Trotter after ten years service was granted a year's Testimonial to run from the end of that season.

The 'Buzzer'

Our coach, the master tactician, was nothing but inventive with the ways by which he tried to give his team of 'cut price' heroes the advantage. One 'Special move' that Doyle-Davidson came up with was called the 'buzzer' which we used to great effect on several occasions in that great season. It was used I remember in a game against Whitehaven at the Boulevard and it went something like this. We were awarded a penalty 20 yards out from the Whitehaven line. Five FC players lined up shoulder to shoulder just behind Chris Davidson who tapped the ball. He then passed it to the first man as all five players turned their backs on the advancing defence. The players passed the ball along the line completely confusing the Whitehaven players who could not see who had it, and then, all of a sudden, Boxall turned and as the other FC players ran off in different directions he charged at the advancing defenders who were by now totally confused and in disarray and taking three players with him he crashed over the line. Whether it was named the 'Buzzer' because of the way that the players buzzed out of the line, or because of the ripple of excitement that went round the crowd when we set up for it, we will never know.

The Club's balance sheet showed that the increase in our gates and the hard work of Ernie Mason and his programme sellers had led to the match day publication and the 'Souvenir Shop' showing their first profit of £329. Most significant though was the fact that the Speedway franchise was still keeping the Club afloat, bringing in an income of £6138.

Back up where we belong ... for now anyway!

Wednesday 31ˢᵗ August 1977   *Hull 19 – Leeds 11*

So we were set for our first season in the top Division for several years and although little had been spent developing the team pre season we were optimistic that in 1977/78, buoyed by the inspirational pre match eloquence of David Doyle-Davidson, we would survive. The first games were played as part of the Yorkshire Cup Competition and after a good victory over Division One side Bramley we were again, as was ever the case, drawn against Leeds, something we should by now have expected. The game was at Headingley and we drew, before winning a great return game at the Boulevard attended by almost 5000 by 19-11. We started our Division One campaign with an away game against Leeds which meant that we had played our arch nemesis three times in seven days. This time though we lost 25-13 but got our first league points the following week with a home draw against Workington.

However, one vivid memory of that season was setting out from Sutton at around 5.30pm one damp and misty Tuesday tea time to watch Hull play Castleford in the BBC 2 Floodlit Trophy. It was 19ᵗʰ October and the drive down to Holderness Road was fine but once I got near the River Hull, which I had to cross, a thick and clinging fog reduced my speed to just ten miles an hour as I crawled along in a long line of traffic. I had just bought a new car to replace the old Ford Anglia and

I was still getting used to a much bigger Ford Cortina Mk 2 in metallic 'Blue Mink'. PRH 703G was a really nice vehicle but with the windscreen wipers going full pelt and the fog lights on by the time I got to Carr Lane in the City Centre I could not see more than five yards in front of me, as a mixture of fog and industrial smog descended like a curtain.

By the time I got to the Boulevard conditions were much better, although once in the ground I had hardly had a chance to get a cup of that beefy hot water that passed for Bovril, (and no doubt burnt my tongue as usual), when the fog caught up with me. As the floodlights worsened the situation as only they can, the referee appeared out of the gloom had a quick walk round the touchlines and despite the pleas for a further delay by the BBC crews there to televise the match, he called the game off with half an hour to go to the kick off.

We all got our money back or a ticket for the re-arranged fixture as we left and I returned to East Hull and Sutton in that long crawling line of traffic until I got to North Bridge and crossed the river when the pall lifted and by I was back in Sutton the weather was as 'clear as a bell'. That week the fog actually came and went for three more days after that and as the City shivered under a shroud of smog, the TV newsreaders further increased the feeling of depression with their favourite subject, the bread shortage which was due to a national baker's strike. There were stories of housewives walking miles trying to get their hands on some of the diminishing supply of bread loaves and all the talk between everyone seemed to be about where it was possible to get that illusive loaf the next day. It was described as the 'Great Bread Strike' by the Hull Daily Mail who also claimed that it was 'Starting to bite'. They always did have a knack of writing naff headlines.

The night after the aborted Castleford game things were just as bad with thick fog again descending right across the City, although I again battled into the town centre this time to take Mum and Dad on a rare family outing to the Dorchester picture house in George Street to see the chart topping Rock and Roll revival band Showaddywaddy. Despite the fog it was great to see Mum having a good night out and she was up dancing 'Under the Moon of Love' with the kids before the end of the concert. As for the Castleford game, well that was rearranged for 30th October when we lost a close and exciting encounter 7-10.

If the game of Rugby League was a great spectacle to watch it was still really hard for those who played it. If ever there was a good example of this it had to be Steve Portz the 24 year old centre who signed for Hull from local Rugby Union outfit Old Hymerians. Steve, like most players, as well as playing rugby, held down a full time job. He was a really nice guy who always had time for a chat with the fans when we met up in the pubs and clubs of the City. However that October he was injured when he dislocated his right shoulder for a second time in twelve months and that after a severe ankle injury had also side lined him for twelve weeks. Previous to that in 1973 he had to get over a serious operation when he dislocated the other shoulder. With employers refusing to continue paying players injured in games and the recompense and insurance payments from the clubs little more than a pittance, it was certainly still a tough life for Steve and professional rugby league players in general in 1977.

The End of 'The Doyle'

Thursday 28th December 1977   *Hull 3 – New Hunslet 23*

Whilst the rest of the Country was dancing and singing along in the cinemas to the John Travolta movie and the Bee Gee's album 'Saturday Night Fever', back in those more sanitised surroundings of the Boulevard two defeats by Featherstone and Widnes meant that the going was getting really tough in our first season back in the top flight. We had simply not made the signings we needed to make the transition. However Coach Doyle-Davidson had been able to make one significant move into the transfer market and after Mick Crane left the Club for Leeds commanding a fair sized transfer fee, he was able to bring in Vince Farrar in mid October. He was an International prop forward from Featherstone who 'The Doyle' immediately made Club Captain. Some of the players had simply had enough, Chris Davidson had threatened to quit the Club and then Mally Walker, the local born second rower, walked away from the Boulevard, telling the local media that he had left because the players had been "let down by the Board with their failure to bring in new players".

This of course saddened the fans because Mally was well liked and we seemed to be witnessing the Club fall apart just when we had all been looking forward to life in the top division. The Coach, who after all those years of inspiration and motivation seemed to have lost the players, struggled on but our displays got worse and worse. Finally on 28th December 1977 we were beaten by New Hunslet at the Boulevard 3-23 in an abject display that lead to the supporters running out of 'Christmas spirit' all together and mounting demonstrations on the pitch and outside the Board room after the game. In fairness it was one of the most spineless and disjointed Hull performances anyone had seen for years.

I didn't join in with this demonstration, I never have because it was all just too sad really and as is my wont on these sorts of occasions I just tramped back to the car to get away from everybody else and grieve on my own. We were all fed up about the lack of signings that the Club had been able to secure, although in fairness the Board had done their best but once again our geographic position and the jobs that potential signings already had in other parts of the country made luring players to the Club a difficult business, before you even considered the wages they wanted.

After the game David Doyle-Davidson, (to everyone's surprise, simply because we thought he would get sacked) resigned as Coach saying, "We insulted the fans with the most gutless and heartless performance I have seen in my life". He also indicated that he could no longer motivate the players and the decision he was making was not for himself but for the good of the Club. Our Chairman who was visibly shocked by the coach's actions "accepted his resignation with regret". Although Charlie Watson had stood by 'the Doyle', we all sort of got the impression when we read the newspapers next day that several other members of the Board had at last got what they had wanted for a while; the head of David Doyle-

Davidson. So Kenny Foulkes was put in charge of the team for the next game whilst the Board started the search for a replacement coach to take over a de-motivated and unhappy playing staff.

Arthur Bunting: The start of a new dynasty

Mum was still really ill and getting less and less mobile but she seemed to rally a bit that Christmas so much so that I was able to take her out just after New Year to the January sales in the City Centre. It was just as we left Binns Department Store in Paragon Square that she noticed a Daily Mail placard announcing 'Hull name New Coach'. So it was that on the 3rd January Arthur Bunting who had, until two years earlier, been Rover's coach, took over as our supremo and although of course we had no idea of the fact back then, the first green shoots of the 'The Golden Years' of the late seventies and early eighties were about to start to appear.

There was in fact all sorts going on at the Boulevard, and the very next day the local paper was full of the fact that Hull Vikings whose franchise payments for holding Speedway meetings at the Boulevard were still playing a major part in keeping us going as a Club, had signed the most famous speedway rider in the world, Ivan Mauger. More worrying though for us FC fans was the fact that the Hull Daily Mail revealed that he had only signed after he and the promoters had met with the Hull Board and agreement had been made to widen the track on all four corners. The pitch was narrow enough as it was and although we all liked the money it brought in, this action was seen by many fans as a step too far. Still with Billy Bremner plying his trade and packing them in down the road at Hull City, many of us just felt pleased that Speedway was there helping to keep our Club in business during what was turning out to be another depressing season.

'Hull Sign Norton', read all about it!

Vince Farrar was doing a great job as captain on the field, but he needed some support, and some poor results indicated to the fans that as far as First Division survival was concerned we already needed a miracle. Vince and Arthur Bunting could not save our Club alone so the board looked to getting some 'instant class' into the team and using Jimmy Crampon as a make weight in the deal, we made an audacious bid for one of the country's best forwards. At the same time the game's weekly paper the 'Rugby Leaguer' reported that Leeds and Bradford Northern were chasing and expected to sign, probably the best loose forward in the world. Then to the surprise of everyone in the RL, up popped little Hull, the 'sleeping giant' struggling at the foot of the table, to beat both these top clubs to the signing. That player was of course the great Steve 'Knocker' Norton.

It was with some disbelief that we received the news of the signing in late January 1978, and I myself saw it again advertised on a Hull Daily Mail 'board' this time outside a newsagents on James Reckitt Avenue, as I drove home from work. It read "Hull sign Norton" and I was dumbfounded, so much so that I did a three point turn in the road and went back to make sure I hadn't miss-read the placard. We had paid the struggling West Yorkshire club £25,000 and lost one of my favourite players Jimmy Crampon in the deal. But this was one of the best players in the world and he was class! 'Knocker' Norton was a prodigious talent and when at 26 years of age he arrived at the Boulevard, he was definitely in the prime of his playing career.

Steve had joined Castleford, his hometown club, from local amateurs Freestone Juniors in 1968 and learned his trade at Weldon Road under the great Malcolm Reilly who was the West Yorkshire club's loose forward at the time. In 1970 Mally left for Australia and 'Knocker' made the Castleford number 13 shirt his own. So successful was he that for the next two 'closed seasons' he followed Reilly to Australia and even played for Manley in their Grand Final in 1976. On his return his success in Australia made him the target for the two top Yorkshire clubs at the time. He must have been aware of the demand for his services as he asked Castleford for a transfer and in stepped Hull. That was probably the point at which the greatest and most successful era in the history of our Club began for real, and Arthur Bunting with his excellent tactical awareness and contacts throughout the Rugby League world, was to mastermind it.

Mick Ronson doesn't make a personal appearance

Music was still a very important part of my life and I regularly went to the Queen's Hall in Leeds and The Spa in Bridlington to watch the country's best bands, although I was finding the new wave and punk movement a bit too much for my musical tastes which then included the likes of Genesis, Yes, Barclay James Harvest and Mike Oldfield. 'Pomp' rock or A.O.R. I suppose the experts of today would call it. However in early 1978 I went to an eagerly awaited concert at the Blind Institute on Beverley Road in Hull to see a band that I had first come across in a pub on Greatfield, the housing estate in the east of the City, back in 1975. Dead Finger Talks were local lads who the local paper told us were about to make it really big and who I guess you would say were in the somewhat dated genre of 'Glam Rock'. In the early part of the decade that whole scene was started of course by Lou Reed, the New York Dolls and David Bowie and the Spiders from Mars.

However the 'Dead Fingers' had apparently seen an opportunity to revisit this great musical era and were best known as a band that satirized the homophobic attitudes of that early punk era. They were great fun to watch on stage as well. They returned to a small venue in Hull simply because it was coming back to their roots, although their first album was released nationally and produced by none other than my old pal Mick Ronson. Rumours abounded in the City that Mick would be at the gig, so I went along hoping to see him again but of course he wasn't there. However the band was excellent and promised much but unfortunately the media seemed to misunderstand completely their motives and the satirical aspects of their music and branded them dated, a slur from which they never really recovered. I still have a copy of that album, 'Nobody Loves You when you're Old and Gay' somewhere in my loft to this day.

Rebuilding for the future

Tuesday 11th April 1978   *Hull 21 – Leeds 14*

At the Boulevard Arthur Bunting had struggled at first to make any headway at all victory wise and the Club sank deeper and deeper into the mire at the bottom of the division. He had a lot more contacts across the game than our previous coach and so he used his influence to start to explore the market. Money was tight of course but he had a lot more success on the field when he changed the team's tactics and took us on a run which saw ten wins in our next twelve games. However what had gone before was just too much to overcome although we really had a good shot at overturning the odds and staying up.

Around then my partner at the time the one of Hull Cheese fame, was working up at the new Job Centre that had opened at the Bransholme District Shopping Centre and one of her colleagues was the future Hull City Councillor Tom McVie who was (and probably still is), as Hull FC 'barmy' as I am. Every time I went to pick her up we would end up getting home late because Tom and I had been discussing the finer points of the Club and their fortunes. In fact it was Tom who rang me at work back on 21st November to tell me that we had signed Vince Farrar. That's what it's like though when fans get together isn't it? It happened back then at Bransholme Job Centre and it still does to this day when I bump into my pals in say Morrisons or the Library, we can make no difference whatsoever to what happens on the field but we can talk about it for hours.

So successful was that late season surge in our form that we moved off the bottom of the league table, and with four games to play we met Leeds at the Boulevard knowing a win would put us just a point away from New Hunslet, Castleford and Warrington, the three clubs above us. It was a critical game and one that brought a crowd of 5,411 to the Boulevard on a spring like April evening. This was said to be a must win game but when you're at the bottom, there are a lot of those games around.

On the 'Threepennies' we had taken Norton, Farrar and Bunting to our hearts and all three had already gained hero status in our eyes. A brilliant 21-16 victory at Featherstone two days earlier had taken its toll and we were playing with six players that were injured and had been 'patched up' for this important match.

Hull started slowly and looked to be suffering as a couple of players highlighting their unfit state, took an age to get up after tackles. Leeds who were really throwing the ball around soon scored a great try that saw five players touch the ball before Gibson strolled in at the corner. Things looked very ominous indeed. The thing about Hull at that time was that in recent games, like the one at Featherstone, they had blown the opposition away with short sharp 'purple patches' in which they raised their game and the tempo of the play and scored a few tries in the process.

From the kick off after the unconverted Leeds try, we swept back down the field and a smart inside pass from Norton found Brian Hancock who, although in a tight situation, managed to shake himself loose from a tackle by Hague and Dickinson and touched down near the posts for Boxall to convert. Next, four minutes later in the 24th minute, Farrar changed direction to find Salmon who passed onto Norton whose looping pass wide out saw Turner take the ball, draw Smith, kick ahead and touch down just before the ball bounced dead.

This time Boxall missed the goal but soon we were in again. Our next try was scored just as Leeds got the ball back. Their half back Haigh looked one way, ran the other and dropped the ball behind him as Barr moved in. In a flash Barr was on the ball, picked it up and galloped downfield drawing and brilliantly beating Leeds full back Murrell, to cross the line. The next ten minutes saw Leeds pressing as first Atkinson and then Sanderson were felled by brilliant last ditch tackles by the Hull full back Marshall. The second effort left our last line of defence out cold and he had to be replaced just before half time by George Robinson.

With seconds to go to the interval, with Hull 11-2 up the FC struck again. Leeds were pressing and as the ball went across the line and Sanderson looked likely to put winger Smith in at the corner, up popped

Turner to intercept on our 25 yard line and blaze downfield with the Leeds defence in his wake to score the try of the night. Boxall who was having an off night missed the conversion again, but we went in leading 14-3.

The second half started with Tim Wilby, the player that was soon to join Hull and who had an 'interesting' part to play in the Club's future in the forthcoming years, taking over at full back for the visitors. In fact after 43 minutes it was his head high tackle on Hull winger Graham Bray that led to Boxall 'finding his kicking boots again' to further extend our lead. As Farrar went off injured we lost our direction and although his replacement Chris Davidson worked hard, Leeds piled on the pressure. A foul by Salmon led to Gibson hitting the left upright with a penalty kick after 50 minutes and he followed up, collected the ball and from the next play Leeds shifted the ball wide for Dickinson to storm in wide out and for Gibson to convert the score from the touch line. Our eight point lead started to look a bit vulnerable but Tony Dukes our hooker that night brilliantly won the next four scrums 'against the head' to ensure that we were able to 'steady the ship'. Fittingly it was the outstanding player of the night who finally made the game safe after 79 minutes.

Following two great 'busting' runs from Salmon and then Tindall, 'Knocker' Norton got the ball from the acting half back position and ghosted through to score, showing the ball left and right as only he could. Although Sanderson scored four minutes into injury time and Gibson goaled it made little difference and as the stewards did their best to prevent us from getting over the fences and onto the pitch, our battered heroes went off to a standing ovation and a score line of Hull 21 Leeds 14.

Although most fans really believed that the 'Great Escape' was on, sadly the following week we lost at Bramley (again) and despite a good 18-4 home win against Salford in our final Division One match we were relegated to the Second Division. We had almost done the impossible though and on the eve of the Tony Duke and Brian Hancock Testimonial game on 28th April, Arthur Bunting was rewarded with a three year coaching contract at the Club. That game, which was against Wakefield

Trinity, ended up being drawn 31-31, with both players receiving £1000 towards their Testimonial payouts. It was a great way to finish the season but it goes without saying that we the fans were all pretty 'gutted' that after all those years trying to get back to the premier Division we came back down at the first attempt, however little did we know what was to follow under the guidance of our new coach, in that next record breaking season.

Chapter Ten

Season Tickets; just buying the right to grumble!

There is no doubt that 1978/79 at Hull FC was a golden season. We were to break records and go undefeated in the League, something that the average Rugby League fan across the world could never have even dreamed of. It was also the season that I started buying a season pass on a regular basis again. After subscribing in the sixties and early seventies I had bought one for some seasons and not bothered for others, but although missing very few home games if any at all, it never seemed a major priority. I was now heading for thirty and I think I was starting to plan things better and perhaps even mature a bit. Sensing that something big was happening at the Club I was now intent on making all the away trips that I could get to, I was just as 'FC Barmy' as ever, but now investing in a season ticket seemed to have become a priority, although that season certainly did nothing to diminish my intake of alcohol and over that year Hull's success and a few beers seem to go hand in hand.

I explained earlier in this book why since the 1978/79 season I have without fail bought a pass. Us season ticket holders think we are a bit special don't we? I mean, year in, year out, we invest in advance in the team we love when mere mortals just pay every week for their fix of Rugby League. Of course that's a jaundiced view and not true at all because more often than not it's the economic pressures of everyday life that make the initial outlay for a season ticket feasible or otherwise. For me personally though, and providing that you can afford to do it, what you get with a season ticket is increased ownership of the 'Being part of it' elements of being a sport's fan. Having read this account of an average fan's obsession with his Club, I hope that you can see why a pass every year is still a must for me.

At the time of writing this book I have a season ticket for a seat in the East Stand of the KC Stadium, I have my own seat and my own environment around me. However back in 1978 I got myself a standing pass at the Boulevard and started watching games from the end terracing. I can recall the many times that I arrived at my spiritual home on that terracing at the Airlie Street end, to find some 'Pies' fan or Leeds 'moron' standing on my 'lucky step'. That position was where I had laughed and cried, despaired and sulked, got rained on, been disappointed and oh so frustrated! It was where, as far as rugby was concerned I did it best and it was MY place. Now at the KC I have a seat, my own home in the Stadium, surrounded by the folks I have grown to know and respect and with whom I enjoy sharing and discussing common interests like, the current coach, our Board's inefficiencies, the quality of the beer and the players' private lives.

So, I believe that in the end all you are doing when you buy a season ticket is upping the belonging a notch, it's all about that feeling that perhaps you're now a 'stakeholder' and own a bit of the experience, the success and of course the abject despair. You can celebrate with 'YOUR' team when they do well and have every right to condemn and complain about them when they don't. That's the deal and if you get a 'pass' that's your right and for me, it should explain that fact in the small print on the back of the season ticket book!

Arthur Bunting makes his mark

That closed season, before we even got started playing in the Second Division the papers were rife with rumor, conjecture and occasional facts about future signings for the Club. Chairman Charlie Watson certainly led from the front and Roy Waudby was without doubt instrumental in sourcing the finance necessary to get us a reputation as the big spenders of the Rugby League, as they and the rest of the Board which included Warren Weintraube, Peter Darley, Keith Moses, Mike Page and Dick Gemmell worked hard behind the scenes to build a winning team. The Club got the cheque book out again and brought in Sammy Lloyd and Clive Pickerill from Castleford, Charlie Stone from Featherstone and Paul Prendeville from Welsh Rugby Union. It was also 'Super' Alf Macklin's Testimonial Year and we were certainly all looking forward to the Division Two opener against Bramley away, before which we dispatched Rovers in the pre season 'Friendly' game and beat both Featherstone and Bramley away in the Yorkshire Cup. Confidence on the terraces was sky high and even the most skeptical of fans could see nothing but a return to the top flight at the first attempt. Our intention was it seemed, to build a pack worthy of the top flight while we were in the Second Division, and then to use it to stay up there.

On supporting your team away from home

In that amazing season I saw every game home and away and as it meant that I was part of a historical event in the annals of Rugby League worldwide I am so pleased that I did. I learned some lessons too because every other week we travelled the north of England like a massive mobilized army and it was then that I started to notice the subtle difference that there is between the fans attitude to their team at home, as opposed to when they are playing away.

For example to this day when you're behind at home after half an hour, everyone's moaning and when you're in front they are all panicking because you probably won't be that way for long. But, I find that travelling fans seem to be always right behind the team. Generally speaking, it's all one big happy family when you're away and everything about it promotes a sense of 'us all being in it together'; the strip, our colours, 'Old Faithful' the banter during the warm up, those great celebrations at the end when you have won and the usually warm applause when you haven't. There is no doubt at all that standing in the 'Away' end in isolated surroundings and supporting the team you love is a great place to be.

When I'm watching a game away I always feel that somehow the FC crowd are more knowledgeable, more passionate and more supportive than the home crowd and although everyone is of course equal in their love of the team, it's hard to imagine anyone being more committed and dedicated than you are when you're a travelling fan. So that season of 78/79, my first 'every gamer', was not just a record breaking occasion that I will remember forever, but also part of my learning curve as a fan.

We of course, as supporters, could not have guessed what was to follow when the season started with another pint or two at the Barley Mow pub in West Leeds and a tight 17-9 win over Bramley. That victory was followed by a comprehensive 61-10 defeat of Oldham at the Boulevard. In that game Sammy Lloyd actually equalled the Club's all time goal kicking record for goals in a game. The record had stood since 1921 when Jim Kennedy set it against Rochdale. Lloyd went on to attain the Club record for goals kicked that year with a massive total of 170, which is now unlikely ever to be equalled. He passed that milestone on a wet afternoon at Blackpool, but more of that later.

Waiter service on the pitch

Sunday 17th September 1978   *Hull 28 – Doncaster 7*

One highlight I particularly remember that year was a trip we all made to Doncaster early in the season. The FC 'Faithful' were there in force and we took over one side of the ground as we sang the 'FC Aces' song to the tune of Blaydon Races. The struggling home club had not seen their Tattersfield ground so full for years, nor were they prepared for the 4000 fans that travelled from Hull that day as the security consisted of just two policeman! A couple of things were memorable about that game, firstly we got to 'cross swords' with Tony Banham who had of course been a Hull player of some repute both on and off the field, but who had also been a victim of the clear out that had to take place to make way for all the new signings we had recently brought into the Club.

The second was the fact that we won the game by 28-7 a score that did more to reflect Doncaster's valiant defensive efforts than it did our attacking prowess. We played the majority of the game in the home team's quarter and they rarely got out of their own half. The bar however was right across the other side of the ground in the Club house and I will always remember the sight of one FC supporter obviously fed up of walking all the way round the dilapidated terraces in his rather inebriated condition, taking advantage of our incessant pressure on the Doncaster line and walking across our twenty five line with a tray of drinks as the game continued up the other end. Dressed in flared trousers and suede safari jacket he captured entirely the Bodie and Doyle look from the popular TV series 'The Professionals' and his waiters act was accompanied by loud cheers from the Hull fans who watched in amazement as he continued on his way back to the Stand. It's a priceless memory, in a year when there were so many.

A new home from home

Sunday 6th August 1978   *Hull 28 – Hull Kingston Rovers 24*

So there I was three games into the 1978/79 season and going down to the Boulevard to watch a game against Batley. It was 1st October, and we won 42-9, but for this fan the game and the result paled into insignificance when the importance of what happened before the game is considered. Ian, a good pal of mine who hailed from the West Riding, who had married a Hull lass and been converted to the cause of Hull FC (as much I would now suspect, for the social aspects that was such an important part of the proceedings that year, as for the quality of our rugby) and I were riding down Hessle Road on the No.73 bus. We were intent on our usual four or five 'pre-drinks' in Raynors the pub at the corner of Hessle Road and West Dock Avenue. This was a short lived tradition which started with the need for a pint or two before the campaign's opening game, the old Eva Hardacker Memorial Trophy match against the 'Old Enemy' which we had won that year 28-24!

Ian was, I remember, extolling the virtues of his other great love Leeds United and commenting on the poor state of the Elland Road pitch (and the Boulevard), when we noticed that we had missed our stop and before we realised, we were a couple of stops and six hundred yards further down Hessle Road, and well past our intended destination. We alighted from the bus and were contemplating the walk back to Raynors when Ian spotted a pub at the other side of the road and we decided that with just two hours of drinking time on a Sunday lunchtime, there was little point of wasting any more of it walking about and so we had our first encounter of the hostelry that was to be both my spiritual, and actual home for the next year.

The Half Way was a traditional West Hull pub, frequented by the remnants of the fishing industry that had not yet been moved away to the newly built housing estates that surrounded the City. It was also, we soon discovered, a regular meeting place and watering hole for the 'travellers', (or gypsies as they were known in those days), that lived in caravans on the open spaces and pieces of spare land where some of the dwellings in the area had been demolished. These streets with famous names like Subway, Gillett, Havelock and Scarborough had formed the heart of the fishing community and of course, in the past, Billy my pal from my apprenticeship days hailed from Gillett Street. He was in a minority however, because for generations few who lived there worked anywhere besides on the trawlers or in the industries that surrounded St Andrew's Dock.

Sadly these homes had been demolished under a scheme that the council disparagingly called 'Slum Clearance'. This not only coincided with the demise of the fishing industry but also decimated the fabulous community spirit that existed in the area. Occasionally families that really wanted to stay on would arrange what was called an 'Exchange' which saw a family from a condemned house taking over someone else's home in say St George's Road or Hawthorne Avenue with those people moving to the first family's designated new home on an estate. However generally folks moved out of the area which not only saw an end to that great spirit that once existed but also meant that a large proportion of the Hull FC 'Family' that had for generations been concentrated in the area, were scattered to the four corners of the City.

The Half Way Hotel was a welcoming place where the smell of hops mingled with that of strong disinfectant from the toilets. The juke box in the lounge included the mandatory singles and pub classics like Pete Smith and Wildwood County's 'Hessle Road', Dean Martin's 'Little old Wine Drinker Me' and of course the most selected record in all the pubs on that most famous of thoroughfares, Hank Williams' 'The Crystal Chandeliers'. Back then Joan and Barry Nicholson were the landlord and landlady and we were made welcome the moment we crashed through the front door! They both chatted to us and Joan a 'large women' who had an even larger bust, (which was to lead to her nick name of 'Mrs. Bus Shelter'), even treated us both to a free drink before the 'session' was over. By it was time to leave for the game, Barry, a big FC fan himself, had got us signed up for the pub bus that was going to the game at Station Road Swinton the following weekend and in fact our new pal accompanied us to the game at the Boulevard, as he was to do to many matches in the next few years.

Travelling with the Half Way 'Fun Bus'

Our biweekly coach trips to away games with the Half Way bus were some of the greatest times I have had in my life. They attracted all manner of people. Some couples, some folks who were out of work, others who had never worked, those who were single, divorced, rich and poor, in fact all of life was there, but for six or seven hours on a Sunday all those personal circumstances and differences were suspended in a haze of pure fanaticism and alcohol! I say six or seven hours however there were times when it was a bit longer than that. Occasionally the bus would break down, invariably on top of the Pennines and there were always lots of 'toilet stops', (particularly on the way back), to slow us down too. The regulars on those trips had knick-names usually linked to their favorite 'liquid' pastime, like 'Trevor the Fish', 'Sauce' and 'Stagger' Lee but they were all 'Black and White' rugby fans and as passionate about their team as they were about their beer.

The toilet breaks were usually taken on the hard shoulder of the motorway with nine or ten individuals ending up covered in mud at the bottom of some moor side motorway embankment! It was a ritual acted out time and again because the participant's inebriated state would usually dictate that once back up at the road level it was a good idea to push someone else down the bank, and so it went on!! Barry the Landlord had an unfortunate habit, probably alcoholically fuelled, of counting the punters off the bus once we were back at the Half Way, rather than onto it before we set off on the journey home. This led, on three occasions, to folks being left in Wigan, Salford and worst of all Whitehaven!! My claim to fame was once getting back from a Sunday game at Warrington on a Tuesday afternoon but that's another story.

Food for thought at away games whilst sampling the local delicacies.

Barry had always telephoned ahead during the week to some pub or other in the town where we were playing that Sunday. This ensured that there would be an 'Early Opening' and usually the reputation of the Half Way bus trip's ability to consume vast amounts of alcohol in the hours before a game, prompted landlords to not only welcome us with open arms, but more often than not they would throw in a free buffet too.

It was funny really because each destination seemed to have its own gastronomic specialties. It was always Crab sandwiches in Keighley (in the Sam Smiths pub next to the brewery), Saveloy's in Widnes and St Helens and Curry (which was quite a departure for some of the lads from the Half Way) from Mr. Sing who was landlord of a little pub just off the main road into Dewsbury! The latter was always looked forward to with great relish and enjoyed on the day, but often blamed for any sort of gastric problems that were experienced in the following weeks and months. In fact it was not unusual to pass the Gents toilets in the

Half Way and to hear, "That's bloody Mr. Sing's curry for you" drifting out of the door.

Mum and Dad were managing alright at home and after I experienced a brief sortie into the world of co-habiting with a lady which was great whilst it lasted but didn't work out when my rugby obsession started to hit the home economics, I moved back into Potterill Lane but was, I felt, getting a bit in the way. The last thing that a couple who are spending all their time looking after each other need is someone coming in at all hours drunk or at least merry. Mum always used to lie awake until I got in, as Mums do, but her condition, which was certainly deteriorating and the fact that I had got used to living away from the family home made me feel that it would be best for everyone if I moved out and got my own place.

One rather quiet night when Ian and I had made the trip from East Hull to Hessle Road for a few quiet drinks, we were invited to stay for the mandatory 'Lock in' at the Half Way and the discussion with Barry and Joan got round to how things were for me at home. At once Joan asked me if I would like to lodge with them and with what was probably an element of undue haste, that was decided upon. To let Mum and Dad down gently I told them that I was helping out at the pub which I guess, with the amount of my Council wages I was putting into the till, I was in a way. A week later I took up residence in a massive room with high ceilings and faded grey walls on the first floor above the Lounge. Living in a pub, it was like a dream come true.

In that amazing year, whilst I lived 'over the shop' and went to work at the Council bleary eyed every morning, we went through the whole season undefeated, with our record at the end of the year showing, played 26 won 26. They were great times indeed, we appeared invincible and the fans had a ball, none more so than those who travelled to away games on the Half Way coach trips. We got left by the coach at Oldham, congered out of the supporter's club at Blackpool, got drenched to the skin at Whitehaven, and then there was Mabel the bar maid at the Barley Mow at Bramley. But then again, she's probably best left unwritten about!

Beating Leeds again this time in the Floodlit Trophy

Tuesday 10th October 1978   *Hull 14 Leeds 8*

The season was up and running, and despite a narrow defeat in the Yorkshire Cup at Bradford, the First Division team that actually 'booted' us out of all the Cup competitions that season, we were to go on and never see a 'L' against a fixture in the Division Two list that year.

Of course getting back up to the First Division in one season was the fans and the Club's top priority but the cup games had to be played and so it was in October that we all boarded the coach from the pub and set off for a night match at Headingley in the first round of the Floodlit Trophy. It was Leeds in the Cup again and as we drove out of the City along Boothferry Road we passed lines and lines of cars queuing in the other direction all going to Hull Fair. In those days no area of the Leeds ground was sacrosanct as far as visiting supporters were concerned, and so having called for a swift three pints in the Three Horse Shoes on Otley Road, before kickoff, we took up a vantage point in the South Stand.

Despite the fact that the second half of the game was televised and it was Hull Fair back home, around 2000 Hull fans made the trip and soon the strains of 'Old Faithful' were drowning out the shouts of 'Leeds Leeds' that was the only chant the home team seemed to know. Headingley was pretty devoid of chants or atmosphere back then, it was just accepted that, as the 'Mighty' Leeds they won at home, simple as, particularly when, as was the case that night, they were playing a team from the lower division.

We started badly with Charlie Stone being penalized and a penalty success to Leeds but shortly after that Crowther sent the whole of the Leeds line the wrong way with an outrageous dummy and walked in to score and put us in front. Sammy Lloyd converted and when he planted over a 'Lloyd special' penalty from fully 52 yards we were 7-2 up. Two players with strong Hull connections were apparent in the next Leeds move though, when down in front of us, clever play straight from the kick off by Mick Crane, sent Kevin Dick in to the right of the posts and the conversion leveled the scores. Just before half time a Ward drop goal edged Leeds in front and we were a point down at the break.

It was likely that we had Bovril and a Wagon Wheel at half time, as the bar was right round the other side of the pitch and usually packed to the doors. For those confused gastronomes reading this, Wagon Wheels were a marshmallow biscuit that you only seemed to be able to get at rugby grounds and right up to just a few years ago the Leeds refreshment stands always had a shelf full of them.

Our half back pairing of Newlove and Hepworth combined quickly at the start of the second half and 'Knocker' Norton was twice held up close to their line. The wily skills of our veteran scrum half Hepworth were to the fore throughout the half as he tried everything he could. As the rain started to fall with just ten minutes to go, he kicked through the Leeds defence and was just about to re-gather the ball on half way when Oulton stepped in front of him. It was an obvious obstruction and despite facing the elements Sammy Lloyd banged over the penalty to put us back in front.

The game was sealed just three minutes from time when Macklin sent the Leeds fans pouring towards the exits. 'Knocker' Norton started the move then Boxall gave a long looping pass to Lloyd, who found 'Super' Alf with a short outside pass that put him one on one with their winger Atkinson. Macklin then did what he had done so many times for us over the years and turned him first inside then out to score in the corner. Lloyd's tremendous touchline conversion broke the Leeds players' hearts as it sailed through the posts, the final whistle went and we had won 14-8, in a game where Farrar, Stone, Tindall and Sammy Lloyd were towering figures in our defence.

I have said in here many times that despite often being well below them in the rankings in those days we had the 'Indian Sign' over the 'Loiners' both at Headingley and the Boulevard and this was a season when although we were ourselves outside the top flight, we actually beat the high fliers twice. Later that year, in February, we were drawn against them again, this time in the first Round of the Challenge Cup and we knocked them out of that competition too.

Were you at that Huyton Game? Everyone else was!

Sunday 22nd October 1978   *Hull 18 – New Hunslet 6*

I was taking Mum to hospital on a regular basis now for all sorts of treatment and it was obvious that her Cancer was spreading, we still talked a lot on those trips about rugby and she regularly related the details of that day at Odsal when the miner 'saved her life' and her being carried out of the Boulevard without her feet touching the ground. At the 'Half Way Hotel' life was a bit of a blur really although I would regularly find myself going to bed at around 2.00am with the strains of 'The Crystal Chandelier' or 'From a Jack to a King' thumping through the floor from the Lounge Bar below.

Another game that was a memorable occasion was when we played at the Elland Road Greyhound Stadium in Leeds against New Hunslet on 22nd October. That day as it got dark towards the end of the game, one by one the floodlights went out until the game ended in the gloom illuminated by just 4 of the 8 columns surrounding the ground. However whenever we played and whatever the surroundings, we appeared invincible and the thousands of travelling fans had a great time.

It was at this time that some of us die hard supporters were starting to pinch ourselves a bit as to what was happening with the team building and the increasing gates and no doubt we would, in our quieter moments mid week in the snug of the Half Way, look back fondly to that day in 1975 when 980 of us were in attendance at the Boulevard for that Huyton game. Still we were not on our own because by now everyone you spoke to had been there, it was a sort of measure of your loyalty to the team and if you weren't there you weren't a fan.

It was not all plain sailing in the league and some games were tight, as hosting Hull FC, or a visit to the Boulevard, was seen by most of the rest of the clubs in the Division as their 'Cup Final'. There was a gulf between the 'haves' and 'have nots' too and a couple of teams (Huyton and Batley) even transferred their home games to the Boulevard, so they could make more money out of them.

Beating Leeds (the Cup holders) again!

Saturday 10th February 1979   *Hull 17 – Leeds 6*

With Leeds, the Cup winners from the previous two seasons and Hull now up there at the top of the Second Division undefeated, the BBC recognized the importance of this game and no doubt sensing an upset, decided to broadcast the second half of the match from the Boulevard as their featured First Round (proper) Cup game. The proceedings started in the usual fashion with the traditional haranguing of Eddie Waring and the BBC commentary team as they paraded around the touch line and up the ladder to the gantry built over the Threepenny stand. They were always greeted with a 'Traditional Welcome' which featured hoots of derision and much doubting of parenthood from the assembled 'Faithful' in the tin roofed edifice below.

The place was packed that day and I watched this ritual as it unfolded, for a change, from the South end of the 'Threepennies'. I remember too the regulars wolf whistling and hooting as three fashionable 'Punks' walked along the front of the stand dressed in vivid pink T shirts over laid with string vests and sporting necklaces made from safety pins!! Things were still very traditional on that stand.

The game started with Hull making all the running, in fact as far as I can remember George Clarke and Brian Hancock were both held up inches short of the line in the first seven or eight minutes. Sammy Lloyd finally opened the scoring after ex FC favourite Mick Harrison lost his cool and was penalized for a high tackle on Keith Tindall, who had 'accidentally' hit Mick twice under the ribs in previous tackles. The game then settled into a typical end to end blood and thunder Cup tie. Finally Leeds took a great chance when another FC exile Mick Crane scored after Kevin Dick and Adams had carved out an opening on the left. With the conversion being missed we turned round at half time and welcomed the BBC Grandstand audience watching at home, trailing 3-2.

As I have said previously in this tome Leeds were always seen as the big spenders, or 'Toffs' of the competition and predictably, as many of the Loiners fans changed ends at half time and walked behind the Threepennies, they were met with the usual chants of "Spent a fortune Won F*** All, Leeeeeds Leeeeeeds". Even though they were the Cup holders it made little difference to the Hull fans. Where it not ever so?

As the BBC Grandstand viewers looked on we soon reclaimed the lead. 'Knocker' very uncharacteristically put a kick straight into touch, however Clive Pickerill who had moved to a makeshift hookers role, won the scrum against the head, and a flowing move saw 'Taffy' Prendeville bundled into touch inches from the line near the corner flag. This time Tony Duke who had by now recovered from a knock and returned to hooker, won the scrum against the head, and the pressure was just too much for the Cup holders as Pickerill himself almost got over wriggling like an eel in a three man tackle to be held inches short. However from a play the ball, he played a great one/two with 'Knocker' Norton who ran in unworried between the posts. Lloyd made no mistake with the two points and it was 7-3 to Hull FC. From the restart we surged up field again with a great Tindall drive and on the 5th tackle Norton dropped a goal to extend the lead.

As usual Leeds were fine whilst they were bossing things, but opposing teams knew that once they got 'ruffled' they started to drop the ball and this game was no exception. We could not capitalise on this panic however but a foul on Tony Duke led to a penalty and once again Lloyd slotted it over to extend the lead to 10-3. As has happened so many times once we had got ourselves into a lead we became sloppy and 'forced' the ball a bit too much in the tackle, and back came Leeds as somehow we all knew that they would. They got a quick unconverted Les Dyl try following a flowing move between Joyce and Ward that made it 10-6. On the terraces we started to doubt that we could finish them off and the crowd started to get at the referee and the officials every time a decision went against Hull.

It was our turn to panic as Pickerill, Hancock and Norton tried drop goals, which all flopped and fell well short of the mark. As Hull coach Arthur Bunting stood arms aloft besides the dugout, victory to the 'Black and Whites' was confirmed by the referee granting us an obstruction try. When Sammy Lloyd kicked through only to find his way to the line blocked by an elbow in the face from Keith Hague, the referee that day Mr. Naughton, no doubt fearing a lynching from the already antagonistic home crowd, immediately awarded the try, and that was it.

The game was completed when 'Knocker' tricked Bryan Adams at the play the ball, causing the Leeds player to be adjudged to have moved off side and Lloyd kicked another penalty and won £500 from sponsors State Express for kicking 5 out of 5 goals in one game. We had won a memorable cup tie against the cup holders in what was turning out to be the most memorable of seasons.

Skating on thin Ice; Mount Pleasant comes to the Boulevard

Tuesday 20th February 1979   *Hull 20 – Batley 0*

Anyone who watched the Club that year will remember that to try and raise some much needed cash for the struggling West Yorkshire team the Batley game was transferred from their Mount Pleasant home and played at the Boulevard in February, but it was almost called off ten minutes before it took place because of ice on the pitch.

We all left the Half Way wrapped up in scarves, 'Bobble' hats and big coats but by we reached the Division Road turnstiles we were 'nithered!!' There was an on field inspection as the pitch glistened in front of the Threepenny Stands but the referee took one look at the size of the crowd, no doubt heard their baiting cries in his direction and decided to go ahead anyway. The game was played in conditions more akin to ice-skating than rugby, and the players at times seemed incapable of keeping their feet, but we won 20-0. There were some close calls too that year. We had just scraped past Blackpool at the Boulevard in November 14-13, we just beat Bramley 8-5 at home in January and we went on to just squeeze past Oldham at a rain sodden Watersheddings in our penultimate game of the season in May. Boy the weather was bad that day!

Oh we do like to be beside the seaside!

Those great Half Way trips to away games continued unabated and there are many stories of the bus getting lost, people being left behind and folks losing their trousers and even their false teeth. These are just too numerous to catalogue here. However there was one great day out when we set off at 7am from Hessle Road for a day out at Blackpool to enjoy the sea, the sun and a game against Blackpool Borough that would not only extend our unbeaten run but also guarantee us the Championship and promotion.

We arrived in Blackpool at around 11am having consumed an ample amount of canned beer on the way and as the pubs and clubs were still shut we got 'Fishy' our regular bus driver to drive up and down the promenade as we all waved 'affectionately' to the locals with various gestures and salutes!!! At 12 noon on the dot we rolled up at the rugby ground which I have to say was decidedly run down, (it had in fact doubled as a greyhound stadium for the past few years). However if Borough Park was a sad looking place, the Social Club under the stand was well furnished and decorated to resemble a tropical beach with giant plastic palm trees and table umbrellas covered in synthetic grass, whilst in the middle was a small dance floor that was surrounded by tables and chairs.

One old timer in an orange Blackpool football scarf told us that the rugby club had only survived over the past years from the takings of this Social Club which was a draw for locals and holiday makers alike, particularly, he said, when they had their Sunday night Hawaiian evenings!! I can still remember one young lad who was around twelve and who had purchased a latex lady's bust from a joke shop on the promenade, having to explain this regalia before he was let through the turnstiles, yet once inside he walked straight past the security and into the Social Club unchallenged.

By 12.15pm the place was crammed with the 'Black and White Army' who, anticipating a historic occasion had travelled in great numbers for a day by the sea. 2,500 fans made the trip most of whom appeared to be in that one clubhouse singing along with the Jukebox to 'I will Survive'.

We had to start 'doubling up' on rounds so difficult was it to get served, and the atmosphere of excitement and anticipation was fantastic. It was however a lot better than the weather outside because when you looked through the one long panoramic window that stretched down the pitch side of the room, you could clearly see the rain lashing down and several seagulls in a row across the centre line looking like beleaguered players waiting for the kick off.

Fancy dress ... not for me thank-you

There were quite a few fans in fancy dress that day who had certainly made an effort for the occasion, there was a crocodile, a couple of Beef Eaters and several Hawaiian 'Beauties' who fitted in well with the decor. One bus load, I think from the Tiger Inn in Cottingham, were dressed up as 'St Trinian's' girls, which was not a pretty sight at all. Now a quick note on fancy dress; I never get involved in that sort of stuff at rugby and my philosophy is pretty simple. You see it's OK as long as you can guarantee you are going to win, but when you follow sport and particularly when you follow Hull FC there are just no guarantees on that at all, so for me it has to be avoided at all costs. I mean to say there is simply nothing in the world to compare with the humiliation of being stood at the JJB Stadium in Wigan, losing 34-0 with 15,000 'Pies eaters' chanting 'Who are you' when the answer is 'Donald Duck' or 'Batman'. As for grown men painting their faces, dear oh dear that's not for me either, let's face it we're following Hull F.C. not bloody Braveheart!

Anyway, after a rather good session and a bit of 'flirting' with the St Trinian's crowd, we finally got outside, (where the rain had stopped) and into the stand where we stood in the Well with hundreds of other FC fans. Those of us who worried about those sort of things knew that this game was not going to be easy, Bak Diabera their player coach and main play maker (who was the only Moroccan playing in the RL at the time), had been born in Hull and his enthusiasm and will to get one over his home town club had never been more obvious than in the home game at the Boulevard earlier in the season, when we just managed to scrape past 'The Seasiders'.

In addition to all that, the local press in the week leading up to the match had made us painfully aware that Sammy Lloyd, our prolific goal kicker, was just 12 points short of toppling Mike Stacey's Division 2 points record of 266. So that game, that day, in a somewhat sleepy Blackpool, had quite a lot riding on it.

Blackpool's rocking; Champions! Champions!

Sunday 29th April 1979   *Hull 27 – Blackpool 7*

A strong wind was blowing down the ground and winning the toss the hosts elected to play with it at their backs in the first half. The game commenced with a penalty to Hull that Lloyd despatched to give us a slender 2-0 lead but then a blistering set of forward drives from the Blackpool pack pinned us back on our line. It was no surprise that when we eventually managed to break out, their Loose Forward Norman Turley constantly used the wind to drive us back into our own 25 yard area with some excellent kicking. Our full back that day George Robinson pulled off a try saving tackle on Redford after just five minutes but eventually under mounting pressure and two penalties from the referee Mr Court, Blackpool scored under the post through second rower Molyneux.

The home sides only claim to fame in what was for them a disappointing season, was their quite amazing drop goal tally, which at that point of the campaign stood at an incredible 33. It was therefore hardly surprising that first Fairhurst and then Diabera popped the ball over the cross bar and by the 29 minute mark we were 7-2 down and the travelling supporters who had started in such a confident mood, were getting a bit 'Twitchy'. As Lloyd kicked another penalty we started to get a foothold and as the early Blackpool enthusiasm started to wane a little, we had three or four chances to score. All these we sadly spurned through over elaboration. The breakthrough came when Stone, Lloyd and Newlove combined to send Prendeville scooting down the wing, he rounded two defenders, before running behind the sticks to touch down and with a Lloyd conversion and a penalty goal, we were 9-7 in front at half time.

During the break we all feared another onslaught from the Blackpool forwards come the start of the second half, but instead it was our six who, with the wind at their backs, pulverised the opposing pack. Farrar led well as Captain and Tindall and Stone drove into the host's ranks time after time. After 50 minutes a rib injury saw hooker Tony Duke leave the field but our reorganised front row of Tindall, Farrar and Stone took complete control. Boxall started to find some space and three times broke out down the middle with those spectacular runs that were for many years the second rower's trade mark. One of these storming excursions down field saw him pass on to Turner who scored a tremendous individual try, and then Newlove superbly dummied and fed Tindall who scored another which Lloyd converted.

Boxall was not to be denied and he blasted through a two man tackle and ran right over full back Doug Robinson to go careering in under the posts for Lloyd to add on the extras again. Minutes from time Lloyd kicked his sixth goal to break Stacey's record and so frustrated was the host's hooker Clarke when he dropped the ball from the restart that he picked it up and threw it at the referee. His sending from the field to a chorus of "Just because you're losing" from the 'FC Faithful', was the last act of the game and we were over the flimsy greyhound fencing and onto the field as the final whistle went. With three matches to go we were Champions and promoted and just 240 minutes away from that dream of going through the season having played 26 and won 26.

After the game, it being Sunday, all the pubs and clubs were shut, so we walked up and down the promenade singing 'Old Faithful' and eating ice cream and hot dogs. It was cold but dry by then and the atmosphere from the thousands of FC fans there on the sea front was just amazing. At 7pm we returned to the club house for a couple of last drinks and continued the singing of "We are The Champions" much to the disgust of the regulars, who had all turned up in their finery, and garlands, for a Hawaiian evening. You sort of got the impression that they were glad to see the back of us lot when, an hour later, we all 'conga'd' out of the door and back onto the bus for a sleep and a long but happy journey back to the Half Way.

We beat Halifax and Oldham in the league and then as a way of giving the players a chance to get away from the pressure before the 'massive' last game of the season against New Hunslet, Bunting took all the staff away to France for a few days. The next Friday thirty players and officials boarded an Air France jet at Heathrow and flew to Bordeaux. They landed at 10 at night and three hours later the whole town centre was ringing to the strains of 'Old Faithful' the first of many impromptu renditions that were to be heard over the next two days. Next day after a game of football on the beach the team played a rather low key match against Tonneins and District which we won 12-10 and apparently the after game hospitality saw few of the players make bed at all that night. The rest of the trip was mostly relaxation and partying although the team had to leave early on Monday morning to get the flight home and it was only when he got back to England and opened his case that Steve Norton realised that he had forgotten to pack any of his clothes in it before he left the hotel room! That game was chalked up as another win but was just academic to us fans as we all looked forward to the last match of what was already a historic season.

Touching the Dream!

Friday 18th May 1979   *Hull 6 – New Hunslet 1*

One of the great successes of that season had been the Programme and Souvenir shop which had been started three years earlier by our vice Chairman's son Roger Waudby. We always called into the cramped little unit before home games and joined many other fans that fought their way to get to the counter. It was certainly doing well and the takings during that record breaking year were six times those of that disappointing First Division campaign twelve months earlier. Run by volunteers it included in its stock, signed photographs of the players, dart flights, key rings, bob hats and car stickers, whilst a replica home shirt with a 42 inch chest would cost you £10-80.

So the scene was set for the biggest game of the season and possibly one of the biggest in the history of the Club, and our chance of a place in the Guinness Book of Records, by going through a whole season undefeated. During the week ahead of the game, I couldn't concentrate at work at all and by Friday arrived I realised that I was in the grip of some sort of madness that would be with me until our victory and place in the record books was confirmed or otherwise. I really couldn't get the match out of my head at all. It was with me all day, when I woke up, when I went to bed and no doubt when I was asleep too. It was just so significant. At work when people were talking to me I would drift off into a world of 'Knocker' Norton, record breaking and Trophies. When this happens and it did more recently when we went to Cardiff in the Cup Final in 2005, I just can't shake it and its simply no good trying! It's always the same before the 'Really Big' games.

Although we were already promoted, I remember the Hull Daily Mail revealing that Arthur Bunting, our coach, had decreed that the team would not be parading the Second Division Trophy around the ground before the kick off. He wanted nothing to take the teams' minds off this last, important and possibly historic, game. Apparently Arthur had seen a similar situation when he was coach at Hull Kingston Rovers end with the hosts losing the game and he was risking nothing this time. There were a couple of presentations already planned for the start of proceedings however as the 'A' Team was to be presented with the Yorkshire Senior Competition salver as Champions and the Colts received the Runners up shield for finishing second behind Hull Kingston Rovers in the Colts league.

After a couple of pints in the packed Humberside Sportsman's Club which was then run by my childhood pal Tony Roberts and which was the new 'guise' of the old Supporter's Club, we joined 12,424 people crammed into the Boulevard. I went back to my roots that night and watched the game from the Gordon Street end of a packed Threepenny Stand where the atmosphere was electric. Hunslet really did not offer much at all on attack but their tenacious tackling soon subdued even the passionately loud fans around me, as the visitors did everything they could to keep us out. Lloyd, our record breaking kicker, missed four goals in the first half and at half time the scores stood at 1-0 after Norton had dropped a solitary goal. The thorn in our side that night was Tony Dean, a little general and a player who was to sign and star for us two years later. He was known as the 'drop goal king' of British Rugby League. It's surprising he didn't play for Blackpool and although he missed with two attempts he slid one over in the second half to level the scores.

It looked likely that the game was going to end in a draw although Hunslet plugged away and another Dean drop goal could never be discounted. Could we lose out at such a late stage? I was 'in pieces' in the stand and was hardly able to watch when following a foul on John Newlove, Sammy at last found his kicking boots and slotted over a penalty. We were in the lead at last, but it was still touch and go, with the whole place holding its breath every time Tony Dean got the ball in our half! It was then left for the most unlikely of heroes to score the only try of the game and seal a place in the record books. Charlie Stone, who only scored eight tries in 200 appearances for the Club, side stepped his way over the line and although Lloyd missed again with the conversion, we were home, we were the champions and now as Vince Farrar and the team paraded the trophy round the ground, we were real record breakers!

It was certainly not a classic game, but for sheer tension and ultimate ecstasy, with so much at stake, it still ranks as high as that win in 2005 at Cardiff. I say ecstasy again and should probably apologise to the reader for going over the top at this point, but then I have spent quite a bit of this tome apologising for being a fanatical follower of what is a largely unobtainable dream, perhaps that night as in the Challenge Cup in Cardiff and at Elland Road in 1982, I got as close as I ever will to grasping it. That night the depression I had suffered at so many games and through so many bleak seasons, packed its bags and moved out! It felt great, we were the Champions and what's more we had done it in such a way that the whole sporting world had to sit up and take notice.

Perhaps in my short lifetime Rugby League and Hull FC has come to mean too much to me and to represent far too many things. I have probably watched too many games, spent too much money and fretted and worried far too much for my own good. Perhaps at times I should have worried about other things but just like that night at the Boulevard against Hunslet the fact of the matter is that at times like that, there is simply nowhere else in the world I would rather have been. Perhaps all those none descript dour, heartbreaking defeats over the years make those moments of sheer bliss..... just that! That season we scored more tries than any other team in the whole competition and although only playing Second Division teams in the League, we still managed to beat Leeds twice in the Cup and draw with Bradford away in the same competition. We of course went up into the top division and thus started that 'Golden Age' in the history of Hull FC that was the early 1980's!

Back up where we belong, where everyone loves a 'Psycho'

Sunday 7th October 1979   Hull 20 – Hull Kingston Rovers 20

Of course as fans we simply couldn't wait for the new season to start but at home Mum's health continued to decline, and we were really worried about her. She was now house bound and struggling to walk at all and although still living in 'The upper room' of the Half Way I was trying to spend as much time as I could at Potterill Lane. The 1979/80 season commenced with Vince Farrar again being given the Club Captaincy and the Board continued to spend money building a side that they and the fans hoped would stay up in the First Division this time around. New signings joining the Club included Tim Wilby, Charlie Birdsall, Graham Walters and Trevor Skerrett. However in addition to these inspired captures we also took on Paul Woods a Welsh full back who I would best describe as having the heart of a lion, the looks of a bulldog and who was simply as hard as nails.

'Psycho' Woods was just mental when he was out on the field and soon became feared across the world of Rugby League. A smallish guy, he was a real hero of mine, as he hurled himself at rampaging forwards without a thought for his own personal safety. Paul made his debut on 23rd September at Blackpool but it was later that year on 7th October that we drew with Hull Kingston Rovers 20-20 at the Boulevard when the fans saw just what we had signed. Woodsey revelling in the tension and passion of his first local Derby was soon in a running battle with Rovers scrum half Alan Agar. They clashed in the middle of the field as the opposing scrum half managed, accidentally, to inflict a nasty gash on 'Psycho's' leg with his studs. This prompted Woods to reluctantly retire to the touch line where he stood having his blooded leg bound with a bandage. Spotting this situation and the lack of a full back in the backfield behind our defence Phil Hogan kicked over the top of our line and chased after the ball. Woodsey suddenly made a dash towards him from the touch line, with his still unsecured bloody binding trailing for about ten feet behind him. He ran and leapt on Hogan's back before he could collect his kick and a real fist fight broke out. From that moment onwards 'Psycho' Woods was a folk hero down at the Boulevard.

Woodsey was a real comedian too and I remember well an incident in a game against Huddersfield at the Boulevard when we were awarded a try in the corner adjacent to the Threepenny Stand. Woods was to take the conversion attempt which was right on the touch line at the Gordon Street end. He looked at the referee who was talking to one of the injured opposition players and sneaked about six yards further in and placed the ball. The referee spotted what was happening and ordered Paul to move it back. He placed the ball with much ceremony right on the whitewash of the touchline and then took three steps back to the perimeter fence, climbed over it and continued his backwards paces up the terracing to the amusement of the supporters and indeed the rest of the players. When he returned to the pitch side he addressed the ball, looked at the muddy pitch and shouted to the crowd in a broad welsh accent, 'Anybody got a carpet?' Paul Woods was a 'one off' alright, oh and by the way, he missed the goal.

Down at the Half Way Hotel something had to give

For once, for me personally the happenings on the pitch at the Boulevard were to be eclipsed by developments in my own life. Living at the Half Way was fine but you could only take so many 'Lock Ins' until two in the morning before getting up for work at 7.30am and it was apparent that I needed to find somewhere else to live. I could have moved back to Potterill Lane, but Mum's cancer was making her life very difficult and Dad was just about managing to look after her, but they certainly did not want a 'partying' 29 year old rolling in at all hours singing 'Old Faithful', that would just not have been fair at all. A pal of mine from work was thinking of leaving the Parks Department and buying a fruit and vegetable shop over in the north of the City in Endike Lane and as there was a flat above the premises that seemed like an ideal solution, but sadly that fell through, however almost immediately a new possibility raised its head when I read the City Council's 'Job Circular'. In there I found an advert for 'Manager-Hull City Hall' which outlined a myriad of duties, but concluded with the words 'Flat available on the Premises'.

This would, I thought, be a massive career change, I knew nothing about the business and back then, in all honesty, it took me all my time to write a letter. I probably didn't stand a chance of getting the position let alone the flat but I was tiring of the new management methods adopted on the Parks Department and the bonus and incentive schemes that had been introduced and my love of music in general and pop music in particular prompted me to fill in an application form.

A new job and a flat in Victoria Square

No one was more surprised than me when I got an interview in September 1979 and if that was not a shock, when I got there, the panel was 'chaired' by Tom Hawkesley, who had all those years previously given me a job as an apprentice gardener. This time the interview was more difficult with no questions at all about my cricketing ability but on leaving I thought that I did OK, however having seen the other candidates in the waiting room as I left, I felt that I would be best employed looking for flats elsewhere.

To my amazement three days later I received a call at work to offer me the job and without thinking I accepted. I was to start in two weeks and to collect the keys for the flat from the Guildhall reception desk. Then, I had a few drinks to celebrate and panicked, what the hell had I done? When I took up my new position as City Hall Manager, I had an office in the City Hall and one in Ferensway (no doubt so that the 'centre' of the organisation could keep an eye on me) but I couldn't write a business letter or understand the accounts and ledgers and although I was fine with the staff management, timesheets, pay etc. I had absolutely no idea at all about catering or booking acts. Still the flat was nice!

It was an opportune time to move really because Barry and Joan at the Half Way had just got a new pub themselves 'The Mermaid' on Boothferry Estate in the West of the City and so instead of taking up their offer to go with them for more late 'lock ins' in what were slightly more salubrious surroundings, I moved into the flat at the City Hall. My new home was situated on the front of the building overlooking Victoria Square and had two bedrooms, a kitchen, bathroom and a big lounge with little 'cottage like' leaded windows. A door led out onto the roof where there was a patio area surrounded by high walls which I was to convert into a roof garden, complete with greenhouse and barbeque. I soon had my new flat looking like home and made good friends with Albert and Mary the Landlord and Landlady of the Punch Hotel across the road. The beer in the bar there was first class and I was strangely pleased to find out that they shut at 11.00pm prompt, so no more 'Lock ins'...... thank goodness.

I did of course visit Barry and Joan at the Mermaid from time to time and often on a Sunday night they would invite the Hull team down for a buffet tea and a few beers. I had some good times back then meeting the players and having a laugh. One night just after we had signed Terry Day I remember winger Paul 'Taffy' Prendeville telling our new recruit that if he was to be playing at centre to the Welsh wide man he would have to be quick because, Taffy said, "I'm a flyer Boyyo!". Paul was fast but perhaps not quite that fast. They were great nights, particularly a few years later when the jokers of the team Ronnie Wileman and Tony

Dean used to do their brilliant Cannon and Ball impersonations to the delight of the regulars.

Learning new skills, and hitting the floor running

If it was a tough job trying to develop the City Hall business and one that was not helped by the staff I inherited. Don't get me wrong the Foreman, Ted Puckering, and the lads were all hard working blokes and really nice guys, who all became instant friends too, but there were only five of them and their average age was 58, so when I booked 'Souxie and the Banshees' as my first big concert it was certainly a culture shock. Looking back I bet after years of Choral Union and Hull Philharmonic Orchestra concerts, they wished me in hell.

I had to start from scratch and build up a team of 'Humpers' who brought the concerts in and 'Bouncers' who chucked the public out. Bob Marriott, a big Hull fan and legendary doorman and steward in the City, was in charge of the Bouncers and would bring an interesting array of staff for rock and pop events which often featured retired local boxers. There were also plenty of ex rugby players like FC stalwarts Shaun O'Brian and Allen Wardell who could be found in the 'pit' in the front of stage at most concerts. The next part of this saga, should I ever get it written, will no doubt include my adventures with pop groups, impresario's, Councillors, Mayors, strippers, comedians and those bouncers during the next ten years.

I got drunk with Rick Wakeman, played Darts in the Punch Hotel with the Three Degrees, was propositioned by a Chippendale, got stuck in the lift with Big Daddy the wrestler, received a written agreement from the LA Centre Folds to keep their tops on, and had to ask David Soul's body guards to leave their guns in the dressing rooms. It was a manic few years when the entertainments business and my love of Hull FC went hand in hand. That first autumn, although I worked most nights, the vagaries of the Sunday Entertainment laws that had years earlier had us all buying programmes to get into the Boulevard, usually meant that the City Hall was shut on a Sunday and so I was able to get to most games home and away.

My 'Old Faithful' retires from the game for ever

After three months of working every day and most nights I was absolutely out on my feet, so I decided it would be a good time to jet off for the first time to the Canaries. I had some holidays owing, and although Mum had been admitted to hospital after degeneration of her bones had led to a broken hip, she was doing reasonably well and so I booked a week in Los Cristianos in Tenerife from Saturday 3rd. November 1979. Then life was to change forever.

I remember it so well really because that morning I had finished my packing and gone down stairs to the City Hall office to make some phone calls and try and persuade the promoter of the Joy Division's latest tour to consider bringing it to the Hall. They were on a sell out tour with the Buzz Cocks and thinking of adding some extra dates. As it was, our electrical supply was not big enough for their production and so, as often happened, my attempts to lure them to Hull were unsuccessful. I went back upstairs and contemplated leaving for the airport at around 6pm that afternoon. I must have dozed off on the settee when there was an almighty banging on the oak front door of the flat. I ran down the corridor to see what all the fuss was about presuming it was one of the staff with a problem when I was confronted by my Dad, in tears saying, 'I've got some terrible news Pete....Your Mother died this morning' Apparently she had tried to get out of bed took a few steps, collapsed and died. It was I guess, looking back, a blessed relief for her but at the time it was just a devastating experience and an unthinkable turn of events. Aged sixty four my Dad had just three days earlier taken early retirement to look after her when she got out of hospital. In an instant, just like that, a half of the two things that had been so consistent throughout my life were gone.

Of course I cancelled my holiday and helped Dad make the necessary arrangements. There was a service at St Jame's Sutton and then it was off to Crematorium. The fact is of course that in these situations you just get sort of used to losing a loved one and then all the 'embers are raked over again' as you have to go through the ordeal of the funeral. Dad took it all with tremendous grace acting in a fashion that he had often explained as displaying a 'Stiff upper lip' although since Mum had passed away he had developed a bad chesty cough, that I just put down to him being at a low ebb with everything that was going on. I loved my Mum and it was hard to imagine that she was not going to suddenly walk into the room with a story about Odsal, Johnny Whiteley, Maine Road or getting carried out of the Boulevard without her feet touching the ground. The loss was just immense.

However my next big worry was Dad because they had always been such a devoted couple living just about in each other's pockets. They went everywhere together and when Mum couldn't go out they stayed at home. They were soul mates and completely relaxed in each other's company and that was the way they liked it. The three of us were a sort of unit, galvanised by common interests and our love of each other and our rugby team. Over the years Mum and Dad had changed their ideas and living arrangements but their love of West Hull and Hull F.C. was always with them, they shared it, and yet seemed very content in the knowledge that that they had passed it all on to me, the next generation of the family. It was my inheritance and I was just 'looking after the family's heritage'. At least I had my work and rugby to get me through, but Dad had no work and now no wife, in fact all he had was an empty house full of memories to rattle about in.

Another 'oh so sweet victory' under the lights!

Tuesday 18th December 1979   Hull 13 – Hull Kingston Rovers 3

Things on the rugby pitch continued as they always do, for the fixture list shows scant consideration for personal, local or national tragedy and a few weeks later we were in a final again, and although nothing would ever take away the sadness I felt about losing my Mum, the pressure of my new job and our continued success in the First Division were acting to at least 'numb' the hurt a bit. We had done well in the Floodlit Trophy that year, and luck was with us getting home draws in all the rounds, beating Halifax by an unlikely 8-1, Huddersfield 34-2, Leeds

16-9 and Leigh in a really dour encounter 9-6. That just left two teams in the final Hull FC and the old enemy Hull KR, as once again we came out of the hat first and the final was scheduled for 18th December at the Boulevard. The opposition, as they have so often done over the years, used the media to indicate their perceived ranking as favourites for the game, but we were playing well and we fans all felt that perhaps this time we could beat them. At three o'clock on the morning of the game, I remember thinking that perhaps I was just starting to get my life back on track again after losing Mum, because I had awoken in a cold sweat worrying about the game that was to take place that night.

That Tuesday evening the weather was bitterly cold and I got everything up and running for a Choral Concert at the Hall before departing for the game at about 6.40pm. I was, as licensee of the City Hall, supposed to be there but I was not going to miss this one! I ran down Carr Lane and just got on a bus that was full of FC and Rovers supporters who were packed in like sardines, with about 20 people standing downstairs and people even standing on the back running board. We all literally fell off the bus as at last it pulled up on Anlaby Road at the bottom of the flyover.

As I started off down the Boulevard I remember once again experiencing that magical glow from the floodlights that lit up the rooftops all around the ground. It always reminded me of the time back in 1967 when the floodlights first arrived and we all marvelled at the effect they had on the surrounding neighbourhood. I also wondered whether Mrs Robson ever did get those curtains lined. I ran most of the way there and on arrival an amazing sight faced me, because although the Floodlit Trophy Final between the two Hull Clubs had been sold out for about 2 weeks there were literally hundreds of folks milling around without tickets.

In the end 18,500 of us squeezed into the Boulevard with another thousand locked outside in Airlie Street! There was an amazing atmosphere as I took my place on the terracing at the Airlie Street end of the ground. I was happy there because although I wanted to get into the 'Threepenny's' it was simply impossible, in fact several burly police officers were standing at each end of the stand barring entry because the place was packed to the rafters. That night, for the first time for ages, all the light bulbs were working in the floodlights and the old place looked fantastic.

The game kicked off and was quickly stopped by the referee as a red distress flare, probably smuggled from a trawler, was lobbed out of the 'Threepenny's' to burn and fizzled on the touchline. This was extinguished by a member of the local constabulary who executed his duty by stamping on it until only a plume of smoke was evident. However a couple of minutes later as we let rip with a chorus of 'Craven Park is falling down' our concentration on the game was again interrupted, this time whilst the kids who had climbed on top of the Threepenny stand via the scaffolding of the television gantry were coaxed back down to earth by the 'tannoy' announcer. One lad fell all of 20 foot from the tower, landing in a heap in front of the crowded terrace who all gave a hefty cheer as he got up and ran off down the touchline before the police could lay a hand on him. If the happenings off the field were exciting they were nothing to what was about to happen on it.

We went into the game as massive under dogs. Rovers had dominated the local scene for years and we had just come up from the Second Division in that famous undefeated season. Although big things were just around the corner, we were still building for that future and our ranks were described by one journalist in the National Press as being made up of "triers, and has beens with a smattering of real class" Take our half backs for instance, they were a real veteran 'little and large' act. There was 6ft 2ins John Newlove who was 33 and mighty midget Keith Hepworth who was an incredible 38 years old and who played most of the second half of the game with a broken hand! In the pack we had two more veterans of those tough years earlier in the decade, Keith Boxall and Keith Tindall. Added to these were some real stars in Charlie Stone, 'Knocker' Norton, Vince Farrar and the great Paul Woods. Incidentally Rovers half back combination that night were the fathers of two of our more recent staff at Hull FC, David Hall and Alan Agar.

From the start, the game was played at a high tempo and there was no lack of big hits and high tackles, this might have been a televised final, but it was still a local Derby! Our heroes played out of their skin and yet despite all our efforts we only led 5-0 at half time, and our try when it came was on the back of a Hull KR mistake. The ball came out of a scrum and the Red and Whites flashed it across the line only for Mike Smith to drop the ball. Young winger Steve Dennison, who at 18 years old had the most memorable game of his career, 'fly hacked' the ball through the line and into the space behind the Rovers cover, it stood up for him and to an increasing deafening crescendo of cheering from the crowd he 'legged it' to the line and touched down.

The second half started with Hull trying to press home their advantage and after just two minutes Graham Evans (a man with a gum shield that was always twice as big as his mouth) crashed over for Dennison to convert. The lead up to this score was brilliant with Paul Woods running right over two Rovers tacklers to free our centre with the line wide open. Woods was having a great game, all aggression and suspect tackles and no one seemed to be able to stop him or indeed wanted to be tackled by him. Phil Hogan tried to stop him, but he felt the full force of Woodsy's power and was carted off on a stretcher and straight to hospital!!! As always the crowd applauded the player as he was taken from the field but this was counteracted by the singing of 'Old Faithful' by the hundreds of fans who had been locked out but who had stayed on the car park outside the ground and who had no idea whatsoever what was going on inside.

Next the Rovers winger Phil 'Old Mother' Hubbard scored for the opposition in the corner, before our substitute forward Charlie Birdsall charged through a group of 'Robins' players, scattering them like skittles, to eventually roll over the line to score. This set off a continuous chorus of 'Old Faithful' that lasted long after the final whistle and the presentation of the trophy; we had won the game 13-3!

What a great night that was!! Paul Woods picked up the Man of the Match award and Steve Dennison kept the match ball! The fact that we were playing our 5th match in 16 days and that the game was televised live on BBC 2 took nothing away from what was a night that everyone who was there will once again remember forever!! It was an amazing year and season with such highs on the rugby field and such lows at home where the worst was yet to come!

As the players proudly paraded the trophy round the ground and the Rovers supporters tramped away muttering, an old guy in front of me in a big grey coat and a muffler turned round and said, "Make the most of it son, you may never ever see that again at the Boulevard". "Miserable old Bugger" I thought but he was right I didn't see Hull win a trophy at our spiritual home again; well not a 'proper' knockout trophy anyway. It was the last time that the Floodlit Trophy was contested and Hull got to keep it! Where it is now is the subject of a few conspiracy theories and urban myths, but the winning of it will long remain one of my fondest memories in a life time of watching Hull FC.

I remember saying over and over as I walked up Airlie Street after the game, "That was for you Mum!" and at the time the feeling I got was that we were as fans, in touching distance of living the 'impossible' dream. We were the best, and all the TV watching world had seen us prove it. As I left the game, walking up Airlie Street with the tide of singing, chanting and laughing FC fans, I looked to my left and there, across the road amongst all the smiling faces, was Tom McVie, my pal from back in those days at Bransholme Job Centre. He just smiled across the Street and gave me the thumbs up, there was simply no need to say anything else, because we knew that at last after all those years of failure and hardship, the dream was realised, the FC were back! To win the Trophy in your first year of being back in the premier league, on the last occasion it was to be contested and against the deadliest of enemies, well, it doesn't get much better. As for the Rovers fans, well they were totally despondent and long gone, but, as is always the case with sport, their time was to come!

More Problems, more work, more illness

At home things were not good and although I was now living in the flat at the City Hall, Dad was still struggling to cope with the loss of his life time companion, and so whenever I could I used to get him down to the Hall and he used to 'help out' by tearing tickets at dances, stewarding at concerts and I think that and mixing with the staff who were all of his own age group, at least kept him occupied. His chest and bad cough was giving me cause for concern because it was getting worse and at times he was coughing incessantly. I felt he should go to the Doctors and get it checked out. At last after much coaxing he agreed to go, but the outcome of his visit was not good at all and the doctor sent him straight to Castle Hill Hospital in Cottingham. Within days I was taking him back for more tests and by the end of January he was diagnosed as having gone through, in a couple of months, the symptoms that Mum had endured over about 14 years. He had terminal lung cancer.

Within two weeks Dad was admitted to Castle Hill to undertake a course of Chemotherapy which was really tough, in fact in the end when the doctors said that there was no hope of him pulling through I asked them to stop the treatment and let him have some peace. Everything had happened so quickly and it was hard to take it all in really. I was living in a sort of twilight world where despite everything that was happening around me, nothing seemed real.

Once the treatment stopped he was usually conscious and enjoyed talking rugby and following it in the local paper. On my daily visits I used to bring him up to date with what was going on at the Boulevard and the City Hall, and he enjoyed that, although it was obvious to everyone that he was failing fast. Radio Humberside was great for him, and he loved to follow games and listened every time Hull was playing. I was really busy at the City Hall too, where my first big marketing initiative, aimed at bringing more pop groups to the venue saw concerts by Uriah Heep and Wishbone Ash taking place as well as a frenetic evening when the venue played host to the Damned in a concert that resembled a riot. In fact I had to stop it before the end when someone discharged a fire extinguisher on the balcony sending the foam all over the 'side of stage mixing desks' and everything shorted out. There was feedback, flashes, bangs and chaos and although that night I wished I was back gardening, afterwards I mused that the whole scene was no different to those early 'pyrotechnic' days of The Clockwork Chicken.

The Cup run begins

Sunday 13th February 1980   *Hull 33 – Millom 10*

As for rugby well, I went when I could but that and even work was secondary behind looking after Dad. At the Boulevard, the Daily Mail was telling us, Arthur Bunting had targeted the Challenge Cup which after League survival, (that was by February practically assured) was to be the Club's main priority. Firstly in that competition we played Millom an amateur side who hail from Cumbria and as expected we beat them 33-10 on a cold February afternoon. That date might be seen as unlucky for some, but that year it proved very lucky indeed for Hull FC as we went on to beat York at the Boulevard 18-8 and then, when our amazing run of home cup draws finally came to an end, we still managed to beat Bradford Northern at Odsal in a thrilling quarter final game 3-0. It was a hell of game full of tension, passion and excitement and the crowd had a great time once the final whistle had gone.

It was a time that homemade banners were all the rage too and a lot of mothers and wives were missing bed sheets that season. That day at Bradford, as well as the usual 'Arthur Bunting's Black and White Army' and 'Bank on Lloyd' there was one that appeared at all the rounds of the cup games that year that simply said, 'Hissing Sid is Innocent'. This referred to a campaign by Radio One DJ Noel Edmonds to exonerate the villain in a piece of poetry 'Captain Beaky and his Band' that had reached number 5 in the music charts in February that year. What it had to do with Hull FC is anyone's guess, but it was always there and sticks in my mind to this day.

So after that great win at Odsal it came to pass that on Saturday 29th March 1980, I joined around 12,000 of the FC Army who made the journey over the Pennines to Station Road Swinton to play Widnes in a Cup semi final that, once again, few of the pundits thought we could win.

Station Road again... with so much at stake

Saturday 29th March 1980   *Hull 10 – Widnes 5*

For us the prize was to be more 'history making' with a clash at Wembley against the old enemy Hull Kingston Rovers, who had already reached the final having won their semi final the previous weekend. It was a game filled with expectation but one to which I did not travel to as usual with the Half Way coach party, but instead, so that I could get back to Dad who was still in Castle Hill Hospital but now in a coma, I went by car.

The build up to the game was marred by the loss of two of our best players late in the week prior to the match. Stand-off John Newlove and Winger Paul Prendeville had been injured the previous week in a 20-4 victory over Workington at the Boulevard and the back room staff had been working all week to get them fit. It was thought that Prendeville at least would make it but he failed a fitness test the night before the game. This meant that our Full Back, famous hard man and talismanic champion 'Psycho' Woods, had to switch from his usual position, to fill in down the middle and so at the last minute, George Robinson, local hero, ex ball boy and '100% Black and Whiter' was called up. It's funny what you remember, and one thing that sticks in my mind was George saying to the Daily Mail, 'I was at home watching the Muppet show with my family, when Peter Darley our Club Secretary came round and told me I had to be at the team's training camp at Mottram Hall in two hours'.

Arthur Bunting who was fast becoming the game's master tactician had decided that the only way to beat the 'Cup hardened', flamboyant Widnes outfit was to meet them head on in the middle of the park and stop them from playing any sort of expansive game. Of course we the fans didn't know this was to be our tactics as we arrived at the great old ground in Station Road. The stadium had for years been Manchester's Rugby League answer to Old Trafford and had seen numerous, semi finals, Lancashire Cup Finals and Internationals. However the demise of the Swinton club as a force in Rugby League and difficult financial times for the game itself, meant that it was quickly falling into disuse and the crumbling terraces and antiquated turnstiles that met us that day were a sad, if not accurate, reflection on the state of the game in most parts of the North, away that was from Humberside.

The place had several areas of terracing that could not be used and with almost 19,000 in attendance, the rest of the ground was packed, with several brave Hull fans even climbing the flood light pylons to gain a better view of the game. As the chants of 'Station Road is falling down' rang out from the 'FC Army', we positioned ourselves at one end on the open terracing towards the corner, as 'Bunting's Master Plan' was implemented straight from the kick off.

It was one of the most stunning displays of power rugby I have ever seen, and when the Widnes team got a bit of space and tried to use the wind that was, in the first half, at their backs, it was 'Muppet Fan' George Robinson that was fielding the towering kicks of Mick Adams and Mick Burke as if he were a fixture in the team. The first half was a real arm wrestle and Hull hustled and smothered a Widnes team that was famed for their open flowing rugby. In the first period Widnes' defence stood tall as it repelled wave after wave of Hull counter attacks. They used the strong blustery wind to great effect and put us under periods of sustained pressure, but we swept back at them with hooker Ronnie Wileman and 'Knocker' Norton a constant thorn in the opposition's side.

It was certainly an indicator of the strength of the Hull FC defence that during the entire game Widnes only got within five yards of our line three times, on one occasion they scored and on the other two they were thwarted by Steve Norton hammering Les Gormley as he went for glory, and Ronnie Wileman pulling off what turned out to be a match winning tackle on Brian Hogan. After all their pressure in the first half Widnes finally broke our line and Gormley scored despite the attentions of George Robinson clinging to his back like a limpet and that, and a Burke conversion, saw the much fancied 'Chemics' go in 5-0 up at half time.

The second half was all Hull though. With the wind behind us we laid siege to the opposition line and on one occasion it took 17 tackles for the Widnes lads to get out of their own 25, even then, on the next play, they were pushed back again, to the resounding continuous choruses of 'Old Faithful' that rang round the old ground. In that second half we got just the start we needed as Norton passed onto Walters who first went outside, then in, to open up space for his winger Graham Bray, who shot in at the corner right in front of us. Sammy Lloyd missed the goal and as Widnes tried to come back, Bowden broke down the left, but that last ditch Wileman tackle on Hogan just saved the day. The Widnes player was grounded just short and then penalised for making a double movement, as he strained to get over the line. From then on it was all Hull. Firstly Woods hoisted a massive kick, which caught in the wind and looked to have gone too far, but it was Paul himself who was blatantly obstructed as he chased the ball, and Lloyd was able to level the scores at 5-5 with the resultant penalty.

Widnes returned to the centre spot to kick off, kicked the ball deep towards Bray, and chased it down. Our winger caught the ball and immediately cut inside the approaching Widnes' cover. Walters, and then Wilby took up the running, before Dennison raced down the wing, but as he fly kicked forward, he was halted in his tracks by Keith Bentley with a good old fashioned 'stiff arm' and Sammy Lloyd knocked over the resultant penalty; we were ahead for the first time, 7-5.

With two minutes to go, and our finger nails down to the knuckles, the game was sealed when from nowhere Charlie Birdsall broke the Widnes' defensive line to send out a great pass to the waiting Bray on the wing. Graham drew the whole of the Widnes' cover, as he headed all the time towards the corner flag, before passing back inside across that defence for Ronnie Wileman to score, again right in front of us. That was another of those 'remember it forever' moments when the action seemed to go into slow motion. The crowd went mad though, and although Lloyd again missed the conversion at 10-5 the game was over. However there was a bizarre end to the match that most people who were there will no doubt, like me, still remember.

A sensational final minute saw Walters and Widnes's Hughes ordered from the field. What happened was this. Mick Kendall FC's 'Physio' was treating Walters on the floor after he was floored by a late tackle, when up came Hughes to lay a couple of punches on our 'sponge man'. This made the prone Walters jump to his feet to retaliate and both players were sent from the field by Referee Fred Lindop. It was a disappointing, if not exciting end to a game that had lived up to some of our expectations, and surpassed most of them.

This frenetic, controversial ending saw the massive army of FC fans on the field, celebrating with the players, as once again Arthur Bunting had got his tactics absolutely right. The roads leading back from Manchester were alive with waving fans and decorated busses and cars all with smiling faces pressed against the windows as 'Old Faithful' rang out across the length of the M62. It was one of those joyous 'convoy' moments that we have experienced on such occasions over the years as the FC Army return home from a major victory. Supporters 'tooted' their horns as they passed each other and some even leaned out of the windows and sang 'Old Faithful' as they passed the hordes of fans having a 'comfort break' on the hard shoulder. I bet the Half Way coach was amongst that lot.

Famous Last Words

I drove back through this melee of happy fans and went straight to the Hospital where Dad, my pal, my mentor and a lifelong 'Airliebird' had laid in that coma for the last few days. I sat, as you do in these situations, in a dimly lit side ward and told him what had happened at Swinton in as much detail as I could. Whether he could hear me or not, I really didn't know but when I got to the bit where I said, "So Dad we're playing Rovers at Wembley on the 3rd May", he amazingly came around, stirred and momentarily open his eyes. Taking my hand he said, "Hull and Rovers at Wembley I don't believe it!" and then he drifted away again. He stopped breathing later that night without gaining consciousness, and so, true to everything he had believed in and cherished throughout his life, the last words he ever spoke were about our team and his team, the 'Airlie Birds'.

So it was back to St. James's Sutton and the Crematorium as within four months I had lost both my best pals, my mentors, parents and the people who introduced me to the 'wonderful obsession'. There was no doubt at all that life was going to be really tough without them both but on reflexion I guess there is little doubt about why I am like I am and I'm so thankful even to this day that they gave me such a rich inheritance. Even now as I write this I am just following in my Mum and Dad's footsteps, because they were both fanatics and as for Dad and that last conversation at Castle Hill, well he certainly was 'FC till he died!' I guess Hull FC has always been in my family and it always will be.

Moving On!

Dad's Funeral was a sad affair with plenty of representatives from the butchery trade, Hull FC and of course the congregation of St James's Church in Sutton in attendance. His urn was interned with Mum in the family grave in Western Cemetery on Chanterlands Avenue and that was it, finished, it all seemed so final and pointless really. It was then that I decided to make a will and request that my own ashes be spread on the Boulevard (Something that I had to change years later to 'Wherever Hull FC are currently playing') and at least they might do a bit of good there, just like no doubt Bill Stamps had done all those years earlier when I tasted his at the Boulevard. After the funeral I didn't have a 'do' I just returned on my own to my flat at the City Hall, poured myself a drink, remembered just what Mum and Dad had given me and the tremendous sporting legacy I had received from them and contemplated life without my two best friends.

The Final to end all Finals?

So now we finally come to the big one! It was the final that would see a monumental day for the game of Rugby League when around 60,000 people from the City of Kingston upon Hull would travel down to London for the biggest day in the history of the Challenge Cup, and a game that would even lead to some 'small minded', yet no doubt in their own way passionate individuals, naming a club 'The 10-5 club' after the eventual score line. However I think that if you have got this far in this journal of an ordinary supporter of a very special rugby team, you must have some perception and indeed understanding as to what all this loyal supporter stuff is about. You will therefore appreciate, I am sure, that there are just some things that this simple lad from West Hull finds it impossible to write about. I can only presume too that you really don't want to read about it anyway. Sufficient to say, it was to be a set-back, but for Hull FC and this particular fan the best was yet to come!

To be continued ......

Epilogue

So there we are, the first 30 years, painfully and sometimes a bit amateurishly laid bare for all to see, and I guess that I might just now start work on the next 30. I hope that this story of just one fan's life, has shown how Hull FC was all around me back in those days of the early 50's, grew up with me, moved house with me and became the backdrop to a life for 30 years. It doesn't really matter who you support, it's all just about total commitment and I have always, like millions of other sports' fans been totally immersed in it all and I suppose even at a very early age, not a little obsessed. OK, you have probably screamed at the pages as you discovered that some of the facts are wrong and some of the detail is muddled but it's simply just how an ordinary bloke remembers it.

This is not a history book or a Club anthology it's simply just me and my memories. There was no cross referencing and no confirming the facts, it's just a head full of memories and if I have got it wrong I apologise.

For those of us who lived around the Boulevard when I was a lad, rugby was everything. Perhaps, in hindsight, I should have had counselling then, but in those days this behaviour was just the accepted norm 'round our way', and certainly not seen as a life changing, or sanity threatening problem! As you will have read already, health in general was a bit of a secondary issue back then anyway and at Chiltern Street School the best remedial care you could hope for was the annual visit from 'Nitty Nora'.

One thing's for sure though, if there was anything that my parents, teachers, or friends could have done in those days to rectify my condition, it's too late now!

If that general sports related malaise is one thing, then that nagging nausea before games seems to be a lifelong condition too! For decades I have suffered those awful nervous feelings in the pit of my stomach when a big game looms and I still, after 50 years, find it hard to eat anything before a match. When Hull FC are defeated, desperate to summon up the mandatory enthusiasm and expectation for the next game, I don't want to talk about it, I just want to crawl away and mourn on my own.

I know there are other sports and perhaps as I pass sixty I should try and 'diversify' a bit, but it never worked in the past so why should it now? When Hull's game day started to change from Saturdays to Sundays in the late sixties I even had a mild flirtation with Boothferry Park and the round ball for a few seasons but it was never ever going to be the same, they all seemed so thin, scrawny and fragile and still do! Then there's all that rolling about and feigning injury: I like to think that I watch a sport where the more serious the injury, the more likely the player is to get up and try to get on with it.

So I'll finish as I started and declare that I'm just sadly and irretrievably hooked on Rugby League in general and Hull FC in particular. Personally, I think it takes at least ten years of supporting your team for you to realise that there is one simple fact in all of this. That being, until you have lost a few heartbreaking semi-finals and 'one point' local derbys, had rain running down your neck and out through your shoes at Headingley, lost your best player to the enemy across the river, got food poisoning from pie and peas at Rochdale, travelled all the way to Widnes to find the game postponed and been chased through Warrington by a gang of 1980's skinheads, then, and probably only then, you have the right to take that special and wonderful satisfaction that comes to you, when you win.

All us obsessive supporters have our own such experiences to call on don't we? It is matterless whether you have been going to games for 6 weeks or 60 years, we all have our stories to tell, and all have our memories, hopes and dreams. They make us what we are, and win or lose, even in the darkest days, they keep us believing in Hull FC, Thatto Heath, Inter Milan, The Miami Dolphins or FC United. It matters not who you support because that belonging, suffering and hurting is intrinsically linked to the fabric into which the supporters' lot is woven. Like all long term love affairs, you have your good days and you have your bad days.

Most of us old timers know it always 'Could be worse', because we actually realise through experience it has been, and no doubt one day, in the future it will be again!! I have cried at plenty of games, never ever in sadness but always in unmitigated joy, I just can't help it.

I guess it's a state of total commitment really. If life has taught me anything it is that you can change your, mind, your girlfriend, your wife, your name, your hairstyle, your religion and even apparently your sexuality, but you can NEVER ever change your team! At home even now my family and acquaintances know from long years of wearying experience, that the fixture list always has the last word on any arrangements. Weddings have been rescheduled, parties switched and christenings moved to such an extent that most folks don't even invite me anymore.

My long suffering wife knows that when she gets a new diary I will not settle until she writes in all the season's fixtures. It's just an accepted fact!! It is always with some satisfaction and relief when I hear her on the telephone saying "Oh hang on whilst I see who we are playing", sad isn't it? Holidays are arranged over the 'International weekend' or are planned as 7 day breaks from a Saturday, after a Friday game, to the Saturday before a Sunday game. When we go to book our breaks the travel agent is visibly depressed at the sight of the fixture list coming out of my pocket.

There have still been those occasions when the sheer requirements of marital survival dictate that I have to miss a game for a family holiday. I do it as a matter of duty, a bit like doing jury service or obtaining car insurance and I have for years spent a fortune in phone boxes across Europe, listening to the local radio commentary on the telephone.

Once in Cyprus, in one of those skimpy telephone boxes they have over there, I got my legs so sun burned that I could not go out for the next three days! It didn't matter though because we beat Salford at the Boulevard and David Doyle-Davidson who was commentating said, "It's coming down like stair rods here!" Nowadays on holiday, I hog the hotel computer, and follow the game on there. There too is another amazing fact, in that I can remember that sunburn, who we played, the rain, the Wagon Wheels, the commentary and a myriad of throw away facts about Hull FC but I struggle, as I said earlier, to remember what colour socks I had on yesterday.

When we are three tries up in a game with five minutes to go, whilst my friends talk about the celebrations in the pub afterwards, I just sit there frantically working out how the opposition can score enough points to beat us before the final hooter goes. That's just the way this fan is. So now, in reality, I have come to the conclusion that short of actually climbing over the barrier and attempting to make a tackle on some breakaway opposition winger, I can do no more.

But then again it is heartening sometimes to know that although I may be a bit of a hopeless individual, I am maybe not quite a basket case yet. There is without doubt a reassurance and a safety in numbers. I always take great heart in the fact that although you think you are on your own, there are many, many others, in many, many sports, who feel exactly the same way as you do.

At Hull FC, as with every other sport's club, our great community has been thrown together over the years through joy and adversity and although often we do not even know each other's names we have camaraderie when we meet at away games, and even in the pub, that is second to none. At a game at St Helens a couple of years ago there was a great example of this, when after our (then) centre Craig Hall had run 80 meters for an interception try, a fan who I knew only to nod to, ran 20 yards across the terracing to hug me! That's how it gets you and whoever you support if you can associate with just a little of what I have rambled on about in this humble chronicle of an average fan's love of a sport's team, then you're already probably one of us, and like it or not

I am afraid you're 'hooked'! If you can't then consign this tome to the Charity Shop and get yourself a jigsaw!

Mind you, I respect all those lucky folks who go to the KC, or any sports arena and are not this barmy. They are still fans of 'their' team, they care, and probably still hurt a bit when they lose, but they have 'other fish to fry'! I really, really envy them. They are just lucky it doesn't get them like it always has done me! That is of course until they try and tell me after a defeat by one point in a local derby that we played well or we were 'unlucky'. B*ll*cks to that, WE LOST! And as for the 'Stamp Collectors' and 'Train Spotters' that tell me "It's only a game, get over it", believe me I tell them straight, it is never, ever, only a game and I'll always struggle to get over it.

Thanks for reading my simple story, if you have actually got this far then you've done well because for me this has all just been an attempt to 'Get it out of my System', although sadly it's one that seems to have failed. If nothing else though it has made me realise just what life and the love of a sport's club is all about, something that I hope in part I have been able to put across in these pages. Hopefully the next and final part will be out some day and I promise to try to make the next thirty years a bit more interesting!

Thanks for sharing this journey with me.

'Come on You Hulllllllarrr!!!!!'